ADVANCE PRAISE FOR

A Revolutionary Subject

"Women of Color around the world continue to suffer the devastating impact of racialized capitalism, despite historical efforts to promote gender equality. In *A Revolutionary Subject: Pedagogy of Women of Color and Indigeneity*, Lilia D. Monzó provides a much-needed Marxist-humanist rereading of coloniality and gendered exploitation to her engagement of the woman question, placing the voices and experiences of Women of Color at the center of the discourse. The result is an excellent treatise that challenges bourgeois liberal feminist notions of empowerment by reinvigorating the tradition of historical materialism with revolutionary gendered insights of indigeneity and class struggle."

—Antonia Darder, Leavey Presidential Endowed Chair of Ethics
and Moral Leadership at Loyola Marymount University

"This book is one of the most compelling conceptualizations of Marxist social theory to date, embedded in a captivating personal life story that leaves the reader humbled and challenged by one-sided regimes of truth, entangled in unjust power relations, legitimized by dominant social systems. Having been born in communist Poland, this book rattles my socio-cultural convictions and is a bold pedagogical tool for critical awaking, reaching out beyond national borders, gender, ethnicity, and social class. I sense that this book will raise worldwide interest. It earns a place at the table with bell hooks's works."

—Anna Odrowaz-Coates, Professor at
Maria Grzegorzewska University (Warsaw, Poland)

"Lilia D. Monzó invites us to join her in epistemological encounters with revolutionary women from the past and present. She summons Marx to the table to illuminate a socialist imaginary as an alternative to capitalism and Freire to advise our prefigurative commitment to move in the spirit of *horizontalidad* (humane horizontal relationships that challenge domination). Standing on these shoulders, as a Woman of Color, I feel I can fly and dream of a new world committed to a new humanism. Monzó gifts us with an invaluable compendium of *sheroes* from around the world who we can be grateful for as we launch our futures from their remarkable legacies."

—Suzanne SooHoo, Professor and Jack H. and Paula A. Hassinger Chair in Education at
Chapman University and co-director of the Paulo Freire Democratic Project

"Lilia D. Monzó draws upon Marxist, humanist, and feminist theory, as well as theology of liberation, to develop a new type of pedagogy of the oppressed for the twenty-first century that connects the need to uproot capitalism with the equally necessary uprooting of racism, sexism, and heterosexism. She bases her argument on the writings, life experiences, and struggles of Women of Color and Indigenous women, from the barrios and ghettoes of the Americas to other sites of revolutionary ferment, from France to China and from Russia to Rojava. This remarkable and original work theorizes a type of radical pedagogy that can accompany, help sustain, and help deepen the critical consciousness of some of today's most important movements for revolution and social justice."

—Kevin B. Anderson, Professor at the University of California, Santa Barbara, and author of *Marx at the Margins*

"*A Revolutionary Subject: Pedagogy of Women of Color and Indigeneity* is a tour de force. By moving her analyses beyond a bourgeois reformist agenda, Lilia D. Monzó cleverly and courageously situates her denouncement of patriarchy in a revolutionary praxis that keenly unveils that any authentic empowerment of women must include all oppressed women who come to voice through conscientization rather than through voice-as-gift by those who remain complicit with the privileges inscribed in whiteness. In a revolutionarily eloquent yet accessible prose, Monzó dares us to imagine the voice of Women of Color not as a gift but as a democratic right—as a human right. She challenges all men and women who think of themselves as agents of change to aspire for coherence and deeply comprehend that, in the end, there will be no change without privilege suicide."

—Donaldo Macedo, Distinguished Professor of Liberal Arts and Education at the University of Massachusetts

"*A Revolutionary Subject: Pedagogy of Women of Color and Indigeneity* is an important text. By sharing contemporary and historical examples, as well as relating elements of her own narrative, Lilia D. Monzó has created a book that will help readers learn from stories that are too often unknown or poorly understood. It is a valuable tool for stimulating critical conversations and paths of action among educators, policymakers, and others who are committed to equity."

—Carla R. Monroe, Editor of *Race and Colorism in Education*

"This study of the impact of Women of Color and Indigenous peoples on the social struggles of our time profoundly illuminates the complex relation of class, race, and gender through an open-ended dialectical perspective. It challenges Eurocentric readings of Marx's work while showing that all social theories must be re-thought and re-developed anew in light of the ideas and perspectives being generated by Chicanx and Latinx women, Indigenous peoples, and the Black Freedom Movement."

—Peter Hudis, Professor at Oakton Community College and author of *Marx's Concept of the Alternative to Capitalism* and *Frantz Fanon: Philosopher of the Barricades*

A Revolutionary Subject

Narrative, Dialogue, and the Political Production of Meaning

Michael A. Peters & Peter McLaren
Series Editors

Vol. 10

The Education and Struggle series is part of the Peter Lang Education list.
Every volume is peer reviewed and meets
the highest quality standards for content and production.

PETER LANG
New York • Bern • Berlin
Brussels • Vienna • Oxford • Warsaw

Lilia D. Monzó

A Revolutionary Subject

Pedagogy of Women of Color and Indigeneity

PETER LANG
New York • Bern • Berlin
Brussels • Vienna • Oxford • Warsaw

Library of Congress Cataloging-in-Publication Data
Names: Monzó, Lilia D., author.
Title: A revolutionary subject: pedagogy of women of color
and indigeneity / Lilia D. Monzó.
Description: New York: Peter Lang, 2019.
Series: Education and struggle: narrative, dialogue,
and the political production of meaning; vol. 10
ISSN 2168-6432 (print) | ISSN 2168-6459 (online)
Includes bibliographical references and index.
Identifiers: LCCN 2018034337 | ISBN 978-1-4331-3407-4 (hardback: alk. paper)
ISBN 978-1-4331-3406-7 (paperback: alk. paper) | ISBN 978-1-4331-5919-0 (ebook pdf)
ISBN 978-1-4331-5920-6 (epub) | ISBN 978-1-4331-5921-3 (mobi)
Subjects: LCSH: Minority women—Education. | Indigenous women—Education.
Educational equalization. | Critical pedagogy.
Classification: LCC LC3715 .M66 2019 | DDC 371.829—dc23
LC record available at https://lccn.loc.gov/2018034337
DOI 10.3726/b14401

Bibliographic information published by **Die Deutsche Nationalbibliothek.**
Die Deutsche Nationalbibliothek lists this publication in the "Deutsche
Nationalbibliografie"; detailed bibliographic data are available
on the Internet at http://dnb.d-nb.de/.

The paper in this book meets the guidelines for permanence and durability
of the Committee on Production Guidelines for Book Longevity
of the Council of Library Resources.

Printed in the United States of America

To my mother, sister, and niece;
and to Women of Color and Indigeneity across the world whose
courage and wisdom inspire me every day.

The beautiful art on the book cover is a graphic by artist-activist Melanie Cervantes titled *Dreams are Stronger than Fear*. Cervantes is co-founder, with Jesus Barraza, of Dignidad Rebelde (dignidadrebelde.com), a graphic arts project based on principles of Xicanisma and Zapatismo. Their website states:

> We recognize that the history of the majority of people worldwide is a history of colonialism, genocide, and exploitation. Our art is grounded in Third World and indigenous movements that build people's power to transform the conditions of fragmentation, displacement and loss of culture that result from this history. Representing these movements through visual art means connecting struggles through our work and seeking to inspire solidarity among communities of struggle worldwide.

Consistent with the work of so many revolutionary Women of Color and Indigenous women depicted throughout this book, Dignidad Rebelde is revolutionizing the ways in which we think about and engage with art for social change.

CONTENTS

ACKNOWLEDGMENTS

This has been probably the most difficult project I have engaged in as a scholar because in writing it I had many moments of clarity about my life experiences, who I am and who I want to be at this stage in my life, and about the many contradictions with which I live. There are many people that have supported me intellectually, academically, and in the day to day struggles of surviving as a Latinx woman to get me to a point in which my subaltern voice could be heard. Still many others have also supported this work. To all of you I offer my profound gratitude.

I still carry the voices of my doctoral mentors who helped me develop a body of knowledge, writing, and research skills that I continue to draw on. These include Robert Rueda, Nelly Stromquist, Reynaldo Baca, Pierrette Hondagneu-Sotelo, Gretchen Guiton, and Laurie MacGilivray. Robert Rueda deserves special mention since it was by his side and with his guidance that I became a scholar. His words of wisdom and his research rigor will forever mark my work.

Suzanne SooHoo has been a rock of support as I navigated the tenure process and learned to disrupt rather than adjust to the academy. From her I have learned to listen more, to quiet the chatter of doubts that infiltrate our minds, and to engage the difficult process of self-reflection. The Paulo

Democratic Project has been a social space and a physical place (Angie and Peter McLaren's home) of sanctuary for me. Our members remind me everyday that our work becomes a creative labor of love when we walk alongside others who share our goals for a better world, who lift us up and recognize our strengths while balancing our weaknesses, and who just love us as we are. In particular I want to thank Tom Wilson, Suzanne SooHoo, Anaida Colón-Muñíz, Peter McLaren, Angie McLaren, Miguel Zavala, Cathery Yeh, and Jorge Rodriguez; know that no matter what, in me you have a sister who will stand up with you always.

I owe a world of gratitude to Peter McLaren for taking me under his huge wings and showing me the way to a Marxist revolutionary critical pedagogy. He challenged me to think bigger and dream grander and he lay a world of opportunities at my feet. Most importantly, he showed me how to look beyond the capitalist haze that clouds our being and glimpse the moments of selfless love that reveal the possibilities that lay within our species being.

I also want to thank my comrades of the International Marxist-Humanist Organization with whom I have discussed Marx's work and many of the ideas expressed in this book at public and private meetings. I have learned a great deal from each of you. I especially want to thank Kevin Anderson.

I am very grateful for the invaluable feedback and encouragement I received from the people who read chapters or earlier versions of chapters, including Charlotte Evenson, Ndindi Kitonga, Peter McLaren, Anaida Colón-Muñíz, Suzanne SooHoo, Kevin Anderson, Donaldo Macedo, Samuel Hassbinder, Kemal Inai, Peter Hudis, Paulo Magcalas, Angela Arzubiaga. Sandy Grande provided invaluable feedback and mentoring in regard to Indigenous peoples and current debates. Kevin Anderson provided significant guidance on Marxist theory and the history of specific movements. I am also very grateful for the friends and comrades who read and provided beautiful blurbs for the back cover, including Anna Odrowaz-Coates, Antonia Darder, Sandy Grande, Suzanne SooHoo, Carla Monroe, Kevin Anderson, and Peter Hudis.

I appreciate the many friends, colleagues, and students who have given of their time to discuss or listen to me think aloud about the topics contained herein, offered opportunities to share my work in public venues, which has allowed me to gauge audience reaction, receive questions and formulate responses, and overall sharpened my thinking, or have been a constant and important source of support for me and my work. These include many already mentioned but also long-time friend Dina Hernandez, the International Critical Pedagogy Conference Organizers at Northeast Normal University in Changchun, China, the Ethnic Studies Summit Committee at Chapman University, Don Cardinal who hired me at Chapman University when he was the Dean, Margie Curwen, Kimberly White-Smith, Dean Margaret Grogan who supported my sabbatical leave, Dave Hill, Meng Zhao, Eman Almutairi, Tim Bolin, Kim Diew, Kevin Stockbridge, Paola Zitlali Morales, Alisha Heinemann, Gerry McNenny, and Anat Hertzog.

I am deeply grateful to Barry Kampol, who first facilitated my contract with Peter Lang. Although the writing of this book was put off for many years and shifted focus as I developed further, it was his initial recommendation and encouragement and his influence with Lang that got me the contract, which was later revised with a new focus.

I thank the Latinx women activists featured in Chapter 6: Anaida Colón Muñíz, Marisol Ramirez, Cheyenne Reynoso, and Martha Sanchez, for sharing their painful and beautiful stories with me, reviewing the narratives I constructed, and helping me think more deeply about what it means to be an activist.

I owe a special thanks to the editors and support staff at Peter Lang: Sarah Bode, Megan Madden, and especially, Luke McCord for their support of this project, tremendous patience, dedicated assistance, and attention to detail.

Most importantly, I thank my family. My mother and father and my sister have never floundered in their belief in my ability to achieve. Spending time with family—my mother and father, my sister, brother-in-law, my nephew and niece, my mother-in-law, and my husband and son—is a necessary sanctuary in an otherwise too often dehumanizing world. I must especially thank my husband and my son for their love and support and for their understanding of the times—too often—when I have been literally or metaphorically absent while writing. My husband and life partner, Michael Roybal, has always stepped up to champion and support my career and personal endeavors, taking up my slack when necessary, as part and parcel of our partnership. You have been my rock for almost 25 years. I love you and I'm grateful for you every day of my life. This book would not have been completed without you. My son, Miguel, is my inspiration; he provides me with the belief in the goodness of our youth and in their willingness to stand up in the future. He is a constant source of laughter and joy in my life and as he has grown up has aided my thinking with his questions and his insights into communism, capitalism, racism, sexism, and numerous social issues. His life and his person are a blessing to me everyday and I am so proud of his gentle and caring spirit and of his emerging engagement with social justice and human dignity.

PREFACE

Walking With Grace, Fighting With Courage: Lilia Monzó's Marxist Humanism

Peter McLaren

Throughout educational institutions as well as the media across the United States, American history is too often shoehorned or cherry-picked such that we are directed to attune ourselves with its grandiosity and ignore its mendacity. Thus, it is far too easy for history to pay us back in its own coin when we elect a president like Donald Trump. The baleful, hate-filled actions of the Trump administration, such as creating jails for children forcefully separated from their asylum-seeking parents who are desperate for refuge from the violence plaguing their native countries, seek justification behind a wall of dissolute rhetorical alchemy, blind fanaticism and bitter and unremitting rage that echoes older and more forlorn feudal dispensations. Trump's ranting against immigrants, globalization and the deep state appears across the stage of history as a mixture of the soberly engineered dismissal of a reality show contestant from *The Apprentice* and the blind vehemence of a screeching Roland Freisler presiding over the Third Reich's Blood Tribunal. Well-thumbed regulations dating back to the invasive leaders of America's settler colonies—you know, those lawmakers and enforcers who designed checks and balances supposedly to keep tyrannical leaders at bay—have been shredded by new weaponized forms of interconnected media governance such as ruling by strident and belligerent twitter rants, or designating journalists as lie-mongering enemies of the people (with the exception of those who work at Fox News, now transformed into a proxy form of state television) or re-tweeting and cross-referencing social media websites dedicated to ludicrous conspiracy theories designed to keep Trump's electoral base in a perpetual feeding frenzy. The ethos of the democracy, enshrined in the fundamental, entrenched and organic laws of the Constitution has been seared away by contempt for immigrants, asylum seekers, and people of color (currently the primary victims are black men whose abuse by law enforcement has spiked since Trump was elected). Trump doesn't need to beta test his political ideology or policies with his cult base, since he himself has proclaimed he could shoot somebody in cold blood and his base wouldn't flinch.

In our post-truth world, occupied by the smoke and mirror catechism of capitalist catachresis and sealed inside indoctrination factories known as schools that are built to siphon away creativity, attempts by investigative journalists at understanding local, national and international events that do not serve the special interests of our president are now dismissed as "fake," collapsing fact into value and acting like sieves for seizing the moral high ground. Truth, which was once assumed to be metastable, has been mongrelized by Trump's self-referential and exceedingly ungraceful attempts to manipulate and control it, blaming opposition to his presidency on the machinations of the deep state and mixing fear, xenophobia, racism, misogyny and white supremacy in the toxic cauldron of his patriotism. In Trumpland, an unreflective opinion carries as much weight as rational, discerning judgment. Our competence as citizens of society is to be judged by how our juridical, political, economic and cultural practices are in line with Trumpism. Fascism has well and truly found its way, even in this age of "woke" leadership.

Self-enriching Republicans who demonically clap their eyes on the dollar sign like your hungry pit bull clasps its jaws on the rack of ham it ripped from your slow cooker, are happy to support Trump's base as long as their property is protected from high taxes and their firms from regulation. The arrival austerity capitalism/neo-serfdom doesn't faze them as long as they are kept safe from having to pay benefits to their workers.

The alt-right, who self-righteously oppose government-enforced equality of outcomes and other affirmative action practices seemingly have no problems with the sexual abuse of asylum seekers by ICE agents but nevertheless are obsessed with blaming feminism, multiculturalism, globalization, atheism, affirmative action, diversity, LGBTQIA rights, and social justice activists who are part of movements such as Code Pink, #MeToo, Black Lives Matter, and

Idle No More, and socio-cultural constructivism, on "cultural Marxism"—a wide net term used by conspiracy theorists who are part of both the alt-right and center right. It is the alt-right who will find their archetypal opponent in Lilia Monzó, a Marxist-humanist feminist whose unrelenting courage and brilliant ideas stoke the flames of revolution on every page of this timely and important volume.

According to alt-right historians, cultural Marxism made its way into the United States after World War II with the Frankfurt School scholars and other writers allegedly bent on destroying the long established patriarchal, white supremacist, fundamentalist Christian political system in the United States from within, thereby making it vulnerable to one-rule corporate domination by masters of a globalist super state.

I've written elsewhere about some of the ludicrous conspiracy theories emanating from the alt-right. These conspiracy theories form part of the dark side of the American Dream. For the last several decades one of the most pernicious conspiracies revolves around the role played by Frankfurt School theorists in the United States as a "protean right-wing boogeyman responsible for queer studies, globalization, bad modern art, women wanting a life on top of baby making, African American studies, the 1960s, post-structuralism (essentially everything that isn't nationalist, 'white,' and Christian)"[1] The theory has been picked up by the extremist Tea Party, rock-ribbed fascists, white nationalists calling for the U.S. to be transformed into a white ethno-state and other alt-right groups, including libertarian Christian Reconstructionists, members of the Christian Coalition, the Free Congress Foundation and neo-Nazi groups such as Stormfront. They maintain that blame for the cultural degradation and corruption of the United States can be placed at the feet of the Institute for Social Research, initially housed at the Goethe University in Frankfurt and relocated to Columbia University in New York during the rise of Hitler in 1935. Philosophers Theodore Adorno, Walter Benjamin, Max Horkheimer, Leo Lowenthal, Erich Fromm and Herbert Marcuse were some of the luminaries of this group, whose works are still frequently studied in philosophy, political science, literary theory and cultural studies classes—not to mention courses on critical pedagogy. Peddlers of this crackpot theory about the role played by these thinkers include Jordan Peterson, Michael Minnicinio, Paul Weyrich, Pat Buchanan, Roger Kimball and other prominent conservatives. Promoters of the cultural Marxist conspiracy theory hold that these "cultural Marxists" (all of whom are Jewish intellectuals) promoted modernist forms of cultural pessimism that shaped the 1960s counterculture—and this "cultural Marxism" set the stage for forms of "political correctness" that have destroyed the cultural and moral fabric of U.S. society through the development of feminism, anti-white racism and revolutions in understanding sexuality. But it is the fringe writings of William S. Lind in particular that have had the most chilling effect. In 2011, Lind's writings inspired Norwegian neo-Nazi mass murderer Anders Behring Breivik to slaughter 77 fellow Norwegians and injure 319 more. Lind and his ilk blame the Frankfurt School theorists as a Marxist project to destroy the West, in particular for a litany of crimes that include the deindustrialization of America's cities, neoliberal free trade policies, affirmative action, immigration, sexual liberation, gay marriage, multiculturalism, political correctness, the welfare state, and the privileging of the concerns of African Americans, feminists and homosexuals over those of white heterosexual citizens. Of course, these became common tropes sold to Americans through the efforts of the Tea Party and media outlets such as Breitbart and Andrew Jones' *InfoWars*. Anyone familiar with critical pedagogy knows that the writings of the Frankfurt School are foundational to its social justice theoretical framework. If you are attacking cultural Marxism, you are *de facto* attacking critical pedagogy. Lind and his followers have certainly influenced the thinking of Donald Trump who is notorious for berating political correctness and feminism and for his scathing disregard for African American groups such as Black Lives Matter.

Scott Oliver captures the logic of this conspiracy theory when he writes:

> On July 22, 2011, in downtown Oslo, the right-wing extremist Anders Behring Breivik—who once gifted his mother a vibrator—detonated a bomb outside the prime minister's office, killing eight. He then drove 25 miles to Utøya island, where the ruling Labour Party's youth rally was being held, and began an hour-long shooting spree that ended with 69 more dead, most of them teenagers. That morning he had electronically distributed a 1,520-page tract, *2083: A European Declaration of Independence*, decrying the "rise of cultural Marxism/ multiculturalism in the West." Later, he said the massacre had been a way of publicizing his manifesto.[2]

Oliver explains,

> So the theory goes that "cultural Marxism" was the master plan of a group of émigré Jewish German academics—widely known today as the Frankfurt School of Critical Theory—who fled Nazi Germany in 1936, decamping to New York. What's certainly true is that, in an attempt to understand why the objective conditions of the European proletariat had failed to trigger widespread revolt, they concluded that religion—that great "opium of the people"—and mass culture served to dampen revolutionary fervor

and spread "false consciousness." So adding a splash of Freud to their Marxism, the likes of Theodor Adorno, Max Horkheimer, Herbert Marcuse, and Walter Benjamin trained their eyes on the subtle intertwining of social and psychic/sexual repression, believing that a revolutionary consciousness could be engendered through psychic liberation and more enlightened cultural forms and attitudes.

While these were the staunch views of a handful of left-wing thinkers writing in the middle of the 20th century, it does not follow that they have been the ideological architects of a wholesale takeover of Western culture.[3]

Oliver is correct to report that the "cultural Marxist" conspiracy has "spread feverishly through the murkier, more hyper-masculinist and libidinally challenged corners of the web"[4] and its exponents lack a basic understanding of the relationship between historical process and the requirements of international capital. He comments on the feverish crypto-fascist "awakening" of Andrew Breitbart when he finally realized the plot to destroy America:

In his autobiography *Righteous Indignation*, Breitbart describes the discovery of cultural Marxism as his "awakening"—redolent of the "red pill" that all conspiracy cranks feel when the vast, anxiety-inducing complexity of the universe becomes pacified in the paranoiac, pattern-seeking mind, reduced to the imaginary order of some joined-up plot (the irony of "red pill," of course, being that it's taken from *The Matrix*, whose makers, the Wachowski Brothers, are now the Wachowski sisters—trans politics being another plank of cultural Marxism). Grasping its effects, *he said* shortly before his death in 2012, was like "putting the medicine in the sherbet ... My one great epiphany, my one a-ha moment where I said, 'I got it—I see what exactly happened in this country.'" The self-righteous zeal animating Breitbart's subsequent *kulturkampf* drips through almost every *interview*, illustrating the propensity for the internet to enable a single person's prejudices, ignorance, and resentments to seize the cultural narrative—to resonate in echo chambers, free of intellectual checks and balances.[5]

Absent a nuanced and granular appreciation for the apparatuses of capitalist exploitation and its immanent relation to popular culture, the cultural Marxist conspiracy theorists fail to recognize that capital grounds all social mediation as a form of value, and that the substance of labor itself must be interrogated because, as Monzó underscores in her work, doing so brings us closer to understanding the nature of capital's social universe out of which our alienated subjectivities are created and how the objective conditions under which we live and labor are structurally maintained and reproduced. As a Marxist-humanist, Monzó clearly recognizes that because the logic of capitalist work has invaded all forms of human sociability, society can be considered to be a totality of different types of labor. What is important here is to examine the particular forms that labor takes within capitalism. In other words, Monzó reminds us that we need to examine value as a social relation, not as some kind of accounting device to measure rates of exploitation or domination. Consequently, labor should not be taken simply as a "given" category, but interrogated as an *object of critique*, and examined as an abstract social structure.

Marx's value theory of labor does not attempt to reduce labor to an economic category alone but is illustrative of how labor as value form constitutes our very social universe, one that has been underwritten by the logic of capital. Again, here we are considering value as monetized wealth. Value does not exemplify a purely reasoned and reasonable calculus but destabilizes the very ground of our being because it requires constant productivity in order to survive. The production of value is not the same as the production of wealth. The production of value is historically specific and emerges whenever labor assumes its dual character. This is most clearly explicated in Marx's discussion of the contradictory nature of the commodity form and the expansive capacity of the commodity known as labor power. In this sense, labor power becomes the supreme commodity, the source of all value. For Marx, the commodity is highly unstable, and non-identical. Its concrete particularity (use value) is subsumed by its existence as value-in-motion or by what we have come to know as "capital" (value is always in motion because of the increase in capital's productivity that is required to maintain expansion). Raya Dunayevskaya, one of the philosophers that has greatly influenced Monzó, notes that all the contradictions of capitalism occur within the embryo of the commodity form precisely because of the contradictory nature of labor.[6] What kind of labor creates value? Abstract universal labor linked to a certain organization of society, under capitalism. The dual aspect of labor within the commodity (use value and exchange value) enables one single commodity—money—to act as the value measure of the commodity. Money becomes, as Dunayevskaya argues, the representative of labor in its abstract form. Thus, the commodity must not be considered a thing, but a social relationship. Dunayevskaya identified the "soul" of capitalist production as the extraction from living labor of all the unpaid hours of labor that amounts to surplus value or profit.[7] If the proponents of the "cultural Marxism" conspiracy theory factor capitalism into their analysis, their emphasis is usually on the market, betraying very little understanding of the process of production itself, including the fetishism of the commodity form. The issue that the Frankfurt School theorists understand, and their alt-right critics do not, is not simply that workers are exploited for their surplus value but that all forms of human sociability are constituted by the logic of capitalist work. Labor, therefore, cannot be seen as the negation of capital or the antithesis of capital but capital's human face. Capitalist relations of production become hegemonic precisely when the process of the production of abstraction conquers the concrete processes of production, resulting in the expansion of the logic of capitalist work. Oliver writes: "Apparently it hasn't occurred to them [the alt-right conspiracy theorists] that the system of nation states, with their tax havens and labor-cost differentials, is intrinsic to the technocratic global order."[8] Using the example of noxious al-right media personality Paul Joseph Watson to emphasize how the alt-right promotes capitalism, Oliver (2017) writes:

> In one of Watson's blustering sermons, *we hear*, over a montage of mainstream-media logos, the following endorsement of capitalism: "A competitive market creates quality, because businesses fail if they don't please the consumer." Among the many ironies that Watson fails to grasp—aside from being a ceaselessly haranguing critic of mainstream-media bias making his pro-capitalist point over a montage of MSM logos—is that the culture industry is precisely the result of … [extreme Paul Joseph Watson voice] … CAPITALISM. This point was perhaps most forcefully made by … [extreme Paul Joseph Watson voice] … THE FRANKFURT SCHOOL.[9]

Moving beyond a notion of ideology as a vulgar distinction between truth and falsity based on membership in a particular social class, Monzó's concern with education challenges many of the mainstream visions of the educational establishment—that its sole purpose is to equalize educational opportunities and outcomes, that it plays a fundamental role in advancing democratic goals and values, or that the purpose of education should be to achieve personal happiness through hard work, personal achievement, and comparative success in the competitive world of commodity capitalism. As Monzó is acutely aware, the "gospel of happiness" proposed by consumer capitalism can blind us to the suffering of the masses. As Adorno notes,

> Only when sated with false pleasure, disgusted with the goods offered, dimly aware of the inadequacy of happiness even when it is that, can men gain an idea of what experience might be. The admonitions to be happy, voiced in concert by the scientifically epicurean sanatorium-director and the highly-strung propaganda chiefs of the entertainment industry, have about them the fury of the father berating his children for not rushing joyously downstairs when he comes home irritable from his office. It is part of the mechanisms of domination to forbid recognition of the suffering it produces and there is a straight line of development between the gospel of happiness and the construction of camps of extermination so far off in Poland that each of our own countrymen can convince himself that he cannot hear the screams of pain. That is the model of an unhampered capacity for happiness.[10]

This is not to say that happiness is an empty concept, an example of false concreteness, but rather exists as an after-image that suddenly captures us without warning. Again, Adorno writes:

> To happiness the same applies as to truth: one does not have it, but is in it. Indeed, happiness is nothing other than being encompassed, an after-image of the original shelter within the mother. But for this reason, no-one who is happy can know that he is so. To see happiness, he would have to pass out of it: to be as if already born. He who says he is happy lies, and in invoking happiness, sins against it. He alone keeps faith who says: I was happy. The only relation of consciousness to happiness is gratitude: in which lies its incomparable dignity.[11]

As a Marxist feminist, Lilia Monzó is the perfect foil for the alt-right who become enraged when Marx's ideas are favorably discussed in America's university seminar rooms. Recognizing the dangers of capitalist social relations and how its impact on education has created a neoliberal nightmare for millions of students, parents and teachers, Lilia Monzó creates another horizon for those who seek ontological, ethical and epistemological clarity, a crucially illuminating horizon that highlights how the taken-for-granted world is constructed, transforming what is traditionally excluded into a framework for discriminating among contextually specific social relations such as those engendered by capitalism, racism, sexism, homophobia and misogyny, making these antagonisms uncomfortably co-present with the reality one is both living and observing.

As a capitalist, you can employ the acidic rhetoric of a Donald Trump, be as bloodthirsty as the Ming Emperor Yongle, who slaughtered 2,800 people in his harem to suppress a sex scandal, or assume the sanguine and avuncular manner of television personality Mr. Rogers, but none of this would fundamentally effect the portentous, auspicious role that capitalism plays in the world. Capitalism is not driven by the meanness of the corporate boss, and it cannot be tempered by kindness and made into something that it is not (of course, a corporate head who is personally kind, fair, and righteous would be preferable in any case). But the main issue is not the personality or individual characteristics of the capitalist (we've all read Hannah Arendt's work on the banality of evil and understand how perpetrators of genocide can be kind and loving family men),[12] but the social relations of capitalist production, which is dependent upon value augmentation at all costs. A complex social structure such as the economy obviously continues to rely upon the existence of individual human beings able and willing to exchange their labor power for wages in order to reproduce itself. Human beings and both producers and consumers are necessary for a functioning economy. But capitalism can function without taking into consideration an individual's species being or "whole personality." Social structures follow their own logic. Interpersonal domination and exploitation are grounded in impersonal structures of domination, which is one of the reasons that social being determines thought.

You don't have to have the searing insight of an Albert Einstein or the precocity of Hokkien polymath Su Song to recognize that capital's performative subsumption of use value by the process of abstraction—remember that abstraction is a concrete material force—has colonized the life world of planet earth. Understanding all of this makes Monzó a dangerous educator.

Monzó's work reminds us that none of us are born into a world absent other people's meanings. We enter a world already populated with different horizons of possible understandings, only some of which have been made accessible, even to the discerning observer. The discourses which we inherit (depending on all kinds of factors, including but not limited to geopolitical location, our gender, race, position within class society, education, religious affiliation) and which "color" our ideologies, embody specific representations of the historical environment in which they are embedded, representations also conditioned by the limitations of the milieu that served as our life-world at certain points in time, and thus they cannot insulate us from the reality we are attempting to understand. The discourses that have been made available to us and which we use to understand the world are necessarily self-referential. In other words, they mediate the very reality we are attempting to understand. If we choose to characterize these systems of intelligibility as "lenses" then we can say that discourses refract rather than reflect the world. No single discourse can offer a completely objective explanatory framework for understanding the complexities of the world. This does not mean that there is no truth that can be discovered in our efforts to understand our world, our place in it, and ways to transform the social relations that bind us to oppression. But it does mean that such truths will necessarily be partial and, as new evidence mounts over time, we may need to revise our theories and also challenge the misconceptions that frame existing theories and cause them to be excluded from serious consideration prima facie.

Monzó is, first and foremost, concerned with how educators draw upon mediated relationships between subjects and objects, between social structures and human agency, and the consequences which follow various forms of sense-making as these pertain to the construction of the revolutionary subject within socially constructed relations of domination and dependency. She is also concerned with opening up semiautonomous spaces where taken-for-granted social relations can be problematized and put under critical scrutiny. She is concerned with the structurally conditioned ways in which history has endowed capitalism with overwhelming legitimacy among educators. Her dialectical analysis of the role of Women of Color in the world-historical march towards liberation advances a necessary political resolution to the class-race debate in part by demonstrating how urgently and cogently Marx speaks to grave concerns at this current historical moment. In doing so, Monzó revitalizes Raya Dunayevskaya's assertion of the important role to be played by the black masses in contemporary social movements and what kind of political subjectivity is necessary for these social movements to be successful.

Monzó's pedagogy is deeply rooted in solidarity with Indigenous peoples in their struggle for sovereignty. Indigenous women and Women of Color form the centerpiece for a new struggle that is eminently political and spiritual and not only committed to bringing down capitalism and the patriarchal and racist structures that support it, but dreaming a new world into existence through revolutionary struggle worldwide.

While acknowledging the difficulties in addressing issues affecting Women of Color across a wide variety of communities, Monzó makes a strong theoretical case for an important collective role to be played by Women of Color as revolutionary subjects, fortifying her arguments through powerful illustrations of the historical role played by Women of Color in revolutions throughout the world. Monzó challenges the postmodern emphasis on the incommensurability of discourses, challenges misconceptions about Marx's perspectives on women, non-western societies and the concept of liberation, while at the same time recognizing diverse ways in which identities are formed in capitalist societies. Recognizing that class struggle alone cannot liberate People of Color, Monzó suggests that rallying around the struggles that hold the greatest traction may be the most propitious way to move forward since these inevitably must lead back to class struggle to eradicate race oppression. As Monzó writes, race exploitation "is not likely to cease so long as capitalism is the mode of production but neither can we wait for capitalism to fall before we begin to challenge oppression and exploitation based on sexism, racism, sexuality, gender fluidity, religion or any other identity."

What Monzó has achieved in her powerful manifesto cannot be underestimated, especially its role in deepening as well as making more expansive the project of revolutionary critical pedagogy, in bringing new insights,

intellectual sustenance and vitality to the project of revolutionary critical
pedagogy, and gleaning new strategies and tactics to begin the struggle. Her
pedagogical work has been greatly influenced by the work of Indigenous
educators such as Sandy Grande and the contributions of Paulo and Nita
Freire. Monzó's recounting of an engagement she had with Nita Freire is as
riveting as it is profound. Here, Monzó speaks of the importance of "grace" in
engaging everyday life. By this she means moving in the world with humility,
generosity and kindness, while at the same time being connected in a spiritual
sense with this movement. Honoring spirituality in this way neither man-
dates for Monzó a necessary connection to established religious traditions, nor
does it exclude such a connection. Monzó describes cultivating the presence of
grace and reflecting this grace in everyday actions in and on the world as prac-
ticing a "spiritual humanism" which may "bring forth the subaltern knowledges that western imperialism has destroyed or submerged." Monzó further
integrates the idea of spiritual humanism with Antonia Darder's writings on
political grace rooted in community and collective ways of knowing. Monzó
writes that "to walk with grace … means to move in the world with a deep and
uncompromising commitment to creating a new humanism" in the service of a
broader decolonizing project. It also means "walking without the fear and guilt
that is running us ragged."

In a world in which humanity has been erased by the commodity form,
and human agency crushed like a mustard seed under a giant road roller at
a Mumbai construction site, Monzó's project of bringing humanity back to
life is not only important but urgent. The seeds of life she has planted with
this book cannot be crushed because its roots are not just found in the fertile
dampness of the earth but in the ineffability of spirit.

Notes

1. Scott Oliver, "Unwrapping the 'Cultural Marxism' Nonsense the Alt-Right Loves," para.
   17.
2. Oliver, "Unwrapping the 'Cultural Marxism,'" para. 1.
3. Ibid., para. 3.
4. Ibid., para. 5.
5. Ibid., para. 7.
6. Raya Dunayevskaya, Marx's 'Capital' and Today's Global Crisis.
7. Dunayevskaya, Marx's 'Capital'.
8. Oliver, para. 9.
9. Ibid., para. 11.

10. Theodor Adorno, *Minima Moralia*, 62–63.
11. Adorno, *Minima Moralia*, 112.
12. Hannah Arendt, *Eichmann in Jerusalem*.

Bibliography

Adorno, Theodor. *Minima Moralia: Reflections from Damaged Life*. Translated by E. F. N Jephcott. London and New York: Verso, 2005.

Arendt, Hannah. *Eichmann in Jerusalem: A Report on the Banality of Evil*. New York: Viking Press, 1963.

Dunayevskaya, Raya. *Marx's 'Capital' and Today's Global Crisis*. (Pamphlet) Detroit, Michigan: News & Letters, 1978.

Oliver, Scott. "Unwrapping the 'Cultural Marxism' Nonsense the Alt-Right Loves." *Vice*, Feb. 23, 2017. https://www.vice.com/en_us/article/78mnny/unwrapping-the-conspiracy-theory-that-drives-the-alt-right

· 1 ·

AN INTRODUCTION

Proletarian women, the poorest of the poor, the most disempowered of the disempowered, hurry to join the struggle for the emancipation of women and of human-kind
from the horrors of capitalist domination! Social democracy has assigned you a place
of honor. Hurry to the frontlines, into the trenches!

—Rosa Luxemburg[1]

Women bring a bounty of strength and courage to social movements and
civic action that springs from our historical experience of oppression and
exploitation.[2] This is especially true of working-class women across the world,
of whom the vast majority are Indigenous women and Women of Color.[3] We
have fought for better working conditions, against slavery, in socialist revolutions, and for the right as women to be recognized as fully human. Our
blood, tears, and sweat have made an undeniable contribution to the path to
freedom that history has laid. Restrained by men and their laws (and sometimes
bourgeois women) we have nonetheless revealed ourselves to be resourceful,
determined, and unrelenting in charging against the world's inhumanities.[4]

Through genocide and conquest the White man proclaimed the right to
define humanity in his own image and rendered all "Others" subhuman and
animalistic—led by instinct and emotion.[5] White bourgeois women have generally been torn between sisterhood and their own class, race, and imperialist

interests, and historically sided with the latter, adopting a liberal agenda for gender equality rather than developing an anti-capitalist agenda that would improve conditions for poor and working-class women.[6] Of course, there are also bourgeois racialized women across the world who have sometimes opted to support and enforce the exploitation and dehumanization of working-class women and embraced a women's rights agenda that has only benefitted middle and upper-class women. Thus, amidst gains for women's rights, it is working-class, Indigenous women and Women of Color[7] across the world who continue to be most exploited, dehumanized, humiliated, patronized, and treated as second-class beings. Yet out of this oppression grows an unparalleled indignation and impetus for revolutionary change. Building on Raya Dunayevskaya's words, I argue that Indigenous women and Women of Color represent an extraordinary "revolutionary Reason and force."[8]

This book has emerged as an outcry to what I see among the organized radical left in the United States as a profoundly western and male-centric culture, even among those who condemn imperialism and proclaim to be anti-racist and anti-sexist.[9] It is not surprising that unless explicitly founded to address racism, radical left organizations struggle with internal tensions surrounding class reductionism and the so-called "identity politics." Further, Indigeneity is rarely addressed among non-Indigenous scholars or activists beyond the critique of the history of colonization and current imperialism, with little discussion of existing settler colonialism, neo-colonial relations with the Global South, or western ways of defining humanity, epistemology, and organizational structures. This can be significantly disheartening to radical Indigenous women and Women of Color who recognize that although the capitalist mode of production demands an exploited class and thus holds explanatory power, racism and sexism and the naturalized superiority and hierarchies of Christian doctrine were equally significant structures used to justify the colonial conquest and enslavement of the Other that spurred the further development of capitalism and created the White supremacist capitalist class from which working-class Whites also benefit. For those of us who experience racism and sexism first hand, to be told by White men that we "need to get past our resentment and distrust," is not only patronizing but also reveals their significant privilege. This privilege is so entrenched that too often Women of Color and Indigenous women are "benevolently" ignored or dismissed when we bring to bear our insights and our sense of fairness and justice—sensitivities that we have developed through personal experiences and which male comrades often lack. At other times we are patronizingly asked or *expected* to contribute "our perspectives" and "teach" an anti-racist and anti-sexist "sensitivity" that takes a lifetime of self-reflection and epistemological de-centering to achieve. Generally, organizational structures inhibit dialogical epistemologies[10] that support an ontological clarity rooted in the lived experiences and theoretical insights of the most oppressed and exploited peoples on Earth. It is, thus, not surprising that we often find it difficult to attract Indigenous women and Women of Color to these organizations, even though at the local community level Women of Color and Indigenous women predominate in community organizing.[11]

I am aware, of course, that lumping all racialized women together can be highly problematic given that experiences of oppression and exploitation vary significantly and internal conflicts and contradictions between and among diverse racialized groups exist. However, it is my belief that while recognizing our many differences in terms of identity, beliefs, forms of exploitation, and also the contradictions wherein some Women of Color benefit from the exploitation of others, our similar experiences of exploitation and dehumanization can be a starting point for building solidarity and organizing against broader capitalist structures that benefit from our continued divisions.[12] I believe strongly that working-class Indigenous women and Women of Color can create epistemological encounters to support each other's interests and come together to challenge the broader capitalist structure that creates the hierarchical relations of domination that keep the vast majority of us dehumanized.[13] Certainly, I have found an important sense of sisterhood with other Women of Color with whom I have forged an authentic sense of "curiosity" in the critical pedagogical sense of wanting to see *with* them (not as the zoo-watching practice that manifests from the White, male, or bourgeois gaze).

It is with this goal of building solidarity and creating radical spaces for collective learning that I have embarked on this project that attempts to bring together the experiences and interests of working-class Indigenous women and Women of Color. Certainly, it is not my intention to minimize the differences or homogenize us in ways that have historically been done to make us invisible. There are important differences, contradictions, and debates being forged within and between many of these groups. Although I reveal some of these contradictions and point to the on-going debates, many of these debates are beyond my expertise. A deep understanding of these contradictions and debates as well as of the specific interests and concerns of specific communities must be *learned from and engaged through the important work of scholars and activists from these same communities.* The ideas and theories they develop through their specific histories, cultures, and sociopolitical and economic conditions cannot be replicated by outsiders. In no way do I present myself as an "expert" of the issues and concerns within these communities. Rather, my goal in this book is to consider the commonalities we share as oppressed racialized women and to point out the importance of learning about each other, working together, and taking the reins of history. How exactly we work this out and charge against the world's inhumanities for the betterment of all is yet to be seen but I do strongly believe that to achieve a new world we will need to listen to each other, love each other, and fight together.

In this vein, I have attempted to write a book that highlights our shared experiences of being hyper exploited and simultaneously courageous revolutionary actors while also providing examples, interspersed throughout, of the diversity of our experiences, pointing readers, whenever possible, to the scholars and activists of said communities. In my view it is in this dialectical relation between the overall experiences of hyper exploited women and the diverse forms this exploitation takes that we may develop the questions and insights that have thus far alluded the mostly western men who dominate the radical left in the U.S. What has always been missing is the wisdom and vision of racialized working-class women whose multiple axes of oppression connect us across a wide spectrum of the population but also support the theoretical sophistication necessary to find creative ways to struggle to change the course of a world in crisis.

And in crisis we are. Consider that the world today is guided by the horrors of violence and greed. Capitalism has run amuck, churning its way through the vestiges of humanity left in a world in which on any given day there are bombs being dropped somewhere in the world, children going hungry, and schools being attacked by their own students. Yet as devastating as the world has become, I continue to hope. In the Marxist-Hegelian tradition, the positive always exists within the negative. This is what led Karl Marx to profess that when the people's oppression became unbearable and they recognized it to be directly related to the capital accumulation of the capitalist class, united they would rise up against the structures that enslaved them.[14] Indeed, time and time again we have seen the oppressed come together to fight against injustices. Today, we find ourselves once again in this predicament—with a growing constituent of disaffected citizens worldwide clamoring against a capitalist structure that continues to drain the life blood of the people— claiming austerity while the richest few increase their lot tenfold without remorse or apology. In the United States the Trump age of hateful slander and repressive policies against all but White men has proven that when people feel particularly moved to resist, they can and do rise up. People are not just marching and protesting; they are organizing. The radical left has been especially revitalized as more and more people are recognizing that life is getting harder and harder for the majority of people in the world and are looking for a new approach to the crisis of humanity. This is a prime time to be talking about anti-capitalism, socialism, and other alternatives. It is also a prime time to be galvanizing different groups to work together in solidarity and to seek out the people with the greatest impetus for social change and the experiences and insights that might bring us new knowledge and new courage.

Marx's communism was a fundamentally humanist philosophy. Inherent in his goal to eliminate exploitation and create a class-free society is an anti-imperialist, anti-racist and anti-sexist imperative with a commitment to recognize the human right of every individual to engage in creative and life-affirming labor, beyond necessity, that would provide the conditions for real freedom, equality, social responsibility, and unfettered love based on a mutual respect of our many differences. I argue strongly in this book that this "new humanism" that Marx professed (unlike the deformed versions of communism that claim to be rooted in Marx), can be achieved, but only when all forms of oppression are recognized as dialectically related to the class structure of our society. To reiterate, I argue in this book that Indigenous women and Women of Color bring a source of untapped "revolutionary Reason and force" that may lead us to freedom.[15]

A World of Unfreedoms

It is astonishing that the horrors that exist across the world today have been normalized. Wars waged in the non-western world, often in the service to empires, are killing hundreds of thousands of not only soldiers, often sent to fight under false pretenses, but also civilians—entire villages, including the children. Across the world and even in the most industrialized nations there are people living in crushing poverty, hunger, and homelessness. In the United States hate crimes against People of Color, Indigenous peoples, women, Muslims, and the LGBTQIA community are not only committed by individuals with lost souls but have been institutionalized in the form of mass incarceration, travel bans, massive deportations, and hate-based legislation.[16] The wealth gap across the world is greater than ever before in history and is even greater in the most advanced capitalist nations.[17] Even when we face financial crisis and the masses grow more impoverished and their lives become more precarious, the wealthiest individuals see their total wealth grow.[18]

This global wealth is highly concentrated in the West, which has never ceased to maintain its chokehold on the Global South—whether through territorial claims, economic sanctions, or the mighty threat of military invasion.[19] But in the age of globalization, transnational capital and the North American Free Trade Agreement (NAFTA) have facilitated the intensification of corporate exploitation of the Global South, wherein they find the greatest exploitable labor and government allies willing to lift restrictions and cheat their own people. Any government or people's movement that troubles this oligarchy is quickly slandered and discredited, and economic, political, and military resources are quickly funneled to quash their efforts.[20] Without question there is something that exists even beyond wage exploitation and can be found even in the richest countries in the world—entire communities of color considered expendable and left to rot.[21] It is not accidental or coincidental that the people across the world who experience the greatest inhumanities are Indigenous peoples and People of Color. Certainly, there are many exploited and impoverished working-class White communities and many forgotten homeless and unemployed or underemployed White persons. However, racism is a critical aspect of capitalist social relations and value production. Although the horrific genocide and enslavement of Indigenous peoples was procured for the sake of land and resources, and that of Black peoples for free labor, the dehumanizing and atrocious savagery that characterized their treatment at the hands of the White man can only be explained by the internalized superiority of the western imperial being.[22] For me this means that we have to look beyond the classical Marxist tendency of class reductionism to a dialectical critique of capitalism that recognizes the significant role that racism and other antagonisms play in maintaining capitalist relations. It also means that as Marxists we have to ask crucial questions of reparations for this history of genocide, slavery, and colonial relations. The atrocities that identified the *Indio*, as Sandy Grande proclaims, "a conquered people earmarked for extinction,"[23] and the historical legacy of this humiliating and painfully exploitative existence, must be addressed beyond the goal of a future utopia that presumes equality renders the past forgiven and forgotten.

Women are clear casualties of capitalist relations, more so Indigenous and Women of Color. The kinds of violence endured among women has an altogether different character but one that is equally deadly and that seems to withstand reform efforts. We have billion dollar industries rooted in the commodification of women's bodies—the beauty industry, sex trafficking, pornography and prostitution, and even international surrogacy as well as laws in every nation that control in varying ways women's bodies. While certainly many gains have been made among women in the last century, including the right to vote in almost every country. Women's oppression cannot be viewed merely as gendered phenomena. Race, Indigeneity, class, sexuality, and other forms of oppression affect women's lives in a multitude of ways. Indeed, the greatest progress for "women" has generally been for middle- and upper-class women who have been able to lighten their burden of oppression and exploitation by shifting it onto poor, predominantly racialized women.[24] That all of us in the United States and in other countries who are not Indigenous to those regions live, work, and play in stolen lands and have benefitted from the slaughter of Native peoples is a sobering thought that must fill us with rage at our own, even if unintended, complicity (see below more on the concept of theft as property).[25]

The general population is led to believe that these crimes against humanity are necessary to secure our "freedoms," which are clearly tied to capital interests and ultimately to the interests of the capitalist class. Even when we recognize the fallacies inherent in these "truths," we fail to recognize or act upon our agency to change the course of history. Hegel argued that freedom is always a social construction rooted in a particular social and historical moment and that it is our "unfreedoms" that restrict our self-actualization and establish the "freedoms" that serve existing structures of domination, including the specific mode of production.[26]

The capitalist system that we have been led to believe is the "best" and only "natural" outcome of "development" has always been vastly destructive. From its early "so-called" primitive accumulation, capitalism and the capitalist class grew out of and is maintained through the dispossession of the masses. Western capitalism developed through the genocidal wars forged against Indigenous peoples of the Americas and African nations that allowed the development of empires that pillaged and enslaved its colonies.[27] Although some scholars have misinterpreted Marx's description of "primitive accumulation" to refer to an *initial* period of colonial expansion in the early stages of capitalism, this is a misreading of his work. Rather, Marx in *Capital*, Vol. I challenges this interpretation referring to "so-called primitive accumulation" to infer that capitalism is a system of *continual* thievery. Indeed, we continue to see the appropriation of lands and resources with which Indigenous communities, often the most vulnerable, have lived for thousands of years.

The West continues to infringe upon Native sovereignty for its million dollar development projects that extol vital resources and threaten the water and well-being of all.[28] This "land grabbing" has been increasing to such an extent that it is being termed "the new colonialism."[29]

In the United States most people have little understanding of capitalism, how it developed and how it functions. Its workings are kept obscure to the people through ideologies about the need for specializations and degrees to understand "difficult concepts." With this narrative, we fetishize capitalism, markets, money, and all other concepts and accept the explanations given to us by the "experts," many of whom have an interest in maintaining the status quo. We have come to believe with surprising naïveté that, even as we evidence the atrocities that go on within the United States and in international contexts in the name of preserving "our way of life," this is the "best" system that exists. As my son at the age of ten declared, having gleaned it from his schooling and other socialization processes, "it is the only system that works." The question I posed to him in response is one he had never encountered in school. I pose it here to any reader who still believes this lie. How is it that we define endless wars, a racism that hunts Black and Brown bodies, the continuous displacement of Native peoples, the devastation of the Earth on which we depend, and an obscene inequality that leaves millions across the world homeless on the streets as "something that works"?

The institutions that could be playing an integral part in shedding light on the root causes of our social problems and providing explanations and drumming up alternatives are, for the most part, so deeply implicated in reproducing these unfreedoms that they too present capitalism as an inevitable conclusion to history. Education and the media—one an arm of the state, the other a corporate entity—psychologize social ills, turning them into individual flaws including prejudices or lack of motivation. As Peter Joseph explains, we are taught to examine problems from the symptoms that are created and that are directly evident rather than being taught to examine the complex contradictions from which they arise and the ways in which they relate to broader social structures.[30] The truth is sought through "evidence" that is directly apprehended through our senses rather than understood through deep analysis. Our minds and bodies are fragmented such that we think through narrow specializations that perceive our world in pieces rather than as a complex holistic system. The dialectical approach developed by Hegel and grounded materially by Marx is, not surprisingly, absent in our schooling.

With this lack of conceptual clarity comes a belief that poverty, war, racism and other social forms of human suffering are natural and inevitable.

Rather than demand change, we strive to do whatever it takes so that our families and friends do not become victims too. Beyond this personal circle, however, we create a psychological distance that allows us to empathize on an abstract level but without much personal investment. This is not human nature but what we learn within a system of value production that alienates us from each other as human beings.[31]

For example, when we learn that millions of young girls in the "developing world" don't have access to education, we are troubled but relate this problem to sexist attitudes within those countries and lack of economic development. We perceive the problem as an isolated phenomenon within particular countries rather than one that functions within a global capitalist economy and which developed from a history of colonial relations that enriched the West by dispossession of the Global South. Rarely is it clear to the general public that the transnational capitalist class, many based in the West, benefit greatly by maintaining a large workforce of undereducated and financially desperate women who can fill their highly exploitative factory jobs.[32]

For those who take the time to make these structural connections, we have created narratives that support ideologies that justify the horrific conditions that many people experience by placing blame on the victims. For example, the worn-out myth of meritocracy continues to drive most discussions of inequality in the United States, suggesting that the American dream is real and attainable for anyone who simply tries hard enough. The idea that any obstacle can be surpassed is so entrenched in our psyche that we have developed an entire industry of self-help to support the individual as if structural obstacles to well-being did not exist. The American structural unconscious is well at play in our society since we continue to believe these narratives even when we are bombarded everyday with the evidence that they are lies.[33]

Capitalism: A System of Exploitation

There is no doubt that the mode of production is key to the structure of any society as it sets up the system by which a society survives and reproduces itself through the production of foods and other resources. Capitalism is a class system of value production wherein workers produce for the capital accumulation of a much smaller capitalist class. Exploitation and inequality are inherent to capitalism because workers' wages are always set at the minimum amount that can be earned in order for them to subsist at a level where they return the next day. These wages amount only to a portion of the labor power put to use each working day; the remainder of the working day is surplus, unpaid labor.[34] Most of us presume that we make a fair trade by selling our labor for an hourly wage and that the profits made from our labor are made at the market in the sale of the products we produce. Marx demonstrated, however, that while some profit is made in this way, capital is accumulated at the point of production through the exploitation of labor. A part of the surplus value produced at the point of production is turned into capital when it is invested into another cycle of production. This continuous churning of capital to produce ever-increasing amounts of capital is what defines the system of capitalist production.[35] The greed and alienation that is developed through this mode of production drowns out any sense of human compassion. Human beings become mere workers or commodities and treat each other as such.

In order to understand how capitalism distorts our humanity, which allows us to merely accept the atrocities we evidence everyday, we must recognize that we live our lives as alienated beings unable to fully develop the essence of our humanity, as Marx characterized it—our social nature and our ability to labor creatively for both our individual and collective well-being.[36] Alienation is the sense that aspects of our own humanity have become foreign to us. Under capitalism, production ceases to be an act of creative labor that draws on our intellect and physical selves to produce something of use value for society. Instead, the things we produce become "thingified" such that they are no longer recognized as embodying our creative labor. They are perceived as something outside of our human productive capacity that often turn against us, controlling us, even though they were made by us, in a process of production that robs us of our human agency to think and act as Subjects.[37] We are also alienated in the process of making production cheaper and more efficient, with factory work being increasingly fragmented so that workers are often engaging only in a fraction of the job to actually produce something of value. In this sense, human beings labor in an abstract realm where they are often unable to see or experience the final product and are rarely able to purchase the products they produce. The production of machinery, which had the potential to support greater production while minimizing the physical labor of workers, became instead a source of further exploitation and alienation as workers were pushed to produce more and became mere appendages to the machine. In this process, factory work has lost any sense of laboring to produce something a human being can be proud of and become instead a routine of meaningless tasks in which neither the human capacity for creativity, intellect, or varied physical movement are necessary or allowed.[38] Nothing is more dehumanizing than to limit for extended amounts of time a human being's use of those aspects of their being that differentiate them from non-humans—their agency, intellect, and creativity.

Perhaps more frightening is that under capitalism we cease to recognize how the process of production, including buying and selling and market competition, are all based on social relations. Instead, commodities are made to appear as things, market competition seemingly occurs between things, and even services and other activities and relationships are perceived as things that can be bought and owned. As John Holloway effectively explains, capitalist production processes in which we make large quantities with the cheapest materials and under the worst of working conditions in order to compete with other producers significantly inhibits any sense of pride for one's labor. On the other side, the buyer has little recognition or appreciation for the way the product was made, the labor that was put into it, or the person that produced it. They seek merely the cheapest price and have little concern or inclination to worry about whether or not the products were produced under safe and fair working conditions.[39]

I am not blaming anyone in particular for the problems that capitalism creates. Capitalism is a totality that affects every aspect of our lives. As long as we are encased within global capitalism we are highly limited in the extent to which we can function outside of the logic of capital. The majority of the world now lives in urban centers and must work for survival, wage slaves to a system that exploits people at almost every turn. The poor cannot purchase items that are made well by socially conscious companies that offer living wages and are environmentally friendly. While this is certainly a short-term solution it will not change the exploitation and the demand for capital accumulation that is inherent to capitalism.

Consider, as an example, the recently developing industry of outsourcing gestational surrogacy. Couples unable to carry their own child are seeking surrogates to carry and give birth to their babies. While the process costs approximately $100,000 in the United States, it can cost as low as $6,000 in poor countries.[40] This topic raises important moral questions about whether babies should be produced for sale as any other commodity. Yet in our capitalist society there seems to always be someone who is willing to develop production for anything that has a high demand. As our society maintains a value for the nuclear family (perhaps without a clear understanding of its patriarchal roots) couples who cannot conceive on their own (women with fertility problems, same-sex couples) are often desperate for non-traditional ways to have children. The first examples of surrogacy involved family or close friends willing to do this for someone they loved. However, as the demand has grown it has become a highly lucrative business that is outsourcing the surrogacy process to the developing world, with poor Women of Color carrying babies to term and giving birth for a fraction of the cost to couples.

In one report of a case that is representative of others, an Israeli gay couple contacted an agency that made arrangements for them to have a woman from Nepal to be their surrogate. One of the men was hesitant, being conscious that this practice constitutes a form of exploitation of the women surrogates, but agreed upon learning that the surrogate from Nepal would earn $12,000. They believed that this was acceptable because this amount in Nepal could actually provide a "life changing" opportunity to the woman. However, they later learned that what the woman had received was only about $5,000. This seems to be the average going rate for female surrogates in countries, such as India and Nepal. It functions like a purchase. The surrogates receive a small amount (about $50) each month that they carry the child and a final lump sum at the point of delivery. If they miscarry, the amount they have not received is returned to the buyer.[41]

This "job" involves pregnancy-related risks, emotional and psychological turmoil related to signing away all rights to a baby that they carried and nourished and gave birth to and potential social stigma in some countries. Yet the surrogates interviewed explained that they needed this job—the only way that they could make enough to send their children to school, buy a small piece of land or, if they already had a little land, to build a small mud house.[42] For women who live in precarious economic conditions, making a "choice" to be a gestational surrogate is not a choice at all. Although I balk at any use of a woman's body for profit, I recognize that the need for our own and our children's survival comes before any sense of morality. This example evidences how the capitalist system and its dialectical relation to sexism and racism, deforms our humanity, placing the poorest women in the position to welcome the use of their bodies as sources of income. The exploitation of the women and the manipulation of couples' desires for a baby is just business as usual—it is what defines our capitalist process of creating desires and exploiting production for capital accumulation. It does not escape me that it is because I have other financial supports that I can moralize about whether a woman's body ought to be for sale. Capital does not only structure our material conditions but also our values and beliefs by limiting choice and opportunities.

Many recognize the horrors that have been created under capitalism but blame greedy individuals, arguing that there's nothing wrong with capitalism per se and that capitalism can be made into a benevolent system that is socially responsible to workers and to the environment. These reformists argue that we can provide social services to everyone without limiting competition and growth. Others argue that we can legislate upper limits to growth. These suggestions fail to grasp the fundamental defining characteristics of capitalism—accumulation of capital.[43] Accumulation requires the constant production of surplus value and therefore the constant exploitation of producers. Yet there is an internal contradiction—the tendency toward a falling rate of profit—that needs to be continuously corrected in order to accumulate more capital by cutting wages or squeezing more surplus value out of the workers. Capitalism has been able to correct this internal contradiction and remain viable at different times in history in different ways but it will not be able to do so forever.

Neoliberalism has been the latest strategy for correcting this internal crisis—a series of ideologies and policies ushered in during the Ronald Reagan and Margaret Thatcher administrations in the early 1970s. Neoliberalism posits that the government is inefficient and all programs are better served through the competition that comes from unfettered privatization. It seeks to increase accumulation of capital through the elimination or privatization of social service programs, wage cuts, and through the expansion of free trade with reduced regulations. In its claim to efficiency it also highlights standardization, conservatism, and accountability as key necessary components of effective programs. This then set the stage for challenging welfare programs for the poor and diversity initiatives. It also fosters notions among the working and middle classes that economic problems are a result of increased government spending on "minorities" and provides the context for scapegoating People of Color and immigrants for economic stagnation. This neoliberal age is also at the heart of school choice programs and funding cuts to most social programs. It's also responsible for the significant increase of corporations moving their factories to poor countries where workers are paid next to nothing and made to work in unsafe working conditions. The consequences of free trade are also felt among the working people in the developed world who are left without jobs.[44]

It is hard to predict how far people are willing to sacrifice to maintain a system that increasingly devastates them and the rest of the world. However, the scientifically-predicted environmental apocalypse we are facing in the not too distant future may finally wake us up to the need for an overhaul of the capitalist mode of production. According to scientists, we are consuming our world into destruction and this impending doom is looming in the horizon.[45]

The premise of capitalism as unlimited growth is not possible within a world of limited resources. The problem of fossil fuels is not going away that easily. Richard Smith points out that even though we may begin to operate on renewable solar, wind, and waterpower, saving the planet will require:

> 'immediate and severe curbs' on fossil fuel production and consumption in the industrialized countries, which could only be achieved by shutting down entire sectors of the economy around the planet—not just fossil-fuel producers, but all the industries that consume them and produce GHG emissions—autos, trucking, aircraft, airlines, shipping and cruise lines, construction, chemicals, plastics, synthetic fabrics, cosmetics ... and many more ... this would unavoidably mean mass bankruptcies, global economic collapse, depression and mass unemployment around the world.[46]

Capitalism cannot be slowed down. Growth is fundamental to capitalism. We have to constantly produce. The only solution is to shift to a completely different system that is founded on sustainability or the production of only those things we actually need. Smith continues:

> To be sure, we need food, clothing, housing, transportation, and energy to run all this. But ... most of what corporations produce today is produced not for the needs of people but for the needs of corporations to sell to people. From the ever-more obscene and pointless vanities of ruling class consumption—the Bentleys and Maseratis, the Bergdorf Goodman designer collections, the penthouses and resorts and estates and yachts and jets, to the endless waste stream of designed in obsolescence-driven mass market fashions, cosmetics, furniture, cars, "consumer electronics," the obese 1000 calorie Big Macs with fries, the obese and overaccesorized SUVs and "light trucks," the obese and ever-growing McMansions for ever-smaller middle class families, the whole-house central air conditioning, flat screen TVs in every room, iThings in every hand, H&M disposable "fast fashion" ... not to mention the appalling waste of the arms industry, which is just total deliberate waste and destruction.[47]

Samuel Fassbinder calls out the corporate and legislative capitalist reformists whose sole plan for saving the planet is the reduction of CO2 emissions, naming this strategy "fantasy climate change mitigation."[48] According to Fassbinder, "no medium-term progress toward climate change mitigation has in fact been made even by the standards of the carbon dioxide measurement fetish." He points out climate change mitigation is being constructed as a market-based problem rather than a problem inherent to the capitalist system that seeks continuous accumulation in a finite world. Fassbinder points out that rather than seeking to manipulate nature to fit the logic of capital, we should be asking, what kind of society will save our planet?

This question undoubtedly points us toward sustainability rather than unlimited growth and this, by definition, directs us to move beyond capitalism. The change from production for the sake of production to production of only what we actually need is part and parcel of a larger change in what we value and how we think about humanity and our place in the world. An especially vital approach to making sense of the destruction of capitalism and creating a sustainable alternative is one that integrates, both theoretically and practically, the exploitation of nature to the exploitation of human beings into a more comprehensive analysis of our economic, social, and ecological relations under capitalism. Peter McLaren elaborates:

> The crises of global capitalism, including grotesque inequalities and ecocide, are not self-standing—they form an organic unity. In capitalist societies such as ours, self-alienating subjectivity is always already social alienation linked to the social relations of production, to racialized and gendered antagonisms, and to the normative constraints of what Best, Kahn, McLaren and Nocella (2011) refer to as "the global power complex" that reduces everything to production and consumption. It is this alienation that generates the self which remains isolated from its Other, including the natural world. Living within the state of planetary eco-crisis so aptly characterized by Richard Kahn (2010) as constituting "geographies of genocide, ecocide, and zoöcide" we cannot experience our self-presence except through the anamorphically distorting mirror of capital.[49]

Eco-socialism, which began developing in the early 1990s under the guidance of James O'Connor and Joel Kovel, has supported important and fruitful lines of analysis and practical applications across the world but has also met with significant political resistance.[50] As can be expected, a movement that explores the interconnections of diverse forms of exploitation to the capitalist system can begin to align multiple and diverse interests in ways that develop mass unity against capital. Indeed, this approach recognizes that Marx did not support the unchecked and exploitative human domination of nature as some have suggested, but a dialectical one, wherein human beings are recognized as products of nature but with the capacity to affect nature.

Indigenous scholars write extensively about the ways in which their peoples recognize the dialectical relations between human beings and the rest of nature. Relationality and the decolonial politics that it informs is understood as the fetter to the violence of settler and capitalist logics.[51] This approach emphasizes using only what is necessary and developing a strong sense of gratitude to the gifts that nature provides for our nourishment and our well-being. Unfortunately, eco-socialism has drawn little from the Indigenous movements and decolonial scholars that have been growing in Latin America, which aim specifically to develop a sacred relationship to nature and values for interdependence and sustainability. Walter Mignolo points out that western scholars often fail to recognize and/or acknowledge scholars and theories in Latin America or other parts of the Global South, privileging a Eurocentric western perspective that undercuts the accomplishments of non-western scholars.[52] Particularly notable is the case of Bolivia and Ecuador, which have inserted the concept of *buen vivir* into the national conversation and into their constitutions. *Buen vivir* is the Spanish translation used to convey *sumak kawsay*, a Quechua expression that translates to English into "the good life" but has little to do with the western notion that signals continuous economic growth and the amassing of goods. Eduardo Gudynas points out that *buen vivir* strives instead for harmony between human beings and between humans and nature, a sustained standard of living rather than continual growth, and collectivism.[53] Similar movements, rooted in Indigenous notions of development, have emerged in other parts of Latin America. Although this is an important step resulting from more progressive governments and key leaders that gained popular support in response to the devastating effects of the neoliberal policies implemented during the 1980s and 90s, such movements, even national ones, within global capitalism are generally wrought with internal and external pressures that often result in little actual changes. Gudynas points out that *buen vivir* is not necessarily incompatible with capitalism; yet it is clear that its values challenge those upon which capitalism is founded.[54]

It is critical that Marxist and others on the radical left *work with and learn from* the Indigenous peoples and communities of color that are actively engaged in developing alternative social relations than those which sustain capitalism and that they suspend the Eurocentric and androcentric perspectives that have been privileged for far too long. Gudynas argues that organizing society around the principles of *buen vivir* is not an attempt to return to precolonial times nor a rejection of western thought. Instead it is an attempt to bridge western philosophy with Indigenous knowledges.

Race, Class, and Gender: A Marxist-Humanist Approach

Although we often think of capitalism as an economic system, Marx argued that the mode of production and our material conditions structure our social relations in ways that impact almost every aspect of our lives. This has led many to mistakenly accuse Marx and all Marxists as class reductionists, meaning that Marx and Marxism relegated other antagonisms to secondary importance. This classical interpretation stems from Marx's important critique of Hegel's philosophy that ideas and consciousness became the basis for material reality. It is highly discussed in Marxist literature that "Marx corrected Hegel" and "stood him upright" by instead developing a historical materialist philosophy in which material reality—objective reality such as class and material conditions outside the self—was the base (materialism) from which the superstructure (consciousness) was determined. Here we have what Raya Dunayevskaya critiqued—a misrepresentation of Marx that fails to recognize his dialectical method and the humanism inherent in his entire project.[55]

Raya Dunayevskaya, whose interpretation of Marx's work took serious note of his early humanist work in the *Economic and Philosophic Manuscripts of 1844*, developed a Marxist-humanist interpretation of Marx's work.[56] She challenged the narrow ways in which Marx's work has generally been characterized as a critique of capitalism and instead draws on his entire body of work to argue that he developed a philosophy of revolution, a theoretical and practical path to a new humanism. In this interpretation, Dunayevskaya and other Marxist-humanists recognize women's oppression, racism and other antagonisms as intricately connected to class and the maintenance of capitalism.[57] Furthermore, Marxist-humanists understand that class struggle involves the struggle against all forms of oppression and exploitation and that at times it is these struggles that must take precedent as we build an alternative to capitalism. Indeed, Dunayevskaya placed significant emphasis on the potential of the Black liberation movement to lead us toward revolution.[58]

A Marxist-humanism recognizes Marx's dialectical materialist approach in which he documented how varying oppressions took shape for the purposes of capital accumulation. This does not make a class analysis more important or primary but gives it explanatory power. Indeed, the treatment of women is recognized as the first form of exploitation and oppression but one that takes on particular specificity within capitalism. However, while each antagonism is structured differently within society, it is clear that we cannot eradicate one without eradicating the other—they work dialectically to support each other. Certainly, capitalist systems retain some features that may be thought of as socialist and it is likely that an end to capitalist production will not necessarily immediately eradicate class, gender, or race relations nor automatically obliterate notions of "normalcy" that target the LGBTQIA communities. However, a mode of production founded on collective social development and responsibility, creative labor beyond necessity, and a humanist approach to all living things can create the conditions of possibility for equality, free-dom, and real social democracy—the new humanism Marx sought.

Unfortunately, just as the class reductionism that I previously challenged, the cultural turn, with its postmodern and post-structural emphasis on differ-ence, has discursively deployed extreme versions of an identity politics that preclude any sense of shared essential qualities in either our humanity or the oppression and exploitation of oppressed communities, precluding any possibil-ity of working together across differences to transform social conditions.[59] In one version, identity politics highlights the multiplicity of singular identities based on diverse experiences and infinite intersectionalities. This is the so-called post-colonial hybridity that renders culture defunct as a political category. At the other extreme is the development of definitive markers of cultural identity that can become exclusionary and has also been used to proclaim a "politics of recognition," that can ultimately serve the status quo. An important example of this comes from Indigenous struggles for self-determination in settler-colo-nial states. Glen Sean Coulthard makes an important and convincing argu-ment that the "politics of recognition" has become the dominant expression of self-determination among Indigenous communities. He critiques that this mode plays into the liberal politics of settler-colonial states and is increasingly used to further displace Indigenous peoples and further encroach on their land rights. Coulthard points out that recognition supports a "politics of reconcilia-tion," which functions *as if* actual reparations or a "transitional stage" wherein colonial relations, including state-sponsored land encroachment and material inequalities, have been transcended, when in actuality these continue to define relations between the settler-colonial state and Indigenous communities.[60]

Certainly, I support neither the amorphous post-colonial position that rejects any notion of shared identities or the restrictive and exclusionary politics that do not address the intersectionalities within groups. And cer-tainly, I understand that it was through the material reality of dispossession that the White man instituted the era of colonialism, American slavery, and the settler colonialism that continues to exist in the United States and in other parts of the world and created for himself a legacy of wealth and power that continues to this day and clearly positions Indigenous peoples and People of Color squarely within the working class and limits their social and economic opportunities. Nor have I forgotten how White middle-class women betrayed their sisters of color, opting for an equal rights agenda instead of liberation for all, within which their own successes were gained through the hyper exploitation of Indigenous women and Women of Color.

Any Marxist-humanist perspective is one that must acknowledge this reality and keep it at the forefront of our agenda for change and liberation.

Yet there is an important ideational element to oppression that is dialectically related to the material impact. Frantz Fanon has brilliantly depicted the psychological impact of oppression;[61] most working-class People of Color and Indigenous peoples, myself included, have every reason to feel ill at ease among White peoples. In the United States for example, not only do we know few White persons at a personal level, being racially segregated in working-class neighborhoods and work spaces (Indigenous persons living in American Indian reservations may know even fewer),[62] but we also experience White persons mostly in positions of authority over us—our teachers, our doctors, our bosses and often these people perpetrate against us because they have not been taught the cultural and historical sensitivity to understand or draw upon our ontological and epistemological differences and instead operate under the very system of power and privilege that historically rendered us less than human. While there are many White persons today and even throughout history that have and continue to challenge these atrocities, we can still see across every sphere of life that our material conditions reflect a racism that is deeply rooted in the American unconscious—and manifested in education, housing, employment, health, politics, and the arts. While People of Color are often rendered incapable or unworthy; Indigenous persons are often conveniently made invisible as if they no longer exist, the atrocities perpetrated against them mythologized into a celebration of "thanksgiving" that is a violent denial of the genocide of their ancestors and a consistent attempt to eradicate their cultures and languages. We have every reason not to trust White peoples. We also have every reason and every right to seek out social spaces that reflect our experiences of oppression and exploitation, our concerns and interests and where we can feel at ease and be recognized as worthy, smart and beautiful, just as we are.

Identities are formations that reflect our history of oppression and exploitation. We still have to find a way to work through these very real fractures among us because the divisions only support the maintenance of the White supremacist, patriarchal capitalist class. We have to start building bridges by acknowledging and accepting that racism, sexism, and other antagonisms exist and that people have an important need and desire to embrace their identities and have them validated. While this alone will not create the material conditions for us to thrive, it is a necessary (although not sufficient) step for us to claim the reigns of history.

Hegel, Marx, and the Making of Freedom

It is critical to understand that many of Marx's ideas originated with Georg Wilhelm Friedrich Hegel, whose work reveals the human search for freedom to be the object of history. According to Dunayevskaya, Hegel was the first to recognize that the increase in production brought about through industrialization and the machine would result in greater alienation of labor.[63] However, this understanding did not lead Hegel to develop a philosophy of working-class revolution—this was for Marx to take up later following and further developing Hegel. Instead Hegel's work focused on the Subject— whom he brought to life by making visible her agency and development in the realm of ideas. For Hegel freedom lay in the ability to reach the absolute idea, or what could be considered truth. Hegel elaborated a highly theoretical path toward this truth from consciousness (a direct apprehension of the world as it appears to be) to self-consciousness (in the case of slavery, the recognition of our state of unfreedom and enslavement through consciousness) to the final stage of the absolute Idea, which would then produce absolute Mind—a state in which the human mind were free from the clouding that ideology produces. Yet unlike many who have dismissed Hegel's important contribution to freedom because of his focus on the idea, Dunayevskaya has argued that the historical and the material were always present in Hegel's dialectic of the Subject even though he chose to focus his work exclusively on the stages of human consciousness.

While the Hegelian dialectic has been widely discussed and analyzed, a very brief summation is that it is a form of reasoning that lays the path toward freedom by recognizing that our conditions of unfreedom exist through concepts and ideas rooted in an internal contradiction of presumed opposites, one negative and one positive. Freedom thus lies in the resolution of these contradictions and in their unity, after which the process starts up again, until the subject reaches full liberation or freedom. For Hegel the path toward liberation lies in negation and Absolute negativity. In fact, freedom lies in the negation of the negation, a double or absolute negation. The first negation results in a destruction of the old but this does not in itself dissolve the contradiction or produce a new and positive path. A second negation is necessary to challenge the existing structure all together, unify, and present a new and creative step forward. This process of dual negation he calls absolute negativity.

Marx certainly recognized the significance of this dialectic and sought to develop a path to freedom that incorporated the material plane along with the ideational, and sought the heightening and eventual overcoming of contradictions. Unlike the crude materialists who argue that Marx "corrected" Hegel's focus on consciousness by setting him "upright," I would argue that instead Marx developed a philosophy of revolution that is truly dialectical, recognizing the material and the ideational as presumed opposites that must be unified in the Revolutionary Subject. Thus, in Capital, Ch. 7, Marx writes of "free conscious activity" as the hallmark of being human, something that the worker under capitalism is denied. Freedom must be sought dialectically—in body and mind, objectively and subjectively—and that the process of becoming free on both these planes must be recognized as one process—a unity of presumed opposites (like idealism and materialism)—wherein our consciousness is liberated in the process of developing freedom from material constraints. By grounding the Subject in their material conditions—their body in an objective reality, but also writing of the "quest for universality" of those same workers trapped in the material reality of capitalism, Marx introduces the proletariat as the Subject of revolution and class struggle as its fundamental objective in history.

Although Hegel's analysis is fundamentally western, Hegel's understanding of continuous movement and evolution in history is crucial to our goal of freedom for it recognizes that what comes next is always held within that which came first. Hegel was convinced that it was in the dialectical method that we would find Truth and Absolute Mind—Freedom. He stated, "To hold fast to the positive in its negative, to the content of the presupposition in the result, this is the most important factor in rational cognition ..."[64]

The potency of this premise, as Marx recognized, was that we did not need to create something completely new to call Freedom. The positive lay dormant within the negative and it would surely evolve through the struggle to negate the negative in our society. Capitalism could be challenged because within it lay the positive—the capacity and willingness to struggle and the vision and hope for a better world. We can see it in everything we can conceive of—in the capacity to organize that is inherent to factory spaces where highly oppressed people work closely and create solidarity; among those who work to create better schools and offer better health services to underserved and otherwise oppressed communities; in the self-activity and agency of these oppressed groups; and in the hundreds of thousands that have finally begun to use their voices and their bodies in protest, in sit-ins, in marches all around the world. It is easy to think that there is nothing we can do but if we look around there are many people who recognize our conditions of unfreedom and who are trying to develop a sense of collective solidarity, vision, and courage.

Importantly for this work is that Hegel made clear in his famous example of the master/slave dialectic that full positive freedom of self-consciousness could come not to the self-satisfied complacent masters, but only to the slaves—only the slave would be able to gain "a mind of his own" because the slaves were the ones whose unfreedoms could hold fast the positive within the negative—the absolute Mind. Dialectically speaking, then, we can see the significant promise for freedom that lies within the people who experience the greatest unfreedoms—working-class and poor Women of Color and Indigenous women whose exploitation and oppression at a global scale is unparalleled.

Fanon, with his analytical brilliance and personal experience, critiqued and extended Hegel's master/slave dialectic to the colonial context. Fanon understood that the "reciprocal recognition" that Hegel professed necessary for freedom was premised on the master also seeking recognition from the slave. Fanon understood that the master's desire for recognition as an essential "being for itself" cannot be met by the slave, since the slave's recognition is nonessential and dependent, thus not actual recognition at all. Fanon's brilliant analysis reveals that relations of domination preclude mutual recognition, such that the slave will never gain actual recognition from the master. Instead the slave must *struggle* for self-recognition in the process of changing material conditions. For Fanon, recognition or material reparations cannot be given by the colonial power since this act merely confirms the colonized subject's position of dependency. The colonial subject ceases to be thus only when she finds self-recognition as true independent Subjects, assert their independence, and demand conditions of freedom on their own terms.[65]

Drawing on Fanon's insights, the liberal "politics of recognition" that seems to be leading the movement for Indigenous rights, must be reconceptualized as self-recognition, independent of the state's seeming willingness to acknowledge or concede to Indigenous interests but must be sought independently of the state and its colonial representative. The race studies version is a "politics of inclusion" which seeks to have racially diverse bodies and voices included in dominant spaces as a form of 'recognition." The same logic applies here that racialized groups or other marginalized groups can only come to know their worth as Subjects independent of what the dominant group think through self and collective action that evidences our human essence as active agents of history.

Revolutionary Critical Pedagogy

Education can play a prominent role in developing a praxis of liberation. As dialectics would have it, we must recognize that material conditions influence and are also influenced by ideologies. Education is the realm of what Antonio Gransci called the war of position—an ideological war waged against the masses to challenge the hidden ideologies that support the ruling class.[66] In schools and classrooms, unions and local clubs, work spaces and in homes we can begin to question and create conditions that allow the oppressed, and in particular the voices of Indigenous women and Women of Color, to be heard and seen, to recognize that their life experiences of oppression may bring insights on how to create a better world, and to challenge the normative assumption that capitalism and the structures of racism and sexism and other antagonisms are inevitable.

Critical pedagogy is a philosophy of praxis that interrogates conditions of oppression and exploitation and creates conditions of possibility for developing new social relations that are founded on equality, human dignity, and solidarity with all peoples and all living things, including the Earth that sustains us. Critical pedagogy recognizes that freedom and the struggle to achieve it is a human vocation. In Peter McLaren's words:

> Praxis ... is the ontological process of becoming human ... denouncing oppression and dialectically inaugurating new forms of social, educational, and political relationships.[67]

Unlike the simplistic and presumed neutral "application" of critical pedagogy as "teaching methods," pedagogy is a much broader ontological and epistemological *process* through which social relations are developed, sustained, and or challenged toward particular economic, social, and political ends. A critical pedagogy, then, engages this process to recognize, denounce, and ultimately transform the systematic oppression, exploitation, suffering, and indignities to which the majority of life is subjected within the capitalist mode of production and which have significantly intensified under neoliberalism, strangling the many who were already experiencing a chokehold from which they could find no escape.

Based on the work of Paulo Freire and others who have developed his ideas, including Peter McLaren, Antonia Darder, Henry Giroux, and Donaldo Macedo, and bell hooks, critical pedagogy demands that we engage in a humanizing education wherein our humanity is affirmed by becoming socially conscious of the world as it is and as it could be.[68] Inherent in this project of becoming more fully human is that we are actors in history and always in the process of becoming—an unfinished project of nature's creation that we are tasked, as human agents, with the awesome responsibility of continually struggling to perfect, that is, to become more fully human. If liberation is a human vocation, certainly we must be endowed with all the necessary capacities—human capacities: knowledge, hope, dreaming, solidarity, and courage—to actualize this awesome goal and charge forward with revolutionary intent.

This dialectical view of humanity as both products and makers of nature and human-made culture recognizes the interdependence of humanity with nature. Freire and many critical pedagogues engage what from a western lens would be presumed "a pedagogy of the non-rational (if not irrational)." The deployment of such embodied concepts as love, hope, and courage (the locus of which may be in the heart) as capacities that must be socioculturally developed toward a transformation of objective material conditions cannot be crudely diagnosed as a western and androcentric tradition. While certainly critical pedagogy remains seeped in generalizations that have throughout history served to erase the experiences of those most oppressed among the oppressed, through its failure to focus on the specific concerns of particular groups or recognize the contradictions that are sure to emerge in seeking liberation for all, it is without a doubt that critical pedagogy has from inception engaged with the spiritual and socio-emotional dimensions of our human nature.

Although liberals have taken to domesticating Freire's work by removing his revolutionary intent and reducing his philosophy to a method of dialogue, Donaldo Macedo points out that Freire's pedagogy was always intended to challenge class relations but he was true to Marx's dialogical method and recognized that no one axis of oppression should be reduced to another.[69] Dialogue in a Freirian sense was not a method for communicating but an epistemology, a way of knowing, that could draw on the ontologies of the oppressed, often submerged through the violence of colonizing relations.

A Marxist revolutionary critical pedagogy as developed early on by Paula Allman but more prominently in the last few decades by Peter McLaren highlights the Marxist roots in Freire's works and his goals for transforming the world.[70] This approach is insistent that capitalism cannot be reformed and must be eradicated for our liberation. McLaren states:

> Revolutionary critical pedagogy is a mode of social knowing that inquires into what is not said, into the silences and the suppressed or the missing, in order to un-conceal

operations of economic and political power underlying the concrete details and representations of our lives. It reveals how the abstract logic of the exploitation of the division of labor informs all the practices of culture and society. Materialist critique disrupts that which represents itself as natural and thus as inevitable and explains how it is materially produced. Critique, in other words, enables us to explain how social differences—gender, race, sexuality, and class—have been systematically produced and continue to operate within regimes of exploitation—namely within the international division of labor in global capitalism, so that we can fight to change them.[71]

McLaren remarks that revolutionary critical pedagogy is like the "night shift" of critical pedagogy, less valued and in constant need to defend its existence as a viable force for creating a better world.[72] I would argue, following in this vein, that a revolutionary critical pedagogy that addresses the emancipation of women, and especially Women of Color, as a necessary conjoined effort to class struggle is the "second shift" of critical pedagogy and of the feminist movement. Yet, precisely for this positioning, developing a critical pedagogy of Indigenous women and Women of Color is of crucial significance to our plight for liberation. Sandy Grande points out in *Red Pedagogy* that while a revolutionary critical pedagogy recognizes the need to decenter western epistemology and draw upon Indigenous wisdom, knowledge, and spirituality, there is still the need to breathe into it the distinctions that Indigenous Peoples and other marginalized communities bring. This includes developing a praxis that attends to the rights and material interests of Indigenous communities and communities of color, whose interests and experiences remain at the margins of its pedagogy.[73] Importantly, this includes responding to the contradictions among and within the various communities in regards to land rights, immigration, and other diverse interests that sometimes splinter racialized communities.[74] This is our task to fulfill, as the marginalized Others, by infusing revolutionary critical pedagogy with our insights and further theorizing in ways that stretch its reach and develop the nuance that will allow it to speak to more communities while also creating bridges that will unify us and make us strong enough together to bring the monster of capitalism to its knees.

A revolutionary critical pedagogy can also engage us in the necessary practice of dreaming and developing courage. We are unlikely to take the necessary risks of revolution without an imagined alternative beyond class and a strong faith in possibility. But this dream must reflect the epistemological diversity that exists. A Eurocentric western notion of a classless society will surely be short-lived as inherent in it would be the existing hierarchies of knowledge and power that have defined history. As Freire often noted, hope is essential to the process of liberation.[75] For many of us, hope is found when we see evidence of dialogic encounters wherein the dominant group is willing to hear our truths, recognize these as significant, *and*, most importantly, to engage with us in transforming conditions. It is also found in the moments of collective praxis wherein we act and reflect alongside others with a similar hope and desire to breathe in deeply of the sweet scent of freedom.

Organization of the Book

Although I provide some background to Marx's philosophy in this introductory chapter and in the following two chapters, it is not my intention in this book to detail or analyze Marx's significant contributions to social theory. There are hundreds of books by numerous authors that do that. My goal in this book is to provide a little theoretical background for readers to appreciate why Indigenous women and Women of Color, as well as others, might find a philosophical home in Marxist-humanism. Although Marxism is often quickly rejected by those who proclaim it a White man's game, as I once did, I implore you to read through Chapters 2 and 3 and make a more informed opinion and then to pore over many more books and learn all you can.

Chapter 2 focuses on the exploitation and oppression of Indigenous women and Women of Color and notes the significant impetus for revolutionary action that these conditions create. I trace the beginnings of women's oppression, drawing on the important work of Maria Mies and other feminist scholars. I also discuss briefly the role of colonialism according to Rosa Luxemburg and decolonial theorists in order to develop a dialectical understanding of the oppression of Women of Color and Indigenous women and their experiences with class, race, and gender.

I recognize that still many people will question why an Indigenous woman or a Woman of Color would embrace a framework that was developed by an "old White man," that has been touted as both androcentric and Eurocentric and was said to espouse the human domination and transcendence of nature. I discuss this at length in Chapter 3, drawing specifically from Marx's writings to show what he wrote on the human-nature relationship and on women's oppression and racism. Although his early writing does evidence a Eurocentric perspective, it is clear from his later writings that he learned and grew in this respect throughout his life, finally recognizing the significant impetus for struggle and agency of non-western and Indigenous peoples and learning to appreciate what could be learned from their ways of living to develop a better world. Here, I discuss why it is not contradictory to espouse a Marxist-humanist philosophy and also challenge western dominance and support non-western thought and development. Indeed, Raya Dunayevskaya who developed Marxist-humanism was a proud Jewish woman from the Ukraine and it is perhaps *because* of her unique ways of "reading the world and the word"[76] that she saw a humanist and dialectical philosophy in Marx's works that escaped many other Marxists. I believe that to build a humanist society we must not reverse existing systems of domination by repudiating the brilliant and significant work of Marx merely because he was a man. His work aimed toward the liberation of all and offers not only a sketch of how to move forward but also the hope and vision for us to believe it can happen.

Chapter 4 is an autobiographical sketch that traces my experiences and ways of seeing the world as a working-class Latinx immigrant woman. People have often asked me how I came to radical politics given my background as an immigrant from Cuba and growing up amidst the realities of the Cuban diaspora and anti-Castro dogma. My story challenges us to look closely at what a Marxist philosophy can teach us about hope and possibility. Sharing one's life story can be a humbling experience. It makes us vulnerable in ways we rarely dare to be within this world of competition and commodified relationships. But how can I ask the world to be courageous and audacious enough to question history and to struggle for freedom without putting myself in that same vulnerable space? Yet personal stories have to be more than a mere cathartic experience; they should be tools that help move us forward on the path to creating a better world. My analysis at the end sheds some light on what I perceive to be key learnings from my story.

Chapters 5 and 6 profile revolutionary women in history and today. Specifically Chapter 5 explores some key roles that women have played in radical revolutionary movements, highlighting specific events, activities, and in some cases particular women. In Chapter 6 I explore the concept of the revolutionary Subject and argue that the characteristics and courage of the revolutionary Subject are learned and develop out of experiences of oppression. Here four local Chicanx/Boricua/Latinx women activists share their stories of struggle and impetus to change the world. These stories were collected through recorded conversations and then reconstructed into narratives. The women co-authored this chapter with me since the stories are told in their own voices and make the heart of the chapter.

I added Chapter 7 upon the recommendation of Sandy Grande, whose critical and insightful analysis recognized that in my attempt to underscore the common reality of hyper exploitation that the vast majority of racialized women experience as a point from which we could create solidarity across differences, I had ignored the many tensions that exist between and among us. The chapter is not comprehensive of the many tensions that exist but rather focuses on key points of contention. What I found in reviewing this work is that, in general, there are strong bonds of solidarity, when we see parallels across our experiences of oppression and when we come to see how our "racisms" are linked to maintain the settler-colonial state and the broader capitalist system.

I end this book by calling for a "pedagogy of dreaming," referencing the important work of Paulo Freire and other critical pedagogues who have attempted to move beyond the western lens of "rational" thought to an embodied knowing that draws on our human capacity for love, hope and courage. In pedagogy of dreaming I discuss the significant role of dreaming, envisioning, and prefiguring a world beyond capital to shake us out of our alienated stupor of resignation and move us to act as agents of history. Chapter 8 introduces Paulo Freire and the emotional and spiritual dimensions of his revolutionary praxis for transformation and sheds light on his Marxist and humanist roots. Freire was a master dialectician who brought together the macro goal of transforming structures of oppression with a humanizing pedagogy at the level of interpersonal relations between teachers and students and oppressed and oppressors. I also explore how dreaming guided Marx's humanist vision of a new society and Freire's humanizing pedagogy. A pedagogy of dreaming challenges western hierarchies of humanity, temporal assumptions and notions of "Truth" and creates spaces for Indigenous women and Women of Color to recover and develop ways of being that may develop the social relations that lead to revolutionary transformation and a new humanity. Grace is explored as a spiritual concept that we can draw upon to gain collective and community impetus and force to challenge the life-killing reality of our world and establish a socialist alternative that honors our full capacity to be human.

Notes

1. Rosa Luxemburg, "The Proletarian Woman," 245.
2. Although the woman/man gender and sexual binaries are narrowly defined social constructs that establish hierarchal relations of domination and obscure the dialectical relation between them. I use the term woman to refer to anyone who is or has been defined as such by society and thus has experienced oppression and exploitation on this basis. Although postmodernism has importantly problematized the practice of essentializing

human beings, it is Marx's concept of the negation of the negation that we can potentially employ to liberate society of such binaries. Until then, however, I believe that while
recognizing, learning from and celebrating our differences, it is also imperative that we
recognize our common experiences of oppression as working-class women, Indigenous
women and Women of Color, women of the LGBTQIA community, Muslim women,
Jewish women, and women of all other oppressed peoples. The term woman and its plural
women is sexist language because it positions women as an appendage to men. Some people address this sexism by changing the spelling to womyn or womxn. However, this shift
has not caught on among the majority of the population. I have opted to retain the traditional usage so as not to alienate readers and also as a reminder that we continue to live
lives subordinate to men in both material condition and in the way we are perceived and
treated. While changing language to reflect our goal for greater equality can be a positive
step forward, it can also have the unintended consequence of rendering society blind to
the persistent and in some ways increasing exploitation of women across the world. I have
been thoughtful in how to use these terms, attempting to make this work as inclusive as
possible. It is important that we not allow the ways in which we use terminology to divide
us. Divide and conquer is the oppressors greatest tool. All of these terms are evolving
to reflect our increasing understanding of different identities and ways of being in the
world. Some people are more proficient in these new developments than others based on
generation, personal experience, schooling, and other factors. This work is a contribution
to developing a more humanist world. Part of a humanist approach is accepting that we all
travel on this journey at different speeds and enter at different points.

3. I use the term Women of Color inclusive of all women-identified peoples who are racialized as other than White, ethnic and religious minorities, and women from non-western
   societies. Although Indigenous women *are* Women of Color, I follow the current practice
   of naming them independently given that too often they have been forgotten in statistics
   of "major groups" and to highlight their unique experiences of colonization and genocide
   and their continued struggles with state legitimized land thefts and for self-determination.
   Indigenous women refers to women whose ancestors were the first peoples or native to a
   particular region.

4. Sonia Kruks, Rayna Rapp and Marilyn B. Young, eds. *Promissory Notes: Women in the
   Transition to Socialism.*

5. Maximiliano Valerio López, "The Empire of the Written Word."

6. bell hooks, *Feminism is for Everybody.*

7. In this work I capitalize most identity markers in order to avoid perpetuating relations of
   domination, including the terms Women of Color and Person of Color are appear at times
   in juxtaposition to the White dominant group.

8. Dunayevskaya refers to women and Black masses, and in particular Black women as "revolutionary Reason and force" to signal not only workers' collective force but also and
   importantly their capacity for ideas, for developing theory grounded on their lived realities as exploited workers and on their movement in struggle (see Raya Dunayevskaya,
   Rosa Luxemburg, Women's Liberation, and Marx's Philosophy of Revolution). Dunayevskaya
   often capitalized Reason to signal this important dimension of revolution, which cannot
   be forged by force alone, but also to highlight that women and Black women, historically
   relegated to "unthinking followers" were leading the women's movement for liberation

though their own consciousness, agency and impetus. It is important to point out that Dunayevskaya, as Marx before her, was a dialectical thinker. She rejected the traditional rationalist views of reason as the positivist abstraction of thought dismembered from the knowing body, which defines reality as only that which can be quantified mathematically and renders all other ways of knowing as "irrational." Dialectical reason rejects this binary that has been created between rational and non-rational or intuitionalist thinking. Dialectics embraces multiple forms of thinking and knowing, including emotions, feelings, and intuition (see Peter Hudis, "The Ethical Implications of Marx's Concept of a Post Capitalist Society").

9. Jocelyn Cohn and Eve Mitchell, "No Safehouses: Patriarchy on the Left."
10. Paulo Freire, *Pedagogy of the Oppressed*.
11. Susan Stall and Randy Stoecker, "Community Organizing or Organizing Community? Gender and the Crafts of Empowerment."
12. It is important to note that this book centers on the experiences and interests of working-class Women of Color. Bourgeois Women of Color experience oppression by race and gender but their class privileges significantly mediate these. More importantly, this work is geared towards the vast majority of Women of Color and Indigenous Women whose experiences of exploitation and dehumanization support an interest in revolutionary change.
13. I use the term working class in the way that Karl Marx used "proletariat"—to refer to those whose labor is exploited in the service of the capitalist class or other dominant groups. Although some scholars have suggested that Marx used the term only in reference to those who directly produced surplus value for the capitalist, I follow more contemporary scholars who note that Marx not only recognized use value but argued for a socialist alternative wherein labor was the production of use value. With this understanding in mind, I use working class or workers to refer to women who labor for wages, those who labor in the home without wages, and those who work in the informal market; in short, all the women who do not belong to the capitalist class.
14. Karl Marx and Friedrich Engels, "The Manifesto of the Communist Party."
15. Raya Dunayevskaya, *Rosa Luxemburg, Women's Liberation, and Marx's Philosophy of Revolution*; see also note 8, this Chapter.
16. Lilia D. Monzó and Peter McLaren, "Challenging the Violence and Invisibility Against Women of Color—A Marxist Imperative."; See also Andrea Ritchie, *Invisible No More*.
17. Rupert Neate, "Richest 1% Own Half the World's Wealth, Study Finds." *The Guardian*.
18. Neate, "Richest 1%."
19. Noam Chomsky, *Optimism Over Despair*.
20. William I. Robinson, *Global Capitalism and the Crisis of Humanity*.
21. Lilia D. Monzó, Peter McLaren and Arturo Rodriguez, "Deploying Guns to Expendable Communities."
22. Ramon Grosfoguel, "The Structure of Knowledge in Westernized Universities."
23. Sandy Grande, preface to *Red Pedagogy*, x.
24. Grace Chang, *Disposable Domestics*.
25. Robert Nichols explores deeply the complex issue of conceptualizing land as having been "stolen," which presumes a property relation to land that many Indigenous communities reject. Nichols points out that land was reconceptualized as property after capitalist relations were established and that a more apt conceptualization can be drawn from Marx who

conceptualized land enclosures and appropriation of the land in which others resided as a process by which people were separated from their means of production, Nichols critiques, however, that this definition of the process of displacement of Indigenous communities does not get at the entirety of the process for Indigenous communities for whom land was and is more than a means of production. He argues that a more useful conceptualization that would cut through the debates around seeking sovereignty through land treatise may be conceptualizing the relationship of Indigenous peoples to land as one of "responsibility." See Robert Nichols, "Theft is Property."

26. Georg Wilhelm Friedrich Hegel, *Hegel's Phenomenology of Spirit.*
27. Fred Magdoff, "Twenty-First Century Land Grabs: Accumulation by Agricultural Dispossession," *Monthly Review.*
28. Melanie K. Yazzie, "Unlimited Limitations."
29. Stefano Liberti, *Land Grabbing: Journeys in the New Colonialism.*
30. Peter Joseph, *The New Human Rights Movement.*
31. Karl Marx, *Economic and Philosophic Manuscripts of 1844.*
32. Barbara Ehrenreich and Arlie Russell Hochschild, *Global Woman: Nannies, Maids, and Sex Workers in the New Economy.*
33. Richard Lichtman, *Essays in Critical Social Theory.*
34. Marx, "The Working Day."
35. Karl Marx, "The General Law of Capitalist Accumulation."
36. Marx, *Economic and Philosophic Manuscripts.*
37. Ibid.
38. Ibid.
39. John Holloway, *Crack Capitalism.*
40. Emily Harris, "Israeli Dads Welcome Surrogate-Born Baby in Nepal on Earthquake Day".
41. Harris, *Israeli Dads.*
42. Ibid.
43. Marx, "The General Law of Capitalist Accumulation."
44. Arturo Rodriguez and Kevin R. Magill, eds., *Imagining Education: Beyond the Logic of Global Neoliberal Capitalism.*
45. Richard Smith, "Capitalism and the Destruction of Life on Earth."
46. Ibid., section "Emergency Contraction," para. 1.
47. Ibid., section "Wild Facts," para. 3.
48. Samuel Fassbinder, "Climate Change Mitigation in Fantasy and Reality."
49. Peter McLaren, "Seeds of Resistance," 85
50. Joel Kovel, *The Enemy of Nature: The End of Capitalism or the End of the World?*
51. Sandy Grande has pointed out in personal communications that Indigenous relations to nature are commonly misunderstood among non-Indigenous peoples. She argues that there is little language in English to convey this relationship but that it is closer to kinship than any form of reverence or worship. See Enrique Salmón, "Kincentric Ecology: Indigenous Perceptions of the Human-Nature Relationship."
52. Walter Mignolo, "Epistemic Disobedience, Independent Thought and Decolonial Freedom."
53. Eduardo Gudynas, "Buen Vivir: Today's Tomorrow."
54. Gudynas, "Buen Vivir."

55. Dunayevskaya, *Marxism and Freedom*; Raya Dunayevskaya, *Rosa Luxemburg, Women's Liberation and Marx's Philosophy of Revolution.*
56. Dunayevskaya, *Marxism and Freedom.*
57. Dunayevskaya, *Rosa Luxemburg, Women's Liberation and Marx's Philosophy of Revolution.*
58. Dunayevskaya, *American Civilization on Trial.*
59. Dave Hill, Peter McLaren, Michael Cole and Glenn Rikowski, *Marxism against Postmodernism in Educational Theory.*
60. Glen Sean Coulthard, *Red Skin, White Masks.*
61. Frantz Fanon, *Black Skin, White Masks.*
62. American Indian reservations, Canadian reserves, and other tribal lands are federal designations resulting from treaty relations.
63. Dunayevskaya, *Marxism & Freedom.*
64. Georg Wilhelm Friedrich Hegel, *The Science of Logic*, p. 744.
65. Fanon, *Black Skin, White Masks.*
66. Antonio Gramsci, *Selections from the Prison Notebooks.*
67. Peter McLaren, "Being, Becoming, and Breaking-Free," para. 2.
68. For a collection of works by critical pedagogues see Antonia Darder, Rodolfo D. Torres, and Marta P. Baltodano, eds., *The Critical Pedagogy Reader.*
69. Donaldo Macedo, introduction to *Pedagogy of the Oppressed, 30th anniversary ed.*
70. McLaren, Peter, *This Fist Called My Heart: The Peter McLaren Reader*; Paula Allman, *Revolutionary Social Transformation.*
71. Peter McLaren, "Critical Pedagogy against Schooling: An Interview," PM response 3, para. 8.
72. Peter McLaren, *Pedagogy of Insurrection: From Resurrection to Revolution.*
73. Sandy Grande, *Red Pedagogy.*
74. For some of these contradictions in interests among racialized communities see Iyko Day, "Being or Nothingness: Indigeneity, Antiblackness, and Settler Colonial Critique" and Manu Karuka, "Black and Native Visions of Self-Determination."
75. Paulo Freire, *Pedagogy of Hope: Reliving Pedagogy of the Oppressed.*
76. Paulo Freire & Donaldo Macedo, *Literacy: Reading the Word and the World.*

Bibliography

Allman, Paula. *Revolutionary Social Transformation: Democratic Hopes, Political Possibilities, and Critical Education.* Santa Barbara, CA: Praeger, 1999.

Chang, Grace. *Disposable Domestics: Immigrant Women Workers in the Global Economy.* Chicago, IL: Haymarket Books, 2016.

Chomsky, Noam. *Optimism Over Despair: On Capitalism, Empire, and Social Change.* Chicago, IL: Haymarket Books, 2017.

Cohn, Jocelyn and Eve Mitchell. "No Safehouses: Patriarchy on the Left—Part 2 of 4." *Unity and Struggle*, December 3, 2015. www.unityandstruggle.org/2015/12/patriarchyontheleftpart2/

Coulthard, Glen Sean. *Red Skin, White Masks: Rejecting the Colonial Politics of Recognition.* Minneapolis: University of Minnesota, 2014.

Darder, Antonia, Rodolfo D. Torres, and Marta P. Baltodano, eds. *The Critical Pedagogy Reader*. 3rd edition. New York: Routledge, 2017.

Day, Iyko. "Being or Nothingness: Indigeneity, Antiblackness, and Settler Colonial Critique." *Critical Ethnic Studies 1* (Fall 2015): 102–121.

Dunayevskaya, Raya. *American Civilization on Trial: Black Masses as Vanguard*. Chicago, IL: News and Letters Committees, 2003.

———. *Marxism and Freedom: From 1776 until Today*. Amherst, NY: Humanity Books, 2000.

———. *Rosa Luxemburg, Women's Liberation, and Marx's Philosophy of Revolution, 2nd edition*. Chicago, IL: University of Illinois Press, 1991.

———. *Women's Liberation and the Dialectics of Revolution: Reaching for the Future*. Atlantic Highlands, NJ: Humanities Press International, 1985.

Ehrenreich, Barbara and Arlie Russell Hochschild. *Global Woman: Nannies, Maids, and Sex Workers in the New Economy*. New York: Henry Holt & Co., 2002.

Fanon, Frantz, *Black Skin, White Masks*. New York: Grove Press, 1952

Fassbinder, Samuel. "Climate Change Mitigation in Fantasy and Reality." *Knowledge Cultures* 4, no. 6 (2016): 250–271.

Freire, Paulo. *Pedagogy of the City*. New York: Continuum, 1992.

———. *Pedagogy of Hope: Reliving Pedagogy of the Oppressed*. New York: Bloomsbury, 1994.

———. *Pedagogy of the Oppressed, 30th anniversary edition*. New York: Bloomsbury, 2000.

Freire, Paulo and Donaldo Macedo. *Literacy: Reading the Word and the World*. Westport, CT: Bergin & Garvey, 1987.

Gramsci, Antonio. *Selections from the Prison Notebooks*. New York: International Publishers, 1971.

Grande, Sandy. *Red Pedagogy*. New York: Rowman & Littlefield, 2004.

Grosfoguel, Ramon. "The Structure of Knowledge in Westernized Universities: Epistemic Racism/Sexism and the Four Genocides/Epistemicides of the Long 16th Century." *Human Architecture: Journal of the Sociology of Self-Knowledge 11*, no. 1 (2013): 73–90.

Gudynas, Eduardo. "Buen Vivir: Today's Tomorrow." *Development 54*, no. 4 (2011): 441–447.

Harris, Emily. "Israeli Dads Welcome Surrogate-Born Baby in Nepal on Earthquake Day." *National Public Radio*, April 29, 2015. https://www.npr.org/sections/goatsandsoda/2015/04/29/403077305/israeli-dads-welcome-surrogate-born-baby-in-nepal-on-earthquake-day.

Hegel, Georg Wilhelm Friedrich. *Hegel's Phenomenology of Spirit*. London: Oxford University Press, 1977.

———. *The Science of Logic*. Cambridge, UK: Cambridge University Press.

Hill, Dave, Peter McLaren, Mike Cole, and Glenn Rikowski, eds. *Marxism Against Postmodernism in Educational Theory*. Lanham, MD: Lexington Books, 2002.

hooks, bell. *Feminism is for Everybody: Passionate Politics, 2nd edition*. New York: Routledge, 2015.

Hudis, Peter. The Ethical Implications of Marx's Concept of a Post-Capitalist Society. In Constructing Marxist Ethics: Critique, Normativity, Praxis, edited by Michael J. Thompson, 336–356. Boston, MA: Brill, 2015.

Joseph, Peter. *The New Human Rights Movement: Reinventing the Economy to End Oppression*. Dallas, TX: Benbella Books, 2017.

Karuka, Manu. "Black and Native Visions of Self-Determination." *Critical Ethnic Studies* 3 (Fall 2017): 77–98.

Kovel, Joel. *The Enemy of Nature: The End of Capitalism or the End of the World?* New York: Zed Books, 2002: 123–124.

Kruks, Sonia, Rayna Rapp and Marilyn B. Young, eds. *Promissory Notes: Women in the Transition to Socialism*. New York: Monthly Review Press, 1989.

Liberti, Stefano. *Land Grabbing: Journeys in the New Colonialism*. London: Verso, 2013.

Lichtman, Richard. *Essays in Critical Social Theory: Toward a Marxist Critique of Liberal Ideology*. New York: Peter Lang, 1993.

López, Maximiliano Valerio. "The Empire of the Written Word: Modernity, Humanism, and Colonization." *Lapíz* 1 (2013): 32–64.

Luxemburg, Rosa. "The Proletarian Woman." In *The Rosa Luxemburg Reader*, edited by Peter Hudis and Kevin Anderson, 242–245. New York: Monthly Review Press, 2004.

Luxemburg, Rosa. *Accumulation of Capital*. Eastford, CT: Martino Fine Books, 2015.

Macedo, Donaldo. Introduction to *Pedagogy of the Oppressed, 30th anniversary edition*, Paulo Freire, 11–27. New York: Bloomsbury, 2000.

Magdoff, Fred. "Twenty-First Century Land Grabs: Accumulation by Agricultural Dispossession." *Monthly Review: An Independent Socialist Magazine* 65, no. 6 (2013). https://monthlyreview.org/2013/11/01/twenty-first-century-land-grabs/

Marx, Karl. *Economic and Philosophic Manuscripts of 1844*. Translated by Martin Milligan. Moscow: Foreign Language Publishing House, 1961.

———. "The General Law of Capitalist Accumulation." In *Capital*, Vol. I, translated by Ben Fowkes, 762–870. New York: Vintage Books, 1977.

———. "The Working Day." In *Capital*, Vol. I, translated by Ben Fowkes, 340–416. New York: Vintage Books, 1977.

Marx, Karl and Friedrich Engels. "The Manifesto of the Communist Party." In *The Marx-Engels reader, 2nd edition*, edited by R. C. Tucker, 469–500. New York: W. W. Norton & Co. Inc, 1978.

McLaren, Peter. "Being, Becoming, and Breaking-Free: Peter McLaren and the Pedagogy of Liberation." *Teoría de la Educación. Educación y Cultura en la Sociedad de la Información* 10, no. 3 (2009): 256–281.

———. "Critical Pedagogy Against Capitalist Schooling: Towards a Socialist Alternative. An Interview with Peter McLaren." *Global Education Magazine*, April 7, 2013. http://www.globaleducationmagazine.com/critical-pedagogy-againstcapitalist-schooling-socialist-alternative-interview-peter-mclaren/

———. *Pedagogy of Insurrection: From Resurrection to Revolution*. New York: Peter Lang, 2015.

———. "Seeds of Resistance: Towards a Revolutionary Critical Ecopedagogy." *Socialist Studies*, 9, no. 1 (2013): 84–108.

———. *This Fist Called My Heart: The Peter McLaren Reader*. Edited by Marc Pruyn and Luis Huerta-Charles. Charlotte, NC: Information Age Publishing, 2016.

Mignolo, Walter. "Epistemic Disobedience, Independent Thought and Decolonial Freedom. *Theory, Culture & Society* 26, no. 7–8 (2009): 159–181.

Monzó, Lilia D. and Peter McLaren. "Challenging the Violence and Invisibility Against Women of Color—A Marxist Imperative." *https://iberoamericasocial.com/challenging-the-violence-and-invisibility-against-women-of-color-a-marxist-imperative/*

Monzó, Lilia D., Peter McLaren, and Arturo Rodriguez. "Deploying Guns to Expendable Communities: Bloodshed in Mexico, U.S. Imperialism, and Transnational Capital—A Call for Revolutionary Critical Pedagogy." *Cultural Studies/Critical Methodologies* 17, no. 2 (2017): 91–100.

Neate, Rupert. "Richest 1% Own Half the World's Wealth, Study Finds." *The Guardian*, Nov. 14, 2017. https://www.theguardian.com/inequality/2017/nov/14/worlds-richest-wealth-credit-suisse

Nichols, Robert. "Theft is Property! The Recursive Logic of Dispossession." *Political Theory* 46, no. 1 (2018): 3–28.

Ritchie, Andrea. *Invisible No More: Police Brutality Against Black Women and Women of Color*. Boston, MA: Beacon Press, 2017.

Robinson, William I., *Global Capitalism and the Crisis of Humanity*. New York: Cambridge University Press, 2014.

Rodriguez, Arturo and Kevin R. Magill, eds. *Imagining Education: Beyond the Logic of Global Neoliberal Capitalism*. Charlotte, NC: Information Age Publishing, 2017.

Salmón, Enrique. "Kincentric Ecology: Indigenous Perceptions of the Human-Nature Relationship." *Ecological Applications* 8, no. 5 (2000): 1327–1332.

Smith, Richard, "Capitalism and the Destruction of Life on Earth: Six Theses on Saving the Humans." *Truthout*, November 10, 2013. https://truthout.org/articles/capitalism-and-the-destruction-of-life-on-earth-six-theses-on-saving-the-humans/

Stall, Susan and Randy Stoecker. "Community Organizing or Organizing Community? Gender and the Crafts of Empowerment." *Gender & Society* 12, no. 6 (1998): 729–756.

Yazzie, Melanie K. "Unlimited Limitations: The Navajos' Winters Rights Deemd Worthless in the 2012 Navajo-Hopi Little Colorado River Settlement." *Wicazo Sa Review* 28, no. 1(2013): 26–37.

· 2 ·

INDIGENOUS WOMEN AND WOMEN OF COLOR ON THE TRENCHES OF FREEDOM[1]

When Black women stand up—as they did during the Montgomery Bus Boycott, as they did during the Black liberation era—earth-shaking changes occur.
—Angela Davis[2]

For the property-owning bourgeois woman, her house is the world. For the proletarian woman the whole world is her house. …
—Rosa Luxemburg[3]

The vast majority of Indigenous women and Women of Color live lives ruled by violence.[4] As women we face an insidious (and sometime blatant) attack on our right to exist—economically, physically, sexually, politically, ideologically, symbolically and psychologically. Compounding this assault are experiences of racism and White supremacy, which is an especially brutal structure that manifests through imperialism and colonial relations, land theft, anti-immigration, the hegemony of English, hyper exploitation, unequal access to education and health care, hyper-policing, and violence, including the violence against ancestral lands.[5] This violence against Indigenous women and Women of Color has been a strong historical impediment to self-determination, opportunities, and potential. Although some fare better than others, none can completely escape this racist misogynist exploitation within global capitalism. It is embedded in every institution and will continue to be as long as capitalism remains the global force it is today. Sexism, racism, and colonialism, including settler colonialism, are inextricably intertwined with the forces of production to hold up capitalist social relations.

As I pointed out in the Introductory chapter, I am very aware of the contradictions that exist among and between racialized groups, Indigenous peoples, immigrants, and other oppressed communities as well as the fact that gender as a category and women among these communities may face different treatment and experiences. My goal is not to homogenize women in ways that invisibilize them and their particular interests. Joanne Barker makes a strong statement in this regard:

> [The] ... discursive elision of Indigenous and 'of color' women and their communities only further displaces the history of Indigenous women's disidentification with feminism and 'of color' identifications for failing to distinguish Indigenous collective rights and struggles for sovereignty and self-determination—and Indigenous women's roles within those struggles—from the liberalist individualism of civil rights.[6]

It is to honor the specificity of issues that concern Indigenous communities that I have not collapsed Indigenous women into the more collective "Women of Color." And of course, many other women may feel that their specific identities are lost in this generic identity. However, my goal in this work is to shed light on the fact that the capitalist system feeds off of our oppressions, even though these are manifested differently. As such, I believe strongly that it is through understanding and challenging capitalism and its imperial and colonizing imperative that we may develop an alternative that allows all life forms to flourish in ways supportive to the particulars of diverse cultures and peoples. While we may need to contend with contradictory interests, I believe many of these, in so far as they are effects of capital and empire, may be dialectically engaged in our collective confrontation against capitalism. The work of scholars and activists who focus on understanding and changing the social conditions that particular communities and the women among them experience is critically important and necessary. In no way does this work suggest otherwise. However, this work attempts to provide a holistic view that encourages us to look across our differences to see the ways in which we can connect. Capitalism is a monster that is adaptive and flexible and, thus, has eluded destruction from within (the internal crisis) and without (revolutionary efforts). Globalization has created conditions wherein bringing down capitalism will require collective transnational and international movements. This requires that we learn about and from each other; and that we create empathy for each other and build bonds together.

Consider the vast array of contexts in which working-class women around the world, mostly Indigenous and of Color, find themselves exploited.[7] At a global scale only half of working-age women participate in the formal sector of the labor economy, with Indigenous women having the lowest participation rates.[8] Other working-age women and many young girls work as "contributing family workers" without direct pay or in the informal sector, which is often extremely poorly paid and unregulated.[9] Furthermore, the division of labor continues to be a significant factor across the world with women doing more than two times the amount of unpaid domestic work than men. For example, according to a 2015 United Nations report, women in rural Malawi spend over eight times more hours than men completing the same domestic chores and women in Sub-Saharan Africa spend about 40 billion hours per year collecting water.[10] In the United States married women without children do seventeen hours of housework a week while men do seven hours.[11] For many women, this domestic labor is completed after having already put in a full day of work. This exploitative second shift leaves women physically and mentally exhausted at the end of the day.[12]

In addition to the cost-free labor that women perform, their paid work is devalued. A wage gap exists in every nation across the world.[13] Although in the United States The Equal Pay Act was signed by President Kennedy in 1963 it has been consistently difficult to enforce, such that women, on average, continue to be paid 20 percent less than men.[14] Of course, this percentage worsens significantly when race enters the picture, with Black and Latinx women earning significantly less than White women; pay rates for Indigenous women are rarely even documented.[15] It is important to note that the push for women to join the waged labor force is not a solution to women's liberation, especially for racialized women who often labor in the worst working conditions. In fact, although the incomes may alleviate poverty (which is a good enough reason to support it), it nonetheless increases their exploitation. Although there is some evidence that waged work can grant some women greater power in the household, this is truer for women whose wages are sufficient to support them. Unfortunately, wages earned among the poorest women across the world are generally insufficient to leverage their incomes for greater gender equality in the family, especially for women with children.

Among Indigenous communities, the increasingly shrinking land base has resulted in a greater need for women and men to supplement traditional occupations in cultivation and crafts with waged work.[16] This situation is made more difficult given the reduced educational opportunities that Indigenous peoples experience and the rapid changing labor market.[17] Indigenous women across the Global South are increasingly migrating to urban centers and emigrating to the industrialized centers of the Global North. In Bangladesh and Nepal, for example, many Indigenous women are taking jobs in the garment and textile industries. In Latin American they tend to concentrate in domestic work. Most Indigenous women take jobs in the informal economy, which renders them ineligible for labor law protections, health care, or longer term planning systems like social security.[18]

Clearly, a blanket approach to describing women's experience worldwide hides the fact that class, racialization, and colonialism have a significant impact in the life opportunities of women. Poor women, Women of Color, and especially Indigenous women in the so-called "developing" world but also increasingly in "expendable" communities of the "industrial world" bear the greatest negative impact of capitalism. Globalization and the neoliberal policies that have dominated the world for the past half-century have been especially brutal to racialized women, exacerbating their conditions of precarity, further cheapening their labor, and creating social conditions that victimize them in a host of ways.[19]

In countries where healthcare is not universal, poor women's health suffers most since they have less access to paid medical benefits and fewer financial resources. A woman in Sierra Leone, for example, is 100 times more likely to die during childbirth than a woman in Canada. Among poor families and especially rural families in the "developing" world, girls have fewer opportunities than boys to access education since the perception (often a reality) is that they may be less likely than boys to find paid employment, making girls' education a greater financial burden to the family than boys' education. Since Indigenous languages are rarely taught in schools, Indigenous women in Latin America are twice as likely to lack literacy skills than a non-Indigenous woman.[20]

In addition, working-class racialized women often have the most physically demanding jobs and labor under extremely poor working conditions. Reports of labor law abuses abound across industries. Consider, for example in export manufacturing, the Bangladesh garment industry that employs predominantly Bangladeshi women. In 2013 the Rana Plaza factory collapse that claimed 1100 lives brought international protests from workers demanding wage increases, better working conditions, and a stop to human rights violations in the more than 5000 garment factories belonging to such corporate giants as GAP and Walmart. Although the legal minimum wage was subsequently raised from $39 per month to $68 per month, this was still significantly less than the $100 workers had demanded and still many companies fail to comply with the new legal minimum wage.[21] It is important to understand that abuses against workers, especially in industries that employ predominantly poor women, are the standard rather than the exception.

The world is finally coming to recognize the significant phenomena of domestic violence, sexual assault, and sexual harassment as common to women's experiences. Poor women are especially vulnerable to these experiences because they lack the economic and social resources that protect more affluent women. Transgender Women of Color are experiencing a period of brutal violence in the aftermath of increased legal rights and social acceptance for LGBTQIA communities.[22] The severe violence against Native women's bodies in settler states, including rape, disappearance, and murder, is finally being recognized, via the #Am I next movement.[23] In addition, the billion dollar horrific industry of sex and human trafficking targets predominantly the most vulnerable women.[24] In some countries women may lack the legal means to defend themselves against this violence.[25]

There are also institutionalized forms of violence against women. In the United States for example, racialized women, especially Black women, are over-represented in comparison to White women in incarceration rates. The so-called beauty industries, including the weight-loss industry, are billion dollar industries that create and profit off of women's emotional and psychological distress.[26]

Consider also the significant increase of immigration from peripheral countries to the industrial world. The displacement of peoples as a result of poverty, war, and environmental disasters has and continues to push large numbers of women and families to seek safety and a better life in the industrialized world. Immigrant women, especially undocumented women, have often faced physical, psychological, and sexual violence and wage theft under the threat of deportation or other negative consequences.[27]

Today immigrants and refugees are increasingly facing a hostile reception in the "developed" world. While this is in part due to the scapegoating that occurs during periods of increased economic precarity among the working and middle classes, there is no doubt that racism and xenophobia are important elements to this rejection. The United States election of Donald Trump is an instructive case of racism given that he was elected despite persistently espousing a racist narrative against immigrant, Indigenous, Black, Muslim, and Latinx communities (in addition to misogynist and anti-LGBTQIA narratives). He has since made evident his White nationalist agenda by shutting down refugee programs, attempting to reverse the Deferred Action for Childhood

Arrivals (DACA) program, launching a massive deportation project against Latinx, predominantly Mexican, undocumented persons, demanding a wall at the US-Mexican border, attempting to drastically change immigration law against family reunification and toward a selective immigration that excludes the neediest persons, and tearing apart families seeking asylum through child theft and the criminal prosecution of parents.[28] These policies and attitudes against immigrant and refugee families especially target Mexican and Central Americans and are particularly painful and trying for Latinx women and children.

Although this violence reflects current conditions, it is important to note that these are not new phenomena. The exploitation of women can be traced back to the development of "tools of destruction" in the hunter-gatherer age.[29] The hyper exploitation of Indigenous women and Women of Color is a product of colonial relations and its ties to capitalist development.[30] Seemingly as we improve the condition of women's lives in certain areas, society finds new alternate ways of increasing the exploitation and the oppression of women. The discussion above makes one thing clear: The oppression of Indigenous women and Women of Color is clearly a function of a complex interplay between gender, colonialism, race, class, and other antagonisms. It is my contention that this violence against Indigenous women and Women of Color will not be eradicated unless we develop a struggle that is anti-capitalist, anti-imperialist, anti-sexist, anti-racist as well as against all other forms of oppression, and that seeks to decolonize not only through equitable material conditions but by engaging with Indigenous knowledges, cultures, and ways of being in the world and with nature.

Class and the Mode of Production

The historical materialism that Marx developed demands that we trace the development of women's oppression through the changing modes of production. This approach posits that the mode of production is the key enduring feature of any society because it sets the conditions for its own reproduction through the material necessity of food, water, and other necessary resources.[31] Materialism does not refer to class per se but to conditions that are set up through societal structures that are outside of our consciousness.[32] Unfortunately an ahistorical approach to women's oppression has led to explanations founded on biological determinism and the attribution of specific characteristic to human nature without examining how patriarchal relations have shifted and developed along with changing material conditions.[33] In like manner, a historical materialist perspective on racism examines the material contexts under which the White man defined himself superior. As I will show below, in both cases we find systems of domination put in place to support the accumulation of capital.

It is important to note that tracing the development of gender and racial oppression through the mode of production does not mean that everything is reduced to class nor does it give class primacy over other antagonisms. Further historical materialism does not develop a causal relationship to gender, racial, or other oppressions. The misrepresentation of materialism as the "base" and idealism as the "superstructure" fails to recognize Marx's dialectical method. Rather than simply turning Hegel "right side up" as many have claimed, Marx attempted to bring in the material along with Hegel's notion of consciousness to explain existing conditions, recognizing that each was an aspect of the other.[34] Joel Kovel makes this argument:

> This discussion may help clarify a vexing issue on the left as to the priority of different categories of what might be called 'dominative splitting'—chiefly, those of gender, class, race, ethnic and national exclusion, and, with the ecological crisis, species. Here we must ask, priority in relation to what? If we intend prior in *time*, then gender holds the laurel—and, considering how history always adds to the past rather than replacing it, would appear as at least a trace in all further dominations. If we intend prior in *existential* significance, then that would apply to whichever of the categories was put forward by immediate historical forces as these are lived by masses of people: thus to a Jew living in Germany in the 1930s, anti-Semitism would have been searingly prior, just as anti-Arab racism would be to a Palestinian living under Israeli domination today, or a ruthless, aggravated sexism would be to women living in, say, Afghanistan. As to which is *politically* prior, in the sense of being that which whose transformation is practically more urgent, that depends upon the preceding, but also upon the deployment of all the forces active in a concrete situation. ... If, however, we ask the question of *efficacy*, that is, which split sets the others into motion, then priority would have to be given to class, for the plain reason that class relations entail the state as an instrument of enforcement and control, and it is the state that shapes and organizes the splits that appear in human ecosystems. Thus class is both logically and historically distinct from other forms of exclusion (hence we should not talk of 'classism' to go along with 'sexism' and 'racism', and 'species-ism'). This is, first of all, because class is an essentially man-made category, without root in even a mystified biology. We cannot imagine a human world without gender-distinction—although we can imagine a world without domination by gender. But a world without class is eminently imaginable—indeed, such was the human world for the great majority of our species' time on earth, during all of which considerable fuss was made over gender. Historically, the difference arises because 'class' signifies one side of a larger

figure that includes a state apparatus whose conquests and regulations create races and shape gender relations. Thus there will be no true resolution of racism so long as class society stands, inasmuch as a racially oppressed society implies the activities of a class-defending state. Nor can gender inequality be enacted away so long as class society, with its state, demands the super-exploitation of woman's labor. Class society continually generates gender, racial, ethnic oppressions and the like, which take on a life of their own, as well as profoundly affecting the concrete relations of class itself. It follows that class politics must be fought out in terms of all the active forms of social splitting. It is the management of these divisions that keeps state society functional. Thus, though each person in a class society is reduced from what s/he can become, the varied reductions can be combined into the great stratified regimes of history—this one becoming a fierce warrior, that one a routine-loving clerk, another a submissive seamstress, and so on, until we reach today's personifications of capital and captains of industry. Yet no matter how functional a class society, the profundity of its ecological violence ensures a basic antagonism which drives history onward. History *is* the history of class society—because no matter how modified, so powerful a schism is bound to work itself through to the surface, provoke resistance ('class struggle'), and lead to the succession of powers.[35]

As Kovel notes above, class struggle alone cannot liberate women, racial minorities, or any other group. As well, it would be very difficult to achieve a classless society without attending to the liberation of all oppressed groups since these systems of domination work in tandem to sustain capitalist relations. These antagonisms also keep people divided ideologically and materially and truncate possibilities that we might work together to create class consciousness. Even if we were able to work together across hierarchical differences to bring down the capitalist class, without significant commitment and resolution to eradicate other oppressions any classless society would be short-lived because the ideologies that support systems of domination would remain.

Clearly Marx's work cannot possibly be considered deterministic since his was a call for the workers of the world to rise in unison against capitalism and establish a path to freedom. Marx posited that the material conditions set up conditions of possibility—that is, we are neither condemned to live a predetermined life nor are we completely free to choose from endless possibilities. Structural constraints exist but within these we have agency to act and change the world. As Marx professed in his Thesis on Feuerbach:

> The materialist doctrine that men are products of circumstances and upbringing, and that, therefore, changed men are products of changed circumstances and changed upbringing, forgets that it is men who change circumstances and that the educator must himself be educated.[36]

The argument that economic restructuring has not resulted in women's liberation is an accurate one. Although socialist revolutions initially brought about great improvements in women's rights and gender equality,[37] establishing favorable laws and, in the case of long-lasting revolutions, such as Cuba, have made significant economic changes that support women, changes in sexist and racist attitudes have not developed as quickly.[38] It is thus evident that while a socialist revolution is a necessary condition for women's liberation, it is to be expected that changes in social relations take time to develop. The attitudes and values of the revolutionary leaders must be aligned with gender and racial equality and with the equality of Indigenous peoples and this must not be a "false generosity,"[39] or a "politics of recognition"[40] but an actual commitment to the process of transforming gender and race relations of domination in ways that put racialized women in leadership positions and their ideas into policy.[41] We ought to be mindful of four important points when we critique the idea that class must be abolished for women's liberation: 1) women's liberation and the development of a socialist consciousness have not been given the prominent role necessary in past or current revolutions; 2) socialism is not merely the economy that is established after seizing the capitalist state but a process of economic and ideological changes that may take many years to establish itself to a significant degree; 3) many so-called socialist revolutions or "communist states" have diverted significantly from what Marx envisioned as "communism," developing instead forms of state capitalism, such that we must be careful of claims made based upon these "models"; and 4) capitalism is a global economic order and any nation that attempts to develop an alternative is limited by its need to continue to take part in a global economy. A viable alternative to be fully realized will require a transnational effort.

The Rise of Gender Exploitation and Class Relations

Maria Mies traced women's exploitation through modes of production and argues that women's exploitation and subjugation has been the global precondition for the development of capitalist production.[42] Mies argues that historical accounts suggest that the first division of labor was between men and women and dates back to Indigenous hunter-gatherer societies and to the "tools of destruction" developed initially for hunting animals.[43] Mies recounts the gender relations in these societies, which consisted of a division of labor wherein women cultivated fruits, vegetables, and grains while men went out in long expeditions to hunt animals for food and other goods. Mies argues that men depended on women's production to survive during hunting expeditions that sometimes took months at a time. Meat was, thus, not a daily staple but rather a luxury item and therefore it was women's food production that supported the tribes. Hunting as an economy of risk, Mies argues, could not have been considered the primary basis of subsistence and women's roles as primary subsistence providers gave them significant power.[44] While Mies takes almost a reverse position to the traditional male-centered depictions of hunter-gatherer bands wherein men were central figures responsible for the tribe's welfare and women were passive and inconsequential, Linda Owen, taking a much more balance approach, providing significant detail about the significance of women's contributions to subsistence and also points out the likelihood that the presumed division of labor was not as strictly defined as traditional anthropological accounts suggest.[45] Indeed, there is growing documentation that Indigenous hunter-gatherer societies were much more egalitarian and some were matriarchal.[46]

Mies points out that while "women's activity" was productive and generative of life, "men's hunting" was destructive of life. The tools they designed were meant to kill animals for food and other products. Eventually these tools began to be used by men not only against animals to secure foods but also as weapons against other tribes. According to Mies, the advantage that women had as the producers of daily staples for subsistence in hunter-gatherer societies was lost when men began to realize that they could use their tools of destruction not only to kill animals but to kill or coerce other human beings to doing their will, including forcing women to work for them and to control the production processes.[47] It is imperative to debunk the sexist myth that men, with their "natural" aggressiveness and hyper sexuality, have always dominated women and that women were dependent on men for protection and food. Historical research does not support this myth. Instead it records women's early engagement over production and shows them agentic and very capable of working collectively to ensure their own and their children's subsistence.[48]

Hunting and gathering gave way to a pastoral economy based on domestication and animal breeding.[49] According to Mies, when men became aware of their own productive capacity to impregnate women, rape increased, and sexuality became much more controlled. It is generally accepted that pastoral societies had greater gender inequality than hunter-gatherer societies. The agriculturalists who followed in this vein of coercion and domination of women established marriage laws to bind women, whose main responsibility was farming and having children.[50] At this time a man's wealth was based on marriage and the number of wives he had, since more women and children meant greater production. Women (and to a lesser extent young men) were often kidnapped, enslaved, and forced to marry. These were also the origins of polygamy.

According to Mies, class relations seems to have emerged when violence or the threat of violence began to be used by men to forcibly take women from other villages and enslave them in order to accumulate a surplus of goods—more than necessary for subsistence. The Chiefs usually were able to secure the greatest number of female slaves and/or wives. Here we see the beginnings of class divisions and additional forms of domination due to lineage. The men who were not able to secure as many female slaves were seen as weaker beings.[51]

This history suggests that class relations developed alongside the exploitation of women with the impetus being the accumulation of goods and services. Here we can deduce that while gender relations of domination precede class relations, the domination of women is nonetheless from inception based upon men's desire to amass foods and gain prominence as a result of his production prowess. The modes of production shifted upon technological innovations but retained class as a defining factor in relations of production as well as gender relations that came to be a relation of exploitation and domination. An important note to stress, however, is that while tools of destruction created the conditions of possibility that developed into gender power relations and the exploitation of women, other possibilities existed and could have taken shape. This is to say that we, as women, were not fated to be exploited but rather specific historical circumstances took shape that evolved into relations of exploitation and domination.

Industrialization and the Family

Other materialist feminists, even when they critique Marx on other grounds, have taken up a historical materialist analysis and provided important insights into the development of women's exploitation and oppression. For example, Silvia Federici traces women's current conditions to industrialization, which led to the nuclear family and shifted the division of labor into the specific forms established under capitalism today.[52] She argues that as industrialization pushed the people off land subsistence and into waged work a much starker contrast was created between women of the working classes who necessarily had to find waged work and bourgeois women who remained in the home. Given the brutal working conditions of factory work and the difficulties that having to work away from home presented for women who were pregnant or lactating, women, whenever financially possible, generally opted to stay at home tending to housework and children. Although the gender division of labor existed prior to industrialization, the separation of work into separate physical spaces made performing non-gender specific work more difficult.[53]

At the same time that the gender division of labor was becoming solidified as appropriate, necessary and even "natural," the nuclear family was developing as a result of families moving to the industrial city for waged work. Given that prior to waged work, families had pooled their resources for subsistence, it followed "naturally" that the wages of the worker in the family would be used to support the family, making domestic work unwaged. "Women's labor power," thus, became devalued as unpaid labor.[54]

Silvia Federici's important work on the witch hunts of the 16th century adds a new dimension to this examination of the material conditions that led to women's exploitation.[55] She documents that before capitalism took off as the mode of production, women lived more open and sexual lives and that they were perceived to hold natural powers (as a result of their child-bearing capacities) that could potentially sway men to challenge the capitalist order. In an era of changing economic conditions, older women were increasingly facing land enclosures that left them begging for subsistence on the streets. Since these older women held the collective memory of pre-capitalist times they presented a strong threat to the new economic order. Western Europe launched a crusade against women that was also taken up in Latin America and the United States. Women, who were made to be "witches," were massacred in the hundreds of thousands and their ways of life were significantly changed for generations to come. To avoid persecution women were relegated to the safety of the home and to a repressive association to their sexuality, further entrenching the woman to a space of servitude under the nuclear family.[56]

Here we have a dialectical historical materialist interpretation of the development of stereotypes about "women's nature," that recognizes both the role of capitalist development and the need to secure its growth along with supernatural beliefs about women. Here material and ideational reality conjoin to develop a massive persecution of women and eventually to entrench them as meek, unassertive, asexual, and best suited to the private sphere of the home.

Heather Brown demonstrates that Marx's notes on the history of women and the family in non-western societies from his ethnological notebooks loosely concur with this interpretation.[57] His research led him to discover that women's oppression throughout history took on specific characteristics that differed according to family conditions. Indeed, Marx's notebooks point to shifts in the family, from clan to patriarchy to nuclear, developing alongside economic changes. According to Marx, the shift to the nuclear family increased the isolation of women, making them more vulnerable to the abuses of husbands, which gave men greater control over women and secured their reproductive roles within the family and within capitalism.[58] Federici critiques Marx's masculine lens, arguing that it limited his ability to clearly examine the historical conditions that have led to their oppression. I completely agree that Marx did not develop a complete analysis of women's oppression and as a man was likely blind to aspects of women's labor and experiences. Importantly, however, Federici's contributions do not contradict Marx's argument that women's condition of oppression and exploitation related to the gender division of labor and the development of the nuclear family under capitalism. Rather, her work adds a new dimension to the entrenchment of women in the home and the greater concretization of the division of labor. Undoubtedly there are many more contributions to be made to further develop Marx's ideas. Drawing on his work as a foundation for understanding the oppression and exploitation of numerous groups does not preclude us from continuing to study and learn about the varying ways in which particular social relations have developed. Indeed, we need this more than ever, especially regarding our understanding of the roles of Indigenous women and Women of Color.

A Marxist interpretation of women's oppression, thus, is dialectical, recognizing their exploitation within both work and family and in the productive and reproductive spheres. The division of labor, women's depressed wages, and their free domestic labor secures cheap or free labor for the capitalist and also keeps women under strict control by men and families, in order to secure what Marx called the special commodity, the production and reproduction of the next generation of workers, including their labor power and the attitudes and values necessary for a society that functions off their exploitation. It is important to note here that too often feminist analysis has failed to capture the reality of poor women and Women of Color who have never been able to live "normalized" bourgeois lives and who also entered the waged workforce during industrialization, even while under persecution as witches.

Today, women's workforce participation has grown significantly but the devaluation of their labor power, their cheap wages, and the entrenched ideologies
that their "place is in the home" creates for most women, poor and middle
class, a double shift that inhibits the transformation of gender ideologies and
equitable material conditions. These conditions both reflect and hold up the
capitalist system.

Coloniality, Slavery, and Primitive Accumulation

Racism is dialectically related to capitalist relations. There is a long-standing
feud between race and class theorists regarding which oppression came first
and caused the other.[59] This feud is especially prevalent in discussions regarding the development of western imperialism, the colonization of most of the
non-western world, and American slavery, which resulted in mass genocides
and an unwarranted horrific brutality against Indigenous, Black, and Brown
peoples and created sub-human ideologies of non-western peoples that have
been sustained for over five hundred years. Certainly, the genocide and
conquering of foreign lands, the establishment of colonies throughout the
Global South and settler colonialism was and is an economy of dispossession
meant to enrich and support the "development" of the west.[60] It is important to note that the differential level of economic "development" that is
found between the west and the non-western world is a direct result of this
dispossession.

Race as a category was developed during the plantation era to justify the
transatlantic slave trade and the enslavement of Black peoples in perpetuity.[61]
Although the slave economy had existed in various parts of the world, it was
based on class. In the "new world" White slaves were indentured until full
payment was rendered.[62] There is no doubt that American slavery and the
construction of racism were economic constructions. Indeed, industrialization
in the United States developed on the backs of Black slaves who built the
cotton industry.

Marx's critique of capitalism recognized "dispossession" as an essential
aspect of capitalist production.[63] One of the most commonly known aspects
of Marxist theory, detailed in *Capital*, is the process of extracting unpaid labor
(creating surplus value) from workers who are paid only for a portion of the
working day. It is this surplus value that is turned into capital when it is invested
in new cycles of production. Marx states, "The production of surplus-value, or
the making of profits, is the absolute law of this mode of production."[64]

With the growth of wealth that accompanies accumulation, we see more and more concentration of the means of production in the hands of capitalists who either confront each other in competition or consolidate their property. In competition, we have then an increase in exploitation, the demand for greater and greater surplus value, and an attempt to beat out the competition. Wealthier capitalists buy out smaller capitalists in a process of centralization. While the process of accumulation is slow, centralization is capable of quick tremendous growth and is responsible for the growth of specific industries. In our day, we see this in the concentration of capital among billionaires and multi-billion-dollar corporations, creating a withering away of the middle class and leaving a large portion of the population as workers. Centralization accelerates growth by increasing the use of machinery and automation, which increases the productivity of labor but also eventually decreases the necessary labor power, pushing large numbers of workers into permanent or semi-permanent unemployment.[65]

Colonialism became and continues to provide the greatest form of hyper-exploitation, with significantly cheap labor and horrific working conditions. Marx uses the example of Ireland which was at the time experiencing a significant depopulation due to the potato famine of 1846, wherein one million people died, and to a significant exodus from Ireland to the United States. At the same time, farms were being highly centralized with the wealthiest capitalists buying off smaller farms. While workers lived under extreme pauperization, the total social capital of the country was significantly prosperous. Marx argued that the capital growth of Ireland was especially beneficial to the English aristocrats who sought to buy meat and wool from Ireland at the cheapest possible prices for the English market but more importantly the unemployed population of Ireland was especially beneficial to the English bourgeoisie who employed them as cheap labor, which in turn brought down the wages of the English working class.

In *Capital*, Vol. I, Marx also links dispossession to colonialism through the concept of "so-called primitive accumulation," which depicts the horrific process of transition from feudalism to capitalism in western Europe, focusing specifically on England, and its violent appropriation of the means of production of non-capitalist communities and societies through "conquest, enslavement, robbery, and murder."[66] Glen Coulthard in *Red Skin, White Masks* brings an important Indigenous lens to Marxism. He states:

> In *Capital*, these formative acts of violent dispossession set the stage for the emergence of capitalist accumulation and the reproduction of capitalist relations of production

by tearing Indigenous societies, peasants, and other small-scale, self-sufficient agricultural producers from the source of their livelihood—*the land*.[67]

This separation of the people from their means of production, which was their means of subsistence, opened up territories to private enterprise and forced the people into the labor market, creating a class of workers in direct distinction from those who owned the means of production—the capitalists. Coulthard argues that it would be a mistake for Indigenous communities to reject or ignore the insights of Marx but he posits three critiques that are worth addressing. The first Coulthard critique is that Marx ascribed a temporal association to his concept of primitive accumulation, articulated as an *initial* process of capitalist development. The most famous critique of Marx's temporal emphasis came from Rosa Luxemburg, in *The Accumulation of Capital*, which was a brutally honest portrayal and unequivocal indict-ment of imperialism and the colonizer's barbaric pillaging and murderous treatment of Indigenous peoples.[68] Luxemburg was a vital and extraordinary revolutionary figure who courageously denounced imperialism and set out to demonstrate the *spatial* dimension of capitalism. She argued that Marx con-fined himself to *temporal* dynamics and, thus, missed the *integral* relationship of imperialism to capitalism.[69] According to Luxemburg, capitalism "depends from its inception on absorbing and destroying non-capitalist strata" in order to correct the internal crisis of capitalism that Marx articulated as "a tendency of the falling rate of profit."[70] The increase of production through machinery (constant capital), which pushes workers into unemployment or semi-unemployment, as discussed above, creates a crisis of overproduction, wherein production is accelerated while also limiting workers' purchasing power. According to Peter Hudis and Kevin Anderson, "Rosa Luxemburg argued that the fundamental contradiction of capital lies in the 'unlimited expansive capacity of the productive forces' and the 'limited capacity of social consumption.'"[71] Luxemburg argued that this contradiction necessi-tates buyers from outside capitalist societies or from pre-capitalist societies.[72]

Although clearly accurate in her understanding that capitalism drew heavily on the non-capitalist world for its development and growth, Luxem-burg perceived that the only way to increase means of production (constant capital) was by first selling the product of labor and turning it into "pure value" or the money form. She argued that with little purchasing power in the capitalist world the capitalist must turn to the non-capitalist world for expan-sion of the "market" and find additional buyers. Her approach was market driven and gave too much power to notions of supply and demand.[73]

Hudis, however, convincingly points out that Marx did not ignore spatial dimensions of capitalism. This is evident in his chapter on "so-called" primitive accumulation wherein he articulates the dispossession of the non-western world as the "chief moments of primitive accumulation."[74] What Marx argued, which Luxemburg did not grasp, was that in certain industries the product itself—in its use form—is inserted as means of production into new cycles of production; it need not be realized in its abstract value form through the market (money) prior to insertion into capitalist production. Not only that, but according to Hudis, Marx argued, "the material or use-form of the product is of decisive importance in pre-determining the destination of the elements of expanded reproduction."[75]

What this suggests is that the conquest of territory or the appropriation of lands are often used as capital in the development of new industries of production. Luxemburg correctly articulated that imperialism and the colonial appropriation of land was essential to accumulation but she gave too great an emphasis on the need for new markets to address overproduction in capitalist states. This is the common supply and demand model. Certainly, markets must sometimes be expanded in consequence to overproduction but this is not internal to the process of capitalist production as is what Marx pointed out as the tendency of the falling rate of profit. This internal crisis, wherein the increase in production diminishes value while at the same time greater and greater production is needed to create increasing amounts of surplus value and accumulation, is, according to Marx, why imperialism and colonial relations remain a permanent feature of capitalism.

That Marx articulated this internal crisis supports the idea that he was well aware of the fact that capitalism would continually need to seek out new sources for the creation of surplus value. From this interpretation, Marx's theory of accumulation explains from an economic standpoint the devastation that western capitalism erected on the non-western world, a devastation that continues today, even as much of the non-western world has itself become capitalist.

The second critique that Coulthard posits has to do with the Eurocentricism and racism against non-western peoples that Marx evidenced in his early work and the misrepresentation of his work as depicting a specific developmental path that would lead each nation in turn from its particular mode of production through capitalism and onto communism. This critique is answered more fully in Chapter 3. Here I merely say that while the early Marx was a product of his time, there is evidence that as he came to learn about non-western societies, he became less Eurocentric, naming the colonizers the "barbarians," and emphasizing that his theory of capitalism was intended to depict capitalist development in England, not throughout the world. Coulthard acknowledges that toward the end of his life Marx was engaged with understanding what he called the Asiatic Mode of Production and with trying to learn from the more egalitarian elements of non-western societies.[76]

The third critique that Coulthard levied against Marx is that the focus of his philosophy was the critique of capitalism and that he was interested in colonialism only in so far as it illuminated a defining aspect of the capital relation—the expropriation of the worker from their means of production. In Coulthard's analysis, Marx's main concern with colonialism is in the process of proletarianism, or pushed into selling their labor for subsistence. Coulthard is concerned that this emphasis reduces land to a mere instrumentality rather than understanding that the appropriation of land itself, outside of its material impact on the people, is an act of violence of gargantuan proportions against Indigenous peoples whose relationship to land he proposes is best depicted through the concept of "responsibility."

Although Marx certainly does not write nearly as much about land as he does about the laboring class, it is important to understand that Marx's philosophy had to do not merely with changing the mode of production but with creating a new humanism. In *Capital*, Marx writes from the perspective of the capitalist and from this perspective land is a source of wealth and the worker is the source of value. He describes a "metabolic rift" that occurs when the laborer is separated from the means of production and put to work to create commodities that have not only use value but also abstract value. For Marx the separation of worker and land is not only a violent enactment for the worker who is thereby rendered exploitable but for the land that becomes subjugated and exploited for its resources.[77]

Decolonial theorists have also reached back in history to make sense of the rise of western male domination. Ramon Grosfoguel argues that it is the horrific history of systematic genocide and epistemicide that gave way to the "western imperial being."[78] According to Grosfoguel, it was Descartes' proposition in 1637 of the *ego cogito*—I think, therefore I am—that proclaimed western male thought to be rational and objective "Truth" and severed the "rational thinking mind" from the body politic, as if floating above a body that is grounded. This rational and objective mind was then proclaimed the defining attribute of what it means to be human, rendering all those who fall outside the narrow confines of western man subhuman—irrational, animalistic, led by instinct and emotion. Grosfoguel points out that this logic was made possible by the *ego-conquiro*—I am, therefore I conquer—that began with the western colonial expansion of 1492 wherein western man internalized themselves as superior beings because they had conquered the world. It was the ego *exterminus*—the logic of genocide and epistemicide—that supported and justified the I conquer. Grosfoguel points out that the *ego exterminus* can be situated in the four genocides/epistemicides of the 16th century that were carried out "1) against Muslims and Jews in the conquest of Al-Andalus in the name of 'purity of blood'; 2) against Indigenous peoples first in the Americas and then in Asia; 3) against African people with the captive trade and their enslavement in the Americas; 4) against women who practiced and transmitted Indo-European knowledge in Europe burned alive accused of witches."[79]

While a historical materialist perspective locates the impetus for this genocide on the capital accumulation of the capitalist class, decolonial theorist Walter Mignolo argues that a subaltern approach focuses on both the Subjects that act and those that are acted upon. Deeds do not just happen in the abstract, rather they happen *to* and *by* a racially marked, gendered body that include other characteristics located in a particular space and time.[80] This is a dialectical approach that supports the explanatory power of capital accumulation but also maintains the subjective positioning and the values and beliefs inherent to that positioning of the White man as colonizer of Indigenous peoples. The genocidal atrocities inflicted upon Indigenous communities, women, and others have always been justified by the need to cleanse the Other of their "ungodly" ways. However, this does not change the fact that such ideologies emerge out of conditions that have arisen from the mode of production and the desire of the capitalist class to maintain this system that they rule for their own benefit. Here we see capitalism in dialectical relation to racism, with each an aspect of and supporting the other.

From its beginnings, capitalism has been a world system that has preyed on the racialized and gendered Other and these conditions continue unabated under current global capitalism, especially for Indigenous women and Women of Color, not only in the "developing world," but also for those displaced from their Indigenous lands or communities and who find themselves politically and socially minoritized in the industrialized world. The shifts that capitalism has undergone as a result of the cyclical crisis and recovery that capitalism periodically faces, has not only intensified the oppression, subjugation, and humiliation of Indigenous women and Women of Color but has led to qualitative differences in the ways in which they live in the world. For this reason, of course, it has become clear to me that we must engage the insights, courage, and indignation of Indigenous women and Women of Color to help us find an alternative to capitalism. It is Indigenous women and Women of Color who undoubtedly bear collectively the bleeding hearts and hands of the most oppressed and exploited peoples in existence and it is for our sisters and our children that we will take up the struggle against capitalism that will one day bring this monstrous giant to its knees.

Maria Mies describes the parallels between the gender division of labor and the international division of labor, which led the way to the development of capitalism and continues to be a significant source of its accumulation.[81] That is, the informal labor of women controlled by men via the threat of violence laid the foundations for capitalism to take shape. This informal "women's work" could be any of the following: unwaged, forced, uncontracted, unregulated, and very rarely unionized. What this meant was that women's work was extremely cheap, without benefits, and with few controls to make their work environments safe and sanitary.[82] Under these conditions women's work contributes significantly to production, either directly or indirectly, and allows for substantial profits. In a similar vein, the labor of Indigenous peoples, under colonial rule, was forced and unregulated, and workers were subject to tremendous atrocities that garnered for the capitalist and the colonial government significant riches. What Mies terms the "housewification" of colonized and otherwise marginalized People of Color, especially Women of Color around the world, is the growth variable that has fed the capitalist system, through expanding markets and increased production at cheap costs, which has resulted in favorable results for the capitalist. However, the atrocities committed against women and Indigenous peoples cannot be explained through mere economic gains. Ideology plays a significant part in people accepting the atrocities that were committed against Native peoples.

Whitestream Feminisms

In the United States, the feminist movement as an organized and recognized movement was spurred on by abolition, wherein Black women were the first women to stand up publicly for their rights. On the heels of abolition the Civil Rights Movement sought greater rights for Black people. There is no doubt that many White women allied themselves to the abolitionist movement and supported their Black sisters' and brothers' rights to freedom and civil rights. Yet this is not the whole story. bell hooks points out that if the feminist movement had moved seamlessly from abolition to women's rights, it would have been a movement that recognized the double oppression of Black women and other Women of Color. Instead, hooks argues, White women, while claiming support for greater civil rights for Blacks, were nonetheless fearful and/or indignant that Black men might gain the right to vote before they did on the basis of gender.[83] According to Jesse Daniels, White women leaders took the opportunity to divert the focus on civil rights for their own ends and begin the fight for women's suffrage on the grounds that they were better equipped to the task of voting than Black men.[84] Daniels documents that racism and White supremacy played a central role in the development of the feminist movement. Lori Ginsberg argues that the leaders of the feminist movement, including Elizabeth Cady Stanton, strategically used the racial tensions of the times for her political advantage, making it clear that it was a matter of self-respect to fight for *their* right to vote in the face of the possibility of Black suffrage:

> Elizabeth Cady Stanton's positions on the relative worthiness of black men and white women as citizens … her choice of all-too-familiar racist language had broad and lasting consequences, both theoretical and strategic, for the movement she helped lead. By claiming that some American citizens were more worthy of rights than others, Stanton helped lay the groundwork for a defense of woman's rights based on race, respectability, religion and class that would be hard to shake. Surely Stanton and Anthony understood this when they reported on the formation of a 'White Woman's Suffrage Association' in Washington, D.C., or admitted that the proposed Fifteenth Amendment 'rouses woman's prejudices against the negro' while increasing 'his contempt and hostility toward her as an equal.' Furthermore, this appeal to prejudice, whether it was an intentional strategy or not, worked. One woman wrote Stanton and Anthony's newspaper, *The Revolution*, to declare that she had 'never thought, or cared, about voting till the negroes began to vote,' but now 'felt my self-respect rise.' She went on: 'If educated women are not as fit to decide who shall be the rulers of this country, as 'field hands,' then where's the use of culture, or any brain at all? One might as well have been 'born on the plantation.'[85]

Joanne Barker reports that Susan B. Anthony expressed similar racist ideologies as well as expansionist views in regards to the Philippines and that she expressed views that White women were equally important to voting laws as "Philippinos, Puerto Ricans, Hawaiians, Cubans" who she referred to as "an ignorant and unlettered set of people." Barker also reports on another suffragist, Matilda Josslyn Gage, who expressed racist ideologies in an article she wrote entitled "Indian Citizenship" in response to the suffrage rights conferred on Indigenous peoples, who often rejected this "gift" that went against their rights to self-determination.

> Gage reacted strongly to what she perceived as an attempt to "force [suffrage] on the red man in direct opposition to his wishes, while women citizens, already members of the nation, to whom it rightfully belongs, are denied its exercise ... Can women's political degradation reach much lower depth? ... She educated, enlightened, Christian, in vain begs for the crumbs cast contemptuously aside by savages."[86]

These quotes evidence that the feminist movement used racist and expansionist ideology to rationalizing why White women were more deserving of citizenship than non-White men. This racist history upon which the feminist movement was founded has not been shaken. Sandy Grande points out that although heavily critiqued by Women of Color and despite the rhetoric of inclusion, feminism has remained loyal to the vantage point and interests of a predominantly White middle-class base, what she more accurately terms "Whitestream feminisms."

While the first wave of feminism focused on securing the right to vote, the second wave of feminism was aimed at challenging inequities between men and women, including increasing educational opportunities for women, equal pay, increasing workforce participation, and reproductive rights. This agenda was meant to secure better living conditions for women. The problem was that it defined women's oppression from the vantage point of middle-class women and, therefore, was blind to the different forms of oppression and exploitation that poor women and Women of Color were subjected. Amidst this second wave of feminism, poor White women and Women of Color were rendered invisible. The power relations between women of diverse social and racial backgrounds and the differing material conditions secured privileges to White middle-class women while subjecting Women of Color to a position of subordination and humiliation. Feminism became a dirty name, a signal of White women's racism, wherein they chose to side with the White supremacist capitalist class in order to retain their privileges, even though the structure of capitalism was complicit with their gender exploitation. Here bell hooks is worth quoting at length:

> Ideologically, thinking in this direction enables Western women, especially privileged white women, to suggest that racism and class exploitation are merely an off-spring of the parent system: patriarchy. Within the feminist movement in the West, this has led to the assumption of resisting patriarchal domination as a more legitimate feminist action than resisting racism and other forms of domination. Such thinking

prevails despite radical critiques made by black women and women of color who question this proposition. To speculate that an oppositional division between men and women existed in early human communities is to impose on the past, on these non-white groups, a worldview that fits all too neatly within contemporary feminist paradigms that name man as the enemy and woman as the victim.[87]

hooks points out that although the economic independence gained through waged work and equal pay that takes primacy within the feminist political agenda is an important *step* to gaining liberation for women, this alone cannot be the end goal since it does not address the specificity of oppressive and exploitative conditions affecting Women of Color.[88]

The critiques hurled at this Whitestream feminism led the way to a third wave of feminism or feminisms that sought to be more inclusive of poor women, Women of Color, Indigenous women, Lesbian and Transgender women, Muslim women and all others' identities to which women subscribe. Sandy Grande points out that this third wave, however, continued to be deeply implicated in normalizing White middle-class experiences of oppression and exploitation, while relegating the experiences of Other women, poor and of Color, to the margins. She notes that instead of drawing on intersectionality for explanatory reasons or platform agenda, a multiplicity of feminisms were developed each related to a gendered version of a particular social identity.[89]

Materialist feminists, sometimes also Marxist feminists, developed during this third wave and, like other feminisms, expounded theories that primarily took into account the experiences of White middle-class women. From this perspective the key to understanding women's oppression and exploitation lay in "women's work" under capitalist production. They argued that the key to women's oppression and exploitation lay in the naturalization of "women's work" as caretakers, which is perceived as naturally developed rather than involving particular skills. As a natural result of our capacity to give birth and nourish life, women's caring work has been devalued and their laboring outside the home cheapened given the perception that women are less committed to laboring for wages and more likely to regard this work as supplemental to their more natural caring work. It is presumed that women will one day take maternity leave and take time off of work when children become ill or other family related issues arise. Their commitment to wage labor is seen as waning. From a materialist perspective women become a potential cheap labor reserve that can be induced to work when necessary and in this way keep men's wages down and restrain their attempts to make demands for better pay and working conditions. These conditions are reinforced through the high cost of childcare that often demands women (whose wages are lower than men's) stay home. Here ideologies about women's nature and the material conditions work in tandem to maintain women subordinate to men.

While this Marxist feminist interpretation develops a theory in which women's oppression is clearly related to capitalist relations, as exemplified in the historical materialist analysis presented above by Mies and Federici, it too fails to recognize how these material and ideological conditions differ among racialized, Indigenous, or otherwise marginalized women.

The notion that women's labor is devalued because they are primarily a reserve labor force is a middle-class assumption that is based upon the experiences and privileges of White middle-class women whose White husbands' wages are significantly higher than that of working-class men. Around the globe capitalism has ensured that the poorest women, mostly Women of Color and Indigenous Women without land and living in industrialized areas, have to work for wages. These families differ significantly from the presumed "ideal" bourgeois family. Furthermore, the legacies of colonization and slavery, and the social ills associated with poverty, have established patterns that differ significantly from that of the White middle-class family.

For example, the western logic that divides humans from nature and develops relations of domination between them, defines White men as human and relegates Woman of Color to the sphere of nature, which is perceived as sub human. As such Women of Color and Indigenous women are made into "natural mothers" and clustered in the domestic service industry, working predominantly for middle-class White women who, as the person typically in charge of domestic issues in her home, becomes their boss, setting up relations of domination between Women of Color and White women.[90] It is thus the domestic waged labor of Indigenous women and Women of Color that becomes the source of White women's privilege to work for wages outside the domestic sphere without worrying about her children's welfare and/or without taking on a "second shift" of childcare and housework.[91] The waged domestic worker, in contrast, whose job is generally unregulated and without benefits also faces the psychological trauma of having to care and love other people's children while her own are left either unattended or in free latchkey programs with little personal attention of the type she provides for her employer's children.[92] In this example we see clearly how the interests of waged Women of Color and those of middle-class, generally White, women, come into conflict.

For these waged domestic workers, the emphasis on equal pay, which has long been a priority of the feminist movement, does not change their conditions of subordination and exploitation nor the parental absenteeism their children sometimes endure. Although increased wages support everyone, equal pay with men does not necessarily mean increased wages for working-class Women of Color and Indigenous women whose male counterparts do not make that much more income than they do. Only a classless society that draws heavily on the values and knowledges of Indigenous women and Women of Color will be liberating. Of course, this presents for many White middle and upper-class women a contradiction since the risk and uncertainly of a new society is perceived less necessary to those who experience adequately comfortable lives and are positioned higher up the social hierarchy.

An important understanding about the role that gender relations plays in sustaining capitalism is that men's wages are also depressed by the devaluation of women's work. Since women present a cheap labor force, the capitalist wants women to enter the workforce. This provides the capitalist with a labor force of cheaper workers that could easily replace men who may wish to demand higher wages. This is a strategy that keeps workers controlled under the threat of job loss. However, ideologies about women's natural roles as mothers and men's misogyny hide the capitalist interest in maintaining unequal pay between men and women. This is of special significance since it relegates the gender division of labor and unequal pay to the ideological sphere, making people seek to change traditional gender values and beliefs rather than focusing on how capitalism triumphs under these gender divisions. This circumvents the potential of men and women recognizing their common interests and joining forces against a system that exploits all workers.

The focus among feminists for waged work and equal pay also evidences western notions of equality that completely ignore the interests of Indigenous women. For Indigenous women who have been uprooted from their ancestral lands and made to forgo the life-affirming labor and more egalitarian relations that characterized tribal life, waged work and equal pay is just another way to further entrenching the settler-colonial logic of individualism, production, and accumulation and the devaluation of Indigenous ways of knowing and being, which prioritize community, sustainability, and a sacred relationship to land and nature. According to many Indigenous scholars, emancipation for Indigenous communities is sought via self-determination and the recovery of stolen lands. This is completely incompatible to feminist calls for equal pay, which seek to merely improve conditions within the existing settler-colonial state.

In addition, Whitestream feminists often perceive men to always be the oppressors. However, for Women of Color and Indigenous women, the oppressors are both men *and* White women. Indigenous women may also perceive Mestiza women as the oppressors given their mixed Indigenous and colonial ancestry, and their positioning in relations of domination to Indigenous peoples.

Thus, Indigenous women and many Women of Color may be more prone to side with their brothers of color. This is especially true in the United States where Men of Color experience grave conditions of racism, hatred, violence, and murder. Under these circumstances, Indigenous women, Black women, and Latinx women recognize their need to do whatever it takes to keep their fathers, husbands and male children safe from police shootings, prison, and detention centers. The unbelievable racism and xenophobia evidenced in the attitudes, statements, and policies of the Donald Trump administration and the fact that he has received the support of a majority of White women is not lost on Indigenous women and Women of Color and is likely to increase the divide between White feminists and Feminists of Color.

Women of Color and Indigeneity in the Settler-Colonial State

The brutal history of oppression of Women of Color under slavery and colonial rule has left a legacy of pain and destruction that continues to impact affected communities. For example, Black women's experiences of oppression can be directly related to the material conditions of the plantation era that imported approximately 500,000 slaves from Africa to what is now the United States between 1619 and 1807.[93] The horrific experiences that women, men, and children endured under slavery cannot be over-emphasized. To speak of women's oppression without recognizing this history endured by Black families is to give mere lip service to the ideals of equality and social justice. Black women's oppression in the family cannot be understood without considering how gender relations among them were dictated by White plantation owners who determined almost every aspect of their lives, including their familial relations and their reproductive practices. Consider that enslaved women bore an average of 9.2 children at the demand of plantation owners who used them to breed more children that would become their property.[94] In the concept of "spirit murder," Patricia Williams develops a striking depiction of the legacy of pain and humiliation that the slave era left on Black families.[95]

The material condition that developed the slave trade also had further material repercussions for Black men and women, who upon their emancipation needed to find waged employment amidst racialized ideologies that had been developed to justify slavery and then continued to define the value of their labor power and access to jobs during the following Jim Crow era.[96] We continue to see evidence (finally made more public in the media) that Black women's oppression cannot be isolated from the oppression of Black men, and more generally, Black communities, who continue to be terrorized and targeted for death and incarceration, increasingly at younger ages through the school-to-prison pipeline, in what is now being recognized as, "the new slavery."[97]

The oppression of Black women is not merely related to their economic necessity, although the loss of income that is felt when family members are killed or incarcerated among poor families that depend on multiple incomes cannot be underestimated. However, the middle-class experience of women serving as a reserve labor force for men, and this being an aspect of their labor power depreciation and subsequent dependence on men, is not typical in poor communities of color where men are more often than in middle-class communities to be absent, unemployed, or underemployed. Furthermore, Black women's oppression also results from the senseless loss of loved ones and the lack of opportunities, discrimination, and trauma of racism. Addressing the oppression of Black women must consider the oppression of their entire communities, including their fathers, husbands, and children. In the face of impending genocide, a focus on "equal pay" seems far removed from a commitment to the liberation of all women, much less to that of all human beings.

In a similar vein, Indigenous women's experiences of oppression is tied to the colonial project of dispossession and appropriation that resulted in an unparalleled history of genocide and epistemicide, upon whose backs the White supremacist capitalist class emerged and with which we are all complicit as we live in (and some of us purchase) settled land. The history of oppression and exploitation of Native peoples in settler states that ensued after initial "conquest" is one of continual land encroachment and displacement and cultural and linguistic hegemony. Schooling has served the state well in the continual land theft, displacement, and epistemicide of Indigenous peoples. In the United States, the history of Indigenous boarding schools, the subsequent integration of Indigenous children into public schooling, the Americanization movement, and the "termination period," wherein Indigenous peoples were "freed" from the reservation system and integrated into urban centers and vocational training programs were systematic attempts to de-Indianize and de-Mexicanize communities by erasing their languages and cultures and thereby encroaching on ancestral lands and resources and developing Indian labor.[98] The academy has also been complicit in the dispossession of Indigenous resources by building universities on American Indian reservations, Canadian reserves and other federal or state-designated tribal lands and taking resources earmarked for Indigenous peoples but systematically failing to substantively admit and/or offer them scholarships.[99] This encroachment has never ceased, with Native peoples consistently having to fight the state for their rights to land and other human rights. Sandy Grande points out that the feminist movement has never been able to adequately address the fact that for Native women, their oppression is first and foremost seen as a product of colonization and that White women have failed to recognize their own complicity in the colonial project and global capitalism.

It is important to understand that the colonial project of land appropriation through genocides and epistemicide is also about the consistent attempt to negate the continued existence of Native peoples in order to normalize the White supremacist settler-colonial project as the "immigration experience." In so far as the settler-colonial process is likened to "immigration" and perceived as the "natural" human engagement and freedom to move and resettle makes invisible the reality that immigration is significantly a *consequence* of capitalist imperialism and colonization. The majority of immigrants around the world immigrate in the hopes of finding relief from crushing poverty, wars, land grabs and dispossession, or (often human induced or exacerbated) environmental disasters. Immigration is rarely, as often defined, a choice.

Native scholars and activists, including Audra Simpson, Sandy Grande, Mishuana Goeman, and The Red Nation[100] often discuss the systematic erasure of Indigenous peoples under settler colonialism, where Indigenous peoples are fictionalized as either the "barbaric" first peoples or the "victims" that were wiped out. This positioning is not only a violent continuation of the dehumanization that they "experienced (past tense)" in a presumed colonial past, but also creates a mythical narrative of justification for a reinterpretation of these settler-colonial relations as no longer colonial because Indigenous communities no longer exist. The narrative is thus that the "unfortunate mistakes" against Indigenous communities are a thing of the past because they no longer exist in sufficient numbers to reclaim the lands in which they lived and breathed for thousands of years before invasion. The invisibility of the Indigenous peoples in settle-colonial states is a structural phenomenon meant to ease the social conscience of the settler state and simultaneously increasingly infringe upon the lands and sovereignty of Indigenous peoples. As Nick Estes of The Red Nation states, "Settlement and colonization are never complete processes; they always have to be re-enacted."[101]

The continual existence of Indigenous people in settler states creates overwhelming cognitive dissonance with ideologies that relegate the brutal conditions of colonization and dispossession to the past. According to The Red Nation, the Albuquerque Police Department has the largest percentages of fatal police shootings, eight times as high as NYPD, and the majority of these are killings of Native peoples.[102] Melanie Yazzie explains:

> Colonization presumes the disappearance [of the Native] and the finality of settlement, but Indians are ubiquitous. That fact that we're present makes us anachronisms. We're not supposed to be here, but we're here in really large numbers. That increases the amount of violence necessary to contain us.[103]

In the American unconscious, Indigenous peoples are presumed ghosts of the past. White folks move through the land as if it were theirs with little recognition that Native peoples continue to exist among us. This myth is perpetuated through a persistent Eurocentric curriculum, media, and other state exclusionary tactics.

Indigenous women live out this invisibility as doubly oppressed peoples— oppressed as Indigenous peoples and under the patriarchal relations sustained and enforced through Indigenous Nations. Importantly, it must be understood that the patriarchal structures that exist within Indigenous communities (as well as Black and Latinx communities) are highly linked to the colonial project. Consider, for example, the case of the Mohawk nation, which defined kinship and community belonging through the mother's clan. In the Kahnawake, prior to the Indian Act, community non-Indian spouses of men and women were granted membership in the community, which meant that they could "hold land, operate businesses, and claim tax exemption on the reserve."[104] However, The Indian Act, passed in 1868, supplanted this matrilineal society with a European patrilineal model that aimed to redefine Indigenous women across Canada who married non-Indian men (or non-status Indian men) and their children as non-members, with no rights to hold land or even live in the reservation. Non-Indian female spouses of Indian men and their children, however, were given full rights of membership. Indigenous women fought for over one hundred years to have this sexist provision amended in 1984 through B C-31. However, what this bill does is it allows each community to decide its own membership laws. While in one respect this is a triumph for sovereignty, one hundred-plus years of patriarchal rule and continual land encroachment has led some men to reject this shift to greater gender equality.

Although sexism cannot be solely associated to capitalism and its imperial mandate, physical, sexual, and psychological violence against women is and continues to be one of the most brutal realities of colonization and empire building. Although often exaggerated to demarcate racialized communities as "uncivilized," domestic and other forms of violence against women among Indigenous, Black and other communities of color can be clearly traced back to the colonizer's physical and sexual enslavement of Indigenous, Black, and Mestiza women.

Audra Simpson points out that The Indian Act and other settler-state authorizations are systematic attempts to governmentalize the process of "knowing" Native peoples—a process that is fundamental to conquest and enlisted anthropology and its concept of culture and tools to "mark the end game" of colonial relations by containing difference into "neat, ethnically-defined, territorial spaces that now needed to be made sense of, ranked, to be governed, to be possessed."[105] Simpson challenges the ways in which the state, through its ethnographic knowing, has spoken of and for her people. She explains:

> As an anthropologist I always found such portraits of Indigenous peoples to be strange in light of the deeply resistant, self-governing and relentlessly critical people that I belong to and work with.[106]

Simpson points out that this ethnographic intent was and is more than simply representational, rather a violent act to know and make known Native peoples in ways that do not reflect the voices of Native peoples themselves and in ways that facilitate and legitimize their continual colonization, land theft, and erasure.

This problematic of being made "known" to the White man (and woman) through and for the continual oppression of Native peoples bleeds into notions of recognition, membership, and citizenship. Simpson evidences that the Mohawk peoples "to whom I belong and with whom I work" *refuse* the state "at almost every turn." The contestation of membership with a legal right to land has grown as a result of the continual state encroachment on Native reserves and the limited resources of the community. Of significance is the problem of the disproportionate number of Whites living and holding land in Native reserves as a result of the Indian Act.[107]

The Marxist-humanist goal of liberation seeks a socialist alternative that would eradicate land ownership and state-controlled borders. This is not unproblematic for many Indigenous peoples whose goal of self-determination is heavily based upon the recovery of previously stolen lands. Yet the Marxist-humanist perspective I am drawing upon in this book supports the rights of all peoples to self-determination, recognizing that racialized groups, Indigenous communities, and other oppressed groups have a right to define and struggle for freedom for themselves while we continue to simultaneously support a broader global coalition against capitalism. Kevin Anderson has argued convincingly that Marx in his time supported nationalist movements not only because he argued that these would lead the way toward broader global class struggles, but because all peoples have a right to struggle for their own freedom.[108] Yet the end goal of establishing a Marxist-humanist communism would be to create a society founded on equality, interdependence, and cooperation and in which control of the means of production would be in the hands of the people through democratic processes. Ultimately this approach would challenge land titles. Yet it is without a doubt that Marxist humanism must begin to explore the challenges that notions of reparations poses to the development of a socialist alternative to capitalism. Certainly, Marxists must recognize that establishing equality is not equitable given that certain communities, especially Black and Indigenous communities, have undergone histories of genocide that cannot be easily forgiven or forgotten. At the same time, however, some Indigenous scholars argue "the retention of sovereignty as the ultimate goal of Indigenous politics signifies the ultimate concession to the forces of assimilation."[109] Establishing sovereignty and recovering land rights relinquishes Indigenous notions of land as sacred and instead constitutes western notions of private property that defines land as a commodity—a thing to be owned and used for personal accumulation and production. These considerations are important ones that require continued dialogue among Indigenous and Marxist-humanist scholars, activists, and communities. I discuss this and other contradictions between and among diverse racialized communities further in Chapter 7.

Gender and Racialization Under Global Capitalism

Robinson agrees with Mies' assessment about the role of women and colonialism in the rise and maintenance of capitalism. However, he argues that current trends have shifted from an international division of labor to a transnational division of labor wherein corporations are not necessarily tied to one nation state.[110] This does not negate the continued existence of western domination over the Global South but does mark a new emphasis on colonial relations within the industrial world. Robinson discusses the atrocious realities of the neoliberal age that emerged as a backlash to the gains of the Civil Rights era and Keynesian capitalism. Specifically, neoliberalism has attempted and, in many cases, succeeded in privatizing social services, decreased state controls, and unleashed an unfettered market competition that has impoverished millions around the world and left the poorest in destitute conditions. On the heels of this neoliberal age or perhaps extending it, we are witnessing in the Trump years a growing fascist-like politics across the world that heralds a new age of White supremacy, nationalism, misogyny and conservatism but that retains, with an unmasked disdain, the hyper exploitation of the Global South and its immigrant descendants.

Under these conditions we find that it is women in the developing world that are the most hyper exploited. They are the ones whose lives suffer the most, having fewer opportunities for self-development, which negatively impacts entire communities. Instead, they work under the gun of maquiladora industries that pay little and offer substandard working conditions, while mostly western corporations make millions off their backs.[111] In this new global capitalist economy, where the transnational corporation reigns supreme and a neoliberal ethic of individualism and privatization is the order of the day, the capitalist feels little remorse at the hardships of his workers and no sense of responsibility for the well-being of his fellow citizens (sexist gender here is intentional since capitalists are significantly male). Thus, we are increasingly finding great pauperization among the "disposable communities" of the most advanced capitalist countries. Immigrants are pushed from periphery countries to flee poverty, displacement, and endless wars—ills created within a backdrop of significant economic and political factors that are often hidden from the general population. Thus, we find that many people and governments can swiftly and without remorse turn away women and children (men too, of course) who are running literally for their lives and deny them safety and dignity. This is what many countries in the Global North are doing to the Syrian people.[112]

In the United States, which likes to claim itself "humanitarian," Trump is attempting to rescind existing refugee programs and deport populations that are already receiving asylum for environmental disasters or political persecution and the undocumented communities, especially those from Mexico and Central America, are experiencing a massive deportation campaign.[113] Of course, that the significant immigration increases from the Global South to the developing world is a result of western imperialism is conveniently forgotten as working-class communities scrounge for increasingly limited resources and jobs.

Today's immigrant women, especially undocumented women, face a hostile world in the Global North. Often, they are accused of taking jobs and resources of the host country. Increasingly they are hunted down, detained, and deported—sometimes without due process. Although this practice has been going on for years, today's campaign against immigrants is fierce.[114] The Trump administration's response to asylum seekers—separating families and jailing children—was a heinous crime against humanity. It is critical to understand that problems that may seem isolated to specific parts of the world or disconnected from other issues can be, and often are, part of a broader web of social relations that hold up the capitalist system. Deportations that are often presented to the general population of voters as a way to secure employment opportunities for working Americans are actually related to the maintenance of a highly lucrative prison industrial complex.

Today the prison industrial complex is a multi-billion dollar industry that has become global and in which primarily Black and Brown peoples' bodies are caged and controlled and made to work for close to nothing, while making millions for private corporations.[115] For example, G4S has become the third most profitable corporation in the world by providing a host of security related goods and services to support an industry that includes public and private state prisons, local jails, the juvenile justice system and school policing, the Mexican border patrol and detention centers for undocumented immigrants and asylum seekers. Although under law prisoners are not protected by labor laws, this does not pertain to people in detention centers since they have not been convicted of a crime. Yet public and privately owned detention centers holding undocumented immigrants force them to work for next to nothing, even though outside the detention centers, their undocumented status prevents them from gaining lawful employment. According to a case under review by the ACLU (American Civil Liberties Union), the pay they received was $1 per day for an eight-hour shift.[116] This reality begs the question whether the focus on immigration is merely a ploy for the accumulation of capital.

The incarceration and detention of Women of Color secures an onslaught of terror and destruction against entire communities of color. Since most

Women of Color who are incarcerated or detained are the primary caretakers of children and lack significant resources and support systems, their children's lives are often devastated and entire communities are often affected. Seen from a capitalist perspective this devastation supports the development of expendable communities that are needed to fill the poorest sectors of the economy and to form the next generation of surplus labor. The criminalization of undocumented workers also reinforces the racist ideologies that pathologize communities of color and which justify the inequalities and injustice inherent in capitalism to those people who might otherwise empathize with People of Color. From the perspective of capital that has no human interest, the detention and deportation of undocumented women makes sense when we realize that these women produce more value to the capitalist as slave labor in detention centers or as cheap labor in the maquiladora industries of the Global South.

In the meantime, those immigrant women not detained, whether documented or undocumented, who often work for miserly wages, may not speak English, and may not know their rights. The climate of criminalization and rejection that they are facing, particularly in the United States, is one that makes them especially vulnerable to workplace harassment, sexual assault, physical abuse, and wage theft.[117]

Although there is no way to document the vast issues that racialized women face across the world or the significant variability of experiences that they encounter, there is no doubt that they generally face exploitation in the workplace as well as in the home and that this oppression is class, gender, and race-based. Women of the LGBTQIA face other significant forms of oppression and Muslim women are especially targeted in today's climate that villainizes Muslims across the world. My goal in this chapter has been to give an overview of the development of exploitation among women under capitalism and how imperialism, racism, and global capitalism affect the lives of Indigenous women and Women of Color. Certainly, the hyper exploitation that is documented suggests a long history of struggle without which many of us and our mothers and grandmothers would not have survived. This exploitation is not likely to cease so long as capitalism is the mode of production but neither can we wait for capitalism to fall before we begin to challenge oppression and exploitation based on sexism, racism, sexuality, gender fluidity, religion or any other identity. We cannot claim to support an ideology of liberation and equality while accepting the oppression of any one particular group.

Notes

1. Sections of this chapter appear in Lilia D. Monzó, "Women and Revolution."
2. Angela Y. Davis, *Freedom is a Constant Struggle*, 86.
3. Rosa Luxemburg, "The Proletarian Woman," 243.
4. Indigenous women and Women of Color are categories that encompass significant diversity (for greater explanation of how I use these concepts, see Chapter 1, note 1). Some women may not feel their life experiences are reflective of a systemic violence against women and racialized communities. However, individual experiences can often differ significantly as do the meanings that we attach to these experiences. Although this diversity is important to document, I focus in this book on our collective experience of exploitation. Global and national statistics clearly demonstrate a systemic oppression and exploitation that I would describe as forms of violence.
5. Cherríe Moraga and Gloria Anzaldua, eds., *This Bridge Called My Back*; Maythee Rojas, *Women of Color and Feminism*; Barbara Ehrenreich and Arlie Russell Hochschild, *Global Woman: Nannies, Maids, and Sex Workers in the New Economy*; Incite! *Color of Violence*.
6. Joanne Barker, "Indigenous Feminisms," 2.
7. United Nations, *The World's Women 2015: Trends and Statistics*.
8. Inter-Agency Support Group on Indigenous Peoples' Issues, *Indigenous Peoples' Access to Decent Work and Social Protection*.
9. United Nations, *The World's Women 2015*.
10. Ibid.
11. Ibid.
12. Arlie Hochschild with Anne Machung, *The Second Shift*.
13. United Nations, *The World's Women 2015*.
14. Ibid.
15. Ibid.
16. Inter-Agency Support Group on Indigenous Peoples' Issues, *Indigenous Peoples'*.
17. Ibid.
18. Ibid.
19. Nandini Gunewardena and Ann Kingsolver, eds., *The Gender of Globalization*.
20. United Nations, *The World's Women 2015*.
21. Kanya D'Almeida and Naimul Haq, "Two Years after Rana Plaza Tragedy."
22. Lilia D. Monzó and Peter McLaren, "Challenging the Violence and Invisibility Against Women of Color—A Marxist Imperative."
23. Eve Tuck, "Challenging Whitestream Feminism: Response 1."
24. Siddharth Kara, *Sex Trafficking: Inside the Business of Modern Slavery*.
25. Laura L. O'Toole, et al., *Gender Violence: Interdisciplinary Perspectives*, 2nd ed.
26. Meeta Jha, *The Global Beauty Industry: Colorism, Racism, and the National Body*.
27. Lilia D. Monzó and Peter McLaren, "Women and Violence in the Age of Migration."
28. Lilia D. Monzó, "White Supremacy, Hate, and Violence in Charlottesville."
29. Maria Mies, *Patriarchy and Accumulation on a World Scale*.
30. Mies, *Patriarchy and Accumulation*.

31. Jose P. Miranda, *Marx Against the Marxists*.
32. Paul D'Amato, "Why Was Marx a Materialist?"
33. Nancy Holmstrom, "The Socialist Feminist Project."
34. Karl Marx and Friedrich Engels, *The German Ideology*.
35. Joel Kovel, *The Enemy of Nature: The End of Capitalism or the End of the World?*
36. Karl Marx, "Thesis on Feuerbach," 144.
37. Ana Muñoz and Allan Woods, "Marxism and the Emancipation of Women."
38. Luisita Lopez Torregrosa, "Cuba May Be the Most Feminist Country in Latin America."
39. Paulo Freire, *Pedagogy of the Oppressed*.
40. Glen Sean Coulthard, *Red Skin, White Masks*. For a very brief discussion, see Chapter 1.
41. Margaret Randall, *Sandino's Daughters Revisited: Feminism in Nicaragua*.
42. Mies, *Patriarchy and Accumulation*.
43. Ibid.
44. Ibid.
45. Linda Owen, *Distorting the Past*.
46. Mark Dyble, et al., "Sex Equality Can Explain the Unique Social Structure of Hunter-Gatherer Bands."
47. Ibid.
48. Owen, *Distorting the Past*.
49. Mies, *Patriarchy and Accumulation*.
50. Stephanie Coontz, *Polygamy Fact Sheet: A Historical Background*.
51. Mies, *Patriarchy and Accumulation*.
52. Silvia Federici, *Caliban and the Witch: Women, the Body, and Primitive Accumulation*.
53. Federici, *Caliban and the Witch*.
54. Ibid.
55. Ibid.
56. Ibid.
57. Heather Brown, *Marx on Gender and the Family: A Critical Study*.
58. Karl Marx, *The Ethnological Notebooks of Karl Marx*, 2nd ed.
59. Lilia D. Monzó and Peter McLaren, "The Future is Marx: Bringing Back Class and Changing the World—Revolutionary Critical Pedagogy as Moral Imperative."
60. Fred Magdoff, "Twenty-first Century Land Grabs: Accumulation by Agricultural Dispossession."
61. Alex Callinicos, *Race and Class*.
62. Callinicos, *Race and Class*.
63. See Note 25 in Chapter 1 for a brief discussion of the problems associated with this term, especially in reference to land. For a fuller discussion, see Robert Nichols, "Theft is Property."
64. Marx, *Capital*, Vol. I, 759.
65. Ibid.
66. Ibid., 874
67. Glen Sean Coulthard, *Red Skin, White Masks*, p. 7
68. Rosa Luxemburg, *Accumulation of Capital*.
69. Rosa Luxemburg, *Accumulation of Capital*.

70. Hudis, "The Dialectic of the Spatial Determination of Capital."
71. Peter Hudis and Kevin Anderson, *The Rosa Luxemburg Reader*, 18.
72. Luxemburg, *Accumulation of Capital*.
73. Hudis, "The Dialectic of the Spatial Determination of Capital," 7.
74. Marx, *Capital*, Vol. I, 532.
75. Ibid.
76. Kevin Anderson, *Marx and the Margins*.
77. John Bellamy Foster, "Marx's Theory of Metabolic Rift: Classical Foundations for Environmental Sociology."
78. Ramon Grosfoguel, "The Structure of Knowledge in Westernized Universities."
79. Grosfoguel, "The Structure of Knowledge," 77.
80. Walter Mignolo, "Epistemic Disobedience, Independent Thought and Decolonial Freedom."
81. Mies, *Patriarchy and Accumulation*.
82. Ibid.
83. bell hooks, *Feminism is for Everybody*.
84. Jessie Daniels, "Trouble with White Feminism."
85. Lori D. Ginsberg, *Elizabeth Cady Stanton: An American Life*,
86. Barker, "Indigenous Feminisms, p. 4.
87. bell hooks, *Ain't I a Woman*, 19–20.
88. bell hooks, *Feminism is for Everybody: Passionate Politics*.
89. Grande, *Red Pedagogy*, 182.
90. Pierrette Hondagneu-Sotelo, *Domestica*.
91. Hondagneu-Sotelo, *Domestica*.
92. Ibid.
93. Edward E. Baptist, *The Half Has Never Been Told*.
94. Baptist, *The Half Has Never Been Told*.
95. Patricia J. Williams, *The Alchemy of Race and Rights: The Diary of a Law Professor*.
96. Callinicos, *Race and Class*.
97. Joshua Dubois, J., "Prison: The New Slavery for Black America."
98. It is important to note that the Americanization movement was aimed at not only Indigenous peoples but also Chicanx communities of the Southwest after the Mexican-American war as well as other immigrants, including Italians and Poles, in an attempt to assimilate them into the perceived superior Anglo-Saxon culture.
99. Grande, *Red Pedagogy*.
100. Red Nation is a council of Native and Non-Native activists committed to the liberation of Indigenous peoples. Visit https://therednation.org/
101. Christina Heatherton, "Policing the Crisis of Indigenous Lives: An Interview with Red Nation," para. 2.
102. See Melanie Yazzie in Christina Heatherton, "Policing the Crisis of Indigenous Lives: An Interview with Red Nation."
103. Ibid, para. 3.
104. Audra Simpson, "On Ethnographic Refusal: Indigeneity, "Voice" and Colonial Citizenship," 73.
105. Simpson, "On Ethnographic Refusal," 67.
106. Ibid, 68.

107. Ibid.
108. Kevin Anderson, *Marx at the Margins*.
109. Grande, *Red Pedagogy*, 70.
110. William I. Robinson, *Global Capitalism and the Crisis of Humanity*.
111. Ibid.
112. Neil Hicks, "The Trump Administration Turns Its Back on the World's Refugees."
113. Patrisia Macías-Rojas, *From Deportation to Prison*.
114. Macías-Rojas, *From Deportation to Prison*.
115. Davis, *Freedom is a Constant Struggle*.
116. Alexandra Starr, "At Low Pay, Government Hires Immigrants Held at Detention Centers."
117. Mary Bauer and Mónica Ramírez, *Injustice on Our Plates*.

Bibliography

Alexander, Michelle. *The New Jim Crow: Mass Incarceration in the Age of Colorblindness*. New York: The New Press, 2012.

Anderson, Kevin. *Marx at the Margins: On Nationalism, Ethnicity, and Non-Western Societies*. Chicago, IL: University of Chicago Press, 2010.

Baptist, Edward E. *The Half Has Never Been Told: Slavery and the Making of American Capitalism*. New York: Basic Book, 2014.

Barker, Joanne. "Indigenous Feminisms." In *the Oxford Handbook of Indigenous People's Politics*, edited by José Antonio Lucero, Dale Turner, and Donna Lee VanCott. Oxford University Press, Online publication, 2015. https://www.academia.edu/14991489/Indigenous_Feminisms_2015_

Bauer, Mary and Mónica Ramírez. *Injustice on Our Plates*. Montgomery, AL: Southern Poverty Law Center, 2010. https://www.splcenter.org/20101107/injustice-our-plates

Brown, Heather. *Marx on Gender and the Family: A Critical Study*. Chicago, IL: Haymarket, 2013.

Callinicos, Alex. *Race and Class*. London: Bookmarks, 1993.

Coontz, Stephanie. *Polygamy Fact Sheet: A Historical Background*. Austin, TX: Council on Contemporary Families, 2006. https://contemporaryfamilies.org/wp-content/uploads/2013/10/Coontz2006_Polygamy-fact-sheet.pdf

Coulthard, Glen Sean. *Red Skin, White Masks: Rejecting the Colonial Politics of Recognition*. Minneapolis: University of Minnesota, 2014.

D'Almeida, Kanya and Naimul Haq. "Two Years after Rana Plaza Tragedy, Rights Abuses Still Rampant in Bangladesh's Garment Sector." *Truthout*, April 24, 2015. https://truthout.org/articles/two-years-after-rana-plaza-tragedy-rights-abuses-still-rampant-in-bangladesh-s-garment-sector/

D'Amato, Paul. "Why Was Marx a Materialist?" *SocialistWorker.org*, October 28, 2011. https://socialistworker.org/2011/10/28/why-was-marx-a-materialist

Daniels, Jessie. "Trouble with White Feminism: Racial Origins of U.S. Feminism. Racism Review: Scholarship and Activism Toward Racial Justice. February 18, 2014. http://www.racismreview.com/blog/2014/02/18/trouble-with-white-feminism

Davis, Angela Y. *Freedom is a Constant Struggle: Ferguson, Palestine, and the Foundations of a Movement*. Edited by Frank Barat. Chicago, IL: Haymarket Books, 2016.

Dubois, Joshua. "Prison: The New Slavery for Black America." *Irish Examiner*, June 29, 2013. https://www.irishexaminer.com/lifestyle/features/prison-the-new-slavery-for-black-america-235416.html

Dunayevskaya, Raya. *Rosa Luxemburg, Women's liberation, and Marx's Philosophy of Revolution, 2nd edition*. Urbana and Chicago, IL: University of Illinois Press, 1991.

Dyble, Mark, Gul D. Salali, Nikhil Chaudhary, Abigail Page, Daniel Smith, James Thompson, Lucio Vinicius, Ruth Mace, Andrea B. Migliano. "Sex Equality Can Explain the Unique Social Structure of Hunter-Gatherer Bands." *Science 348* (2015): 796–798.

Ehrenreich, Barbara and Arlie Russell Hochschild. *Global Woman: Nannies, Maids, and Sex Workers in the New Economy*. New York: Henry Holt and Company, 2002.

Federici, Silvia. *Caliban and the Witch: Women, the Body, and Primitive Accumulation*. New York: Autonomedia, 2004.

———. *Revolution at Point Zero: Housework, Reproduction, and Feminist Struggle*. Oakland, CA: PM Press, 2012.

John Bellamy Foster. "Marx's Theory of Metabolic Rift: Classical Foundations for Environmental Sociology." American Journal of Sociology 105, no. 2 (1999): 366–405.

Freire, Paulo. *Pedagogy of the Oppressed*. New York: Continuum, 1970.

Ginsberg, Lori. *Elizabeth Cady Stanton: An American Life*. Hill and Wang, 2009.

Grande, Sandy. *Red Pedagogy: Native American Social and Political Thought, 10th anniversary edition*. New York: Rowman & Littlefield, 2015.

Grosfoguel, Ramon. "The Structure of Knowledge in Westernized Universities: Epistemic Racism/Sexism and the Four Genocides/Epistemicides of the Long 16th Century." *Human Architecture: Journal of the Sociology of Self-Knowledge 11*, no. 1 (2013): 73–90.

Gunewardena, Nandini and Ann Kingsolver, eds. *The Gender of Globalization: Women Navigating Cultural and Economic Marginalities*. Santa Fe, NM: School for Advanced Research Press, 2007.

Heatherton, Christina, "Policing the Crisis of Indigenous Lives: An Interview with Red Nation." In *Policing the Planet: Why the Policing Crisis Led to Black Lives Matter*, Chapter 8. Edited by Jordan T. Camp and Christina Heatherton. New York: Verso, 2016.

Hicks, Neil. "The Trump Administration Turns Its Back on the World's Refugees." *Huffpost*, February 2, 2018. https://www.huffpost.com/entry/the-trump-administration_b_14557092?utm_hp_ref=middle-east

Hochschild, Arlie with Anne Machung. *The Second Shift: Working Families and the Revolution at Home*. New York: Penguin Books, 2012.

Holmstrom, Nancy. "The Socialist Feminist Project." *Monthly Review: An Independent Socialist Magazine 54*, no. 10 (2003): 1–13.

Hondagneu-Sotelo, Pierrette. *Domestica: Immigrant Workers Cleaning and Caring in the Shadows of Affluence*. Berkeley, CA: University of California Press, 2001.

hooks, bell. *Ain't I a Woman: Black Women and Feminism*. Boston: South End Press, 1981.

———. *Feminism is for Everybody: Passionate Politics*, 2nd edition. New York: Routledge, 2015.

Hudis, Peter and Kevin B. Anderson, eds. *The Rosa Luxemburg Reader*. New York: Monthly Review Press, 2004.

Incite! Women of Color Against Violence. *Color of Violence: The Incite! Anthology*. Durham, NC: Duke University Press, 2016.

Inter-Agency Support Group on Indigenous Peoples' Issues. *Indigenous Peoples' Access to Decent Work and Social Protection*. June 2014. https://www.un.org/en/ga/69/meetings/indigenous/pdf/IASG%20Thematic%20paper_%20Employment%20and%20Social%20Protection%20-%20rev1.pdf

Jha, Meeta. *The Global Beauty Industry: Colorism, Racism, and the National Body*. New York: Routledge, 2016.

Kara, Siddharth. *Sex Trafficking: Inside the Business of Modern Slavery*. New York: Columbia University Press, 2009.

Kovel, Joel. *The Enemy of Nature: The End of Capitalism or the End of the World?* New York: Zed Books, 2002: 123–124.

Lopez Torregrosa, Luisita. "Cuba May Be the Most Feminist Country in Latin America." *The New York Times*, May 1, 2012. https://rendezvous.blogs.nytimes.com/2012/05/01/cuba-may-be-the-most-feminist-country-in-latin-america/

Luxemburg, Rosa. *Accumulation of Capital*. Eastford, CT: Martino Fine Books, 2015.

———. "The Proletarian Woman." In *The Rosa Luxemburg Reader*, edited by Peter Hudis and Kevin Anderson, 242–245. New York: Monthly Review Press, 2004.

Macías-Rojas, Patrisia. *From Deportation to Prison: The Politics of Immigration Enforcement in Post Civil Rights America*. New York: New York University Press, 2016.

Magdoff, Fred. "Twenty-First Century Land Grabs: Accumulation by Agricultural Dispossession." *Monthly Review: An Independent Socialist Magazine* 65, no. 6 (2013). https://monthlyreview.org/2013/11/01/twenty-first-century-land-grabs/

Marx, Karl. *Capital*, Vol. I. Translated by Ben Fowkes. New York: Vintage Books Edition, 1977.

———. *The Ethnological Notebooks of Karl Marx*. Marxists Internet Archive. https://www.marxists.org/archive/marx/works/1881/ethnographical-notebooks/notebooks.pdf

———. "Thesis on Feuerbach." In *The Marx-Engels Reader*, 2nd ed, edited by Robert C. Tucker, 143–145. New York: W. W. Norton & Company, 1978.

Marx, Karl and Friedrich Engels. *The German Ideology*. New York: Prometheus Books, 1998.

Mies, Maria. *Patriarchy and Accumulation on a World Scale: Women in the International Division of Labour*. London: Zed Books, 2014.

Mignolo, Walter. "Epistemic Disobedience, Independent Thought and Decolonial Freedom." *Theory, Culture & Society* 26, no. 7–8, (2009): 159–181.

Miranda, Jose P. *Marx Against the Marxists*. Maryknol, NY: Orbis Books, 1980.

Monzó, Lilia D. "White Supremacy, Hate, and Violence in Charlottesville—A Marxist Humanist Response." *International Marxist Humanist Organization*, Aug. 17, 2017. https://www.imhojournal.org/articles/white-supremacy-hate-and-violence-in-charlottesville-a-marxist-humanist-response/

———. "Women and Revolution: Marx and the Dialectic." *Knowledge Culture 4*, no. 6 (2016): 97–121.

Monzó, Lilia D. and Peter McLaren. "Challenging the Violence and Invisibility against Women of Color—A Marxist Imperative." Iberoamérica Social: Revista-Red de Estudios Sociales, April, 2016. https://iberoamericasocial.com/challenging-the-violence-and-invisibility-against-women-of-color-a-marxist-imperative/

———. "The Future is Marx: Bringing Back Class and Changing the World—Revolutionary Critical Pedagogy as Moral Imperative. In *International Handbook of Progressive Education*, edited by M. Y. Eryaman & B. C. Bruce, 643–670. New York: Peter Lang, 2015.

———. "Las Mujeres y la Violencia en la Era de la Migración." *Iberoamérica Social: Revista-Red de Estudios Sociales*, June 10, 2015. https://iberoamericasocial.com/las-mujeres-y-la-violencia-en-la-era-de-la-migracion/

Moraga, Cherríe and Gloria Anzaldúa, eds. *This Bridge Called My Back*. Albany, New York: SUNY Press, 2015.

Muñoz, Ana and Allan Woods. "Marxism and the Emancipation of Women," *In Defense of Marxism*, March 8, 2000. https://www.marxist.com/marxism-feminism-emancipation-women080300.htm

Nichols, Robert. "Theft is Property! The Recursive Logic of Dispossession." *Political Theory 46*, no. 1 (2018): 3–28.

O'Toole, Laura L., Jessica R. Schiffman, and Margie L. Kiter Edwards, eds. *Gender Violence: Interdisciplinary Perspectives, 2nd edition*. New York: New York University, 2007.

Owen, Linda. *Distorting the Past. Gender and the Division of Labor in the European Upper Paleolithic*. Tübingen, Germany: Kerns Verlag, 2005.

Randall, Margaret. *Sandino's Daughters Revisited: Feminism in Nicaragua*. New Brunswick, NJ: Rutgers University Press, 1994.

Ritchie, Andrea J. *Invisible No More: Police Brutality Against Black Women and Women of Color*. Boston, MA: Beacon Press, 2017.

Robinson, William I. *Global Capitalism and the Crisis of Humanity*. New York: Cambridge University Press, 2014.

Rojas, Maythee. *Women of Color and Feminism*. Berkeley, CA: Seal Press, 2009.

Simpson, Audra. "On Ethnographic Refusal: Indigeneity, "Voice" and Colonial Citizenship." Juncture 9, Dec. (2007): 67–80.

Starr, Alexandra. "At Low Pay, Government Hires Immigrants Held At Detention Centers." *NPR*, July 23, 2015. https://www.npr.org/2015/07/23/425511981/at-low-pay-government-hires-immigrants-held-at-detention-centers

Tuck, Eve. "Challenging Whitestream Feminism: Response 1. In *Red Pedagogy: Native American Social and Political Thought, 10th anniversary edition*, Sandy Grande, 213–219. New York: Rowman & Littlefield, 2015.

United Nations. *The World's Women 2015: Trends and Statistics*. New York: United Nations Department of Economic and Social Affairs, Statistics Division, 2015.

Vogel, Lise. *Woman Questions: Essays for a Materialist Feminism*. New York: Routledge, 1995.

Williams, Patricia J. *The Alchemy of Race and Rights: The Diary of a Law Professor*. Cambridge, MA: Harvard University Press, 1991.

· 3 ·

MARX ON WOMEN, NON-WESTERN SOCIETIES, AND LIBERATION

Challenging Misconceptions[1]

I knew I didn't know what the hell communism was, and yet I'd been dead set against it. Just like when you're a little kid and they get you to believe in the boogeyman. You don't know what the hell the boogeyman is, but you hate him and you're scared of him.

—Assata Shakur[2]

Marx answered the questions of his day, not ours, but can we afford, as Women's Liberationists today, to be without a total philosophy, because the greatest philosophy for uprooting the exploitative old and creating ground for the new was formulated by 'a man'?

—Raya Dunayevskaya[3]

Marx developed a philosophy of revolution that offers a path toward a "new humanism"—a way to change not only the economic structure of society but the ways in which human beings relate to each other, what we value, and how we engage in the world.[4] His vision was certainly lofty—to change not only the way the world functions but also who we are as human beings within it. Freedom from capital and its class, race, gender, and other antagonisms would allow us to create a communistic society where every individual would have the resources they needed to engage in creative labor and develop their full potential as a human being.[5] Without commodity fetishism, private property or the need or desire for accumulation, our goals would be tied to meeting the social needs of the community. Marx believed wholeheartedly that we, as a species, had the potential to build such a future—that it was our destiny and that only under these circumstances would we actually fulfill our true "human nature." As C. L. R. James stated of Marx "No man had a more elevated conception of the destiny of the human race.[6]

Capitalism, by definition, is the antithesis of this "new humanism." It is a system designed to produce capital accumulation for the capitalist class through the exploitation of labor. Workers are forced to sell their labor power to the capitalist class who own the means of production.[7] Racialized and gendered divisions cut across these classes and stratify society in ways that minimize our potential strength to change the system that keeps us in chains. The abolition of private property and capitalist relations is absolutely necessary to develop the new humanism Marx envisioned. But central to creating a classless society and to this new humanism is the abolition of rac-ism and sexism. There is a common misconception that Marx gave priority to or reduced everything to class. However, Marx's work, when examined in its totality, reveals that Marx's concern for humanity went far beyond a critique of class relations. He wrote vehemently against the oppression of women, Black slavery in the United States, and, although initially Eurocentric, eventually grew to recognize not only the "barbarism" of western imperialism but also the agency of non-western peoples and he began to value their ways of being.[8]

Marx's theory of value and his dialectical method provide a strong argu-ment and an approach to challenge the oppression of women and People of Color. Indeed, he came to realize through his analysis of non-western societies, that the greatest potential for class struggle lay with the most pauperized and alienated communities who were not blinded by their false hopes of social mobility or inclined to align themselves with the White capitalist class. This is exactly the conclusion that Raya Dunayevskaya came to, which led her to proclaim the Black masses to be the potential vanguard of the revolution.[9] Certainly, history has shown the Black community's courageous capacity to develop a mass movement for social change and to provide a springboard from which other oppressed groups would follow. Of course, other hyper exploited groups have a similar impetus and capacity. Regardless of who leads the way, or if perhaps a more horizontal approach may be in order, it is certain that Indigenous women and Women of Color, will be a vital "revolutionary Reason and force."[10]

Marx on Women, the Family, and Gender Relations

Critiques of Marx's writings as gender-blind and/or sexist and deterministic evidence a failure to understand Marx's dialectical method and his theory of liberation.[11] Heather Brown, in her path-breaking work on Marx and gender, provides a detailed analysis of all of Marx's major works on women, gender relations, and the family—from the young Marx to the *Ethnological Notebooks* that document his research at the end of his life.[12] Brown remarks that it is "… important to look at Marx's theory as a totality—both the positive and the negative aspects—in order to assess its potential in terms of advancing feminist theory and aims"[13] Such analysis reveals that from his earliest works Marx evidenced thinking on gender relations and ways of relating to women that were quite progressive for his time.

There are of course important examples of male chauvinism in Marx's work and a dearth of specificity on so-called "women's work" in the domestic sphere and women's roles in capitalist production. This is especially true in his early work in which his concern for women's oppression sometimes seemed to uphold traditional notions of women's nature. For example, in "The Working Day" Marx argues that for women to be working alongside men through the night is likely to have negative consequence on their character:

> These females employed with the men, hardly distinguished from them in their dress, and begrimed with dirt and smoke, are exposed to the deterioration of character, arising from the loss of self-respect, which can hardly fail to follow from their unfeminine occupation.[14]

Here he is clearly assuming some abstract notion of a woman's natural character.

In many ways Marx was a man of his time. Consider that at the time in which Marx lived women's lives were considerably more restricted than today, socially, economically, and politically (although in many ways women today experience even greater horrors that belie the legal rights many have gained).[15] It was not until 1893, ten years after his death, that the first nation, New Zealand, granted women the right to vote. In England, where Marx spent most of his adult life, women did not gain the right to vote until 1928. Thus, as Brown states, it is undeniable that "in a number of cases, he was unable to overcome completely the prejudices of his own time, especially with regard to women."[16]

Nevertheless, even with a certain level of ambivalence toward women's equality, his writings on women, gender relations, and the family were particularly revolutionary. He fully recognized the dehumanizing treatment of women and was a strong advocate of women's liberation. From his early writings, Marx was challenging traditional gender relations. In his early work, *The Economic and Philosophic Manuscripts of 1844*, Marx notes the different ways in which humans ("*Mensch*") treat men and women and argues that our evolution as a species could be measured by the way in which society treats women, indicating that this should be no less than equal to the way in which we treat men ("*Mann*"). Kevin Anderson notes how inaccuracy in the original English translation of *The Economic and Philosophic Manuscripts of 1844* has obscured Marx's revolutionary thinking on gender and women. Specifically, he notes that in the German language the words man (*Mann*) and human being (*Mensch*) are similar; thus, when, in the original writing, Marx used the German term "*Mensch*," which means human, it was translated into English as "*man*."[17] Taking a more accurate translation from Kevin Anderson, Marx states:

> The direct, natural, necessary relationship of human being [*Mensch*] to human being is the *relationship of man* [*Mann*] *to woman* [*Weib*]. ... Therefore, on the basis of this relationship, we can judge the whole stage of development of the human being. From the character of this relationship it follows to what degree the *human being* has become and recognized himself or herself as a *species being*; a *human being*; the relationship of man to woman is the *most natural* relationship of human being to human being. Therefore, in it is revealed the degree to which the *natural* behavior of the human being has become *human* ...[18]

Although in this passage we witness Marx's heteronormative worldview (he was a man of his time), the passage makes clear that Marx was at least as concerned with transforming gender relations as he was with the eradication of class. Here, he equates gender relations with human relations and thus marks gender relations a central consideration in the development of humanity.

Not long after, in 1848, in *Manifesto of the Communist Party*, Marx and Engels write enthusiastically about the dissolution of the modern bourgeois' family and the development of more communal forms. They point out the inability of the bourgeoisie to imagine women as more than mere capital.

> The bourgeois sees in his wife a mere instrument of production. He hears that the instruments of production are to be exploited in common, and, naturally, can come to no other conclusion that the lot of being common to all will likewise fall to the women. He has not even a suspicion that the real point aimed at is to do away with the status of women as mere instruments of production.[19]

Here Marx and Engels note that men's assumption that communal property would make women into the property of all men evidences men's inability to view women as anything but property. His point is that the men who critique the commune on this basis cannot see beyond their view of women as objects to be owned—if not by one man, then by all men.

Some critics of Marx have claimed that he portrayed women as passive objects rather than Subjects capable of self-determination. However, this characterization likely comes from the book, *Origins of the Family, Private Property and the State*, which Friedrich Engels claimed to have written based on thousands of pages of Marx's notes found after his death. These notes, portions of which comprise *The Ethnological Notebooks*, reveal Marx to have been working on the history of the family in non-western societies. Engels must be commended for taking up the topic of women's oppression, which at the time of publication had lost favor among socialist work, and forcefully denouncing the treatment of women in capitalist society. However, he rendered women passive and unagentic with his now infamous statement, "The overthrow of mother-right was the world historical defeat of the female sex."[20] This proclamation was a fatalistic stance against the possibility of women's emancipation.

Yet it has long been established that Engels was more deterministic and less dialectical in his reasoning than Marx.[21] Various authors have pointed out that very little of Marx's notes on Morgan were actually included in *Origins of the Family, Private Property and the State*.[22] Contrary to the passive positioning that Engels' statement reflects, the early ambivalence to gender equality that Marx displayed, which to me reflects a product of his subconscious socialization into a patriarchal world, shifted and gained much greater clarity as he bore witness to women's revolutionary spirit in the Paris Commune of 1871 and as his studies progressed. His later work portrays him more dialectical in his thinking about women and demonstrates that he came to recognize women's courage, power, and agency. In a letter to Dr. Ludwig Kugelmann in 1868, Marx writes,

> great progress was evident in the last Congress of the American "Labour Union" in that among other things, it treated working women with complete equality. While in this respect the English, and still more the gallant French, are burdened with a spirit of narrow-mindedness. Anybody who knows anything of history knows that great social changes are impossible without the feminine ferment.[23]

Dunayevskaya pointed out that Marx politically favored and fought for the "autonomous existence of women." He closely followed the Paris Commune and applauded the tenacity and commitment of the women of the Commune and attributed their victimization to capitalist structures and institutions:

> The *cocottes* [prostitutes who serviced upper class men or mistresses] had refound the scent of their protectors—the absconding men of family, religion, and, above all, of property. In their stead, the real women of Paris showed again at the surface—heroic, noble, and devoted, like the women of antiquity. Working, thinking fighting, bleeding Paris—almost forgetful, in its incubation of a new society, of the Cannibals at its gates—radiant in the enthusiasm of its historic initiative![24]

Further words leave no doubt that Marx recognized female communards' agency and courage as he compared them to two powerful Greek Goddesses no longer willing to endure their oppression.

> The women of Paris joyfully give up their lives at the barricades and on the place of execution. What does this prove? Why, that the demon of the Commune has changed them into Megaera and Hecates![25]

Here, he applauds the female communards' tenacity and revolutionary spirit. According to Dunayevskaya, Marx considered the Paris Commune "*the* political form in which to work out the economic emancipation of the proletariat."[26]

Biographies of Marx and his family evidence that in many ways he lived his personal life as a man who was in and of the world of his time—married and catered to by his wife and daughters. Yet he shared his intellectual life with them. This he did at a time in which women's roles among the middle classes were believed to be to marry, bear children and stand by their husband's side. He engaged each of his daughters as intellectually capable beings, sharing his work and listening to their ideas even in their youth. Jenny Marx, his wife, came to be known as Marx's sounding board throughout his life. Indeed, he relied on Jenny and his daughters to translate various versions of his work.[27] Rather than shy away from the critique that would at least theoretically confront his privilege and reveal his lived contradictions, he attacked the family and gender relations as a microcosm of capitalist relations:

> The division of labour in which all these contradictions are implicit, and which in its turn is based on the natural division of labour in the family and the separation of society into individual families opposed to one another, simultaneously implies the *distribution*, and indeed the *unequal* distribution, both quantitative and qualitative, of labour and its products, hence property, the nucleus, the first form of which lies in the family, where wives and children are the slaves of the husband. This latent state of the family, though still very crude, is the first form of property, but even at this stage

it corresponds perfectly to the definition of modern economists, who call it the power of disposing of the labour power of others. Division of labour and private property are, moreover, identical expressions: in the one the same thing is affirmed with reference to activity as is affirmed in the other with reference to the product of the activity.[28]

When Marx states that private property and the division of labor are identical expressions, he is referring to the identical process of disposing of the labor power of others, which defines the individual in society, including the woman, solely as worker, as commodity, and in which both the labor and the product of labor turns on the individual and confronts her antagonistically to confine her as a slave.

An important context to understanding Marx's critique of gender relations and abhorrence to the oppression of women are his writings on prostitution, insanity, and suicide.

In *The Holy Family*, Marx provides a discussion of two fictional female characters of the novel *Les Mystères de Paris*, Fleur de Marie, a prostitute, and Louise Morel, a servant who is sexually exploited. In the novel the author portrays the stories of diverse characters. Yet he indicts the women with a moralistic stance that belies the complicity of bourgeois society in the conditions that women face. Marx takes a very humanist position toward these women, recognizing them as agentic Subjects even in light of their circumstances. He challenges the villainizing of women who have few other options for survival, arguing that Marie had more human qualities than the bourgeoisie who would judge and shame her all the while benefitting from her condition.[29]

Marx also investigated and wrote about the phenomena of female "madness." Again, he questioned the general tendency to psychologize the consequences of women's oppression. Marx reported on a case in which husband and son plotted against a woman to have her declared mentally insane and commit her to an insane asylum over a money dispute. Marx publicly denounced both the husband and son for their treacherous plotting but more importantly also denounced the laws that gave men authority to institutionalize women against their will. While blasting the men, he recognized clearly that these horrors become more common as people are strapped materially. It is the hyper exploitation and privation that deforms us to a state of inhumane conduct toward the people we are supposed to love.

Marx also wrote a piece on women and suicide.[30] In this piece Marx focused on the ways that bourgeois society deforms our most intimate of social relations, that of child and parent, wife and husband. Marx argued that the rise in female suicides that was being seen at the time was not due to any particular weakness or mental disorder among women but to the savagely brutal ways in which people learn to relate to each other, ways that reflect relations of property. Hence fear, jealousy, and indignation are all forms of control that define the way we relate to our intimate others. Because women are the subordinates in gender relations it is they who suffer atrocities that are brought on by this deformity, since society has given men the power to control their lives. Under these circumstances suicide, Marx argues, proves to be their only escape, perhaps even the best of all options. In this respect rather than perceiving women who commit suicide as defective or feeble-minded we might consider their suicide to be a final act of agency.

"Productive" and "Unproductive" Labor

The most substantive critique against Marx and Marxism among feminists is Marx's definition of "productive labor," as "abstract labor" or labor that directly produces surplus value. The critique is that Marx was so androcentric that he failed to recognize or gave little import to the array of work that is often termed "women's work," or domestic labor—child bearing and rearing, housekeeping, cooking, and other forms of caring and emotional work. While this work would be considered "concrete" or labor that produces use value, feminists have long argued that this work indirectly increases or makes possible the "productive labor" that creates surplus value by making, generally speaking, men's lives easier and more pleasant after work so they can be physically and psychologically prepared for the next day of paid work.[31] Lise Vogel adds to this analysis by arguing that women's greatest and unique productive activity is the production of the next generation of workers and their labor power—the capacity to labor, which is crucial to capitalist production.[32]

Certainly, these are crucial activities to the survival of any society, including under capitalism. However, Marx was writing from the perspective of the capitalist, such that only the work that created surplus value—profit— would be considered "productive" *to the capitalist*. Marx never minimized the importance of use value. In fact, his new society was to be based on use value. Certainly, Marx could have and should have discussed more fully the role of so-called "women's work" in capitalist production. However, that he did not do so cannot be presumed to mean that his philosophy of revolution cannot speak to women's liberation. The assumption that Capital's focus on "productive labor" is invisible to the work of women, suggests a normalized existence for women around middle- and upper-class standards. Indeed, Marx addressed the oppression of women as wage-workers in "The Working Day." Furthermore, the dialectical reasoning that Marx employed to understand the relationship of humanity to nature is especially relevant to any movement toward women's liberation.

Marx's writings clearly evidence his dialectical approach. Throughout his vast work Marx analyzed concepts that he recognized to be rooted in a constant tension with a presumed opposite that upon close analysis was often each an aspect of the other. For example, he treated concepts such as material and consciousness, use and exchange value, social and nature in this way. Of course, some binaries were deemed hierarchal; the negative needed to be negated for the positive to emerge. In other cases, it was the separation itself that needed to be smashed forcefully in order to destroy the perceived binary and create something altogether new. The dialectic is a critique of dualisms. Brown contends that Marx "sought *Aufhebung*, the dialectical overcoming or even destruction, of the old and its re-emergence in a higher form."[33]

This dialectic is very evident in his discussion of the relationship between nature and culture, which has significant bearing on gender relations and women's liberation. It has long been proclaimed that it is women's nature to bear and raise children—that they have particular essential biological and physiological qualities that give them the natural instincts and temperament for "caring work." Marx's theory of human nature and the relationship of our social being to our nature challenges the biological determinism embedded in this patriarchal and sexist argument. While Marx did not speak to gender or sex-based differences, his theory of human nature presents a significant challenge to conceptions of women's nature as static and biologically determined. According to Marx, human nature is socially constructed and historically specific to the mode of production.[34]

For Marx, our capacity to labor, to produce our livelihood, was an essential characteristic of human beings. Nancy Holmstrom points out that even the biological determinants of human nature take on new forms through history and evolve in ways that stretch its biological ties. "As new needs and capacities are continually being created, biology remains an important determining factor, but human life progressively becomes less directly tied to its biological base.[35] Rather than a narrowly defining determinism, biology merely determines a wide range of possibilities in human beings. As technology develops, biology or nature is socioculturally adapted to serve social and cultural needs. Consider that women decide if and when they will give birth and have at their disposal the ability to considerably reduce the possibility of pregnancy and to terminate an existing pregnancy (regardless of laws). In addition, traditional ways of reproducing are also changing through technology, such that people who, in previous generations, would have been unable to give birth can now be inseminated. Biology is thus always subject to social and cultural conditions.

The gender division of labor has developed particular "natures" among men and women. Yet we can see, given current historical developments in gender fluidity, that the possibilities are much wider than have been made normative. A change in the way we labor will undoubtedly have a significant impact on what human beings develop in terms of temperament, proclivities, instincts, etc. Holstrom explains:

> As the forms of human labor (and the resultant social practices and institutions) change, new mental and physical capacities are developed, some remain undeveloped, and others are destroyed. Hence different behavioral and psychological generalizations will be true of people who do different sorts of labor in different modes of production.[36]

While generally speaking women and men do labor differently and engage differently in the world, there is no evidence that these differences are biological. Rather these "natures" are not essential aspects of human beings but rather products of our social world, created through the possibilities that the gender division of labor establishes. Thus, our natures are constantly changing and evolving and differ across modes of production.

An important misrepresentation of Marx's theory of the human/nature binary fails to grasp his dialectical method. The critique made is that Marx's vision for a free humanity "beyond necessity" reflects a belief in the superiority of the human over nature and that he not only condoned the human domination of nature but believed freedom to be a transcendence from our dependence on nature. While there are some examples of word choices that may be interpreted in this way in Marx's work, this can be attributed to either ambivalence on his part or simple difficulty with expressing that which we have no words to express, given the actual development of human disdain of nature under capitalism. The corpus of Marx's work, however, suggests that while human beings produce their livelihood through the manipulation and appropriation of nature, we are also defined by and dependent on nature. In other words, humanity and nature are interdependent through a dialectical relation that is *mediated* (not dominated) by our labor. This is an important clarification since it is one of the most significant critiques among Indigenous peoples whose traditions and beliefs are based on a view of nature as sacred and human beings as stewards of the Earth rather than the pillagers we have become.

For Marx, labor was the greatest authentically human capacity. Alienating labor was abstract labor in which the product confronted the producer as their nemesis. An important aspect of alienating labor is that it separates mental from manual work, thus creating labor that dehumanizes the worker. In this type of work labor ceases to be a human-affirming activity and becomes only the means to sustain life. But alienated labor confronts not only the laborer but all others as well and thus alienation in work leads to alienation between human beings.

Marx argued that non-alienating labor or human labor was labor that engaged both cognitive and practical activity. In line with this method, the gender division of labor is for Marx the dualism that, if not creates, exacerbates women's oppression and exploitation. Indeed, he argues that the gender division of labor must be eradicated in order to create the conditions for equality between men and women. It is important to note that dualisms are made such to sustain hierarchical relations of domination, which support the class relation by which capitalism is defined. In the gender division two dualisms are operating: (1) a dualism between what has traditionally been considered appropriate women's work and men's work, and (2) the *perception* that "women's work" is predominantly instinctual (non-thinking) and men's work is cognitive. The first dualism must be smashed by negating the idea that women cannot engage in the type of work that men have traditionally done. Generally speaking, women have made some important gains in breaking down this barrier and positioning themselves in traditionally male fields. This is especially true in the "working communism" of Cuba and in other industrialized nations, although the atrocities that continue to be committed against women demonstrate that there is still much work to be done. The second dualism has not even been attempted. Few attempts have been made to negate the perception that "women's work" is purely instinctual or manual and requires little thought. While some aspects of this work may be thus, others, especially the socialization of children into adulthood, require significant cognitive, psychological, and communicative skills. The socialization of "women's labor"—turning childcare and housework into waged work for other women—created opportunities for women to enter traditionally male spaces but it did nothing to challenge the devaluation of childcare and other caring work. Only an increase in wages and status of the labor performed is likely to draw men into the traditionally women's private sphere. Under capitalism, however, wherein the production of surplus value is primary, an increase in wages in the domestic realm is not likely to take place.

Marx on Racism, Family, and the Revolutionary Potential of Non-Western Societies

Paralleling feminist critiques of gender blindness, critiques have argued that Marx was Eurocentric, with a western lens that relegated Indigenous communities and People of Color to the margins of humanity. Connected to this is the argument that his theory of revolution provided a universal path to communism that would be led by the "more developed" world. Inherent in such a claim is the advanced development of the White man whose imperial violence upon the non-western world was both necessary and desirable in order to bring these countries in line to follow western development. While this Eurocentric perspective is evident in his early work, Kevin Anderson has demonstrated that Marx's perception of non-western peoples began to shift as he studied the non-western world and their struggles against western imperialism. In *Marx at the Margins*, Anderson traces the chronology of Marx's work, thereby demonstrating the impact of his studies and his theoretical growth; specifically, Marx developed what Anderson calls an "internationalist" outlook wherein he recognized the great *human* potential for revolutionary action among the most oppressed peoples in the world.[37]

For example, in one of his earliest and most significant works, *The Communist Manifesto*, written in 1848, Marx and Engels deliver a scathing critique of capitalism. However, prior to this critique, they unequivocally praise capitalism and credit the bourgeoisie for playing "a most revolutionary part" in history:

> The bourgeoisie, by the rapid improvement of all instruments of production, by the immensely facilitated means of communication, draws all, even the most barbarian, nations into civilisation. The cheap prices of commodities are the heavy artillery with which it batters down all Chinese walls, with which it forces the barbarians' intensely obstinate hatred of foreigners to capitulate. It compels all nations, on pain of extinction, to adopt the bourgeois mode of production; it compels them to introduce what it calls civilization into their midst, i.e., to become bourgeois themselves. In one word, it creates a world after its own image.[38]

The young Marx mistakenly believed that capitalism would save the world from its "barbarism" and would create the necessary conditions (industrialization) for communism to develop.

Marx made a living primarily as a journalist, although his radical politics did not result in steady and secure employment. However, he did maintain an important position during the years 1851–62 as Chief European Correspondent for the *New York Daily Tribune*. This position engaged his intellectual capacity in the specific sociopolitical context of the time. Marx wrote many articles for the *Tribune* on politics, imperialism, and the national question. He also corresponded regularly through this time with Engels and others and often discussed his work and the political issues of the time. Many of these are available in various collections. Examining them reveals that in the early years at the *Tribune* Marx held deficit views of non-western peoples, referring to India and China as stagnant societies whose revolutionary spirit was spawned by the brutal hand of British imperialism, and toasted the British for bringing civilization to them and being "the unconscious tool of history."[39] In an article on the Crimean War, he referred to the Turks, Slovenians, Greeks, Wallachians and Arnauts as " … a conglomerate of different races and nationalities, of which it is hard to say which is the least fit for progress and civilization …"[40] Anderson argues that his views began to change around 1856 when, at the onset of the Second Opium War, he emphatically denounced the British for *their* savage and barbaric treatment of the Chinese, but continued to believe this a necessary evil to produce the conditions necessary for communism.[41] This young Marx believed in a linear path to communism that would necessarily be led by the industrialized capitalist world.

The orientalism in the *early* Marx is unmistakable and should not be glossed over or excused.[42] However, it is important to remember that this Eurocentric position was especially prevalent during the time of Marx's life and was likely challenged only by those who had significant interactions with or learnings of non-western societies. In fact, White supremacy and racism continue to ravage Indigenous peoples and communities of color today, even in the most multicultural societies, such as the United States and England. But Marx, himself, recognized that he lacked sufficient knowledge to write about Asia and other non-western societies for the *Tribune* and in a letter to Engels dated March 10, 1853, Marx acknowledges his lack of expertise and requested Engels to write under his name.[43]

As a professor of education teaching courses on social justice I encounter Eurocentric students every semester and, although it was initially one of the

most difficult aspects of my work (see Chapter 4), I have learned to think
of these students as potential allies—young people whose social consciousness can begin to develop by critically examining the world and constantly
reflecting on their social position in society. I give these students the chance
that I believe we all deserve to learn and grow into critical human beings
who question the realities that have been normalized under capitalist relations of production. Why should we offer Marx any less consideration? As a
Woman of Color, I was initially put off by some of his early racist references
and sought to find other theorists and theories that would help me fully understand and change the injustices of our world. Yet upon a deep reading of a
large portion of his vast body of work it soon became very clear to me that
Marx was a man who too made mistakes and deserved to be allowed to grow
and evolve. Not only that but, through his studies, he developed a philosophy of revolution that could potentially challenge all relations of domination
and create a new society. Here I wish to echo Dunayevskaya's words above.
Although I recognize that White men secured their place of dominance under
capitalism through genocide and slavery we cannot condemn Marx and his
work for the past atrocities of the White man, especially when his work is
meant to challenge everything that they stood for and especially as he too
lived as a closet Jew and under persecution of the capitalist order. The promise
of freedom and beauty inherent in Marx's philosophy of liberation is much
too important.

It appears that while Engels was writing for Marx on the politics of the
day, Marx was educating himself. Anderson notes that it was after the Second
Opium War that Marx began to really take a close look at China and began
to place the British in the role of barbarians. By early 1857, Marx had completely shifted to an anti-colonial stance, reversing his earlier support of the
First Opium War. In his writings during the same time period on the 1857
Sepoy Uprising in India, Marx condemns British atrocities and begins "to
theorize the self-activity and struggle of the colonized Indians."[44] Marx wrote
significantly for the *Tribune* on the Sepoy Uprising between 1857–58, taking
a definitively anti-colonial stance and formulating the idea that within the
colonial apparatus lay the foundation of a people's struggle. This was a turning
point in which Marx began to consider the possibility of a different path to
communism, writing in a letter to Engels on January 16, 1858, "India is now
our best ally."[45]

Anderson traces a similar path in Marx's writings on Russia, Poland, and
Ireland with his early articles for the *Tribune* reflecting a Eurocentric view.

He wrote disparagingly of the Russian communal villages, characterizing them as despotic social and political systems. Indeed, he wrote particularly disparagingly of Russia and sided with the Ottoman Empire on the Crimean War. The turning point for Marx to recognize the revolutionary potential of Russia coincides, not surprisingly, with his shift in perspective toward India and China. In 1858, Marx begins to see the revolutionary potential of a serf uprising in Russia.[46]

During this same time Marx had been studying and making notes in preparation for *Capital*. In these notes that were completed in 1857–58 and later published as the *Grundrisse*, we find an unfinished comparison of the development of class society in Asia and western Europe. Marx was apparently at the time making sense of his discovery of an "Asiatic mode of production." Anderson discusses that in the *Grundrisse* Marx characterizes the western proletariat as "formally free but largely atomized and stripped of any significant control over its means of production" whereas he characterizes pre-capitalist societies as communal proprietors of land and without the goal of value production.[47] Marx outlined three different communal forms: Asiatic, Greco-Roman, and Germanic. He described each of these as having diverse forms of clan life, including different forms of marriage, lineage, and property rights. Importantly he did not view these as stages, with one following the other. Marx suggested that the Germanic form was a precursor to the feudalism of medieval Europe. Commonalities of these pre-capitalist societies included that they each had a labor system that emphasized use value and individual private property did not come into existence under any form until capitalism had emerged. Marx argued that of all modes of production, the Asiatic form was least like modern capitalism and had a greater life span. As Marx notes in the *Grundrisse*, "Here labor itself still half artistic, half end in itself. … Labor still as his own; definite self-sufficient development of one-sided abilities."[48] Although termed geographically, Marx recognized this Asiatic form in India, Indonesia, Russia, Peru, and Romania. Marx was very taken and impressed with this mode of production and began to consider how specific aspects could be incorporated into the communism that would come after capitalism.[49]

By the time Marx wrote *Capital*, we see him portray the communes and villages in a much better light than previously. In contrast, his loathing of capitalism became increasingly evident. Furthermore, the idea that these different forms suggested multiple paths toward development and eventual communism became concretized for Marx. Anderson points out that Marx sought to correct the misunderstanding of *Capital* as a universal theory of human development and corrected the French edition of *Capital* to clearly read as a critique and analysis of *western* capitalism and not a universal theory of capitalist development. He also requested that Engels make sure this would be the edition used for all future translations. This is of utmost importance because it clearly evidences the fact that Marx no longer saw western society as the advanced developed society from which all other societies must take their cue.[50]

Marx took great interest in the United States Civil War that began in 1861. He wholeheartedly condemned American slavery. Marx recognized slavery to be an economic system spawned of primitive accumulation and pointed out that without slavery the cotton industry in the United States could not have existed, which was instrumental to the development of capitalism. And he proclaimed the intent of the Confederates to continue to amass capital by breaking the souls and bodies of Black peoples:

> The war of the Southern Confederacy is, therefore, not a war of defense, but a war of conquest, a war of conquest for the spread and perpetuation of slavery.[51]

Marx was staunchly in favor of Black freedom and abolition. He stated:

> In the United States of America, every independent movement of the workers was paralyzed as long as slavery disfigured a part of the Republic. Labor in a white skin cannot emancipate itself where it is branded in a black skin."[52]

Although initially hopeful that the working class would unite against the horrors inflicted upon Black slaves in the South, the Serfs in Russia, and the Fenians in Ireland, he finally came to understand that racism and ethnicity were very effective tools for dividing the working class and eliminating the threat of class struggle. In a letter to his friends Sigfrid Meyer and August Vogt written in 1870, Marx explains this division between the working class of England and Ireland:

> Every industrial and commercial center in England now possesses a working class divided into two camps, English proletarians and Irish proletarians. The English worker hates the Irish worker as a competitor who lowers his standard of life ... He regards himself as a member of the ruling nation, and consequently, he becomes a tool of the English aristocrats and capitalists against Ireland, thus strengthening their domination *over himself*. He cherishes religious, social, and national prejudices against the Irish worker. His attitude towards him is much the same as that of the 'poor whites' to the Negroes in the former slave states of the U.S.A.[53]

Marx continues:

> This antagonism is artificially kept alive and intensified by the press, the pulpit, the
> comic papers, in short by all the means at the disposal of the ruling classes. This
> antagonism is the secret of the impotence of the English working class, despite its
> organization. It is the secret by which the capitalist class maintains its power. And
> the latter is quite aware of this.[54]

Marx's comments reflect the three important functions of racism beyond
slavery: (1) to create an ideological ferment against People of Color that
serves to justify inequality, (2) to minimize the value of a segment of the
working class and drive down the wages of all workers, and (3) to divide the
working class and thereby stunt the working-class consciousness and unity
necessary to bring down capitalism. It is true that, considering his vast body of
work, Marx did not write a lot about racism and when he did so it was almost
always in connection to its economic function and the class struggle. This
is because Marx's historical materialism posits that consciousness stems from
material conditions. That is, although racism is ideological, racist attitudes
and beliefs are rooted in the conditions of inequality that exist and these racist
ideologies justify and further entrench these conditions of economic and social
inequality. While the class struggle alone cannot liberate People of Color,
Keeanga-Yamahtta Taylor reminds us "Marxism should not be conceived of as
an unchanging dogma. It is a guide to social revolution and political action,
and has been built upon by successive generations of Marxists."[55]

An important note that must not be left unstated is that Black women
played a very important role in abolition and Black liberation in the United
States, even though their interests for liberation from patriarchal structures
were eventually relegated to secondary importance among Black liberation
struggles. Dunayevskaya has written of this extensively, seeking to establish
the revolutionary potential of Black women.[56] As might be expected, Marx
made no mention of Black women's key roles in abolition. This is likely due
to the fact that these women's remarkable activism and courage went unac-
knowledged even in local papers and Marx was writing on the Civil War from
Europe.

Dunayevskaya points out that in the last decade of his life, disillusioned
with the monstrosity that humanity became under capitalism and inspired by
the diversity in development he encountered in his studies of pre-capitalist
societies, Marx set out to find a new path to communism.[57] Although
incomplete upon his death, his extensive collection of notes, some of which

have now been published as his *Ethnological Notebooks*, gave further credence to women's agency and their species being but also to that of non-western societies and Indigenous peoples. These studies challenged some of his earlier Eurocentric views such that he came to believe non-western peoples would lead the way to socialism.

Marx engaged in very careful readings of the work of Lewis Henry Morgan and other contemporary anthropologists. As discussed earlier in this chapter, Marx took extensive and critical notes on these works, especially Morgan's, and these were partly published as *The Ethnological Notebooks*, which detail the relationship between the family, gender relations, and the mode of production in non-western societies. Through these works Marx learned that gender relations had evolved throughout history and differed according to family type, which developed in response to or alongside the particular mode of production.

In particular, Marx noted the greater gender equality and freedoms that women enjoyed within the gens (clan) under the Asiatic mode of production, especially the Iroquois women, than in the later patriarchal and modern nuclear family. He noted that a strict division of labor existed wherein women were primarily involved in food preparation while men were out doing the hunting. However, Marx noted that food preparation was a highly valued and status activity.[58] Peter McLaren points out that the extensive notes that Marx took of Henry Lewis Morgan's work, especially on the Iroquois people, and his excitement over their more communal and egalitarian society. McLaren is worth quoting at length:

> Many passages of these *Notebooks* reflect Marx's interest in Iroquois democracy as expressed in the Council of the Gens, that 'democratic assembly where *every adult male and female* had a voice upon all questions brought before it,' making special note of the active participation of women in tribal affairs. In this area as elsewhere Marx discerned germs of stratification within the gentile organization, again in terms of the separation of the 'public' and 'private' spheres, which he saw in turn as the reflection of the gradual emergence of a propertied and privileged tribal caste. Marx was nonetheless unmistakably impressed by the fact that, among the Iroquois, women enjoyed a freedom and a degree of social involvement far beyond that of the women (or men!) of any so-called civilized nation ... It was not only Iroquois social organization, however, that appealed to him, but rather *a whole way of life* sharply counter-posed, all along the line, to modern industrial civilization. Whatever reservations Marx may have had regarding the universal applicability of the Iroquois 'model' in the analysis of gentile societies, the painstaking care with which he copied out Morgan's often

meticulous descriptions of the various aspects of their culture shows the power of their impact on his thinking.[59]

Marx was clearly looking to learn from the Iroquois, not necessarily to move backwards in history but to perhaps consider how Iroquois way of life could inform a new communistic society.

Marx perceived that women had greater power in clan society because their food gathering and preparation activities were the clans' primary source of subsistence whereas the meat men hunted was predominantly a luxury item. The detailed examples of life among various peoples support Maria Mies' theory that "tools of destruction" led to the theft and enslavement of women to work in food harvesting, which increased food production. Here we find the introduction of private property and class distinctions within the clan. The increased production which made smaller family units possible and the increased conflict within the clan led eventually to the disintegration of the clan system and the establishment of the patriarchal family, defined by property relations in which wives, children, slaves, and servants were all members of the family. This property relation led to a desire to establish paternity in order to determine inheritance rights. Women's lives thus became highly controlled to ensure they would have only one male partner, whereas the same expectation did not apply to men. In addition, Marx noted that women under the patriarchal family were more vulnerable due to the lack of family support that existed within the clan. "Civilization," was thus a process that took away women's freedoms. Marx notes that the strict legal controls over women, however, indicate that they were not complacent in the face of their oppression but likely actively resisted. Thus, Marx recognized women, even under constant threat and oppression, to be historical Subjects.[60]

According to Dunayevskaya, Marx noted that the strife recorded between the chiefs and the ranks was evidence of class struggle already taking place within primitive communism. He recognized this discovery to mean that communism did not first require a linear passage through capitalism. Rather, multiple paths to communism existed and there was a definite possibility that the Russian proletariat could establish a communist state before the West.[61] Of course, we now know that his prophecy came to be only a few years after his death in the Russian Revolution of 1917. As history would have it, this communism, built initially upon Marxist ideals, later took a turn toward totalitarianism. It is critical that we not equate Marx's humanist philosophy of revolution and his vision for a new society with the various communisms that have distorted his ideas and his ideals.

Marx's Humanism and a New Society

From his earliest works, Marx was after something much bigger than a mere change in economic relations. His vision was for the proletariat to take the reins of history and develop a new humanism, a society wherein alienation ceases to exist—the absolute negation of the alienated existence we endure under capitalism and the emergence of a new person and a new society guided by love, dignity, and social responsibility. Dunayevskaya makes this point clearly by quoting Marx's words in "Private Property and Communism":

> Marx's opposition to private property was very far removed from a question of 'property.' Rather his opposition ... was due to the fact that it 'completely negates the personality of man ...'[62]

As noted above, Marx recognized the man/woman relation as a key representation of our humanity, the degree to which we as a species being had reach our full potential. And he was clear that our current gender relations were characterized by tremendous unfreedoms and oppression. Indeed, his studies of pre-capitalist societies demonstrated that capitalism exacerbated gender inequalities and relegated women to a position of servitude within the family. While perhaps subconsciously chauvinistic, Marx was sincere in his desire to support women's liberation and in creating a world that was socially just for women. He came to recognize their revolutionary spirit and potential and to praise their courage and resistance. Although he did not work out a theoretical understanding of the continued impact of patriarchy on capital accumulation, clearly, he understood that his vision for a new humanism could not be accomplished as long as half the population remained enslaved.

Although a clear advocate of all workers, Marx evidenced a strong Eurocentric perspective in his early work. Yet extensive study of non-western societies and active involvement in current global events led him to recognize the revolutionary potential of all peoples and to look beyond preconception to discover that pre-capitalist societies could be the first to arrive at communism, taking diverse paths not necessarily modeled after western Europe. Here, too, Marx came to recognize that slavery had been at the heart of capitalist development and that racism was one of the ruling class's most powerful tools to keeping the working class divided and unable to rise up together against capitalism.

Marx was very aware that his vision of a new humanism would require the transcendence of relations of domination, including class, racism, and women's oppression. Under capitalism all relations are in some way or another property relations. Dunayevskaya points out that instead of all the senses that are considered human we adopt a "sense of possession, which is the simple alienation of all these senses."[63] The dissolution of the entire system serves to free the human senses to human need rather than to wealth and property. Marx's critique of private property was not merely a concern for economic justice. Rather Marx was primarily concerned with the distortion of humanity that results from alienated labor and capitalist production processes. He envisioned a communism in which the species being is a collective of individuals who value the unique contributions of all human beings and create conditions for each to thrive "from each according to his abilities to each according to his needs."[64]

Marx understood from his earliest work that our relation of man to woman would define the relation of human being to human being. He came to understand that our essential human characteristics—our revolutionary spirit as Subjects of history—lay potentially with each of us. But he also came to realize that our social conditions would define our alliances and that it was likely that those who could align themselves with the oppressors would do so. Only the most oppressed with nothing to lose and everything to gain would be most likely to lead the charge of revolution.

Notes

1. Sections of this chapter have been previously published. See Lilia D. Monzó, "Women and Revolution," *Knowledge Culture* 4, no. 6 (2016), https://www.addletonacademicpublishers.com/online-access-kc

2. Assata Shakur, *Assata: An Autobiography*, 152.

3. Raya Dunayevskaya, *Women's Liberation and the Dialectics of Revolution: Reaching for the Future*, 82.

4. Karl Marx, *The Economic and Philosophic Manuscripts of 1844*.

5. Marx, *Economic and Philosophic Manuscripts*.

6. C. L. R. James, "They Showed the Way to Labor Emancipation: On Karl Marx and the 75th Anniversary of the Paris Commune," para. 5.

7. Karl Marx, *Capital*, Vol. I.

8. Kevin Anderson, *Marx at the Margins: On Nationalism, Ethnicity, and Non-Western Societies*; See also Heather Brown, *Marx on Gender and the Family: A Critical Study*.

9. Raya Dunayevskaya, *American Civilization on Trial: Black Masses as Vanguard*.

10. Dunayevskaya, *Rosa Luxemburg, Women's Liberation, and Marx's Philosophy of Revolution*; see also "Chapter 1, Introduction," note 8.

11. See Martha E. Gimenez, "Capitalism and the Oppression of Women: Marx Revisited."; See also Nancy Holmstrom, "The Socialist Feminist Project."

12. Brown, *Marx on Gender*.
13. Ibid., 5.
14. Karl Marx, "The Working Day," 368.
15. Marx lived from 1818 to 1883, a time in which women had few legal rights.
16. Brown, *Marx on Gender*, 17.
17. Kevin Anderson, introduction to *Marx on Suicide*, ed. Anderson and Plaut, 1999.
18. Karl Marx, cited in Kevin Anderson, introduction to *Marx on Suicide*, p. 6; For an earlier translation see Marx, *Economic and Philosophic Manuscripts*, p. 48.
19. Karl Marx and Friedrich Engels, "Manifesto of the Communist Party," 488.
20. Friedrich Engels, *"The Origins of the Family, Private Property and the State,"* 736.
21. Raya Dunayevskaya, *Rosa Luxemburg, Women's Liberation, and Marx's Philosophy of Revolution*, 2nd ed.
22. Anderson, *Marx at the Margins*; Brown, *Marx on Gender*.
23. Karl Marx, "Letter to Sigfrid Meyer and August Vogt," April 9, 1870.
24. Karl Marx, "The Civil War in France," 641.
25. Ibid., 647–648.
26. Dunayevskaya, *Women's Liberation*, 58.
27. Mary Gabriel, *Love and Capital: Karl and Jenny Marx and the Birth of a Revolution*.
28. Karl Marx and Friedrich Engels, *The German Ideology*, 51–52.
29. Karl Marx and Friedrich Engels, *The Holy Family*.
30. Eric A. Plaut and Kevin Anderson, *Marx on Suicide*.
31. Brown, *Marx on Gender*.
32. Lise Vogel, *Woman Questions: Essays for a Materialist Feminism*.
33. Brown, *Marx on Gender*, 16.
34. Marx, *The Economic and Philosophic Manuscripts*, 103.
35. Holstrom, *Socialist Feminist Project*, 457.
36. Ibid., 458.
37. Anderson, *Marx at the Margins*.
38. Marx & Engels, "Manifesto," 477.
39. Karl Marx, "The British Rule in India."
40. Karl Marx and Frederick Engels, "Extracts from the New York *Tribune* on the Crimean War."
41. Anderson, *Marx at the Margins*.
42. Edward W. Said, *Orientalism*.
43. Anderson, *Marx at the Margins*.
44. Ibid., 37
45. Ibid., 41.
46. Ibid.
47. Anderson, *Marx at the Margins*, 156.
48. Karl Marx, *Grundrisse*, p. 497.
49. Marx, *Grundrisse*.
50. Anderson, *Marx at the Margins*.
51. Karl Marx, "The Civil War in the United States," para. 3.
52. Karl Marx, *Karl Marx: On America and the Civil War*, 275

53. Karl Marx, "Letter to Sigfrid Meyer and August Vogt," para 12.
54. Marx, "Letter to Sigfrid Meyer and August Vogt," para. 13.
55. Keeanga-Yamahtta Taylor, "Race, Class and Marxism."
56. Dunayevskaya, *Rosa Luxemburg*.
57. Ibid.
58. Karl Marx, *The Ethnological Notebooks of Karl Marx*.
59. Peter McLaren, "Red Bones," 89–90.
60. Marx, *Ethnological Notebooks*.
61. Dunayevskaya, *Rosa Luxemburg*.
62. Ibid., 81.
63. Ibid., 81
64. Karl Marx, "Critique of the Gotha Program," 531.

Bibliography

Anderson, Kevin. *Marx at the Margins: On Nationalism, Ethnicity, and Non-Western Societies*. Chicago, IL: University of Chicago Press, 2010.

Anderson, Kevin. Introduction to *Marx on Suicide*, Eric A. Plaut and Kevin Anderson, Eds., 3–40. Evanston, Il: Northwestern University Press, 1999.

Brown, Heather. *Marx on Gender and the Family: A Critical Study*. Chicago, IL: Haymarket Books, 2013.

Dunayevskaya, Raya. *American Civilization on Trial: Black Masses as Vanguard*. Chicago, IL: News and Letters Committees, 2003.

———. *Rosa Luxemburg, Women's Liberation, and Marx's Philosophy of Revolution, 2nd edition*. Chicago, IL: University of Illinois Press, 1991.

———. *Women's Liberation and the Dialectics of Revolution: Reaching for the Future*. Atlantic Highlands, NJ: Humanities Press International, Inc., 1985.

Engels, Friedrich. "The Origins of the Family, Private Property and the State." In *The Marx-Engels Reader, 2nd edition*., edited by R. C. Tucker, 734–759. New York: W. W. Norton & Company, 1978.

Gabriel, Mary. *Love and Capital: Karl and Jenny Marx and the Birth of a Revolution*. New York: Little, Brown and Co., 2011.

Gimenez, Martha E. "Capitalism and the Oppression of Women: Marx Revisited." *Science & Society* 69, no. 1 (2005): 11–32.

Holmstrom, Nancy. "The Socialist Feminist Project." *Monthly Review: An Independent Socialist Magazine* 54, no. 10 (2005): 1–13.

James, C. L. R. "They Showed the Way to Labor Emancipation: On Karl Marx and the 75th Anniversary of the Paris Commune." *Labor Action: Newspaper of the Workers Party of the United Sates*, March 18, 1946. https://www.marxists.org/archive/james-clr/works/1946/03/paris-commune.htm

Marx, Karl. "Critique of the Gotha Program." In *The Marx-Engels Reader, 2nd edition*., edited by R. C. Tucker, 618–652. New York: W. W. Norton & Company, 1978.

———. "The Civil War in France." In *The Marx-Engels Reader, 2nd edition.*, edited by R. C. Tucker, 618–652. New York: W. W. Norton & Company, 1978.

———. "The Civil War in the United States." *Marxists Internet Archive.* https://www.marxists.org/archive/marx/works/download/Marx_Engels_Writings_on_the_North_American_Civil_War.pdf

———. *Karl Marx: On America and the Civil War.* New York: McGraw-Hill, 1972.

———. *Capital*, Vol. I. Translated by Ben Fowkes. New York: Vintage Books, 1977.

———. "The Working Day." In *Capital*, Vol. I, translated by Ben Fowkes, 340–416. New York: Vintage Books Edition, 1977.

———. *Grundrisse.* New York: Penguin Books, 1993.

———. *Economic and Philosophic Manuscripts of 1844.* Translated by Martin Milligan. Moscow: Foreign Languages Publishing House, 1961.

———. "The British Rule in India." *The New York Herald Tribune*, June 10, 1853. https://www.marxists.org/archive/marx/works/1853/06/25.htm

———. Letter to Sigfrid Meyer and August Vogt, April 9, 1870. In *Marxists Internet Archive.* https://www.marxists.org/archive/marx/works/1870/letters/70_04_09.htm

Marx, Karl and Friedrich Engels. "Manifesto of the Communist Party." In *The Marx-Engels Reader, 2nd edition*, edited by R. C. Tucker, 469–500. New York: W. W. Norton & Company, 1978.

———. *The German Ideology.* New York: Prometheus Books, 1998.

———. *The Holy Family.* CreateSpace, 2016.

———. "Extracts from the New York Tribune on the Crimean War." In *The Russian Menace to Europe*, edited by Paul Blackstock and Bert Hoselitz. London: George Allen and Unwin, 1953. https://www.marxists.org/archive/marx/works/subject/russia/crimean-war.htm

McLaren, Peter. "Red Bones: Toward a Pedagogy of Common Struggle—Response 2." In *Red Pedagogy: Native American Social and Political Thought, 10th anniversary edition*, Sandy Grande, 83–92. New York: Rowman & Littlefield, 2015.

Plaut, Eric A. and Kevin Anderson. *Marx on Suicide.* Evanston, IL: Northwestern University Press, 1999.

Said, Edward W. *Orientalism.* New York: Random House, Inc., 1978.

Shakur, Assata. *Assata: An Autobiography.* Chicago, IL: Lawrence Hill Books, 1987.

Taylor, Keeanga-Yamahtta. "Race, Class and Marxism." *SocialistWorker.org*, January 4, 2011. http://socialistworker.org/2011/01/04/race-class-and-marxism

Vogel, Lise. *Woman Questions: Essays for a Materialist Feminism.* New York: Routledge, 1995.

· 4 ·

IN SEARCH OF FREEDOM

My Road to Marx

Ya las lágrimas se me han secado …
Ya estoy libre de espantos …

—My mother

Ustedes no saben lo que vivimos—la miseria …
Creen que los libros lo dicen todo!

—My father

I was raised with the echo of my parents' words—messages that guided my actions and views and, sometimes, as in the words of my mother above, proverbs that spoke of more than her own history but of the history of so many women whose lives were defined by sacrifice but also enormous courage and struggle. My parents decided (my mother grudgingly) to emigrate from Cuba to the United States in 1971, 12 years after the victory of the Cuban Revolution. My sister and I were six and four, respectively. I grew up in the United States, observing the pain of the Cuban diaspora and the economic and social struggle that came with the decision to seek "a better life." I was raised with stories of rations and food shortages, long lines, stores with empty shelves, compulsory sugar cane cutting brigades and neighborhood spies that silenced dissent and created distrust. Some were lived experiences, some were exaggerations and some were myths. Most were no different than what happens in the United States, although perhaps more selectively and often to the more impoverished communities of color. I do believe the fear, however, was real. A seething anger toward anything socialist or communist, and especially toward Fidel Castro and Che Guevara, permeated any conversation about Cuban life and politics in our household.

These stories were manifestations of real hardships experienced but without the contextual explanation of the root causes of the depravity Cuba began experiencing at the onset of the Revolution nor of the factors that likely contributed to what has been characterized by critics as repressive political policies. These contributing factors included the U.S. embargo, the *Bay of Pigs Invasion*, over 600 C.I.A. (Central Intelligence Agency)- or Cuban exile-led assassination attempts against Fidel Castro, and eventually the loss of Soviet economic support after its fall.[1] Although U.S. propaganda shamelessly exaggerates and/or mislabels many of the human rights abuses attributed to Fidel and the Cuban Revolution, there is no doubt that some of these abuses were real (Fidel publicly acknowledged and apologized for the persecution of LGBTQIA individuals, not that this absolves him) and that political freedoms were and are often denied to the Cuban people.[2] I am neither dismissing the significance of these nor justifying them. Nonetheless, the stories I grew up hearing and that are often told among the Cuban-American community are often told in a historical vacuum without the political consciousness of the impact of imperialism, global capitalism, or of the significant benefits that the Cuban Revolution—with all its hardships—brought to the Cuban masses, many of whom were Black citizens and/or farmers and ranchers who lacked the most basic human rights, including health care and education.[3] For women, the revolution also brought opportunities for greater self-determination previously out of reach.[4]

My parents do not represent the wealthy or professional class of Cubans who fled to Miami at the first inkling of revolution. My father, with a third-grade education, worked in Cuba in upholstery and my mother completed six years of primary education before moving on to study sewing as a technical trade. However, following gendered traditions, my mother did not work for wages while in Cuba. She married my father and became a homemaker, relegating her economic contribution to the informal sector of caring work and her skill and creativity to the confines of family appreciation, making dresses for her daughters. My mother's father, Abuelito Francisco, owned a mom and pop grocery store and his own modest home. Although the revolutionary government repatriated all foreign owned lands, second homes and rental properties, families were allowed to retain the homes in which they lived and to pass these down to their family members. Upon marriage, my father built an additional room to the back of my maternal grandparents' house and my parents (and later my sister and I) lived there until the day we left for the United States. The home currently remains in the family. The mom and pop grocery store, as all private enterprise, was closed down not long after the Revolution's victory. My paternal grandparents also owned their own home and it too remains within the family.

While I empathize with my parents' experiences of want, their indignation with having their property "taken" and their fear of repression (two uncles served twenty years as political prisoners), I grew up with a different reality. Of course, the "American dream" did not materialize and yet the myth prevailed as truth. I lived a form of schizophrenia wherein I could not see what I was apparently supposed to see. These narratives of American greatness, liberty and justice that everyone believes did not match my own experiences of alienation, inequality and unfreedoms. I would come to recognize this schizophrenia as a form of contrived hysteria wherein we are made to be "crazy" by the power of others to determine what is true. In society at large, in the workplace and the home, it seems Women of Color are often denied what we actually see.

Not wanting to leave her family behind, my father (whose parents and two siblings had already emigrated) had to make additional promises to convince my mother to leave Cuba and move to the United States. Through playful sarcasm I have heard often that these promises included that in the United States my mother would never need to iron another piece of clothing nor deal with cockroaches. Unfortunately, my parents have never been able to afford sending their clothing to the dry cleaners, we have certainly encountered cockroaches, and we have experienced poverty, near homelessness, language barriers and linguicism, racial discrimination, and other economic-related social turmoil. In addition, my mother's sacrifice of leaving her entire family behind, of being absent from all major family events, of the years of absence and disconnect have not been easy. Nor has it been easy for my father to reconcile himself to the fact that the opportunities he believed existed in the United States came with limits and were not equally accessible to everyone.

Like so many other immigrant families, my parents transferred their hopes and dreams of success to their children. They can believe their sacrifice of leaving Cuba was well worth it because their daughters did "make it"—I am a professor and my sister is a schoolteacher. Although we could have done this in Cuba too without separating the family and without the thousands of dollars I accrued in student loans (Cuba's education system is free to all from pre-school to doctorate), there is no doubt that my current U.S., middle-class standard of living would not have been possible in Cuba. U.S. economic sanctions, loss of support from the Soviet Union after its fall, and limited resources and production left Cuba with a decade-long "special period" of privation from which they are still recovering.[5] And perhaps, as a result of a destabilizing economy that must prioritize agriculture, the production of basic needs, and the tourist industry on which the country relies, I may not have been able to work within my field (as many highly educated professionals in Cuba don't) and might instead be working at some unskilled service job for the tourist industry that would pay (under the table) two or three times a professor's salary in Cuba.

My recent visit to Cuba has made very evident to me what my parents believed they were giving their children—greater economic security, presumed greater political and economic freedoms, an "easier" life with an abundance of commodities, especially foods and the promise of presumed limitless possibilities. While these things are certainly currently available to me as a professional woman they were not available to us as I was growing up and they remain elusive to the masses of impoverished people in the United States who face a highly unequal education system, lack medical care and experience chronic unemployment or underemployment, low wages, and poor working conditions. In my view, what we gave up was the opportunity to live in a society that aimed to develop solidarity and interdependence among its people, a work ethic based on community social development rather than individual competition and economic accumulation, and the opportunity, although filled with many hardships, to remain part of a larger project for the betterment of humanity. I do not want to romanticize Cuba—there are serious problems and in many ways it has fallen into the same trap as other so-called "working communisms" by concentrating ownership of the means of production in the hands of the state[6] rather than in the hands of the people (as Marx called for)—but Cuba is an example of the promise in organizing for greater equality and social responsibility and an experiment in socialism that can potentially be redirected toward a Marxist-humanist revolution.

In contrast, the devastation of homelessness and even hunger that we evidence in the United States where resources abound are a product of an extreme and shameful disparity justified through capitalist lies of meritocracy and opportunity. At the same time, this abundance of commodities and higher standard of living found in the United States and other "developed" nations undoubtedly result from the imperial legacy of dispossession of the people and lands in the colonies, the enslavement of Black and Indigenous peoples and from the corporate hyper exploitation of the Global South.[7] We may face, among the population as a whole, less economic need than Cuba but our acquiescence to a world of destruction in the service of a few eats daily at our souls and deforms us into what David McNally calls "monsters of the market."[8] Thankfully, just as in popular culture, the real life zombies that many of us become are capable of rising up and often do so. So how did a Latina Cuban "exile" come to question and challenge all that she had grown up hearing and find her way to Marx?

In this chapter I share stories that have made me who I am today—a Latina Marxist-humanist, revolutionary critical pedagogue with a dream for a world where every life matters equally and where people live, learn and love freely, where our labor reflects the creative activity of individuals working to improve our world. It was recommended to me that I include in this book how, having grown up in an anti-communist environment, I became a Marxist. Through storied narratives I document my political awakening, including periods defined by survival, fear, and hope. Weaved among these stories are the subtext of communist values, feminist pursuits, racial aggression, internalized oppression, the recovery of stolen truths, and an ongoing struggle to breathe deeply at least once in my life. My hope is that my story will not just give readers an understanding of why I've written this book but that it will also offer some instructive lessons that will advance the goal of developing a more humane world. I end this chapter with my own brief analysis of how my story might move us forward. I ask that as you read this chapter, you suspend judgment of my family and appreciate the particular material conditions from which my daily life took shape. I invite you to *see with me*.

Capitalist Delusions: The Immigrant Narrative Confronted

My story starts off with the typical immigrant story of economic struggle. My parents say they left every dime they had and all their personal belongings to our family in Cuba. As most immigrants to the United States, they believed we were coming to the land of plenty. In the United States, my father worked hard painting houses and quickly rose to lower middle-class status—they bought a small home in the suburbs, we went to public school, and we even paid small installments every month for medical care. Yet this "success" did not last long. An economic downturn along with rampant individualism and alienation took their toll and we lost all economic footing that we had gained. Although my parents remain faithful to their belief that this is the best country in the world and grateful for allowing us citizenship status, I saw a different reality.

In my mind's eye I see us walking down the street at night—my father, mother, sister and I. It is a story I have heard often. We arrived with plans to stay with my grandparents (on my father's side) until my father could get a job. Within a few days of arriving, my father and his brother (who was also staying there) had an argument. Letting his pride and quick temper get the better of him, my father rejected their assistance and we walked out with the few things we had brought with us. With no money, no work or even a place to live, we set out into this new land. An apartment manager with a vacancy gave us refuge on the promise to pay the rent as soon as my father got a job. We were lent an old mattress that was placed on the floor and there we all slept until we awoke to the shuffling and yelling sounds of my father's loud booming voice. A large rat had been nibbling at his head. My sister and I watched as my father scurried around the room with a large shoe to kill the rat that got away with a chunk of his hair.

My mother entered the waged work force about five years later when my father's work faltered and the bill collectors started calling. We desperately needed the money. In the States, her talent and craft went unrecognized by the outside world as she joined the hundreds of thousands of women in the garment industry whose days are filled with the mindless, repetitive, alienating, assembly line piecework in sweatshop factories. Still, we lost the house in Miami and moved to Los Angeles. My mother found similar life-killing work in the factories of the Los Angeles garment industry. Soon we would come to see how this work and the material realities (food deserts, lack of medical insurance) that afflicted my family would begin to slowly ravage my mother's body. Fortunately, she continued with the life-affirming creative labor that filled her soul, making dresses for my sister and me as we grew into young women (she made my wedding dress) and now looks forward to making dresses for her granddaughter (my niece).

Finding work was harder for my father in Los Angeles, where the Latinx community did not benefit from the large wealthy Cuban-American community who had left Cuba prior to or in the early years of the Cuban revolution. These early Cuban immigrants built an influential base in Miami, which facilitated employment and other services to later arrivals.[9] The economic challenges we faced in Los Angeles amidst the hyper exploitation of predominantly Mexican and Central American workers were significant. We settled in Bell, a small Latinx immigrant community in the South East Los Angeles metropolitan area. The economic precarity my parents have faced through the years have pushed them to relocate to different apartment buildings within the area nine times.

It isn't hard to see why I could not accept the mainstream narratives my father believed. He was arguing in favor of an economic system that kept us at the bottom of the economic strata and failed to recognize the racialization that marked us as subhuman—deficient, incapable, unworthy, lacking in intelligence—and that justified our exploitation. My mother was often silent in our debates. She lived through some of the greatest struggles a woman endures while my father was socially protected by his gender. Although my mother endured these struggles with tenacity and a quiet calmness that only now I have the life experience to appreciate, I saw her many humiliations, felt her pain and prayed for a different life for myself.

Forty-five years would pass before I returned to Cuba in 2017. My grandmother, whom I was named after, would die before I returned. There was only ever enough money for my mother to visit. Eventually Cuba became just the place where I was born; my aunts, uncles and cousins were a series of faceless names. I learned to identify as a Latina rather than a Cuban woman—connected more to the Mexican and Central American communities that I came to know as a teenager and college student and later as a bilingual teacher and researcher. However, Cuba would remain in my heart as I struggled to understand the contradiction in the accolades from the left and what my father denounced. I've come to understand, as Miryam Yataco wisely articulates, "how deep our identities are …" that " … we can travel thousands of miles but still stay connected to our lands and communities."[10]

My first introductions to Karl Marx and Paulo Freire came during my last year as an undergraduate at the University of California, San Diego. I took a course by a visiting instructor who was working for an organization that helped to develop community banks and micro businesses among low-income communities in Latin America. The course had a praxis component and the instructor invited me to work with him and a community of women in El Florido, a small *colonia* on the outskirts of Tijuana. That experience concretized for me the many critiques I had read about the U.S. government, imperialism and White supremacy—critiques I had gained within the courses of my major in communications and minor in political science. It also concretized for me the sense of alienation I felt as a racialized woman in the United States. Although I was not Mexican I recognized a cultural affinity that I did not share with *"los Americanos"* and the poverty and exploitation my family and I experienced was not alien to them. I felt that my life experiences were validated by their own experiences of precarity. I also felt accepted as an equal (at least equal to the Mexican woman) in a way that I had never felt in the United States.

I was full of indignation (I still am) after learning of the history of horrors that the C.I.A. (Central Intelligence Agency) and the U.S. government perpetrated against Latin America and elsewhere. I attributed the disparities I observed to racism, corporate greed and the U.S. drive for power. This was 1988 when the United States was backing and arming the Contras against the left-leaning Sandinista government of Nicaragua. I wanted to fight alongside the Sandinistas, to free the world of the horrors I was learning about. At this time, my feminist perspectives were also being sharpened by women's studies courses. This was an important time for my development. My politics previously vague became sharply defined to the left. My friends called me a socialist but our understanding of socialism was limited to some vague notion of anti-capitalism and social equity. I did not yet have sufficient theoretical understanding of Marxism to understand how political economy structures the totality of our lives. I lacked the necessary theoretical sophistication to connect the various social ills of our world.

Over two decades would pass before I returned to these roots and pore over Marx's vast body of work and that of other Marxists and other scholars with a vision of an alternative to capitalism. I was a 21year-old working-class Latina woman attempting to survive in a world of alienated social upheaval. Gender relations, economic struggle, racism and internalized oppression defined my life. My interests in political economy were pushed to the sidelines as these pressures intensified.

On Feminist Understandings and the Right to Speak

My experiences and ways of being and understanding the world have all been mediated by my gendered existence. The world had defined me a woman and from that moment on everything took on a specifically gendered meaning— from the presumably little things like what I might wear or what I should eat, to more life-changing things like what I was supposed to be good at or study, to the things that define us profoundly such as when and how to speak and whether I would actually be heard. My earliest conscious experiences of oppression have to do with being a woman. I came to understand at a very young age that my life was defined by, controlled by and always in relation to men. As women we were visitors to *their* world and therefore we were expected to abide by *their* rules. Growing up, decisions, activities, opportunities were always made in relation to my father—because he said so, in reaction to what he would say, because we wanted to hide it from him, because he did or did not approve.

I learned early on that boys could be who they wanted to be. Sure, they got into trouble for it but this was expected. Girls were supposed to be timid, quiet and agreeable. I was none of these things. The pictures of my youth almost all show a curly haired girl with a scowl on her face. I was not happy sitting for hours while my mother made me into the Latina Shirley Temple, I did not want to pose for pictures with animal characters at Disney World and I did not want to perform Cuban dance moves on command at family gatherings. To my family's astonishment I had a mind of my own and wanted to use it. I was a feminist before I even knew what the word meant. As I grew up and my world expanded I realized that the attempts to dominate me were not a function of my family dynamics but our reality as women, and that these social controls were made more stringent and multiplied by race and class.

Women who recognize their agency and resistance within a patriarchal society may reject my portrayal of our lives as hyper exploited and oppressed. I do not deny women's agency and resistance or that women have made tremendous gains within this world controlled by men. Indeed, one of my major goals in this book is to highlight women's agency, especially that of Indigenous women and Women of Color, and their tremendous impetus and courage to act. However, I do not want to deny that often the gains we've made have allowed some of us perhaps a less restricted life but one that remains in the service of what bell hooks calls "White supremacist capitalist patriarchy."[11] Joining the workforce, for example, has allowed us greater autonomy and decision-making power within the family; however, it has also re-affirmed our exploitation by creating a double shift. Further, the perception of progress made by middle-class American women must be interrogated in light of its relation to the increased devastation of working-class Women *and Men of Color* in the United States and across the Global South.

In our family my father was the patriarch with presumed final authority over all matters. However, many challenges to his perceived rule were enacted without his knowledge, often with my mother's support. She recognized my father's expectations of his daughters to be outdated and often intervened on our behalf. I, however, lacking in the art of subtlety, was tagged *"candela"* for my rebellion and willingness to verbally challenge my father by *"contestando"* (literally to contest by talking back). I was not supposed to have my own opinions, much less go against his. This is common in families that employ authoritarian parenting and especially experienced among girls.[12] Yet while I did pay a price for talking back, it was also perceived as daring and they were seemingly proud that I would be able to confront the outside world. My father liked to say, *"Es igualita a su padre."*

I recall much more vividly the many times I held my tongue and felt trapped and voiceless, unable to express myself in order to keep the peace. My expressions of disagreement with my father often resulted in anger and disharmony in the household. To a young girl his loud booming voice in anger sounded like an explosive bark. As I grew older my perceived rebellious nature came in the form of questioning and much later arguing over serious topics, such as racism, class relations, anti-capitalist ideals, party politics, gay rights, etc. My sister would tell me to "stop arguing" and "let it go." Inevitably my mother paid the price for my back talking since it was presumably her job to keep her daughters in line.

Although Latinx women are often depicted as submissive, my mother demanded respect from my father in a way that was subtle but effective. She found resourceful ways to support our needs and respect our individuality as young women within the confines of a culture of *machismo*. My mother was instrumental in transforming gendered expectations for my sister and me. We were sometimes expected to help my mother with a little dusting and laundry on the weekends, not because it was our duty but because it had to get done and she needed help, but our primary job was our schoolwork. Although my mother attempted to teach us how to cook, she did not force us to learn to cook or to do other "women's work," nor were we ever expected to take on these tasks after my mother began working outside the home.

I was certain that I never wanted to become a traditional woman and often said so, refusing to learn to cook even the simplest of dishes. My mother did not seem to put much faith in this possibility but she regarded it as a worthy goal, saying *"Ojala que así sea!"* My father indulged my thinking with quiet amusement. Today, I see pride in my parents' eyes when they note that my husband is the cook in my home, even for family gatherings, and shares the household responsibilities. While they clearly consider mothering to be my first responsibility, they are proud of my academic success and professional role.

While my father expected my mother to be a traditional wife and homemaker (even when she entered the waged workforce—although he "helped" more)—cooking, cleaning, doing the laundry and tending to her daughters, he held a double standard when it came to his daughters. We were expected to get good grades, go to college, and *"prepararse para que ningun tipo cualquiera venga a maltratarlas."* They held high expectations that we would go to college, have a career, and move up the social and economic ladder—that was after all why they had emigrated to the United States. This was an unquestioned expectation even though they had little idea of what this would require, how to build the necessary study habits, or what the financial cost or application process entailed. I never heard my parents express the belief that after marriage my sister or I should become "housewives" nor did they explicitly ever suggest that it was our role to follow our husbands. My grandmother and other family members were not so clear on this and wondered why we continued to work once we married and had children.

We were, however, clearly and explicitly socialized to the repressive sexual standards that have been used throughout capitalist societies to control women's bodies and secure the next generation of workers. The narrative that defines women as virgins or whores was made very clear to my sister and me. We were told that "loose" women were *"hechadas a perder"* (spoiled) and that "no man would want to marry such a woman." That marriage may not be necessary or desired was never considered.

Stories about the proper way a Latina was to behave were inscribed in me very early, often through disdain expressed about other young women's behaviors. As I grew into an adolescent, my parents began to censor my and my sister's clothing and interactions with boys. We were not allowed to wear shorts or short skirts because they were thought to be provocative to men. It was inscribed in the dictates of our behavior that we were supposed to protect ourselves from men who were not capable of resisting temptation. My grandmother would share stories about all the women my father had dated prior to settling down. These comments were followed with stories of meeting my mother and having to visit her in the presence of the entire family and my grandfather's sternness that kept them in line. While these stories were told to entertain and reminisce they also carried important messages about the value of women *"de familia"* as opposed to *"de la calle."* In contrast to women, men were expected to be experienced with sex and unlikely able to resist temptation. Of course, this glorification of men's sexual prowess naturalizes men's sexual predatory behavior. Sex before marriage among boys was to be expected, whereas for girls it was thought to ruin her life.

> I was 11, a budding young woman,
> curiosity and eager for romance.
> He flirted with me. His smile was lazy, pretending to be cool.
> I was pretending too. Not too interested, but loving the attention
> A message of desirability in a world where women's worth is only that
> Who am I?
> A saint? A Whore? Or just a girl?

I hated that we were not allowed to wear shorts in high school. The high school I went to was on a year-round schedule and we were in school during the hottest part of the summer. Sometimes it was 100 degrees Fahrenheit and my sister and I were probably the only two girls wearing pants. As soon as I went away to college I bought myself the shortest mini-skirt I could find. I deliberately wore it on my first visit home from college. I figured since I was no longer living under their roof and they weren't paying for my education, they couldn't say anything. I wore short miniskirts almost everyday for four years. Surprisingly, my father never commented to me about it. I later learned he initially complained to my mother about it but she did not discourage me from wearing them.

As a young woman joining the dating scene, "you're clipping my wings" became a playful mantra I used to rebuke men's negative judgments of my decisions or alternative recommendations, which too often resulted in discouraging me from pursuing my interests. I now recognize this as perhaps an unconscious form of control founded on deficit perceptions of women's "limitations," "idealism" and "irrationality." I recognize that in my youth I allowed men's unsolicited disapproval to temper my excitement, slow me down, and to ultimately affect my self-confidence and self-actualization.

Today my father exhibits important growth in terms of gendered ideas and I too have grown up enough to recognize the many ways in which his wisdom taught me well. He now often takes on the tasks he once perceived to be "women's work." While on the two occasions that my mother had cancer, he stepped up for months at a time to cook, clean, and care for her. His beliefs about gender roles have been significantly relaxed with respect to my son

(13 years old) and my nephew and niece (both 14 years old). Patriarchy and machismo prevail in our society and in our home; I am not suggesting otherwise. However, both my mother and father play out the structural confines of patriarchy in diverse and nuanced ways and these have changed contextually and over time.

In my personal and professional life I live out the objective reality of women's dehumanization, even though many of the men around me try to support women's rights and to treat me as an equal. The dehumanization of women is not merely about the ability to share household chores equitably or about equal pay—these are obvious forms of gender discrimination—but women's dehumanization is a deeply seeded reality that can be evidenced in numerous subtle ways in society, often so normalized we don't recognize it but that lead to the presumption that women don't have sufficient knowledge, need mansplaining and are unlikely to know the best course of action in any given situation. This leads to invisibility, silencing and/or dismissing. Worst of all we begin to do this to ourselves and to each other. My husband who generally takes on an equal share of the workload at home (he is a physician but I work longer hours) is applauded for his "help." While my grandmother would often refer to him as *"un santo,"* I think he is just meeting his responsibility. Still, gender relations of power in society cannot be fully circumvented, even when or if both parties want to do so. Marriage itself is an economic contract that subordinates women and the patterns of our gendered socialization cannot be fully transcended within a capitalist society that bombards us on a minute-by-minute basis with messages that mark women as less than human.

In Survival Mode—Race and Gender as Class Warfare

I came face to face with racism very early in my life. There was little doubt in my almost entirely Latinx elementary school in Miami that the few White kids in the school were different from the rest of us, or more aptly, we were different from them. They represented the people with power—the teachers and doctors and the movie stars and popular singers. Although I interacted with them on a friendly basis, I did not know much about them and presumed that their lives must be very different from my own. There were also very few Black children at our school but there was a Black male teacher, Mr. Brown, whose caring and charisma challenged every negative stereotype about Black men. With him we learned about Martin Luther King, Jr., about slavery, the Civil Rights Movement, and about justice and human dignity. I remember feeling very distraught at the horrors that Black people had been subjected to and, at the time, I did not even know the half of it. Although I recognized, even then, that I did not face the same discrimination that the Black community faced, it was clear to me that whatever I was, I was not "American" and would never belong to the White dominant group that seemed exalted to some form of sacrosanct deity, such that we could not "touch" them. As I grew up I would come to recognize that this untouchability was a social form of deference—it had been ingrained in society that we, People of Color, were somehow beneath them—less worthy, less intelligent, less beautiful.

Racism extends beyond the U.S. borders and has a strong presence in the Caribbean where Africans were also taken and enslaved. Thus, within my own family, I encountered racialized attitudes toward Blacks and other communities of color, which made no sense to me at all until I realized that my parents, having grown up in Cuba, perceived themselves to be of Spanish descent—even though current estimates suggest that the Cuban population could be as much as 70% of African descent. That many people in Cuba chose to recognize their Blackness only if absolutely evident through phenotype is consistent with the racism that inflicts the entire globe, wherein the White man claimed himself human and all Others were relegated to subhuman status to justify their conquest and genocide. Personally, I'm certain (in my own mind) that I have African roots. This is much more consistent with the reality that the majority of the Indigenous Peoples of Cuba were exterminated very early during the Spanish conquest. Of course, whether we are seen as ethnic or racial minorities makes little difference—in the United States everyone that is not of western European background is a Person of Color.

Our move to Los Angeles when I was 14 years old marked an important time in my development as a human being. In Los Angeles the class divide seemed much starker, perhaps because our lives had become much more economically precarious and I was now old enough to not only recognize but to name the injustices I perceived. Whereas in Miami, Spanish had been made an asset by the economic and political influence of the Cuban American community, in Los Angeles with its largely working-class Mexican immigrant and Chicano communities, Spanish was considered a lower-status language and English was a requisite to any good job. My father who had been able to establish his own modest business as a house painter in Miami was not able to pass the required license in Los Angeles because it was available only in English.

In Los Angeles the difference between the poverty of the inner cities and the affluence of Beverly Hills and other wealthy areas reaches gargantuan proportions. There was also much more conflict among diverse communities of color. Poverty, alienation, and lack of opportunity characterized my high school years and were exacerbated in college. These times were so hard that nothing will ever erase those memories of lack from my consciousness— never can I experience a setback without being immediately mentally transposed to that time in which I was not sure I would have a place to live. My family's financial and social problems of the time continue to haunt me to this day. The fear and uncertainty of poverty and the humiliation of the social ills that it generated within my immediate community and family preoccupied my life in those years. Although I dabbled in my early years in the academy with Critical Race Theory, which recognizes the centrality of race and racism in our lives as People of Color, it always seemed to me a bourgeois politics—that is, a politics that comes to light when we, as academics, move beyond real poverty. The reality of having to chose between food or paying the rent, of regular fainting spells because I was not eating sufficiently, of regularly hitchhiking even though I knew the risks I was taking because I had no other option, of phone and electricity cuts, and of constant humiliations of privations in a world in which my peers at UCSD (even those who were Latinx) were economically better off, have a primordial place within my life. Racism, of course, was intricately connected but in times of privations and need it was economic security and stability for which I longed.

It was difficult to move to a new city during high school, where popularity, racialization, national origin, language, and other categories defined particular cliques and marked students as either insiders or outsiders. It was especially disconcerting to me that although my high school, which had and still has a 98% Latinx student enrollment (predominantly immigrants from Mexican, Guatemala and El Salvador), it evidenced significant ethnic conflict. I did not understand why different Latinx groups would turn on each other when we were all equally oppressed and faced very similar forms of dehumanization in the same impoverished communities. I was uncomfortable among the small group of Cuban immigrants that sometimes looked down upon other Latinx groups. I became a chronically absent student and only re-integrated into school upon reaching my senior year, re-defining myself as Latina and shedding a nationalist identity that seemed to stereotype me into a person I did not recognize as myself.

Although chronically absent, I still did quite well academically, particularly in math, in which I had excelled all through my schooling years. Unfortunately to this day I am not sure whether I did well because I excelled or because I attended what was at the time rated as one of the top 100 worst public schools in the metropolitan Los Angeles area. Regardless, someone noticed my potential (perhaps my math teacher) because one day, during my junior year vacation, the school career counselor called me at home and offered me a job. I was surprised to hear from him since I had never been to the career counseling office. It was a job setting up the toy departments at the various Thrifty stores (these were later bought out by Rite Aid). We had moved to an apartment building where my father had arranged to do odd jobs for the owner when we had difficulty making the rent. Since this apartment was too far from school for me to walk my father had purchased a car for me for $500. Although very old, the car ran fine except that very early on I switched gears when I was not supposed to and broke the transmission. From then on when I needed to back up I would have to ask anyone in the vicinity to help me push the car back. Thankfully this was easy since it had a stick-shift transmission. The job gave me responsibility, a little independence and a little needed money. It also got me thinking about what I might do with my life. More importantly, I had come into the career counselor's radar as a student with college potential but lack of instrumental knowledge about schooling.[13] He later helped me apply for a college credit program at CSULA, college application fee waivers, and to complete my college application and financial aid papers. I must add that although this counselor had an important impact on my college path, he was not always able to step outside the racist influence of our society that marks the Other, especially the Mexican Other, as less capable. I recently learned that a brilliant colleague of mine went to my same high school and was met by this same counselor with the rhetoric of unteachability that many Mexican immigrant and Mexican-American students experience.

My time in college was a time to discover myself and to begin the slow and painful recovery of trauma that poverty and social ills had perpetrated against me. I am in no way a victim, of course. I have had opportunities that few have had and I am a result of those opportunities and of my own desire to prove to the world and to myself that I could accomplish what society seemed to yell at me that I could not and to show the silent and sometimes vocal monsters around me and, more importantly, inside of me that they were wrong—that I am just as smart and bright and deserving as every human being.

This was not an easy process. Indeed, it is a narrative I have had to return to too many times in my life, even after I reached what most would claim to be a significant level of success. You see, a predominantly White institution for a young Latina student is a space of particular alienation—where I often felt disconnected from everything that I had grown up valuing. I recognized the invisibility that accompanied my gendered racialization and rendered me voiceless, unworthy of being seen or heard. I recall vividly the endless sea of White bodies, all standing tall, assured a space to speak and other listening bodies. The first time I spoke aloud in class, it was at a women's studies class. I raised my hand to speak, certain that the almost entirely White student body in the class would not be able to comprehend neither my comment nor my English—even though I had been fluent in English for as long as I could remember.

The internal pain and humiliation of having to struggle for that which so many others seemed to have easy access to, including the right to speak and to be heard, played havoc with my confidence. I had learned as a child to lock myself in the bathroom and muffle my screams on a towel to drown out the family arguments that sometimes ensued, part and parcel of a family facing poverty, marginality and fear. I also learned to silence my questions regarding why we could not afford new jeans or another bra and later to not ask at all for the things I needed because it saddened my mother to have to deny me. I learned that when I stood up for myself in school or complained to police officers of their racialized comments—"You need to learn to speak English," they said to my parents with disdain on more than one occasion—I would be labeled "too sensitive," relegating the problem to one of my own making.

Even amidst poverty, sexism and other social ills, my family and community context was a haven. There I was beautiful, smart and worthy of all good things life had to offer but with every step beyond this space of safety, I breathed the contaminated air of racism and marginalization. The silencing now came from without, not out of the inability to make my words grant me what I needed but because my words no longer counted. While I have led a life fighting for the rights of children of color, and increasingly I do my best to fight against global capitalist, racist, and sexist oppression, I have not always done the same for myself. Like my mother, I too learned to recognize and many times to simply accept the injustices that I've endured; *yo también ya estoy libre de espantos.*

A Colonial Legacy

I must confess that my life is much easier than it used to be—my material conditions have been much improved as a result of having a steady income and a job in which I have significant freedom—more so than many others who work in other fields, exploited, with little sense of the value of their own creative labor and who face a constant fear of potential reprimands and unemployment. While I have tremendous privilege as a university professor with a living wage and significant freedom to engage work that is personally fulfilling and that I believe has meaning to others, alienation continues to define my social relations, especially within the White and male spaces of academia. This alienation that has been discussed in terms of people's inability to see the fruits of their labor and to find that the products that are essentially aspects of themselves turn on them and make them slaves to their own production takes on a different meaning in the context of race relations. In this context, it is a process of our inability to recognize the true value of our labor as it is so often diminished and distorted by those who seem not to see or hear us for who we are, people with histories of oppression that inform the way we think and engage in the world and the way others perceive us, treat us, and act around us.

As a Woman of Color, my experiences in dominant spaces are often inscribed with miscommunications, marginalization, dismissiveness, and invisibility. That I increasingly wake up in the middle of the night incapable of sleep even when I am exhausted is a function of spending too much time as a stranger to others and to myself, even though they may believe that they know me well and understand what I am saying. The reality is otherwise. Too often my comments go either unheard because the people instinctively save their concentration and attention skills—the necessary strategies to drown out so much of the many other things that are going on around us and within us—for those they believe will truly have something important to say. Other times, my suggestions, ideas, stories, or comments simply are misunderstood because there is little reference point from which to understand what I am saying. My world, of course, is informed by my own experiences of poverty, racism, sexism, marginalization, and a quest for social relations that are defined by compassion and community. I recognize these miscommunications and although I sometimes try to make myself understood, repeating and explaining, I often simply nod internally—my own recognition that my intended communication was not received. I do not always try very hard anymore—it gets old and I get tired.

As I sat down to write today, I am exhausted from the 2:30 internal wake-up call of the previous night. The incident was nothing to most people but to me it was one of many moments in which my marginality, my otherness, my focus, my gaze is interrupted, questioned not only by others but always by myself, a questioning that occurs even as my rational mind knows that this has happened so often that it cannot be denied. But let me tell the story. A group of us in my college had begun meeting to discuss how to have open conversations across race.

Whiteness pervades because White people set the standard for what is "normal." Half way through the meeting I noted that one of the members of the group was taking detailed notes. It was well intentioned, of course. Why wouldn't we want these conversations recorded? No one recognized that such recording may be unsafe for People of Color in a context in which they must talk about racism and their own experiences. A deep understanding of racism requires that we share personal and private thoughts. I wonder who will see these words that could so easily be held against me if not formally then by virtue of further marginalizing me. Anyway, my morning was filled with thoughts of my otherness and I wondered if these conversations were still buzzing, stressing, taking up space and energy from my White colleagues who had been at that meeting. I wondered if they realized that what I give up in going to these meetings is not just a couple of hours of time, which is bad enough; but that in addition, these discussions cloud my mind for days later.

Of course, this emotional drain takes a toll on my sleep patterns, my ability to concentrate at work, and even on my engagement with my son. The sleepless night catches up with me usually just before it's time to get up to take my son to school and then my son endures a stressful morning with a mama who is running around and impatiently pushing him out the door so that we can make it to school on time. The disturbed feelings of invisibility are lost for a moment to the worry of being accused of "neglectful parenting" for being tardy in a society that highly scrutinizes and defines parents of color as "uncaring" about their children's education.[14] Never mind that both my husband and I have terminal degrees and my son excels in his classes. Of course, these are gendered and racialized encounters since it is typically accusations reserved for Women of Color in urban schools.

We are encased within these stereotypical boxes that limit how we are perceived or imagined and that eventually affect how we see ourselves and who we believe we can become. Most would be surprised to find that they would not recognize me outside the contexts within which they know me.

At the university I am often guarded, unable to express doubt, uncertainty. I must be knowledgeable in a way that challenges my own identity as a growing person whose knowledge is constantly evolving and who wants to be challenged to learn new things and to think of the various nuances that make most things complex. And I wonder if this constant evolution of always on a path toward an undetermined future is only my way of justifying to myself my own ignorance. It is as if my emotions have been cut off from me—leaving me barren—a rational mind that cannot enjoy, almost careful to not become the imposter that I often fear I am. I am always aware of the spaces in which I am perceived not to belong and of the claims to universal knowing that escape me while rarely does the dominant group recognize that what *they* don't know can be of value. I am also keenly aware that no one appreciates when a Latina appears to know more than they and they perhaps unwittingly use punishing tactics to remind me of "my place." Unfortunately, this happens not only with White women but within group as well—jealousy is a painful and destructive emotion that arises out of fear—part of the White man's tools to divide and conquer. It is this sense of competition that guides our everyday reality that makes clear to me the need to uproot capitalism; I have become convinced that it is not part of our innate nature to want to be better than another but rather a deep seeded way of valuing that is learned within capitalist societies.

With family and friends, I am free to be who I am. Well, almost free for I can be thus as long as I limit my academese and withhold my theoretical knowledge, lest I appear to be either showing off or out of touch. Still, this social space of collective learning where every point that is made spurs us to greater understanding is familiar. It is how people function in the real world, outside of the academy where every point must be backed up with statistics or quoted from the greatest theoretical minds—debates where the contenders flex their intellectual muscle only to make a win and exclaim triumph over their opponent. In conversation with family and friends—People of Color whose value is not based on their intellectual capacity, degrees, or other social markers of status—we learn through stories, shared emotions and by listening. Theories develop and holes become evident in light of our lived realities and in the feelings these evoke, drawing on our "cultural intuition"[15] and our deeply submerged knowledges that have for centuries been denied but that live on and emerge at unexpected moments to remind us that although we have been colonized we have not been *vencidas* (beaten). Yet these moments of Indigenous lucidity are icing on the cake. There is freedom in being worthy simply for being that is manifested in joy, in aliveness, in deep breathing and deep laughter—always to be found in long talks with my girlfriends, acting silly with my sister, and playing with my son.

When my son was younger, I was more often seen *running with him* than after him—sometimes in places where adults would frown because we were not "supposed" to be running. Given my work schedule, I much rather spend the time I have playing, talking or even watching TV with my son than the typical "responsible" activities relegated to mothers. I am even okay with playing hooky (skipping school) with him once in a while to do something special. This may seem irresponsible to some people because as a society we ignore the role of play in learning and development and relegate it to "extra" activities, what we do after the real responsible and necessary things get done. Of course, these are the things gleaned to be necessary to socializing children to the capitalist "work ethic" and rule-following behaviors.

These personal challenges to western epistemes and to capitalist social relations have not been planned political acts of rebellion. Rather, these are spontaneous enactments based upon a strong sense of respect for diverse world-views and ways of being learned in my own upbringing. Yet it is exactly this type of challenge to societal norms that establishes the human dignity that John Holloway argues defies the logic of capital.[16] Holloway encourages us to engage in this "other-doing" that brings us joy and dignity and creates the structural cracks that will one day bring down the capitalist system that imprisons us all. I would add that it is not only capitalism that needs to come down but also racism, patriarchy and all forms of oppression and exploitation.

As discussed in Chapter 2, there is currently a contentious debate between proponents of identity politics and some Marxists. This debate is sometimes characterized as the class first or race first debate. I recognize the identity politics of the day sometimes serves as a veil. It supports one of the first rules of capitalist preservations—divide and conquer—by emphasizing the multitude of diverse identities and intersections (and their equally valid singular world views) and thereby rejecting the possibility of having common interests and goals. This approach has the potential (and for some, perhaps the intention) of leading us to become too self-absorbed to recognize that we are all similarly drowning. I do not advocate for the postmodern or poststructural preoccupation with deconstruction and dismissal of the essential qualities in our shared humanity. However, for many People of Color a sense of belonging is visceral. I see the preoccupation with identity among People of Color as a search for community—social spaces where we can be affirmed as human—a place where we can be, as Frantz Fanon argued, "truly seen," and experience what he called "reciprocal recognition."[17]

As Fanon notes in his critique of Hegel's master/slave dialectic the master does not seek recognition from the slave, nor can he, since the slave is not an independent Subject. The mutuality of recognition necessary for freedom, in a Hegelian sense, cannot be achieved within the master/slave relation. Instead, the slave must achieve self-recognition in order to assert themselves as an independent Subject and demand their freedom through material conditions—it is this struggle that allows them to emerge as fully human.

Until then, what we have is the ever-present and heart-wrenching ache of internalized oppression that has been festering in our communities of color for centuries. As Fanon noted, "racism renders the individual anonymous even to [themselves].[18] In Chapter 2, I also discussed Patricia Williams' concept of "spirit murder" wherein the murders committed against a people are not bound to their physical bodies but instead transcend particular lifetimes and generations.[19] In my own interpretation of this concept, I cannot "get past" the racist and sexist atrocities that have been committed to my people, even though I may not have experienced them first hand. I feel the piercing pain of every hunger pang, every rape, and every bullet that my many abuelitas endured.

Who am I?
Not just a woman, a Latina, a mother, a teacher
This is how the White man defines me
I know only what they seek me to know
I have only what they do not want
But I am not only what he is not.

I am more, I search to be more.
But his grip is strong
colonizing my mind and my heart
bending my knees
The other, invisible, in constant jeopardy
Even to myself

A daunting task to reclaim what has been lost
Or claim what is yet to be.

My voice once strong and loud
Now a whisper, a silent scream
She pulls me to Whiteness,

Crowds my mind with her lies
Strangles the Other with threats
Chases my dreams away

Do I deserve this?
Am I ungrateful?
How can I owe someone for what is rightfully mine?

The pain is visceral
I'm very sorry
What did I do wrong?
The silence deafens
The unspoken answer is to exist.

This pain and fear, forever trapped in my body, is especially felt in context where I am not seen, in contexts that are defined by and predominantly inhabited by White men (and to a lesser extent White women)—because of course, it is the failure to truly see me that has led to this history of gendered and racialized assaults. Donaldo Macedo names this experience of "being present and yet not visible, being visible and yet not present" as a form of "cultural schizophrenia."[20] Is it any wonder that we seek out those spaces of sanctuary where someone can *see* us? Without such recognition I cannot know that I even exist. Our endless need to define our identity—*my* endless quest to define who I am—is a testament to my continual search to "breathe" freely.[21]

New Hope and New Courage

I began to develop a structural analysis of our society during the last two years of my undergraduate education when, after switching from a math major to a communications major (based upon my roommate's recommendation that it was "kind of interesting") and adding a minor in political science. There was a sociopolitical strand to the communications major at UCSD in which we examined mainstream media as a tool of the state. I took courses on U.S. politics in Mexico and Central America, women's studies, and racism and ideology. These courses had me reading some of the works of Paulo Freire, Karl Marx, Edward Said, Antonio Gramsci. These readings gave me the theories and language with which to understand my own life experiences. This time on my own in college was a transformational experience. No longer was I restricted from voicing my opinion to keep the peace at home. And there were numerous scholars whose entire body of work was dedicated to making sense of the very same conditions that I experienced. More importantly I worked on a variety of community projects during this time, including with women in Tijuana on cooperative microenterprises and with an immigrant rights organization offering support services to Central American refugees. These activities opened my eyes and my heart to suffering that went beyond my own experiences and I learned to appreciate their diverse world views and their courage in the face of injustice. My own difficulties seemed to pale in comparison—after all I was in college and with this I had the hope of finding social and economic stability. I was humbled by the generosity and kindness that people showed me, even though as a presumed "American" (or raised as such) they could have relegated me to the role of the colonizer. I was also blown away by the wisdom, political savvy, and social awareness of people who may have had little, if any, formal schooling but rooted their analysis not only on their own personal experience but on the history of Latin America vis-à-vis U.S. imperialism and colonial relations. These experiences set me on a path to engage the world as a critical scholar and as an agent of change with the specific goal of challenging the injustices faced by the Latinx community.

Unfortunately, I have long learned that the ability to think and theorize is often a privilege of the middle-class professional. At the age of 21 my parents were struggling with unemployment and near homelessness. My mother was fighting diabetes, hypertension, blood disease, and dental decay without medical insurance or financial means. Thankfully there were doctors in South East Los Angeles who recognized poverty and provided my mother with monthly supplies of free samples of needed medications. My sister and I were barely able to support ourselves in college, often forgoing food to buy our books. My last semester I moved to Tijuana, Mexico where rent was much cheaper in order to finish my undergraduate education. I had to take three buses and ride for approximately three hours to get to campus. Thankfully, I found a job as a bank teller part time near the border. On top of this, I was struggling to negotiate my new-found feminist views with the historical reality ingrained in me, through word and deed, about what it means to be a heterosexual woman and the roles that men play in our lives. Amidst the chaos that is created by poverty and social upheaval, I did not have the time or energy to continue to study these theories. My intellectual pursuits would have to wait. I needed to graduate and find stable employment to support myself and help my family.

Without mentoring in the radical left tradition it was easy to attribute inequality to lack of opportunity, racism to ignorance and stereotypes, and gender oppression to patriarchal tradition and domination. Of course, I recognized capitalism, imperialism, and colonialism to be intricately involved in the mix but did not have a clear understanding of how exactly these fit in. The search to combine a stable income with a career that allowed me to contribute to changing social conditions among the Latinx community led me to teaching. At a time when bilingual education had gained traction, my bilingual skills were in high demand and I was able to immediately get a job in teaching with an emergency credential in South Central Los Angeles. The school enrolled some of the most impoverished Latinx immigrant and Black children in the country. The school demographics have not changed much in 30 years and in 2017 included 98% Latinx and 2% Black. These were children who lived in one-room homes, in garages without adequate electricity or bathroom facilities, and in self-made homes of cardboard boxes. Confronted with the reality that these were *all* children and families of color, Black and Brown, I recognized my niche to be addressing inequality and its relationship to racism. It was clear that these communities were left to rot because they were People of Color.

The field of education has long addressed racial inequality as a function of lack of educational opportunity, cultural diversity, and inadequate teacher preparation for linguistically and racially and ethnically diverse students. Important work has been done to develop and support culturally responsive teaching. Immersed in this work as a doctoral student I set out on a career toward documenting the cultural wealth of the Latinx community and challenging the deficit lens. I believed, or perhaps wished, naively that if we could show the dominant White world that People of Color, and Latinx people specifically, were strong, resourceful, intelligent, and worthy human beings we would begin to see improved educational achievement patterns and bring racial parity and representation in spaces of power. Although this argument sounded hollow to me even then, I could not envision any other way in which we might challenge the oppressive conditions that I had lived in and the even more drastic needs I saw among my students.

The work on culturally responsive teaching and other reform efforts is important work. Although I do not think in the long run it will, on its own, change the overall social conditions of exploitation that afflict predominantly Indigenous communities and communities of color, it has undoubtedly provided important ways to support many students of color within the existing social structure. These students deserve greater opportunities to succeed NOW. They cannot wait for the social revolution that those of us who are economically and socially privileged scholars want to build. We also need to have young people from these communities join our ranks of theorists and activists to develop the vision for an alternative to capitalism that can draw on the strengths and insights of Indigenous epistemologies and other ways of knowing. However, I have come to recognize that a system that depends on the exploitation of the masses cannot be reformed. Even if we create amazing schools and strengthen communities, there will be many more we cannot reach. The production of surplus value occurs only though exploitation. But it took years for my life to become sufficiently economically and socially settled to have the energy and time to think and see more clearly and the coalescing of multiple factors to shake me out of the stupor of comfortable consciousness and challenge me to develop a deeper analysis.

It was 2009 when I received a small grant to do research in Ensenada, Mexico. I spent three years living in Ensenada in the summers and traveling back and forth during the academic years. When in Ensenada my time was marked by a sense of freedom and serenity that I have never known in the United States. The pace of life slowed down significantly and I had time to think and reflect, to exercise and cook, to talk at length with people. I also felt lighter, without the weight of expectations and constraints, without the White male gaze and its judgments.

While I recognized my ability to breathe a little more deeply in Ensenada, I was keenly aware that this was not the case for many impoverished Mexican citizens that could be found by the thousands on a daily basis at the border selling snacks, drinks, and other goods to U.S. travelers. While I was familiar with similar devastation in the United States, our western capitalist education system teaches us to analyze through what can be objectively evidenced and to fragment information into smaller units. From this tradition, we examine conditions within the United States as isolated to particular schools and communities. Rarely does our education system encourage analyzing what the root causes of problems are, which may not be easily evident, but require systemic analysis that transcend disciplinary boundaries and encompass global and transnational relations and conditions. The capitalist value for continuous accumulation, propounded in countless ways, propels the individual to continuously seek more things, higher degrees, more "friends" on social media, more organizations to join, more money, etc.; and as we live with this constant mental drain surrounded by to-do lists that are never completed, the intellectual act of digging deeper for root causes that implicate broader global structures becomes more difficult. This is not an accident.

The study I had planned to conduct in Ensenada—to gain a better understanding of transnational identities—seemed so far removed from the really important questions, questions that I now had the time and energy to ask. Why in a world of significant wealth and resources, did so many people have no other alternative than to beg for scraps from the American tourist? How had it come to be that human beings, my self included, had learned to accept the dehumanization of other people as if this were a natural phenomenon that could not be altered? How had we learned to collectively shut out the horrors of the world and go on with our lives? How would my work that sought to demonstrate the cultural wealth of Latinx immigrant communities change the devastation that I was witnessing—conditions that did not exist only in Mexico but across every country in the world, including in the United States?

At the same time that I was questioning the actual value of my work, I was also struggling as an academic. Teaching was (and is) difficult for me at a predominantly White institution, especially as I teach prospective teachers about conditions of inequality in schools and society. Racism was, of course, a central topic of our readings and discussions and this was difficult content for predominantly White middle-class students who had little understanding of racial dynamics and who bought into and benefitted from the myth of meritocracy and equal opportunity. I did not yet know how to create bridges for my White students to comprehend and empathize with experiences of poverty and racism. My pain at having to discuss my own oppression and hear it dismissed and discussed as a function of perceived limitations was visceral. Further, my student evaluations, like that of many People of Color who teach "difficult conversations," reflected students' resentment over being pushed beyond their comfort zones and the social expectations of who a university professor is supposed to be.

I had not been prepared for this. Having spent all my life in communities of color I had little understanding of what White peoples, much less middle-class Whites, believed or experienced. I also must admit that I was defensive and angry. I resisted any gut-level instinct I may have had to play nice and be deferential and I challenged every deficit-based comment that was made toward racially and culturally diverse students, demanding that students who wanted to be teachers needed to learn to challenge any racist misconceptions and engage an equity-based approach to teaching. I hid my pain at the many insensitive comments I received, "Everyone knows blue eyes are more beautiful than brown eyes."; It's human nature to squash who is in your way as you move to the top."; They get the jobs to meet quotas—not because they're more qualified." I wondered where such venom came from and how they had the audacity to state these as fact without remorse or concern for the dignity of Others.

While less direct I also recognized the whiteness that prevailed at the university wherein I found myself often talking past others—that is we spoke the same language but our contextual experiences differed to such an extent that we could not understand each other. I faced the daily trauma of resisting the temptation to just become another brown face who adopted the expected norms of western classroom dynamics and academia without truly challenging the structure of the academy to become inclusive of not only our bodies of color but also of our experiences, insights, and ways of being as Women of Color.[22]

These issues of institutionalized racism preoccupied my weekdays and on the weekends, I would head down to Ensenada and resume questioning my career goals and my purpose. Although I had excelled in academic writing throughout my doctoral program and been well published upon graduation, I had trouble concentrating on my writing. My fifth-year critical review for tenure came back with the words "inadequate." I felt betrayed by my colleagues because I had explained my historical trajectory to academia as a Woman of Color and my social justice goals but my evaluation had been based solely on the number of publications and student course ratings, with little commentary or recognition of the diverse ways of seeing that I was potentially contributing to my students and to the college. I felt both exposed and invisible. I felt broken and shut myself away from colleagues and friends. Eventually I made my peace with failure. I had grieved and had begun to heal and was quietly working and waiting for the end of the year, seriously considering leaving the academy. I was ready to look for a different path.

Of course, now as a tenured faculty sitting on these committees, I know that critical and tenure reviews are bound to legal issues and must be written in very specific ways that leave little room for misinterpretation. I also recognize that we play right into the game of capitalist logic by dehumanizing people into mere objects of production.

By the hand of God perhaps or of the angels that have kept me safe through horrifying experiences, the dean of our college, then Don Cardinal, suggested I ask Peter McLaren, who was to become named Chapman University Fellow and later joined our faculty as Distinguished Professor, to review a paper that I had been having difficulty getting published. Peter McLaren is a prolific and world-renowned scholar-activist and a founding architect of critical pedagogy. His work emphasizes a Marxist-humanist, revolutionary critical pedagogy. A good friend and colleague, Suzanne SooHoo, who is also an important member of the critical pedagogy community, facilitated this process. I was ecstatic that I would not only get to meet Peter but that he would be reading and giving me feedback on my work. He did much more than that. From that moment on Peter took me under his wing and taught me to fly. He generously shared his work, his knowledge and his many resources with me. Most importantly he shared with me his humanism—his hope and enthusiasm for creating a better world and his belief that we as humans could be, were meant to be, so much better than we were and could create such a world. I was hooked. With quiet precision he guided my reading and pushed my understanding. With his mentoring I believe I read more that year than I had read in all the previous years of my life.

Excited and challenged, intellectually and creatively, I was also resistant to adopt a theoretical framework that was developed by another old White man and that undoubtedly was Eurocentric and androcentric—there was no way that it could not be, given the times in which Marx was writing. I read critically, searching for fallacies, and noted the many critiques hurled at Marxism—class reductionist, racist, sexist, deterministic. With each critique I found to challenge Peter, he listened quietly and then gently but persistently pointed me toward more readings. I felt disloyal, believing that as a Woman of Color I should be seeking theories developed by other People of Color, to challenge the western lens that for so long has dominated and colonized our minds. However, I could not reject the explanatory richness of Marxist-humanism and I could not reject a philosophy of revolution that sought to dismantle the many oppressive realities that I have lived through and to elevate humanity to a more humane substance. In fact, Marxist-humanism freed me from the anger and hopelessness that I felt was slowly choking the life and joy out of me. Without a strong historical and dialectical framework that recognizes the material conditions, racism is ideologically-rooted, something that is conjured up in our minds and hearts—an essential flaw of human beings rooted in some biological or physiological predisposition to prejudice and to seek power. This perspective naturalizes racism and creates an impenetrable barrier to its eradication. Anti-racist or ant-sexist work is a never-ending process. These Marxist readings also brought me to another realization—my goal of eradicating racism is not so that poverty, lack of opportunity, and other social ills may be distributed equally across racial groups. NO ONE should experience poverty, homelessness, indignities, and uncertain futures.

Understanding how our social relations are structured through the mode of production allowed me to see that the alienation, from ourselves and each other, that we experience is a function of the property relation that we internalize as natural and which guides most aspects of our lives, distorting human relations and turning human beings into commodities. As Erich Fromm pointed out, we have come to regard our own capacities, the people we love, and the relationships we build as objects to be owned.[23]

Lilia	I can't breathe (I say aloud without intending to).
Miguel	Why are you having trouble breathing, mama?
Lilia	Because I have to ask for permission.
	(He's 6 years old; he doesn't understand. I smile to soften the blow. My heart aches in anticipation of what he will soon face.)
Lilia	The world is not an easy place.

While this is a horrifying reality it is also one that can be changed. The clear message of Marx's work, often misrepresented, is that we are the makers of history, which refutes any notion of determinism. Indeed, his work as a philosophy of revolution had as its core the purpose to incite the masses to revolution and to offer, through his dialectical materialism, a method or path, unclear and previously uncharted, but a path nonetheless, toward our liberation. Marx did not provide a blueprint for communism, although his work gives us important clues, because he believed fully that it would be and should be worked out by the actual revolutionary Subjects of any given time and place who would lead us toward a future of a more fully human species being, defined by love, equality, and interdependence. The old adage that the future awaits is false. The future can be glimpsed in our actions today.

Yesterday I took a long walk with Peter McLaren, who has become a mentor and a friend. We walked around Orange where we work and where he lives. For three hours we went around zigzagging through the various streets and coming around multiple times without much thought to where we were walking. We contemplated a simpler world where people knew each other over time, kids growing up together in neighborhoods and later meeting up again as adults. He mentioned various films and described the scenes to me. He was lost in his own thoughts but voicing them, a constant sound that held a quiet reassurance to my own thoughts. We wondered aloud why we felt a constant state of disquiet, even anxiety, though our lives were pretty well established. Of course, we knew the answer was related to the deep sense of alienation we experience, an unrelenting distrust within a world guided often by hate and greed. As Marxists we always come back to the pain of the world but at that moment we lost ourselves in our own personal issues—there's a welcoming sense of relief to worry only about ourselves for a little while. I came in and out of his talk. I felt a quiet calm, deep solidarity.

These moments of comradeship with friends and people we care for and respect should be part of the course of living, a necessary component to life—as important as water and breathing. Instead they are generally fleeting moments amidst a lifetime of heartache and chaos, war and destruction. I had come to a point of bleakness in life in which I had lost hope that we could ever find a way out of this nightmare we call living. But I now have a vision for something much grander and the hope and historical knowledge to recognize our capacity to struggle for the sake of the future of the world and of our children. Marx's works and Raya Dunayevskaya's Marxist-humanist interpretation have given me this hope and the willingness to continue to struggle. They've opened my eyes to the many moments, even if random and fleeting, of other-doing that offer glimpses to what we can build together as a society that prioritizes our collective well-being, freedom for all, and the idea that every life is equally worthy.

Heeding the important words of Donaldo Macedo[24] that our stories cannot be merely about the development of voice—mere moments of psychological therapy and instruments of bourgeois complacency, I've taken the time here to reflect on the meaning of my story. A story told for the sole purpose of sharing, especially in this context, is a form of commodification that also keeps us simply tied to the past, paralyzed by our pain. But when we recognize that life is a process of struggle and history is possibility, then stories become tools that provide lessons that move us further along the path to freedom. In this spirit, I recognize my story as one of courage—moments in which I mustered the courage to go against the grain and negate the structures (and its henchmen) that would keep me down; But also, of the many moments in which I *did not act* or *could not act* courageously against the obstacles of my social conditions. The story reveals courage to be developed dialectically in the material conditions that allow us to act courageously as well as in the internal narratives that can either help or hinder.

As I think about my story above I recognize the many times I failed to act on my instincts and suspended my dreams. I was discouraged—literally my courage was taken from me—stolen without remorse or apology. Whether intended or not, these moments were life altering, changing my life path. I wonder also about the cumulative effect of numerous acts of discouraging.

Courage is a necessary part of being human. Every step we take requires some courage since we know not what that step might lead us to. So, we need that much more courage to soar to new heights, to experience new challenges, and to go against the grain.

I also noted that in some cases silence, acceptance, or just waiting can be acts of courage—for acts of courage cannot be abstracted from their implications to family and community nor to the broader political project. There are times when empathy and respect are acts of courage and must take precedence over our individual push to act on our own behalf. Courage, then, is always a social act. It cannot be a feeling but rather must be evidenced in action and developed as we engage with others and determine what may constitute a particular act of courage in a given context. A courageous act must therefore take into account the needs and consequences of a broader community. To act for oneself may not be courageous if it puts others in jeopardy.

Furthermore, to act courageously requires vision. Acting courageously involves risk but to risk without a clear purpose can be foolish. As revolutionary critical pedagogues, we must consider the political project of transformation as a basis for and focus of courageous action. Otherwise we may take risks that negatively affect our transformative goals. The person who individually decides not to adhere to the "strong work ethic" without a conscious understanding of why they are doing so is just "acting lazy," even though it may actually be a form of resistance. But a person who coordinates a non-work effort to challenge the logic of capital and creates a movement that can be publicly recognized is making important waves. This is acting courageously for the social good. This act recognizes how human beings are interdependent and individual interests must also support the collective. It is with this in mind that I move in the next few chapters to share the stories of revolutionary women who have brought this notion of other-doing to the level of struggle.

Notes

1. Duncan Campbell, "Close but No Cigar: How America Failed to Kill Fidel Castro"; Henry Veltmeyer & Mark Rushton, *The Cuban Revolution as Socialist Human Development*.
2. Samuel Farber, *Cuba Since the Revolution of 1959: A Critical Assessment*; Michael K. Lavers, "Cuban LGBT Activists Cite Progress, Ongoing Harassment."
3. Issac Saney, *Cuba: A Revolution in Motion*.
4. Vilma Espín, Asela de los Santos and Yolanda Ferrer, *Women in Cuba: The making of a revolution within the revolution*.
5. Veltmeyer & Rushton, *The Cuban Revolution*.

6. Raya Dunayevskaya, *The Marxist-Humanist Theory of State Capitalism*.
7. Fred Magdoff, "Twenty-first Century Land Grabs: Accumulation by Agricultural Dispossession.
8. David McNally, *Monsters of the market*.
9. Alejandro Portes and Robert D. Manning, "The Immigrant Enclave."
10. Miriyan Yataco, forward to *Red Pedagogy*, xiii.
11. bell hooks, *Talking Back: Thinking Feminist, Thinking Black*.
12. Gloria Anzaldúa, *The Borderlands: The New Mestiza—La Frontera*; See also hooks, *Talking Back*.
13. Robert Rueda, Lilia D. Monzó and Angela Arzubiaga, "Academic Instrumental Knowledge: Deconstructing Cultural Capital Theory for Strategic Intervention Approaches."
14. Lilia D. Monzó, "A Mother's Humiliation: Schools and Institutionalized Violence Against Latina Mothers."
15. Dolores Delgado Bernal, "Using a Chicana Feminist Epistemology in Educational Research."
16. John Holloway, *Crack capitalism*.
17. Frantz Fanon, *Black Skins, White Masks*.
18. Lewis R. Gordon, *Fanon and the Crisis of European Man*, 58.
19. Patricia J. Williams, *The Alchemy of Race and Rights: Diary of a Law Professor*.
20. Donaldo Macedo, introduction to *Pedagogy of the Oppressed*.
21. I have been describing social exclusion as the inability to "breathe" long before I found Frantz Fanon's famous quote "It is not because the indo-Chinese discovered a culture of their own that they revolted. Quite simply it was because it became impossible to breathe, in more ways than one sense of the word." In Fanon, *Black Skins, White Masks*, 201.
22. Lilia D. Monzó and Suzanne SooHoo, "Translating the Academy: Learning the Racialized Languages of Academia."
23. Erich Fromm, *To Have or To Be*.
24. Macedo, introduction to *Pedagogy of the Oppressed*.

Bibliography

Anzaldúa, Gloria. *The Borderlands: The New Mestiza—La Frontera*. San Francisco: Aunt Lute Book Company, 1987.

Bernal, Dolores Delgado. "Using a Chicana Feminist Epistemology in Educational Research." *Harvard Educational Review* 68, no. 4 (1989): 555–582.

Campbell, Duncan. "Close but No Cigar: How America Failed to Kill Fidel Castro." *The Guardian*, November 26, 2016. https://www.theguardian.com/world/2016/nov/26/fidel-castro-cia-cigar-assasination-attempts

Dunayevskaya, Raya. *The Marxist-Humanist Theory of State-Capitalism*. Chicago, IL: News & Letters Committee, 1992.

Espín, Vilma, Asela de los Santos and Yolanda Ferrer. *Women in Cuba: The Making of a Revolution Within The Revolution*. Atlanta, GA: Pathfinder Press, 2012.

Fanon, Frantz. *Black Skins, White Masks*. New York: Grove Press, 2008.

Farber, Samuel. *Cuba Since the Revolution of 1959: A Critical Assessment*. Chicago, IL: Haymarket Books, 2011.

Gordon, Lewis R. *Fanon and the Crisis of European Man: An Essay on Philosophy and the Human Sciences*. New York: Routledge, 1995.

Holloway, John. *Crack Capitalism*. New York: Pluto Press, 2010.

hooks, bell. *Talking Back: Thinking Feminist, Thinking Black*. Boston, MA: South End Press, 1989.

Lavers, Michael K. "Cuban LGBT Activists Cite Progress, Ongoing Harassment. *Washington Blade: America's LGBT News Source*. September 17, 2012. https://www.washingtonblade.com/2012/09/17/cuban-lgbt-activists-cite-progress-ongoing-harassment/

Macedo, Donaldo. Introduction to *Pedagogy of the Oppressed, 30th anniversary edition*, Paulo Freire, 11–27. New York: Continuum, 2000.

Magdoff, Fred. "Twenty-First Century Land Grabs: Accumulation by Agricultural Dispossession. *Monthly Review 65*, no. 6 (2013). https://monthlyreview.org/2013/11/01/twenty-first-century-land-grabs/

McNally, David. *Monsters of the Market*. Chicago, IL: Haymarket Books, 2012.

Monzó, Lilia D. "A Mother's Humiliation: Schools and Institutionalized Violence against Latina Mothers." *School Community Journal 23*, no. 1 (2013): 81–110.

Monzó, Lilia D. and Suzanne SooHoo, "Translating the Academy: Learning the Racialized Languages of Academia. *Journal of Diversity in Higher Education 70*, no. 3 (2014): 147–165.

Portes, Alejandro and Robert D. Manning. "The Immigrant Enclave" In *Social Stratification: Class, Race, and Gender in Sociological, 3rd edition.*, edited by David B. Grusky, 568–579. New York: Routledge, 2000.

Rueda, Robert, Lilia D. Monzó, and Angela Arzubiaga. "Academic Instrumental Knowledge: Deconstructing Cultural Capital Theory for Strategic Intervention Approaches." *Current Issues in Education 6*, no. 14 (2003): 1–11. https://cie.asu.edu/ojs/index.php/cieatasu/article/view/1682/697

Saney, Issac. *Cuba: A Revolution in Motion*. London: Zed Books, 2004.

Veltmeyer, Henry and Mark Rushton. *The Cuban Revolution as Socialist Human Development*. Chicago, IL. Haymarket Books, 2013.

Williams, Patricia J. *The Alchemy of Race and Rights: Diary of a Law Professor*. Cambridge, MA: Harvard University Press, 1991.

Yataco, Miryam. Forward to *Red Pedagogy: Native American Social and Political Thought, 10th anniversary edition*, Sandy Grande, xiii–xiv. New York: Rowman & Littlefield, 2015.

· 5 ·

WOMEN MAKING
REVOLUTIONARY HISTORY

To grant the woman worker the same rights as the man would be to put in the hands of the working class a new and dangerous weapon, to double the active army of the militant opponent; the bourgeoisie is too intelligent to agree to such a dangerous experiment

—Alexandra Kollontai[1]

Throughout history and across the world working-class women have been vital players in revolutionary movements; yet they have generally been absent from historical accounts.[2] In few cases have women risen to the level of hero and been held up as models of courage and greatness, and then only at the local level. Invariably men have eclipsed women and become singular heroes whose extraordinary efforts have become recounted for generations.

We can recognize the centuries-old patriarchal structure of the world at play in this. Certainly, for the most part, stories of past revolutions have been told and studied by men. The erasure of women in these accounts has reinforced the sexist portrayal of women as weak and fragile and has led to the false assumption that during revolution, women have opted to remain home with their children while men courageously stared death in the face with their rifles. In fact, women have not only been involved in all aspects of revolutionary life but also spearheaded and kept the momentum going in some of the most important revolutions in history.[3]

With the growth of qualitative research and more women writing these historical accounts, we are finally documenting women's roles in revolutionary efforts. In particular these accounts have brought attention to the ways in which women's rights intersect with class and race struggles and the possibility that socialist movements may have better traction through a race-first approach, particularly in the United States. Finally, we are learning of the histories and courage of these women and the ways in which they often defied traditional gender conventions to fight for better conditions. They have played a host of roles and they have shaped the initial insurgencies and the goals of revolutions. Contrary to sexist ideologies, women have risked their lives and left their families and children behind to support their vision for a better world.[4]

In this chapter I portray some of the women and the roles they've played in a few of the most important revolutionary movements in history and in some whose historical impact is still in the making. Drawing on women's stories as well as specific revolutionary events, my goal is to demonstrate that working-class women have shaped the goals, strategies, and trajectories of revolutions and also been a strong collective force in moving social movements forward. Here I document that women in revolution have been every bit as courageous as the men that have generally received all the accolades. They risked their lives, put their families on hold, and were completely committed to their cause. However, it is equally important to recognize the women who did not "join the fight" but held their families together, nurtured their children in times of social upheaval and economic depravity, and sometimes gave up their husbands, sons, and daughters to the cause of liberation. Such women hold up a society in turmoil and are as crucial a part of the struggle as those who fight on the battlefields.

Women as Revolutionary Spark and Motor

Only as I began exploring the literature on women in revolution did I learn that in some socialist revolutions women had been the driving force, coming out in larger numbers than men to demand change and representing a larger portion of the organizational membership.[5] This has been true even at times and in places whence men, laws and social conventions more strictly dictated women's lives. Of course, the working women who made up the lot of membership in these socialist revolutions could never abide by middle-class social conventions that relegated women to the home. Poor women have always had to work and have often had to fend for themselves and their children. They have been the ones most affected by economic downturns and, thus, have been drawn to movements that promised better living conditions. It was, thus, not surprising to me that in two of the most important uprisings in history, the Paris Commune and the Russian Revolution, women were the initial instigators and also kept the momentum going.

The Paris Commune

It was "ordinary" working-class women who were up in the very early morning hours on their way to buy bread who sparked the revolt that led to establishing The Paris Commune of 1871.[6] The Franco-Prussian war that began in July of 1870 was causing food shortages and a hike in prices, leaving the Parisian working class to face severe economic depravity. Single women, especially mothers, were particularly devastated. Edith Thomas describes:

> Within the proletariat itself a distinction must be made; women were the more exploited. Most women could earn a living only doing the needlework which had given Paris an international reputation, even if these masterpieces provided them with little more than a starvation wage ... Many working women ate only bread and milk. If one chanced to become ill, there was no way of paying for a doctor or medicine ...[7]

After France declared war, Prussia quickly captured the emperor of France, Louis-Napoléon Bonaparte. The newly established provisional government of national defense, under the leadership of Gen. Adolphe Thiers, turned profoundly repressive and removed all financial support programs for women.[8] According to Carolyn Eichner, André Leo, a socialist active organizer who became an important Communard, proclaimed these women "the true martyrs of the siege."[9]

It's important to note that Gen. Thiers, with the support of the bourgeoisie, had sold out to the Prussians, preferring to give up national sovereignty rather than to allow the Parisian working class to take control. Marx, closely following the Paris developments, observed that this was "the first revolution in which the working class was openly acknowledged as the only class capable of social initiative."[10] In anticipation of the Prussian's advance toward Paris, working-class Parisians, distrustful of this undemocratic provisional government, had moved the city's cannons to the higher grounds of the city, in the working-class neighborhoods of Montmartre and Belleville.[11] André Léo wrote in her unpublished memoirs:

... these canons, now raised up onto the working class buttes, were turned towards the center of the city, toward the city of luxury and palaces, of monarchial plots, of infamous speculators, and of cowardly governments.[12]

On March 18, 1971, General Thiers' government sent in the French National Guard, the people's army, to steal the city's cannons in the very early morning hours, assuming everyone would be asleep. Thiers made one crucial mistake; he forgot the horses that were needed to move the cannons. With their bodies, the women created a barricade to protect the cannons and appealed to the soldiers' sense of loyalty to their own people. When the National Guard was ordered to shoot the women, the National Guard refused, instead disarming and arresting two generals who were later executed.[13]

The National Guard assumed power immediately. Paris declared itself autonomous and proclaimed itself "The Commune" on March 28. It then set forth to create what is considered today the first people's revolution.[14] Among other priorities, they decreed the separation of church and state, abolished night work for bakers, guaranteed the right to develop cooperatives, suspended rents and abolished prior rent debts, and provided pensions for widows and children of those who had died for the Commune.[15] The Commune was exceptionally democratic with the right to recall any elected official and decreed that wages for public officials could be no more than the average wage of skilled workers.[16] The Commune also declared itself internationalist and anti-imperialist.[17] Although initially the Commune had not declared itself socialist, by virtue of being controlled by the working-class people, it was clearly instituting a political and economic agenda of a socialist nature. Keith Mann points out that although women were excluded from leadership positions within the government, "women were involved in much of the daily associational life that gave The Commune its revolutionary energy."[18]

Although the Paris Commune lasted only 72 days before the French army massacred 25,000 Parisians in what is now recognized as Bloody Week,[19] the Commune is recognized as one of the most important examples of workers' uprisings as well as being especially shaped by radical feminist ideology and anti-patriarchal challenge to the status quo. Feminist socialists played both intellectual and popular roles in the revolution as journalists, organizing the people through clubs, churches, and other organizations, marching and protesting, and as nurses and fighters.[20]

The right-wing media (and even some progressives) villainized the women Communards and created an image of them as crazed "furies" who were "more evil than the men because their brains are weaker and their emotions live-lier," falsely accusing them of burning down Paris.[21] Yet despite the misogynist rhetoric that followed the women Communards, they were not deterred and it is without a doubt that their participation shaped the Paris Commune into the most progressive and socially just legislation of its time, which, although short lived, provided a model for what was possible as well as lessons for future socialist revolutions.

The Russian Revolution

The Russian Revolution is a second example of women's fervor for revolu-tion. The Russian revolution is considered one of the most significant events in human history—the first time that Marx's humanist ideas were put to prac-tice. Any mention of the Russian Revolution immediately brings to mind images of extremely powerful and brilliant men who sought to change the world—Marx, Lenin, and Trotsky—but few women. Yet it was women who sparked the first uprising in February of 1917 that later led to the October revolution. On what is now commemorated as International Women's Day, March 8 (February 23, in the old Russian calendar) in 1917, tens of thou-sands of mostly women were found demonstrating in Petrograd for women's rights.[22] According to a report from *The Guardian*, Petrograd's governor at the time had commented that protestors consisted of "ladies from society, lots more peasant women, student girls and, compared with earlier demon-strations, not many workers."[23] By the afternoon that same day, women tex-tile workers had come out on strike and forced their way into factory after factory, calling on the women workers to join them in striking and swelling the number of protestors and strikers to 100,000.[24] The women whose work-ing experiences were abusive, including 12–13 hour workdays for miserly wages, demanded that other women stand together with them in sisterhood. They were also protesting the war, which they recognized to be the source of their increasing privations.[25] Politically astute, they went to the barracks to talk to the soldiers and convinced them that they were risking their lives for a war that they did not create only to later be reinstated in the same factory jobs with the same poor working conditions.[26] This was a brilliant tactic to mobilize the masses of both men and woman for political and economic change.

While it was women who first had the courage to stand up for change in 1917, historical accounts have generally done them a great disservice by failing to recognize or document their contributions beyond that first historic explosion of demonstrations. Recent attempts to gain a greater understanding of the role of women in the Russian Revolution have been able to uncover that it was bourgeois women who abandoned the fight for change when they realized that the Revolution would mean a loss to their own social standing.[27] Instead, but in line with historical reality elsewhere, upper-class women claimed that women's rights were to be won by proving their loyalty to the existing government. In Russia, however, this class division among women became more pronounced even within the socialist camps as it began to reflect different positions on the war, with the Menshiviks in support of the war and the Bolsheviks opposing it.[28]

Working-class and Bolshevik female activists continued to stage strikes and other demonstrations for better working conditions and against the war up until the October revolution.[29] In addition, women's battalions had been established under Kerensky's Provisional Government and they were brought in to defend the Winter Palace against the Bolsheviks who as yet had not gained the people's confidence. Up to 80,000 women are estimated to have served with the Red Forces, many as doctors, nurses, and clerks, but also as soldiers for the Red Army and some held commanding posts.[30] In addition, Bolshevik women were also appointed to provide political education to Red Army soldiers.[31]

The Bolsheviks took women's liberation seriously and Lenin actively supported campaigning among working women. Whether or not they considered women equals, they realized that sexist attitudes threatened class solidarity and that women workers added an important element to the party. Women's active roles in the Revolution and their contribution to its success had much to do with this position and with the continued efforts that brought about significant legislation in support of women in the following years.[32]

Consciousness as Their Driving Force

Some have tried to discredit Russian and Communard women's leadership capacity and/or the critical social consciousness that drove them to act by indicating that these were spontaneous outbursts led by impulse rather than political strategy. Yet in both cases, women had been organizing for years prior to these uprisings. According to Eichner, by 1871 France had become "an incubator for embryonic feminist socialisms"[33] and there were many women's organizations that had been creating consciousness among women on issues of gender equality and its ties to class relations. For example, some of the most visible female figures of the Paris Commune had already been actively involved in feminist socialist politics and organizing women years prior to the Paris uprising. Elizabeth Dmitrieff, André Léo, and Paule Mink, although diverging in their radical leanings, were each members of the International Workingman's Association and each was involved in writing and lecturing on feminist topics and their relations to class. Interest in feminist and class issues had been growing in Paris prior to 1871 and public meetings and discussions drew large numbers of people in Paris. Eichner documents that in one such meeting held in 1870, 20,000 people participated in fourteen different assemblies and the following day another 23,000 attended eighteen sessions, with twice that many people being turned away. Newspapers and journalists recorded that some of the sessions were on feminist topics, such as family life and working women's rights, and that these sessions tended to be packed. Eichner explains:

> An emergent class consciousness manifested itself as the meetings progressed. Recognizing common experiences, conditions, interests, and goals, workers began to develop a sense of solidarity and collective power … In L'Opinion nationale, Léo wrote of the meetings' inspirational impact on female laborers who 'came with their husbands, with their brothers, these working women with their fingers bruised from toiling all day, listen, learn, search with all the strength of their spirit … Several of them also want to speak.'[34]

Thomas's analysis of the role of the Union des Femmes supports this claim.[35] According to Thomas, the Union de Femmes was the women's section of the French International, initially organized by Elizabeth Dmitrieff, who developed a friendship and corresponded with Karl Marx in 1970. Marx, "who was already considered, along with Mikhail Bakunin, the leader of the international revolutionary movement … entrusted [Dmitrieff] with a mission to Paris, doubtless a mission of inquiry, but also of organization."[36] Under Dmitrieff's "stimulus" the Union des Femmes was formed on April 11th, 1971 and from then on held regular meetings. Thomas describes that Dmitrieff recruited "militant" working-class women. Drawing on statutes, the press described the Union de Femmes in this way:

> A responsible organization among the citoyennes of Paris who are resolved to support and defend the cause of the people, the revolution, and the Commune, has just been founded to give assistance in the work of the government's commissions, and to serve at ambulance stations, at canteens, and at the barricades."[37]

Each arrondissement had their own committees responsible for recruiting and mobilizing women for these tasks. They were to remain open day and night and to hold plenary meetings at least daily. The Union des Femmes collected dues equal to the International, which were used for administration costs first and what was left was to be used for "supporting impoverished or ill members of the Union, for paying the committee members who had not the means to devote their full time to the Union, and finally for 'buying kerosene and weapons for the *citoyennes* who will fight … should the occasion arise …'"[38] Thomas points out that the kerosene and weapons were means of combat and that the Union foresaw the possibility of "incendiarism as a defensive measure" but preempted bourgeois morality by pointing out that "it would be equally erroneous to become more indignant about the incendiary kerosene of the Commune than by the incendiary shells of Thiers."[39]

These accounts and many others of the time refute the suggestion that the women who sparked the Paris Commune were not motivated by social consciousness. Indeed, it is unlikely that they would have put their lives in peril to protect the city cannons had they not recognized their national interests and understood its relationship to living conditions.

Elisabetti Rossi documents a similar context for women's development in Russia prior to 1917.[40] As far back as 1870, women in Russia had been members of the Tchaikovsky circles, a socialist organization of student groups that attempted to create awareness of class exploitation among the population and that was particularly egalitarian and focused on emancipation.[41]

Feminism took off years later during the 1905 Revolution with the formation of the League for Women's Equality but this was primarily an organization of bourgeois women. In 1907 at the International Socialist Women's Conference in Stuttgart, Germany Clara Zetkin argued, "Class contradictions exclude the possibility of working women becoming allies of the bourgeois feminist movement."[42] That same year Alexandra Kollontai along with other Bolshevik women organized the Working Women's Mutual Assistance Center with the aim of spreading political education on socialism to working-class women. Years later in 1913, in anticipation of International Women's Day, Kollontai's words appeared in the Bolshevik paper, Pravda:

> The organised army of working women grows with every year. Twenty years ago the trade unions contained only small groups of working women scattered here and there among the ranks of the workers party … Now English trade unions have over 292 thousand women members; in Germany around 200 thousand are in the trade union movement and 150 thousand in the workers party, and in Austria there are

47 thousand in the trade unions and almost 20 thousand in the party. Everywhere—in Italy, Hungary, Denmark, Sweden, Norway and Switzerland—the women of the working class are organising themselves. The women's socialist army has almost a million members. A powerful force! A force that the powers of this world must reckon with when it is a question of the cost of living, maternity insurance, child labour and legislation to protect female labour.[43]

Although Pravda only published a few issues, *Rabonitsa* followed in 1914 as the first socialist women's journal. In May 1917 it became the official women's journal of the Communist Party.

While the women who sparked the Paris Commune and the Russian Revolution of 1917 may not have had a specific plan to rise up, they had been previously politicized with respect to both their sociopolitical context and their potential as women and it is certain that they acted swiftly and courageously to seize the moment and act on their consciousness.

Organizing for Mass Support: Assata Shakur and the Black Panther Party

One of the most important functions of any revolutionary movement and the organizations that form it is developing mass support. Grassroots organizing is critical toward this aim. Exploited peoples recognize their social conditions of oppression and exploitation, often better than those who aim to organize them. The colonizer's greatest tool has always been to make the oppressed believe that our own lack of ingenuity or motivation has created conditions of exploitation and inequality. Building mass support requires challenging these lies and breaking through the walls erected between diverse groups to justify injustices and prevent class consciousness. Organizations must build trust in their ideas and motives, hope and faith that change can happen, and a vision for a better future among the people. If the movement becomes viable, the state will deploy all its power—military, social, economic, and political—to cut a radical organization's potential for growth at the knees.

Women have been instrumental in organizing efforts by working at a grassroots level within their own communities and establishing relationships built on trust. In this case the stereotypes of women as "selfless" and "caring" may be especially useful to gaining community support since their efforts may be perceived as authentically aimed toward improving community conditions rather than self-serving. When women begin organizing and challenging the

state, people recognize the situation to be critical. Women have been socialized, unlike men, to put their families first so when women put their own
partners and children at risk, this is likely to go a long way toward establishing
trust and encouraging others to step up. Successful movements often have
a greater female membership and local female leadership. Women relate to
people differently than men, often focusing on building relationships with
communities and making decisions collectively. Organizing, and especially
providing community services, demands significant time, energy, and commitment but organizers rarely receive the recognition, fanfare or protection that
the leaders of the movement receive. Yet because their work is vital to mass
mobilizing they can become targets of the state.

The case of Assata Shakur is a fascinating and tragic case of state violence against dissenters and of how racism in the United States can become
the springboard for revolutionary potential. Assata became involved with
the Black Liberation Movement in the late 1960s and shortly after joined
the Black Panther Party (BPP), which by the early 70s had grown to have
chapters in every major city.[44] The Black Panthers originated in Oakland,
California with a group of mostly young Black people who decided they were
no longer going to sit by and allow the police to terrorize and gun down their
community with impunity. The Black Panthers began patrolling the streets
with guns in plain sight as a visible threat against police brutality. As the BPP
grew it began providing other social services to the community and developed
an agenda for equity and liberation.[45]

Assata was involved in numerous Panther community organizing and
service activities, including the Harlem branch breakfast program. She was
part of the medical cadre responsible for the health care of the Panthers, was
involved in organizing a free clinic, helped organize the Saturday Liberation
School for children, and supported fundraising efforts. She also participated
in more mundane, but also important, everyday activities such as selling and
passing out the Panther Newspaper. Eventually as the FBI was zeroing in on
them, she organized a safe house for Panther kids.[46] These service activities
and the relationships built with the community contradicted the media's
demonizing portrayals of the BPP. The Black Panther Party was a dialectical
revolutionary party with the goal of a classless society but in its function and
deed it presented itself as a race-first strategy and I believe strongly that this is
why it was so successful at recruiting so many young People of Color.

Assata's story of becoming a revolutionary is the story of an ordinary Black
woman growing up in a racist class society. It is, as Lennox Hinds points out

in the preface to Assata's autobiography, these " ... ordinary experiences of Black people in the United States that have driven millions to despair and many to rebellion ..."[47] Her story reveals grippingly how the personal is always political and how Black revolutionaries are not born but *made* in the context of Black exploitation and oppression, where little Black children grow up learning to loathe themselves without realizing it, seeing only what the White man has structured for all of us to see—an Other—less worthy, less beautiful, less smart, and less good than their White counterparts. In Assata's own words:

> Black revolutionaries do not drop from the moon. We are created by our conditions. Shaped by our oppression. We are being manufactured in droves, in the ghetto streets, places like attika, san quentin, bedford hills, leavenworth, and sing sing. They are turning out thousands of us. Many jobless Black veterans and welfare mothers are joining our ranks. Brothers and sisters from all walks of life who are tired of suffering passively, make up the BLA [Black Liberation Army].[48]

Assata grew up at a time of social unrest. On the coattails of the Civil Rights Movement came demands for justice from the feminist movement, the Chicano movement and the development of the Farmworkers' Union, anti-war activists, and Gay Pride activists. A loud and vociferous call for Black Pride had been stamped into the hearts of Black people all over the country. There was an excitement and hope within the Black community that was infectious and it was coming from highly intellectual people who were calling out racism and capitalism. The BPP supported the growth of social consciousness among Panther Party members and the public. For the first time in her life, Assata was excited to read and learn because it helped her understand her struggles as a Black woman and she came to understand that "Everything is a lie in amerika, and the thing that keeps it going is that so many people believe the lie."[49]

Although she grew up under the subhuman social conditions of racism and Jim Crow, she points out in her autobiography that her mother and her grandparents, especially, had always taught her to have self-respect and stand up for herself:

> Over and over they would tell me, 'You're as good as anyone else. Don't let anybody tell you that they're better than you.' My grandparents strictly forbade me to say 'yes ma'am' and 'yes sir' or to look down at my shoes or to make subservient gestures when talking to white people. 'You look them in the eye when you talk to them.' i was told.[50]

Undoubtedly this upbringing prepared her for the courage and strength she would later muster.

As the BPP grew it came under attack by the FBI and local authorities. Many of the Blank Panther men, including the leaders, were imprisoned. The BPP became a majority female organization and women stepped up as leaders. The Panthers knew that the FBI had infiltrated their organization but they did not know who the culprit was. This led to internal distrust and lack of self critique or reflection, strategically planned by the FBI to disable the BPP from the inside. Assata eventually formally resigned from the BPP. Almost immediately after resigning, she was framed for the murder of a state trooper and a host of other crimes. Her face was plastered on posters and in the news. Assata was forced underground to avoid police capture and worked with the underground railroad (a symbolic railroad of social networks) helping the Black Panthers move from one place to the next undetected and supplying them with basic needs.

Although the Black Panthers created a very cool image of powerful macho men, sporting black leather jackets, black berets and holding up guns, the Black Panther Party got to be almost two-thirds female and women were assigned roles at every level and worked side by side the men.[51] The hyper masculinity associated with the Black Panthers is a reflection of a society that criminalizes Black men and assumes them to be hyper dangerous individuals. Women also dressed in all black, took up guns, and developed a militant public persona in order to show the world that they were a force to be reckoned with and that they would no longer be the victims that they had been made into. Yet Black Panther women dealt with some of the same gender inequities that women have always faced in other organizations. The ideology of equality on a theoretical level was not so easy to implement in interpersonal relationships. Robyn Spencer points out that the women who replaced imprisoned leaders were not as respected as the men.[52] Still, Panther women found their voices and grew in pride and self-confidence in their collective struggle.

Assata was violently targeted by local police and FBI, demonized by the corporate media, charged with seven crimes for which there was little evidence and finally convicted by an all White jury in a trial that failed to secure her legal rights. Indeed, we now have evidence that the FBI was determined to use any means necessary to exterminate what the FBI termed "Black nationalist hate groups." Its counterintelligence program (COINTELPRO) engaged a systematic war of surveillance and attacks on Black groups and individuals to "expose, disrupt, misdirect, discredit, and otherwise neutralize" them, often having undercover agents infiltrate these groups. Indeed, a Black Panther that Assata worked closely with in the medical cadre was later found to have been a police spy.[53]

In her autobiography, Assata lists the various charges she faced, including bank robbery, kidnapping, and murder.[54] Three of these were dropped for insufficient evidence and in three others she was acquitted by trial due to fabricated evidence and false testimonies. The last one she was tried for was for the murder of a police officer during a shootout that, according to medical testimony, she could not have been guilty of since there was no gunfire under her nails and her hand had been so badly broken that she could not have been able to pull the trigger. Although the details of this incident are fuzzy, it is clear that the state did everything it could to make sure she did not get a fair trial, including refusing to allow her attorney to ask critical questions during jury selection and preventing Assata from being present during the process. Assata was sentenced to life in prison.[55] David Goodner states:

> Assata joined the Black Panther Party because she wanted to fight against police bru-
> tality and the other issues oppressing black people across this country, and that is why
> she wound up being labeled a criminal and a terrorist, and why she was ultimately
> captured, falsely convicted, unjustly imprisoned and forced to flee the country and
> seek exile in revolutionary Cuba.[56]

We know from the many cases of police brutality against Black and Brown communities that the justice system in the United States is swayed by an entrenched racism and by a culture of self-preservation within police departments that leads to extreme dehumanization.[57] Assata was denied bail and beaten regularly in prison and even in the courtroom in public view. She was often kept in isolation, fed barely enough to live on, and often denied medical attention even while pregnant.[58] Not long after her transfer to federal prison to begin her life-long sentence rotting away, she was extracted from prison and was not heard of for five years until she resurfaced in Cuba where she sought political asylum and has been living in exile ever since.[59] For five long years her mother and aunt were harassed by police. For five long years she was unable to contact her young daughter, much less see her grow up. She can never again set foot in the United States or anywhere that may have extradition policy with the United States.

While some have speculated that the desire for improved relations between Cuba and the United States may put her in jeopardy, this seems unlikely given that Cuba has long provided refuge for Black liberation activists and has pledged their support for Black struggles both in the United States and in various African countries. Rather than any illusion that the Cuban government may hand her over, the increased hunt for Assata, which placed her on the FBI's most wanted list in 2013, is meant as a threat against any potential whistleblowers and other political activists that they will be prosecuted as hyper criminals.[60]

Although Assata's story is not the typical story of a revolutionary who was able to live out at least for a short time the fruit of her sacrifices, her story is quite common. Revolutions are often cut short by the state militia and other powerful apparatuses. Today the Black Liberation Movement is being revived by Black Lives Matter. The public recognition of police abuses against the Black community and other communities of color serves as a vindication for the pain and humiliation that Assata and her family endured and it serves as a reminder that the Black Liberation Movement may at times lay low but it will rise again and again until the day comes when we can all be free.

The Revolutionary Writing of Ding Ling

Art and literature play a powerful role in revolution. They create images and invoke emotions that can develop social consciousness and inspire people to action. Images, songs, theater, dance, and other art forms can express dissent in ways that have significant and broad impact. In early 20th century China, literature became the medium of revolutionary thought. It became recognized that a new language was necessary to contradict Confucius thought. The May Fourth Movement, which refers to a period that erupted in protests on the 4th of May, 1919, called for greater nationalism, anti-imperialism, and a selective adoption of western ideals. May Fourth feminism was developed by drawing on western notions of women's emancipation but also had a distinct cultural flavor that challenged western binaries.[61]

Ding Ling was a leading May Fourth feminist early in her career and a celebrated Chinese author with over 300 published works.[62] Central in much of her work were feminist ideas, deep questions about what it means to be a woman, the nature of women's sexuality, and the deep psychological effects of societal constraints on women.

Ding Ling grew up ensconced in both revolutionary challenges to current political and gendered ideas but also within a familial context that valued cultural traditions. Her mother, widowed at an early age when Ding Ling was only four years old, made the bold decision to further her own education and enrolled in Changde Women's Normal Academy. There she developed revolutionary ideologies in anti-imperialism, love of country, and gender equality. After graduation she took on various posts in girls' education and maintained a politically active life agitating for women's rights and political causes. Ding Ling grew up with her mother's revolutionary activities as a backdrop and attended all girls' schools throughout her youth. Her closest friendships came from these same revolutionary and feminist social circles.[63]

When her uncles attempted to marry her off, Ding Ling fled to Shanghai with her close friend, Wang Jianhong, on the feminist Anarchist views that women's liberation lay in taking back ownership of their own bodies, which under traditional views belonged to the parents. Anarchist feminism had a short run, which Ding Ling represented as the editor of the Common Girl's School paper, *Women's Voice*. A strike among Shanghai's female mill workers ushered in socialist and Marxist ideologies, which have historically tended to downplay Marx's significant concern for women's emancipation. Thus, not long after in 1922, as has often happened elsewhere, the feminist movement bifurcated into two camps: one with more reformist feminist views focused primarily on family law and women's property rights and one with more radical socialists who joined the Communist Women's Labor Movement that relegated women's liberation to backseat status.[64]

At this time Ding Ling was not yet ready to identity with the Communist Party. After the loss of her friend Wang Jianhong to tuberculosis, Ding Ling, disappointed with life, moved to Beijing. She spent various years drifting in and out of jobs and had various affairs and a "romantic, irregular, common-law marriage" with communist writer Hu Yepin. Barlow points out that in *Mengke*, Ding Ling expressed her belief that the "bourgeois marriage was simply a way of legalizing prostitution."[65] During these years she found herself on the "fringes … of an intensely masculine world of literature."[66] Yet it appears that it was not until 1927 that Ding Ling begins to write herself, producing a series of narratives under the title of "Miss Sophia's Diary" with the central theme that independence was a utopian impossibility.[67]

In 1930, Ding Ling gave birth to a boy. In 1931, Her son's father, Hu Yepin, was murdered along with twenty-three other communist writers and artists. This had a dramatic effect on Ding Ling who sent her son to Hunan to be raised by her mother and took over the editorship of the literary journal of the Communist Front *Great Dipper*. In 1932, she secretly joined the Communist Party. As many other writers of the time, Ding Ling transformed her writing from a form of personal liberation toward revolutionary struggle.

In her new role as revolutionary writer, she gained a level of legitimacy she had previously felt denied when her sole task was writing on gender and sexuality but her focus on gender relations were still evident in her work. According to Barlow, she resolved the contradictions felt at the time between Marxism and feminism by focusing not on sameness between sexes but rather on equal value.[68] Ding Ling's writing at this time described the harsh conditions endured by working-class Chinese women, including alcoholism, wife-beating, and even murder. Invariably in these stories women's oppression was rooted in the monstrosity of the capitalist system.[69]

On May 4th, 1933 Ding Ling, along with her lover Feng Da, were disappeared by the Kuomintang of China. She was publicly presumed dead but was actually detained under house arrest where she gave birth to a daughter. In 1937 she escaped to the Red Army's base area in North China, Yan'an.[70] This was the political capital of the Communist Party located in Shaanxi Province during the Sino-Japanese War. Yan'an functioned as government to Northern China and directed the guerilla defensive against the Japanese, under the leadership of Mao Zedong.

During this time, Ding Ling produced three important works centered on rape. These stories evidenced the reality of rape as a weapon of imperial domination and the significant redress owed to these women upon liberation. In some ways these stories were also about the need to make reparations to the poorest of communities who had borne the greatest deaths and impoverishment as a result of the Sino-Japanese war.[71]

For example, *When I was in Xia Village* is a story told from the first-person perspective of a Communist Party writer who gathers information about a woman who was raped by the Japanese and infected with a venereal disease. After the rape, the woman becomes a prostitute to gather intelligence but when she returns to her village she is rejected. This story poses numerous questions: Who has the power or the right to signify another? Is she a hero or a woman lacking respectability? How would this be a different matter if it were a man? This and other works that she engaged in clearly question the deep contradictions in essentializing women, in party politics, and in a woman's ability to define herself as more than just a woman.[72]

Freedom of writers to express political views became an important source of legitimation for the Communist Party, which often faced charges of repression from the right. The Party feared this new literary depth and how it could divide not only men and women but also the Party leaders from the people.

Mao Tse-tung tightened controls over the arts, literature, and intellectuals, recognizing their significant capacity to shift public perception. On May 2,1942 at the Yan'an Forum on Literature and Art, Mao Tse-tung made this quite clear:

> Our aim is to ensure that revolutionary literature and art follow the correct path of development and provide better help to other revolutionary work in facilitating the overthrow of our national enemy and the accomplishment of the task of national liberation.

He continued:

> The purpose of our meeting today is precisely to ensure that literature and art fit well into the whole revolutionary machine as a component part, that they operate as powerful weapons for uniting and educating the people and for attacking and destroying the enemy, and that they help the people fight the enemy with one heart and one mind. What are the problems that must be solved to achieve this objective? I think they are the problems of the class stand of the writers and artists, their attitude, their audience, their work and their study.[73]

The deep level critiques of any system inherent in feminist writings were seen as subversive, diverting the Party's primary goals of class struggle, divisive within the Party, and possibly embarrassing to Party leaders.

A week after Mao delivered the above statement, in an extraordinary show of honesty and bravery, Ding Ling published a scathing critique of sexual politics within the Communist Party. "Thoughts on March 8," referencing International Women's Day, critiques the roles of women and marriage among party elites and also portrays class differences within the party. Consider her words:

> I am the first to admit that it is a shame when a man's wife is not progressive and retards his progress. But let us consider to what degree they are backward. Before marrying, they were inspired by the desire to soar in the heavenly heights and lead a life of bitter struggle. They got married partly because of physiological necessity and partly as a response to sweet talk about "mutual help." Thereupon they are forced to toil away and become "Noras returned home." Afraid of being thought "backward" those who are more daring rush around begging nurseries to take their children. They ask for abortions and risk punishment and even death ... But the answer: Isn't giving birth to children also work? You're just after an easy life ... What indispensible political work have you performed? ... Why did you get married in the first place? No one forced you to. ... Under these conditions it is impossible for women to escape this destiny of "backwardness." ... It should be self-evident that they are in a tragic

situation. But whereas in the old society they would probably have been pitied and considered unfortunate, nowadays their tragedy is seen as something self-inflicted, as their just desserts.[74]

She continues, addressing party elites directly:

> ... I hope that men, especially those in top positions, as well as women themselves, will consider the mistakes women commit in their social context. It would be better if there were less empty theorizing and more talk about real problems, so that theory and practice would not be divorced and better if all Communist Party members were more responsible for their own moral conduct."[75]

Ding Ling was made to publicly repent in the Communist Party paper, *Liberation Daily*, but her self-criticism did not take back the original claims against the party nor did she accept the criticism that her words represented a "narrowly feminist" perspective. She suffered periodic persecution thereafter, particularly since her work continued to develop a definitive Marxist feminist critique of modern China.

In 1949, Chairman Mao proclaimed the People's Republic of China to be a one-party system controlled by the Communist Party of China. Although generally identified as a communist state, Raya Dunayevskaya's theory of state capitalism clearly defines China as state capitalist, with consolidated control of the means of production at the hands of the state.[76] During this time, Ding Ling regained favor with the Party and developed a traveling theater group to revolutionize local arts that took her into war-torn peasant communities. She became an important representative of the government, sometimes lecturing in Party universities and encouraging young artists to engage in Party politics. She also became editor of the literary column of the Party newspaper, *Liberation Daily. Her most notable literary work during this time was The Sun Shines Over Sanggan River*, a story of the effects of land reform on a rural village completed in 1948.

However, Mao's call for honest criticism of policy and politics during the Hundred Flowers Campaign in 1957, re-engaged Ding Ling to push against the sexual politics of the times. She used this opportunity to express her views on Marriage and the Family and was purged for her efforts from the Communist Party and exiled internally to Manchuria but continued to write with the help of friends and family who would send her paper and supplies.[77] Here we begin to foresee the horrific repression that came later with the Cultural Revolution. In 1966 under this new cultural repression reminiscent of the Confucianism that she had fought against in the May Fourth Movement,

Ding Ling was captured by the Red Guard and endured the ritual humiliation of "capping" (public confessions), and then placed in solitary confinement. She reappeared in Beijing in 1978 and became a symbol of the government's repressive policies toward their artists and writers.

Ding Ling's story is one of incredible bravery, sacrifice, and values for working women's liberation. When reading her literary work, we evidence Raya's insistence that women bore revolutionary Reason—thinking and ideas consistent with a critique of capitalist class and gender relations that pushed farther and deeper than the most enlightened Marxist men of the times.[78]

Critically important is to challenge the bourgeois feminist misrepresentation of Ding Ling's story as evidence of women's repression under communist rule. As noted above, the theory of state capitalism developed by Raya Dunayevskaya clearly evidences China, under Mao and after Mao, as state capitalist wherein ownership of the means of production becomes consolidated at the state level, giving the state significant control over all or almost all facets of the economy and society, and often resulting in the repression of internal critiques. Ding Ling suffered the consequences of state capitalist repression but bourgeois feminists also inflicted their own wounds upon her in a self-serving attempt to represent the violation of women's rights as part and parcel of communism. Yet this misrepresentation of Marx's communism, among both so-called working communism and bourgeois feminism, fully distorts Marx's philosophy of revolution which sought to build a new humanism out of a classless society within which women's liberation, democracy, and free associated labor would be the building blocks.

Women in Leadership: Celia Sanchez and the Cuban Revolution

Men have generally taken control of top leadership positions in almost all major movements that have not been specifically focused on "women's issues," including even when the majority of members have been women. Yet women have nonetheless played important leadership roles in every revolution and in some cases, as in the Black Panther Party, become the default leaders. The complex activities involved in building large-scale revolutionary movements have been managed through coordinated efforts of diverse and smaller units, each with a different organizational structure. Here, women have been able to take on leadership roles and have proven to be intellectually and politically savvy, capable of planning and executing strategy, courageous and decisive. Already we have learned of their leadership capacity, clearly evidenced by Assata Shakur's resourcefulness, the organizing capacities of women in the Russian Revolution and in the Paris Commune, but formal leadership roles, fully recognized by those who answered to them, have been rare.

The Cuban Revolution is an inspiration of hope for many on the left. No one can deny its remarkable achievements in education and health care and its unsurpassed ability to hold off U.S. intervention, escape over 600 assassination attempts against Fidel Castro, and to remain viable for over half a century. Almost invariably the world has lavished its accolades (and sometimes its condemnation) on the male leaders of the time, especially Fidel Castro and Che Guevara. Although women were involved in all areas of clandestine life from inception—sending communication, importing and transporting ammunition and other goods, hiding the leaders—only a small minority held leadership positions and remained in top leadership advisory roles through the years and they remain generally unknown to those outside of Cuba's political circles.[79]

Celia Sanchez was one of these leaders. She was hand-picked by Frank Pais, in command along with Fidel Castro, of what was then called the 26th of July Movement, in honor of the first failed insurgency at the Moncada Barracks on July 26, 1953 wherein many lost their lives. This first failed insurgency created an underground movement that was developed over the course of six years until the final victory in 1959. The death, capture, and torture of the revolutionaries at Moncada drew international condemnation to the dictatorship of Batista resulting in the release of some of these revolutionaries, including Fidel Castro, who proceeded to exile himself to Mexico where he met up with other Cuban exiles and Che Guevara and plotted their return to Cuba to overthrow the government. Another group of revolutionaries, led by Frank Pais, remained in Cuba, working underground preparing for the arrival of Fidel's group. Celia was asked to prepare for the arrival of Fidel and the other revolutionaries, including Che Guevara and Raul Castro, who would be arriving by boat in the Granma from Mexico. She was consulted on the best place to land and was given complete control to plan safe passage for the group into the mountainous area of Sierra Maestra where they would need to remain undetected by the military until the time to advance into the cities. Much of the Sierra Maestra was rural and lacked roads or basic services. It was correctly presumed that the military would not be able to know their way around the Sierra Maestra.[80]

Celia, like many of the other leaders of the Cuban Revolution, was not of the poorest class. She was the daughter of a doctor and dentist. Unlike other professionals who generally opted for the comforts of city life and better conditions afforded them by their profession under capitalist rule, Celia's father had chosen to stay in the rural area of Oriente Province and live in a working-class neighborhood near the sugar mill workers. His service to the community, who was often too impoverished to pay for his medical services and who often came to him for all sorts of other needs that went far outside his medical expertise, was appreciated by the community. When he could not help he listened and provided a comforting ear. He was well respected among the people and Celia, as his daughter, was well known by all. As she grew up Celia was often involved in community service projects and although others also engaged in civic action in those needy parts of Cuba, Celia had a personal touch and care with the community that earned her their love and admiration. She was especially known throughout the region for her gift drive for children. Every year she would take an informal census of the children in the area, including their names, ages, and sizes, so that they would each receive a present for *Dia de los Reyes* that was specific to their needs and wants.[81]

Upon the request form Pais, Celia drew on her large network of friends and neighbors across the coastal cities of Oriente. She recruited militants and set up a network of surveillance of the military garrisons. They knew every military personnel's name, schedules, guard changes, routes, and the guns they had. They knew every weakness of the Batista military as well as when the best time and place to strike would be. She selected and trained herself a clandestine army that was prepared to strike at her command when she received orders from Frank. She was also prepared for any possible contingency. She enlisted a medical doctor friend to train field medics across the province and also trained ranchers and farmers on basic first aid and how to make splints, crutches, and stretchers out of tree branches. She organized for trucks to be ready for pick-up of the men coming in the Granma and take them deep into the mountains. She also had a system for transporting guns and ammunition, food and supplies, and communication to and from Fidel. She designed and ordered construction of Fidel's home in the Sierra Maestra along with escape routes and a lookout room that was used to bring reporters and others that might need to speak to Fidel.[82]

In the rural province of Oriente in the early months, the people did not really know much about Fidel but they knew Celia. "The Dove" (her code name) was the one they trusted and believed in. The military rather quickly figured out that she was the one, via her network of farmers, that was keeping Fidel and the other revolutionaries in the Sierra from capture. In the cities of Holguin and Bayamo there was a larger reward for finding Celia than Fidel.[83]

Although Celia did not meet Fidel until after his arrival in the Granma, both were well informed about the other. It is said that upon their first meeting they spoke alone for hours and that they were inseparable from that day forward until her death in 1980. Celia eventually joined Fidel in the Sierra, becoming the first woman to join the clandestine army. Although the men were initially apprehensive about having a woman in their midst, Celia soon proved to them that she was an asset. She eased communication between them and Fidel, always understanding exactly what Fidel wanted and they soon realized that whatever orders she gave out, Fidel would always back her up completely.[84] Various authors have recognized that they were both completely committed to their revolutionary ideals, to Cuba and to each other. Certainly, this seems an ideal relationship of shared leadership—a model to be emulated.

For many people in Cuba, especially the communities of Oriente, Celia was the heart of the Cuban Revolution and many in the region credit its victory to her leadership and her Farmer's militia.[85] After reading about Celia, Alice Walker states, "Celia was that extraordinary expression of life that can, every so often, give humanity a very good name."[86] Even before the victory of 1959, Celia had started organizing schools for the children of the farmers and ranchers that were selflessly giving themselves to the cause and Celia and Fidel adopted many of the children of the fallen soldiers of the revolution. After the victory, Celia would never forget that it had been the impoverished people of Oriente that had made the revolution possible and developed special scholarships and other programs to bring rural children to the city and facilitate their schooling. She remained a top presidential advisor until her death. Aside from her formal title, it is believed that in all aspects of his life, Celia was Fidel's foremost confidant.

Women in Combat: Zhao Yiman

It is often presumed that women fighting in combat is a modern day phenomenon attributed to the feminist movement's equal rights agenda. Yet women's battalions have been fighting in combat since the Russian Revolution of 1917. Few stories of these brave women have been told in history. They help us recognize the significant contributions that women have and can make to revolutionary efforts. These stories dispel all stereotypes of women as weak, fearful, or indecisive. Indeed, when learning about women in combat we find that they are extremely courageous women, willing to give their life for the causes they believe in, and capable of withstanding tortures and inhumanities for their beliefs and for the safety of their units. While many of the women discussed throughout these various stories have played combat roles, I want to highlight this particular role with the story of one incredibly courageous young woman who fought against the Japanese when they invaded and occupied Manchuria in the early 1900s.

Zhao Yiman was a heroic fighter against the Japanese army during the Manchuria invasion. She was born Li Kuntai in 1905 in Yibin, China to a wealthy family. In 1923 she joined the Socialist Youth League of China and in 1926, she joined the Communist Party (CPC) in 1926 and soon thereafter went to Moscow to study at the Moscow Sun Yat-sen University. There she married before returning to engage in underground revolutionary work in Shanghai, and then in south China's Jiangxi Province.

On September 18, 1931, what has become known to the world as the Manchurian incident sparked one of the most horrific times in Chinese history—the invasion and subsequent occupation of Japan in Manchuria. The Manchurian Incident was a pretext for the invasion of Manchuria. The Japanese military detonated a small amount of dynamite near a railway line owned by Japan's South Manchuria Railway near Mukden (now Shenyang). Although the explosion caused no real harm, the Japanese army retaliated with a full invasion that led to the occupation of Manchuria and the establishment of the puppet state of Manchukuo.

Zhao Yiman was sent to northeast China to start up struggles against the Japanese aggression. At this time, she changed her name in order to protect her family from any repercussions that might have come to them due to her revolutionary activities. Zhao organized strikes among workers and guerrilla forces in the countryside. Zhao also published various articles in revolutionary magazines to spark political awareness.[87]

In November 1935, the Japanese aggressors and the puppet Chinese troops encircled the Second Regiment of the Third Army of the Northeast Anti-Japanese Allied Forces. Zhao Yiman, who had been promoted to the political commissar of the regiment, commanded her troops to fight fiercely against the enemies. She then provided cover for the troops as they broke through the encirclement. Zhao was wounded while covering her troops. She spent several days recovering in a farmhouse but was soon found by the Japanese, wounded again, and captured. She was subsequently cruelly tortured but refused to divulge any information. In the hopes of getting her to talk she was sent to hospital under armed escort to treat her wounds. In the hospital Zhao gave public voice to her principles of resisting Japanese aggression and so greatly moved a nurse and guard that they agreed to help her escape. Unfortunately, Zhao was captured again and endured even more cruelty. On August 2, 1936 she was executed. As she moved to the execution ground she continued to defiantly challenge Japanese imperialism and loudly sang *The Internationale* and *Ode of the Red Flag*. Before her execution she wrote a letter of farewell to her son. Her words resonate with pride and commitment:

> My child, Mum is not going to educate you with words, but with action. When you grow up, don't forget your mother sacrificed (her life) for the country!

The letter along with various photos of her are prominently displayed in a tribute to her heroism at the Anti-Japanese Aggression Museum. Zhao Yiman is also featured as one of the revolutionary heroes in the Northeast China Revolutionary Martyrs Memorial Hall located at 241 Yiman Street, named after her, in the Nangang district of Harbin.

While the story of Zhao Yiman, like that of China's other revolutionary female heroes, is critically important for young Chinese women to learn as well as for the rest of the world in order to transcend the stereotype of the "docile and quiet Asian." Louise Edwards points out that these women are nonetheless popularly positioned within traditional gendered roles, as women who fight for others—the country, in place of a father, or to create freedom for their children.[88] In the case of Zhao her words of farewell to her son are often highlighted, turning her into a dedicated mother, whose revolutionary praxis was a selfless teaching and modeling for her children about patriotism. While this may have been true, it is certain that her revolutionary activities also had to do with her strong communistic ideals and her courageous willingness to fight for those ideals.[89]

Indigenous Women and Women of Color Practicing Horizontalism

Contemporary movements where women have been significantly influential are opting for a radically different, more grassroots, and horizontal organizational or government structure. Women's involvement is clearly influencing this dynamic, which recognizes that traditional top-down leadership and organizational styles derive from western epistemes (White and male) that are highly linked to capitalist systems of domination, imperialism and colonialism and that dismiss subaltern ways of knowing and doing. These new organizational approaches emphasize autonomy and direct democracy as well as the central roles of diverse women. It is no surprise that they have emerged predominantly in Latin America but also more recently in the Middle East and in a resurgence of the Black Liberation Movement in the United States. Here I highlight three of these movements.

The Zapatistas

The Zapatista Movement is an exceptional movement that displays the courage and pride of Indigenous peoples who after centuries of exploitation at the hands of capital, rose up united to fight for an autonomous existence and create a life of hope and equality for their people. Officially, the Ejército Zapatista de Liberación Nacional (Zapatista Army of National Liberation, EZLN) the Zapatistas received overwhelming international support since its initial victory in 1994. It has sustained its autonomy from the Mexican government for over 20 years and in the process developed a strong feminist agenda and collaborative and democratic decision-making processes. The Zapatistas have a strong female presence and influence that has shaped their movement and transformed gender relations in the process.[90]

The Zapatistas became known to the world on Jan 1st, 1994 when they raised themselves in arms against the Mexican government whose signing of the North American Free Trade Agreement (NAFTA) signaled a new era of land theft and economic and social brutality against the Indigenous peoples of Chiapas. Although women were not the initial instigators of the movement and they have a male, non-Indigenous spokesperson, the Zapatistas are led by a significant Indigenous and female presence. From his very first public pronouncement, Subcomandante Marcos pointed out to the world that he is only a subcomandante because the real leaders of the movement are the Indigenous peoples who make their voices heard through a series of democratic councils. The masks represent a non-identity that represents all people living in the ruins of society and the possibility that every community has to stand together and oppose the monstrous structures of greed and hate in the world.

Hilary Klein captures the courage of the Zapatista women as they have demonstrated their ability to rise above centuries of Indigenous oppression to speak eloquently on behalf of their communities and demand their rights and the humility and inspiration that the rest of us feel in the face of their awesome courage and commitment:

> The dignity with which these women carried themselves, set against a backdrop of centuries of racism and exploitation, embodies what the Zapatista movement has come to represent—the resistance of the marginalized and the forgotten against the powerful. Peasants turned warriors, mothers turned revolutionary leaders—dozens, hundreds, thousands of Zapatista women gather, tiny and dark-skinned, with red bandannas covering their faces and masking their individual identities, long black braids hanging down their backs, their fists in the air. They have marched, they have organized, and they have planted seeds—both real and symbolic. They have stood up to the Mexican army and to their own husbands. They have changed their own lives and they have changed the world around them.[91]

A significant aspect of their movement is that they have led it *together*—in what is being referred to as *horizontalidad*.

Although horizontalism is often attributed to the 2001 uprisings of Argentina, Thomas Nail argues that horizontalism was already put into practice in the first Zapatista Encuentro of 1996, which brought together people from all marginalized communities around the world to share their particular struggles and build bridges.[92] Nail argues that *horizontalidad* was developed as an alternative to the party system, which is always fraught with divisions and competition—opposing positions in which there are always winners and losers. In addition to the divisive nature of political parties, is the corruption inherent in a system that functions through a few leaders that "represent" a broader constituent but that can be easily bought off through money or favors.

In contrast, horizontalism functions through *caracoles* that serve as administrative centers that represent three levels of autonomous government: the community, the municipality, and the Council of Good Government. The first two are based on grassroots assemblies. The last takes elected representatives from the prior ones but on a rotational basis in order to have large participation. Assemblies work democratically through open discussions where the goal is for everyone to have a voice and to be heard. The goal is to reach consensus and establish relationships. This is an "effective politics" that is non-hierarchical, anti-authoritarian, and without leaders.[93]

Hilary Klein points out that the EZLN has always had a strong commitment to having women participate at all levels in the movement. While there may have originally been some resistance among men, the response from women was so overwhelming in their insistence to participate that there was little the men could do. The significant participation among women in all spheres of Zapatista life, including as political leaders, insurgents, educators and health professionals, has allowed them to significantly shape the Zapatista movement.[94] Of critical importance here is that even before the 1994 uprising Zapatistas had already passed the Women's Revolutionary Law, which guaranteed them equal rights, safety and dignity in rebel territory. This was crucial to their participation in significant numbers.

Women's participation has also led to significant changes for women at social, economic and political levels but also within their homes and within themselves. For example, Zapatista women recount how joining the Zapatistas not only opened their eyes to the economic, social, and political injustices committed against their communities but also to the abuses they endured as women without even realizing that there could be another way, a more egalitarian way. They point out that by necessity being part of the Zapatista movement required women to take on responsibilities outside the home in ways that required men to step up and take on some traditional female work. Working collectively with other women and making their voices heard through councils has given them both strength and tools to demand women's human rights, including outlawing sexual and physical assaults and outlawing alcohol, which they perceive adds to men's violence against women. Whereas previously women often tended to be married off at early ages and had numerous children, now they have greater choice and voice in the matter. Women express that their participation in the movement and their ability to make changes that positively impact their lives has led to significant increase in personal confidence and agency.

That women have been central in the development of an organizational structure that aims for a non-hierarchical and more democratic way of making decisions and policy is not surprising. After all, hierarchies have sustained unequal distribution and access to resources that have impacted Indigenous communities since colonial times but that also doubly impact Indigenous women. Of course, leadership as it has become defined as a hierarchal practice is a western concept that looks a lot like relations of domination and has clear potential for the abuse of power.

The Zapatistas are not an isolationist movement. From the onset they have developed a dialectical approach to self-sustainability while also remaining a strong model and support for building alternative political, social, and economic structures. This has become more evident than ever as the Zapatistas came forward in 2016 to make the Earth "tremble to its core," initiating the process of creating a National Indigenous Congress that would put forth Mexico's first Indigenous woman presidential candidate for the 2018 election, María de Jesús Patricio Martínez, a Nahua healer more commonly known as Marichuy.[95] Its greatest impact has been, however, on Indigenous groups in Mexico and on Indigenous women who have learned that they can and must engage in a politics that is true to their Indigenous ways and values. Marichuy's campaign was founded on Zapatista values, wherein leadership was meant to represent the voice of the people and governance was defined as a communal process. The campaign *centered* the interests and voices of Indigenous peoples, especially that of women and girls. Although Marichuy did not win the election, her presence in the political scene and her words have important resonance for all racialized women and girls:

> But it's precisely because we are the ones who feel the deepest pain, because we [experience] the greatest oppressions, that we women are also capable of feeling the deepest rage. And we must be able to transform that rage in an organized way in order to go on the offensive to dismantle the power from above, building with determination and without fear, the power from below.[96]

The national attention that this candidacy gave to Indigenous' and women's rights and voices is testament to the ontological, axiological and epistemological strength that the Zapatista women, along with other Indigenous women, provide in Mexico's left politics.

Rojava

Bordering Turkey and Iraq in the northern region of Syria lies the autonomous or semi-autonomous territory known as Rojava, or Western Kurdistan, a region majority Syrian Kurd but that also includes Arabs, Christians, Turks, Syriacs, Armenians, and Chechens and other ethnic and religious groups. The Federation of Northern Syria has chosen to call itself thus in order to be inclusive to the other ethnic groups that fight alongside the Kurds for freedom.[97] Early during the Syrian Civil War in 2012 when government troops withdrew from the region and left it open to possible attack from the self-proclaimed "Islamic State" the various political parties in the region came together to form a governing party and seized the opportunity to declare itself autonomous. This party alliance is the majority Kurdish Democratic Union Party (PYD).[98]

The Rojava revolution founded upon the principles of the PYD has evolved into a "hyprid socialist-democratic confederalism" that organizes grassroots level governing of the people through direct democracy. The PYD, which has close ties to the Kurdistan Workers' Party (PKK), was initially formed as a Marxist-Leninist Party with the goal of creating a Kurdish state. This was in response to a centuries-old repudiation and oppression of the Kurdish peoples whose human rights have been consistently denied in part through their geographical separation into Turkey, Syria, Iraq, and Iran. However, the ideological leader of the PKK and by extension the PYD, Abdullah Ocalan, shifted his thinking and came out in 2011 with a *Democratic Confederalism Manifesto*, which recognizes the greater viability of a grassroots, bottom-up approach and completely rejects the nation state.[99] It seems Abdullah Ocalan spent his years in prison studying and was highly influenced by American anarchist, Murray Bookchin.[100]

Rojava includes three cantons: Afrin, Kobani, and Jazirah. These are protected by the civil protection units, the People's Defense Units (YPG) and the Women's Defense Units (YPJ). The Women's Defense Units fight side by side the People's Defense Units. Although the scenes of ravaged war zones, the cries of mourning parents and children, and the significant privations the people in Rojava currently experience is unimaginable to those of us who live in safety, the people nonetheless live with hope. On the ground as people discuss their vision for the future to a direct democracy that emphasizes communality—the well-being of the community rather than the individual—and guarantees the people universal housing, food, health care, childcare, education, and other basic necessities to live with dignity. They know they are building a model of something beautiful and humanistic—something that is worth dying for.[101]

At the heart of the Rojava revolution, since inception, has been a vision of a better future that includes a secular government, equal participation and political voice for all ethnic minorities, and women's liberation. In Rojava all languages and cultural practices are accepted and each community has the right to honor their own identities.[102] Women form an especially important role in the development of Rojava since it is perceived that without women's liberation there is no possibility of eradicating other forms of oppression. Women's movements in fact predates the revolution. Kongreya Star (Star Congress) is a confederation of women's movements that has been organizing women since 2005 across every sector of society. At the start of the revolution Kongreya Star made sure to keep women's liberation, their voices, and their vision central to the revolutionary goals.[103] Kongreya Star has councils across five specific fields: economics, education, self-defense, women's science, and art and culture.

It is perceived as especially vital that women participate in the economy. Under capitalist rule women were generally excluded from the processes of production but in Rojava Kongreya Star has been actively supporting the development of women's cooperatives in agriculture, animal husbandry, restaurants, and other areas. These cooperatives ensure women that they will be able to care for themselves and their families. Furthermore, in cooperatives the women work but also play an ownership role and make decisions.[104] For Kongreya Star, self-defense is a broad term that encompasses not only women's physical safety but their psychological safety against men and patriarchal institutions, the valorization of women's ways of being and world views, and safety against cultural assimilation.[105]

The cantons of Rojava resemble the "caracoles" in Zapatista territory. They function through popular communes and assemblies of elected representatives.[106] Every neighborhood and town is organized into a commune that comes together to make decisions that affect the entire group. Each commune has an elected administration of three people but these are coordinators not decision makers. They also have assemblies, which consist of elected representatives of the communes.[107]

Rojava's fundamentally democratic and humanist vision is undoubtedly due to the significant role that women have played. Not only are women's equality, dignity, and respect central to the revolutionary goals but also women's participation has been especially significant. At all levels, councils must be at least 40% female and 40% male, with the remaining 20% filled by those with the greatest votes. In addition to this significant participation, women also have parallel councils that are 100% female to discuss issues that are pertinent to women and they have veto power on decisions that affect women.[108]

Women in Rojava are fighting on two fronts—for an autonomous democratic communal society for all ethnic and religious groups in the region but also for the liberation of women. They recognize that their needs are different. They do not necessarily seek exact equality with men because they see themselves as having different experiences. For example, although the women's army (YPJ) fights alongside men and take the same risks, they organize themselves differently. For example, the women who fight do not have children. Those with children are put on other important tasks but not in the front lines because their safety is central to the safety of their children and to society. In

YPJ recruitment is always voluntary. Poor families who lose a family member are financially compensated. A YPJ member explains:

> ... you have to remember we are autonomous. YPJ makes their own decision ... based on their own ideas not just comparing to what men have. That's the difference between here and Western feminism. Feminists are always comparing themselves with men instead of just thinking about what they want and what's best ...[109]

Reporters talking with the women of Rojava have consistently pointed out the courage of the women and their hope and vision for freedom for women and for the people of Rojava.

Black Lives Matter

Black Lives Matter is today's incarnation of the history-long fight for Black liberation that was stalled in the 1970s with an FBI terrorist campaign.[110] Although still in its infancy, Black Lives Matter continues, albeit with different strategies, to address some of the same goals of the 60s and 70s Black Liberation Movement, evidencing that when it comes to the Black community, progress in this country has always been elusive. The Black Panther Party agenda for Black safety from racist police thugs and better economic conditions continues to plague Black and other communities of color. Although obscured to the general White population under the false pretense of multicultural education, affirmative action, and welfare programs, Black communities and other poor communities of color have known that these band-aid programs have been in constant threat or altogether redressed while at the same time other avenues for the continued hunt of Black and Brown bodies have been created. These include the endless war on drugs, three strikes laws, the hunt for highly exploited undocumented people's, and the school to prison pipeline, which all work in tandem to support a highly lucrative prison and military industrial complex that either cages Black and Brown bodies or sends them off to be killed in ruthless imperialist wars.[111]

Black Lives Matter took off in the wake of the social media explosion that has brought national attention to police crimes against Black people. It was founded in 2013 after the killing of unarmed 17 year-old Black man, Trayvon Martin, by a White neighborhood watchman who pursued the victim and yet was acquitted of all charges.[112] Three Black women, Alicia Garza, Patrisse Khan-Cullors, and Opal Tometi openly expressed their horror and pain on social media and proclaimed that Black lives *do* matter.[113]

But it was in the following year after the White cop-killing of unarmed, 18-year-old Black man, Michael Brown, in Ferguson, Missouri that the Black community erupted in agonizing pain and rage over what Keeanga-Yamahtta Taylor has named a lynching. With impunity and no remorse, he was shot over and over and left to rot on the street. But that was not enough. The hate that permeates the racist heart must recognize God's condemnation and wants to obliterate any possible vestiges left beyond the physical by also murdering his spirit and desecrating the memorial of teddy bears and flowers that the community had created in his honor where his body had lain. Only the worst type of disdain toward the entire community can explain why one police officer would allow a dog to urinate on his memorial and another police officer would, whizzing by on his cruiser, destroy the carefully laid out rose petals in the form of his initials that his grieving mother had arranged; or that the same thing would happen again the following evening, destroying once more the memorial of flowers that family and friends were creating.[114]

The predominantly Black community of Ferguson erupted—the pain and rage of centuries of enduring the systemic killing of Black communities through police shootings, incarceration, and a crushing poverty no longer tolerable. Although the media and even some leaders of the Black community condemned the protestors who had turned "violent," the Police's hyper militaristic response against the community and their clear support of the police officer who killed Brown could not be hidden.[115] People all over the country felt the Black community's pain and recognized finally that racism in the U.S. could no longer be ignored or hidden, that those who stood silently watching were just as responsible for perpetuating racism. Sometimes it takes particular events to create mass mobilization.

With the country's eyes and ears open to the incessant police brutality against Black communities, more and more live videos showed clearly that the police's first response in the Black community was to shoot without question or hesitation, even when the victims had their hands up, provoking the now famous slogan, "Hands up, don't shoot." Protests and demonstrations took place across the country and BLM organized a "freedom ride" bringing people from across the country to join protestors in Ferguson. Reporters started investigating and learned that Ferguson's number two source of revenue came from inundating the Black community with fees, fines, tickets, traffic violations, and arrest warrants—all for minor infractions that typically merited no immediate police response in other cities.[116]

In this context of heightened awareness of racism in America, Black Lives Matter became a household name. Community programs to address police "fear" of the Black man and improve police-community relations began operating in the largest and most notoriously racist departments. But BLM has been working also on highlighting that all Black Lives Matter—bringing awareness to the invisibility of violence against Black, Indigenous and other Women of Color, and even more so Transgender Women of Color.[117] It is not only that they too are disproportionately stopped, arrested, and incarcerated and that they experience sexualized forms of violence, but that they are also significantly negatively affected, economically, socially, and psychologically, by the mass incarceration of their fathers, partners, and children.[118] The rebirth of slavery in the context of mass incarceration is decimating Black and Brown communities, solidifying another generation of impoverishment and turmoil among communities of color.[119]

Although women have been central in all previous iterations of the Black Liberation Movement, the recognized "leaders" of these movements have generally been men. The founders of Black Lives Matter are three self-identified Queer Black women.[120] This can, to some extent, be attributed to the mass incarceration of Black men, which has left Black women at the helm of families and communities. Undoubtedly their unique experiences and insights will influence how the movement develops. Certainly, their intersectionality across four axes of oppression—class, race, gender, and sexuality—may connect with a wider spectrum of the population, enhancing its membership and viability. Already the founders of Black Lives Matter have graciously acknowledged the experience and wisdom of long-standing leaders of the Black community, Al Sharpton and Jesse Jackson, but politely rejected their attempts to guide this generation's iteration of Black liberation. Black Lives Matter activists argue that today's technological advances facilitate organizing at a moment's notice and can forgo the hierarchical structure of past movements. Black Lives Matter is describing itself as a movement that is "coordinated" and "organized" but "decentralized." Today Black Lives Matter chapters have sprung up in every major city in the nation. Although their initial mission was to challenge police brutality against Black and other marginalized communities, each chapter has taken on other issues pertinent to their local concerns.[121] One important concern that is being taken up by various chapters is social and psychological healing, which is being addressed by chapters as a necessary part of the Black communities' individual and collective well-being as well as toward building unity and struggle.

Invisible Oppressions: Race, LGBTQIA, and Other Intersections

Although I have discussed multiple ways in which women have been key players in revolutionary efforts, this is far from an exhaustive review. An important point worth reiterating is that many women play multiple roles and engage in numerous diverse tasks in revolutionary activity. Although my focus in this book has been with Indigenous women and Women of Color, I began this chapter describing women's roles in the Paris Commune because of its significance as the first people's revolution. Research on the Paris Commune fails to address the question of racial diversity likely because at the time immigration was not the phenomenon that it is today. We can then safely presume that the majority of the Communards were working-class Whites and their more affluent socialist allies. However, the explosion of immigration from the periphery to the industrialized Global North as well as the colonial history of the Global South has led to a significant conflation of race and class such that most nations are composed of diverse racialized, ethnic, and cultural groups. Unfortunately, only those movements that have had an explicitly race-based agenda document the race of the women involved or how the movement impacted women of diverse racial backgrounds differently. For example, the Russian Revolution treats all women as an ethnic monolith. Similarly, little has been documented about the racial make-up of the Cuban revolutionary women. Not surprisingly, other identities related to sexuality, gender fluidity, religion or other ways in which women differ seem to be absent from these historical accounts. Only when a particular identity becomes an organizing principle do we begin to understand how that particular dynamic played out in the goals and strategies of the revolution and on the women revolutionaries.

The Black Lives Matter Movement whose founders experience oppression on four axes—class, race, sexuality, and gender—brings all four identities to the fore. In a similar vein the Rojava Revolution seeks justice and inclusion along multiple axes of oppression, including gender, class, ethnicity, language, and religion. While identity politics has been a thorn among many on the radical left due to its ties to a postmodern preoccupation with difference and multiple realities, which minimizes the potential for collective consciousness, I believe we can draw on our multiple identities to create a broader base that challenges all forms of oppression. Organizing across differences has a humanist element that aligns well with Marx's new humanism that engenders mutual respect and equality. *Horizontalidad* appeals to women because it challenges the systems of domination that have oppressed us throughout history. In this sense it is especially appropriate for a struggle against all systems of oppression, without any one axis as primary.

Many are questioning whether a movement can flourish without leaders. It's very important to recognize that women have different ways of engaging in the world based on our experiences of oppression and that those of us who experience multiple axes of oppression and exploitation are likely to have important insights into both the ways in which oppression and exploitation work, in their subtlest forms, as well as ideas of how to counter these offensives. It is critical to recognize that many of the critiques come from those whose western views are so entrenched that they can only conceive of hierarchical leadership approaches as "naturally" better. While it may be that horizontalism may not work in all contexts, there is evidence that it has worked for the Zapatistas and thus may work for others as well. Those who negate its potential must be reminded that the western approaches that have thus far led the way for the past 500 years have brought us to the point of unimaginable dehumanization. I must also point out that the critics of these movements, led or highly influenced by today's Women of Color, should be careful in judging our revolutions given that they have not been capable of bringing forth a viable alternative. Furthermore, I would caution that those who live in safety cannot begin to comprehend the violence we endure as highly oppressed communities. This lack of experience, however, must not be a pass to turn away or ignore the painful realities of those who are fighting for their right to be free. The world is much too small and we must learn to perceive the humanity in all of us. While some people turn away from those who suffer it is often those who suffer the most that are looking out for the rest of us. As one young but wise and courageous woman fighter in Rojava explains:

> We fight the war in your place. Because if we were not fighting this war the terrorism of Daesh would come to Europe. We fight the war for our survival but also because we don't want terrorism to spread. We don't want the rest of humanity to be infected by the barbarism of the Jihadis ...[122]

Challenging Backseat Politics

Although in this chapter we see women's extraordinary contribution to revolutionary efforts, it is clear that the gains for women have often come through in spite of a backseat politics. Many women engaged in revolutionary efforts, not only class but also race and LGBTQIA struggles, have argued that their concerns as women have often been relegated to lesser importance.[123] Although women's liberation is often espoused as a central tenet of socialist revolutionary movements, internally women have often been told that "women's issues" will be addressed after the revolutionary party takes power. When women have pointed out gender inequities or even the harassment of women within organizations or the failure to take on such issues, their concerns are either dismissed as insignificant in the face of the "bigger" struggle or critiqued as divisive. In some cases, there have been explicit inequality within the rules of the organization. For example, in the Black Panther Party, women were initially prohibited from dating non-members because it was believed that state agents could infiltrate the organization and gain secrets through dating Panther women. However, Panther men could date anyone they chose, inside or outside the movement. The assumption here characterizes women as more gullible and untrustworthy then men. Women had to challenge these assumptions to have this rule changed.[124] In the Sandinista Revolution, women were often made to feel guilty for taking energy from movements by "complaining" about addressing women's rights. Margaret Randall expresses this frustration among the women:

> First we needed to unite the working class; only then would we be able to rout the dictators. Later there would be time to attend to the "fine points" of social equality, including residual sexism, racism, and, much later, heterosexism. The word "residual" was such a frequently used adjective; it trivialized our concerns as it shamed us for bringing them up.[125]

While espousing a gender equity platform, the leadership itself has often been steeped in traditional sexist attitudes that limit women's contributions to "worker" rather than "leadership." Women express frustration that they end up doing a great deal of the actual work—the daily grassroots level work of mobilizing, organizing, and providing services to and with community—while the men take on the leadership and other visible roles that are traditionally ascribed to men.[126] Here we see that although espousing a Marxist foundation, which seeks not merely gender equity but a broader change in the fabric of society, these movements have often fallen into the trap of developing the movement through traditional hierarchical structures that reflect and produce the same relations of domination that exist in and undergird capitalism.

This does not deny the fact that socialist revolutions have brought about significant supports for women at the level of labor force participation and structures to support this participation, including maternity leave with pay and free childcare, as well as increased rights on a par with men.[127] However, they have generally not been able to fully challenge the deep seeded patriarchal beliefs and values that relegate women to subservient position in gender relations. Even within one of the most gender equitable countries, such as in Cuba that now is third in the world in terms of numbers of women in parliament,[128] gender relations of power have proven to be extremely difficult to eradicate, persisting despite laws and policies to challenging the division of labor at work and in the home. In particular, the man's role as head of household has been difficult to challenge and many women continue to experience the sense that their voice counts less than that of men.[129]

Of significant importance is that probably the longest lasting of socialist efforts, the Cuban Revolution,[130] is lauded as highly invested in women's liberation or as Fidel termed it "the revolution within the revolution."[131] It is clear that a society cannot move to a Marxist communism founded on equality among all its citizens so long as there remains a human hierarchy in which some people are believed intellectually superior, more moral, or having greater leadership capacity than others—these assumed "natural" characteristics endowed to men over women, straight over gay, White over People of Color, cannot be conducive to creating the new humanism that Marx dreamed of.

Notes

1. Alexandra Kollontai, "International Socialist Conferences of Women Workers," para. 4.
2. Vashna Jagarnath, "The Russian Revolution: A Reflection on the Role of Women Revolutionaries."
3. Carolyn J. Eichner, Surmounting the Barricades: Women in the Paris Commune.
4. Sonia Kruks, et al., eds. Promissory Notes: Women in the Transition to Socialism.
5. Two examples: Ashley D. Farmer, Remaking Black Power: How Black Women Transformed an Era; Jane Mcdermid and Anna Hillyar, Midwives of Revolution: Female Bolsheviks and Women Workers in 1917.
6. Eichner, Surmounting the Barricades.
7. Edith Thomas, The Women Incendiaries, 4–5.
8. Ibid., 19–21.
9. Ibid., 21.
10. Karl Marx, "The Civil War in France," 636.
11. Keith Mann, "Remembering the Paris Commune."
12. Eichner, Sorrounding the Barricades, 22.
13. Ibid., 22–23; Thomas, The Women Incendiaries, 52–54,
14. Mann, "Remembering the Paris Commune."

15. Ibid.
16. Ibid.
17. Ibid.
18. Ibid., Section 5, para. 3.
19. Ibid.
20. Eichner, *Surrounding the Barricades*.
21. Gay L. Gullickson, *Unruly women of Paris: Images of the Commune*, p. 4
22. Orlando Figes, "The Women's Protest that Sparked the Revolution."
23. Figes, "The Women's Protest," para. 3.
24. Ibid.
25. Ibid.
26. Ibid.
27. Elisabetta Rossi, "The Emancipation of Women in Russia before and after the Russian Revolution."
28. John Reed, *Ten Days that Shook the World*.
29. Mcdermid & Hillyar, *Midwives of Revolution*.
30. Rossi, "Emancipation of Women."
31. Ibid.
32. Mcdermid & Hillyar, *Midwives of the Revolution*.
33. Eichner, *Surrounding the Barricades*, 18.
34. Ibid., 45.
35. Thomas, *The Women Incendiaries*, 70–87.
36. Ibid., 73–74.
37. Ibid., 76.
38. Ibid., 76–77.
39. Ibid., 77.
40. Rossi, "Emancipation of Women."
41. Ibid.
42. Ibid.
43. Alexandra Kollontai, "Women's Day," para. 3.
44. Assata Shakur, *Assata: An Autobiography*.
45. Robyn C. Spencer, *The Revolution Has Come: Black Power, Gender, and the Black Panther Party in Oakland*.
46. Shakur, *Assata*.
47. Lennox S. Hinds, Foreword to *Assata: An Autobiography*, xi.
48. Shakur, *Assata*, 52.
49. Ibid., 158.
50. Ibid., 19.
51. Ibid.
52. Spencer, *The Revolution Has Come*.
53. Hinds, Foreword to *Assata*, vi–vii.
54. Shakur, *Assata*.
55. Ibid.
56. David Goodner, "Hands Off Assata: Protests Can Protect the Revolutionary Fugitive Again," para. 8.

57. Andrea J. Ritchie, *Invisible No More: Police Violence Against Black Women and Women of Color*; Michelle Alexander, *The New Jim Crow: Mass Incarceration in the Age of Colorblindness*.

58. Shakur, *Assata*.

59. Goodner, "Hands off Assata."

60. Matt Peppe, "Why Cuba Won't Extradite Assata Shakur."

61. Tani E. Barlow, Introduction to *I Myself Am a Woman: Selected Writings of Ding Ling*, edited by Tani E. Barlow and Gary J. Bjorge.

62. Many of her short essays can now be found in the collection Tani E. Barlow and Gary J. Bjorge, eds., *I Myself Am a Woman: Selected Writings of Ding Ling*.

63. Barlow, Introduction to *I Myself Am a Woman*.

64. Ibid.

65. Ibid., 24.

66. Ibid., 25.

67. Ibid.

68. Ibid.

69. Susan Brownmiller, "For Her Pains, She Was Called Old Shameful."

70. Barlow, Introduction to *I Myself am a Woman*.

71. Brownmiller, "For Her Pains."

72. Ibid.

73. Mao Tse-Tung, "Talks at the Yenan Forum on Literature and Art," para. 3.

74. Ding Ling, "Thoughts on March 8," 318–319.

75. Ding Ling, "Thoughts on March 8," 319.

76. Raya Dunayevskaya, *The Marxists-Humanist Theory of State-Capitalism*.

77. The Hundred Flowers Campaign refers to a period in China 1956–1957 when the Communist Party encouraged the people, especially intellectuals, to openly express their opinions and even critique government policies and practices, under the assumption that the ideas of the people and educated classes would result in better policies toward the nationalization of industries. However, when hundreds of thousands of letters poured in, Mao perceived a threat to his leadership and reversed the trend, implementing a "anti-Rightist campaign" meant to silence any opposition.

78. ———. *Rosa Luxemburg, Women's Liberation, and Marx's Philosophy of Revolution*, 2nd ed. Chicago, IL: University of Illinois Press, 1991.

79. Vilma Espín, Asela de los Santos, and Yoland Ferrer, *Women in Cuba: The Making of a Revolution Within a Revolution*.

80. Nancy Stout, *One Day in December: Celia Sanchez and the Cuban Revolution*.

81. Ibid.

82. Ibid.

83. Ibid.

84. Ibid.

85. Ibid.

86. Alice Walker, Foreword to *One Day in December*, 9.

87. Amanda Wu, ed., "Anti-Japanese Fighter Zhao Yiman Unflinching in the Face of Death."

88. Louise Edwards, *Women Warriors and Wartime Spies of China*.

89. Zhu Ying, "Revolutionary Mom."

90. Hilary Klein, *Compañeras: Zapatista Women's Stories*.

91. Hilary Klein, "Women are at the Forefront of the Zapatista Revolution," para. 4.

92. Thomas Nail, "Zapatismo and the Global Origins of Occupy."

93. Marina Sitrin, ed. *Horizontalism: Voices of Popular Power in Argentina*.

94. Victoria Law, "The Untold Story of Women in the Zapatistas."

95. Quincy Saul, "The Core Trembles: New York City for Marichuy."

96. Barabara Sostaita, "Marichuy Could Be the Frst Indigenous President of Mexico."

97. Evangelos Aretaios, "The Rojava Revolution."

98. Petar Stanchev, "From Chiapas to Rojava: Seas Divide Us, Autonomy Binds Us."

99. Stanchev, "From Chiapas to Rojava."

100. Ibid.

101. Rahila Gupta and Kimmie Taylor, "Women on the Front at Raqqa: An Interview with Kimmie Taylor."

102. Tony Iltis and Stuart Munckton, "Rojava's Democratic Feminist Revolution a Source of Hope Among Horror."

103. Kurdistan Solidarity Network, "The Women's Movement in Rojava."

104. Ibid.

105. Gupta and Taylor, "Women on the Front at Raqqa."

106. Stanchev, "From Chiapas to Rojava."

107. Ibid.

108. Gupta and Taylor, "Women on the Front at Raqqa."

109. Ibid., para. 9.

110. Spencer, *The Revolution Has Come*.

111. Alexander, *The New Jim Crow*.

112. Taylor, *Black Lives Matter*.

113. Alicia Garza, "A Herstory of the #Black Lives Matter Movement by Alicia Garza."

114. Taylor, *Black Lives Matter*.

115. Lilia D. Monzó and Peter McLaren, "Red Love: Toward Racial, Economic and Social Justice."

116. Taylor, *Black Lives Matter*.

117. Lilia D. Monzó and Peter McLaren, "Challenging the Violence and Invisibility Against Women of Color—A Marxist Imperative."

118. Ritchie, *Invisible No More*.

119. Alexander, *The New Jim Crow*.

120. Garza, "A Herstory."

121. Taylor, *Black Lives Matter*.

122. Aretaios, "The Rojava Revolution," sect. "Dying for Peace," para 7.

123. Margaret Randall, *Sandino's Daughters Revisited: Feminism in Nicaragua*.

124. Spencer, *The Revolution Has Come*.

125. Randall, *Sandino's Daughters Revisited*, 3.

126. Shakur, *Assata*; Spencer, *The Revolution Has Come*.

127. Ana Muñóz and Allan Woods, "Marxism and the Emancipation of Women."

128. Lopez Torregrosa, Luisita, "Cuba May Be the Most Feminist Country in Latin America."

129. Espín, Santos, and Ferrer, *Women in Cuba*.

130. Raya Dunayevskaya argues that most existing "communisms" are actually state capitalisms. Although many followers of Marxist-Humanism consider Cuba state capitalist, it cannot be ignored that Cuba has maintained a significant emphasis on socialist principles and practices. See Henry Veltmeyer & Mark Rushton, *The Cuban Revolution as Socialist Human Development*.

131. Espín, Santos, and Ferrer, *Women in Cuba*.

Bibliography

Aretaios, Evangelos. "The Rojava Revolution." Open Democracy, March 15, 2015. https://www.opendemocracy.net/north-africa-west-asia/evangelos-aretaios/rojava-revolution

Barlow, Tani E. Introduction to *I Myself Am a Woman: Selected Writings of Ding Ling*, edited by Tani E. Barlow and Gary J. Bjorge, 1–45. Boston, MA: Beacon Press, 1989.

Barlow, Tani E. and Gary J. Bjorge, eds. *I Myself Am a Woman: Selected Writings of Ding Ling*. Boston, MA: Beacon Press, 1989.

Brownmiller, Susan. "For Her Pains, She Was Called Old Shameful." *The New York Times* Book Reviews, 1989 archives. https://www.nytimes.com/1989/09/03/books/for-her-pains-she-was-called-old-shameful.html

Dunayevskaya, Raya. *The Marxists-Humanist Theory of State-Capitalism*. Chicago, Il: News and Letters Committee, 1992.

Edwards, Louise. *Women Warriors and Wartime Spies of China*. Cambridge University Press, 2016.

Eichner, Carolyn J. *Surmounting the Barricades: Women in the Paris Commune*. Bloomington, IN: Indiana University Press, 2004.

Espín, Vilma, Asela de los Santos, and Yolanda Ferrer. *Women in Cuba: The Making of a Revolution within a Revolution*. Atlanta, GA: Pathfinder Press, 2012.

Farmer, Ashley D. *Remaking Black Power: How Black Women Transformed an Era*. Chapel Hill, NC: The University of North Carolina Press, 2017.

Figes, Orlando. "The Women's Protest that Sparked the Russian Revolution." *The Guardian*, March 8, 2017. https://www.theguardian.com/world/2017/mar/08/womens-protest-sparked-russian-revolution-international-womens-day

Garza, Alicia. "A Herstory of the #Black LivesMatter Movement by Alicia Garza. *The Feminist Wire*, October 7, 2014. http://www.thefeministwire.com/2014/10/blacklivesmatter-2/

Goodner, David. "Hands Off Assata: Protests Can Protect the Revolutionary Fugitive Again." *Truthout*, December 22, 2014. Goodner, David. "Hands Off Assata: Protests Can Protect the Revolutionary Fugitive Again

Gullickson, Gay L. *Unruly Women of Paris: Images of the Commune*. Ithaca, NY: Cornell University Press, 1996.

Gupta, Rahila and Kimmie Taylor. "Women on the Front at Raqqa: An Interview with Kimmie Taylor." *50.50: Gender, Sexuality and Social Justice*, February 14, 2017. https://www.opendemocracy.net/en/5050/women-on-front-at-raqqa/

Hinds, Lennox S. Foreword to *Assata: An Autobiography*, Assata Shakur, xi–xviii. Chicago, IL: Zed Books, 1987.

Iltis, Tony and Stuart Munckton. "Rojava's Democratic Feminist Revolution a Source of Hope Among Horror." *Truthout*, November 22, 2015. http://www.truth-out.org/opinion/item/33752-rojava-s-democratic-feminist-revolution-a-source-of-hope-among-horror.

Jagarnath, Vashna. "The Russian Revolution: A Reflection on the Role of Women Revolutionaries" *The Conversation*, October 8, 2017. http://theconversation.com/the-russian-revolution-a-reflection-on-the-role-of-women-revolutionaries-85118.

Klein, Hilary. *Compañeras: Zapatista Women's Stories*. New York: Seven Stories Press, 2015.

———. "Women are at the Forefront of the Zapatista Revolution." *Truthout*, July 30, 2015. https://truthout.org/articles/women-are-at-the-forefront-of-the-zapatista-revolution/.

Kollontai, Alexandra. "International Socialist Conferences of Women Workers." In *Alexandra Kollontai: Selected Articles and Speeches*. Switzerland: International Publishers, 1984. Marxists Internet Archive. https://www.marxists.org/archive/kollonta/1907/is-conferences.htm

———. "Women's Day." In *Alexandra Kollontai: Selected Articles and Speeches*, Switzerland: International Publishers, 1984. Marxists Internet Archive. https://www.marxists.org/archive/kollonta/1913/womens-day.htm

Kruks, Sonia, Reyna Rapp & Marilyn B. Young, eds. *Promissory Notes: Women in the Transition to Socialism*. New York: Monthly Review Press, 1989.

Kurdistan Solidarity Network, "The Women's Movement in Rojava." *Kurdistan Solidarity Network*, November 6, 2016. https://kurdishsolidaritynetwork.wordpress.com/2016/11/06/the-womens-movement-in-rojava/.

Law, Victoria. "The Untold Story of Women in the Zapatistas." *Bitchmedia*, March 13, 2015. https://www.bitchmedia.org/post/the-untold-story-of-womens-involvement-with-the-zapatistas-a-qa-with-hilary-klein.

Ling, D. "Thoughts on March 8." In *I Myself Am a Woman: Selected Writings of Ding Ling*, edited by Tani E. Barlow and Gary J. Bjorge. Boston, MA: Beacon Press, 1989.

Mann, Keith. "Remembering the Paris Commune." *Solidarity*, July/Aug, 2011. http://www.solidarity-us.org/node/3315.

Marx, Karl. "The Civil War in France." In *The Marx-Engels Reader, 2nd edition.*, edited by R. C. Tucker, 618–652. New York: W. W. Norton & Company, 1978.

Mcdermid, Jane and Anna Hillyar. *Midwives of Revolution: Female Bolsheviks and Women Workers in 1917*. London: UCL Press, 1999.

Monzó, Lilia D. and Peter McLaren. "Red Love: Toward Racial, Economic and Social Justice." *Truthout*, Dec. 18, 2014. http://www.truth-out.org/opinion/item/28072-red-love-toward-racial-economic-and-social-justice.

———. "Challenging the Violence and Invisibility against Women of Color—A Marxist Imperative." *Iberoamérica Social: Revista-Red de Estudios Sociales*, April, 2016. https://iberoamericasocial.com/wp-content/uploads/2016/06/Monzó-L.-McLaren-P.-2016.-Challenging-the-violence-and-invisibility-aganst-women-of-color-a-marxist-imperative.-Iberoamérica-Social-revista-red-de-estudios-sociales-VI-pp.-41-47.pdf.

Nail, Thomas. "Zapatismo and the Global Origins of Occupy." *Journal for Cultural and Religious Theory 12*, no. 3(2013): 20–35.

Peppe, Matt. "Why Cuba Won't Extradite Assata Shakur." *Counterpunch*, April 21, 2015. https://www.counterpunch.org/2015/04/21/why-cuba-wont-extradite-assata-shakur/.

Reed, John. *Ten Days that Shook the World*. New York: Penguin Classics, 2007.

Ritchie, Andrea J. *Invisible No More: Police Violence Against Black Women and Women of Color*. Boston, MA: Beacon Press, 2017.

Rossi, Elisabetta. "The Emancipation of Women in Russia before and after the Russian Revolution." *In Defense of Marxism*, March. 8, 2004. http://www.marxist.com/emancipation-women-russia.htm.

Saul, Quincy. "The Core Trembles: New York City for Marichuy." *Counterpunch*, March 1, 2018. https://www.counterpunch.org/2018/03/01/the-core-trembles-new-york-city-for-marichuy/.

Shakur, Assata. *Assata: An Autobiography*. Chicago, IL: Zed Books, 1987.

Sitrin, Marina, ed. *Horizontalism: Voices of Popular Power in Argentina*. Oakland, CA: AK Press, 2006.

Sostaita, Barbara. "Marichuy Could Be the Frst Indigenous President of Mexico." *Feministing*, November 22, 2017. http://feministing.com/2017/11/22/marichuy-could-be-the-first-indigenous-woman-president-of-mexico/.

Spencer, Robyn C. *The Revolution Has Come: Black Power, Gender, and the Black Panther Party in Oakland*. Durham, NC: Duke University Press, 2016.

Stanchev, Petar. "From Chiapas to Rojava: Seas Divide Us, Autonomy Binds Us." *ROAR* Magazine, February 17, 2015. https://roarmag.org/essays/chiapas-rojava-zapatista-kurds/.

Stout, Nancy. *One Day in December: Celia Sanchez and the Cuban Revolution*. New York: Monthly Review Press, 2013.

Taylor, Keeanga-Yamahtta. *From #Black LivesMatter to Black Liberation*. Chicago, IL: Haymarket Books, 2016.

Thomas, Edith. *The Women Incendiaries*. Chicago, Il: Haymarket Books, 2007.

Tse-Tung, Mao. "Talks at the Yenan Forum on Literature and Art." May 2, 1942. https://www.marxists.org/reference/archive/mao/selected-works/volume-3/mswv3_08.htm.

Walker, Alice. Foreword to *One Day in December: Celia Sanchez and the Cuban Revolution*, Nancy Stout, 9–14. New York: Monthly Review Press, 2013.

Wu, Amanda, ed. "Anti-Japanese Fighter Zhao Yiman Unflinching in the Face of Death." April 29, 2015. http://www.womenofchina.cn/womenofchina/html1/special/women_in_war/women_in_war/1504/2959-1.htm.

Ying, Zhu. "A Revolutionary Mom." *ShanghaiDaily.com*, May 27, 2018. https://www.shine.cn/archive/sunday/now-and-then/A-revolutionary-mom/shdaily.shtm

· 6 ·

EN LA LUCHA SIEMPRE

Chicanx/Boricua/Latinx Women as Revolutionary Subjects[1]

Authored With Anaida Colón-Muñíz, Marisol Ramirez, Cheyenne Reynoso, and Martha Sanchez

> Esos movimientos de rebeldía que tenemos en la sangre nosotros los mexicanos surgen como ríos desbocanados en mis venas.
>
> —Gloria Anzaldúa[2]

In many ways my own family dynamics and experiences of economic hardships, racism and gender oppression are common to many Chicanx, Boricua, and Latinx families in the United States. Yet although our experiences are historically specific to a White supremacist capitalist patriarchal structure, they are also complex, nuanced, dynamic and dialectical. As such, there is enormous diversity among Chicanx, Boricua, and Latinx communities in the United States that span citizenship and immigration status, colony status (Puerto Rico) and colonial relations, generations in the United States, Spanish and English fluency, Indigenous identity and languages, national origin, racial diversity, sexuality and gender identification or fluidity, level of schooling, class, and other differences. There is no denying these differences or any need to do so. In the dialectical sense that is central to a Marxist-humanist framing, recognizing the many differences people bring is essential to validating their particular histories and experiences and to the affirmation of self that is critical to developing revolutionary Subjects. We can celebrate these differences and still recognize that most of us have important common interests in the dissolution of racism, sexism, capitalism, and other structures of oppression.

The goal of transforming the world and bringing humanity closer to its full potential requires that we consider who would make the most likely revolutionary Subject, meaning a person with the knowledge and agency—the human consciousness—to act and transform the world. Clearly it is the oppressed and exploited peoples who have the greatest impetus to change the world. The capitalist class that benefits from the existing structure is unlikely to want radical change. In addition, racism has historically proven to be an effective tool for dividing the working class, such that Whites have often opted to support the capitalist class rather than side with racial or ethnic minorities.[3] Marx's recognition that racism was a significant obstacle to class consciousness led him to believe the non-western world to be prime contexts for the development of socialism, although he argued that certain conditions needed to be developed for it to be sustainable, namely the forces of production. Equality and freedom are difficult ideals in a context where all people cannot be fed. He believed that socialism in the developing world would require the support of nations with greater productive capacity. He was correct in his prophecy that Russia might be the first country wherein socialism might emerge and he was also correct that poverty might not sustain the ideals for socialism.[4] However, today's world is increasingly multicultural and in the industrialized world, the poor working classes are made up predominantly of Indigenous peoples, communities of color, and ethnic minorities. This is especially the case in the United States. An important context for developing the next generation of revolutionary Subjects is among Indigenous communities and communities of color.

Dunayevskaya argued that it was the Black masses that would be the vanguard of the revolution, recognizing the potency of the Black Liberation Movement throughout U.S. history.[5] While this community, and the women especially, still have a strong potency, another important revolutionary Subject too often overlooked are Chicanx, Boricua, and Latinx women. The social conditions and stereotypes that affect us have been historically woven from centuries of colonization, corporate and political interests, and the necessity to control our bodies and our minds for capital accumulation.[6] Yet evidence of the struggle, courage, strength, and enduring love that embody Chicanx, Boricua, and Latinx women abounds.

A common stereotype of the Chicanx, Boricua, and Latinx woman is that we are feeble and deferring. Yet for us this characterization has no basis in reality. The majority of the women of these communities are fighters who struggle in a number of rarely recognized ways. In communities with large numbers of Chicanx, Boricua, and Latinx women, we are the heart of most local efforts to change conditions, at all levels but especially at the grassroots level, even though organizations often place men at the helm. Another point I wish to address in this chapter is that too often the left minimizes the importance of local efforts toward micro-level changes and especially those projects that aim at cultural pride and group solidarity. I would argue that although these efforts in and of themselves are not going to bring down structures of oppression and exploitation, they are nonetheless contexts for the critically important work of personal and cultural affirmation that challenges internalized oppression and supports the development of critical consciousness and agency.

In this chapter I explore the potential for social consciousness and revolutionary action of four Chicanx/Boricua/Latinx women involved in local organizing and activities that aim to improve community social conditions. Through my family and friends and through the many Latinx families with whom I've worked as an elementary school teacher, and later, a researcher, I have come to recognize that the women of our communities embody an undeniable revolutionary spirit and history of struggle. I aim to challenge the narrow and stereotypical conceptions that exist about the Chicanx, Boricua, and Latinx woman. Through narratives, I provide a glimpse of the diversity and complexity of experience among the women. Yet these stories also reflect significant commonalities of exploitation and oppression and highlight common interests in creating spaces wherein Chicanx, Boricua, and Latinx women can collectively engage the call for freedom and liberation. Within each woman's history there is evidence of both courage and defeat brought upon by centuries-old constraints and the spirit of struggle that only survival within tremendously dehumanizing experiences can develop. In each case there is a revolutionary Subject—a woman who with the right support systems, hope, and purpose would fight to the death for her family, her children, and her ideals.

This chapter is meant to raise our awareness of the historical legacy of triumph and courage of Chicanx, Boricua, and Latinx women—the exploitation, White supremacy, and sexual domination that we encounter, and the struggle that by necessity we engage to survive in spite of the constant threat we face. This chapter is also meant to honor the important work of local Chicanx, Boricua, and Latinx women activists who are working with community groups, organizations, labor unions, schools, and in other contexts to challenge and improve social conditions. These women make me proud to be a Latinx woman. The four women whose stories are highlighted here make clear the revolutionary potential of the Chicanx, Boricua, and Latinx woman—an impetus for transformation that must be harnessed for the betterment of the hostile world we endure.

The Revolutionary Subject

The revolutionary Subject is not a natural inclination born to particular individuals endowed with what has often been perceived as the Hegelian mystical spirit or the vulgar Absolute Spirit[7]—freedom achieved at the level of consciousness irrespective of material conditions. Rather, the revolutionary Subject is *made* in the process of struggle. That is, particular attitudes, values, and beliefs are learned and developed as individuals take action in processes that affirm their humanity as rational and agentic beings. In Marx's dialectical method, the "revolutionary spirit" is not mystical but rather sensual—emerging out of severely dehumanizing material *and* ideological conditions where people are forced to fight for basic material needs and human dignity. Deborah Kelsh argues that it is our human nature to satisfy our needs and thus, in the face of tremendous exploitation, the individual becomes empowered to resist their conditions of oppression and to fight for their liberation.[8]

Thus, the revolutionary Subject makes itself through its own action and reflection, what Marx termed "revolutionary practice," which Michael Lebowitz notes involves both simultaneously revolutionary change in conditions outside the self and within.[9] Paulo Freire argued similarly that one is transformed through praxis; that is, through acting to change social conditions, the oppressed develop social and political consciousness, which is also a process of humanization.

Lebowitz argues that such struggles are also a process of production—but one that challenges the logic of capital. In Lebowitz words,

> Struggles are a process of production: they produce a different kind of worker, a worker who produces herself or himself as someone whose capacity has grown, whose confidence develops, whose ability to organize and unite expands ... The working class makes itself fit to create the new world.[10]

For Marx the working class was capable of transforming itself into a revolutionary Subject because its deplorable living conditions supported the impetus to transform the structures that are literally killing them but also because the basis of capitalism is the production of value, which is produced through the exploitation of labor. Thus, the working class is the one that must negate their exploitation, stop the process of production, and affirm their humanity. As Freire so aptly stated, "The greatest humanistic and historical task of the oppressed [is] to liberate themselves and their oppressors as well."[11]

However, there is a misconception that the working class only refers to factory workers or those that are highly exploited. Marx used the term much more broadly referring to all those who are forced to sell their labor power for a wage. This includes teachers, doctors, and other professionals, those who produce intellectual labor, and those who work for non-profit agencies or the social service sector. Some may argue that this excludes those who do not work within the formal capitalist system, such as the unemployed or those who work in the informal sector, which involves some of the most oppressed and impoverished communities, most of whom are People of Color. However, these people are an important sector to draw on for revolutionary change. They form the reserve army of labor that the capitalist uses to keep workers complacent under the threat that there are others ready and willing to take your job if you don't comply. Their political awareness and willingness to act for change is critical to any movement.

An important consideration is that the working class is not only diverse in terms of race, gender and other differences that divide their interests but they are also diverse in terms of the kinds of work they do, the alienation they experience, and access to union representation, as well as benefits and job stability. Workers with greater stability, union representation, and living wages differ significantly from the greater mass of precarious employees and autonomous workers of the informal sector who are not guaranteed labor rights, or those who face significant social and economic challenges as unemployed or undocumented workers. Recognizing this fragmentation reveals that we must consider that diverse segments of the working class will be able to organize at different times. The more precarious of the working class will necessarily need be able to organize and strike at only critical junctures, whereas those with more flexible positions must be willing to recognize their position of privilege and step up as needed. Significantly, Charles Post points out that the myth that the more well-to-do workers are generally more reformists as opposed to true revolutionaries does not pan out historically. This is an important realization that leads us to recognize that we ought not to discount anyone in our quest to develop revolutionary potential.[12]

For Marx, struggle was a necessity of the oppressed. He argued that to not struggle when living under dehumanizing conditions would make us "apathetic, thoughtless, more or less well-fed instruments of production."[13] Without struggle we are "a heartbroken, a weak minded, a worn out, unresisting mass."[14] Lebowitz points out that it need not matter what type of struggle one engages in—that it need not be specific to class interests because ultimately all struggles for human development would bring us back to the struggle against capital. Any struggle would reveal the revolutionary Subjects' potential consciousness and their capacity to act. Indeed, Marx championed national and ethnic struggles that may have on the surface seemed unrelated to the fight against capital. He recognized that these immediate struggles for sovereignty and human rights were necessary in the broader struggle against capital.

An important concern is that the working class is significantly divided by racialization. We have seen this clearly in the United States as a result of the Trump administration, wherein a candidate who verbally assaulted communities of color and promised violent policies against them was able to gain enough votes to win the U.S. presidency. At the same time, racism has become a central and unifying experience among People of Color. Under these social conditions rallying the people around the struggle against racism may prove initially more fruitful, especially as anti-racist struggle will inevitably lead to the class struggle since racism cannot be obliterated within a capitalist society.

Freire was not specific about any particular axis of oppression. For him, the oppressed faced a set of interlocking forms of oppression—class, race, gender, and others. When we focus on the goal of freedom as the "historical vocation" of becoming more fully human, then we see that every axis of oppression and exploitation must be challenged toward this goal so that it really matters not around which axis the revolutionary struggle is built since they must dialectically incorporate the struggle against all forms of oppression.

Freire's work also brings to light that revolutionary struggles do not begin at the macro level. Instead they must be grounded in praxis and led by the people. This means that local efforts that improve the social conditions for people are necessary building blocks for the development of large-scale movements. Local efforts not only support people to live with greater dignity and, thus, greater humanization—an ethical imperative, but they also lead to developing political clarity, hope and agency among those who walk with others in struggle. In light of this realization, in the next section I present the stories of four Latinx women engaged in grassroots efforts that address a variety of local and community needs.

Boricua, Chicanx, and Latinx Women *en Acción*

The women in our communities have always had to struggle. As a people whose histories stretch back to the genocidal conquest of the Americas and to the enslavement of our Indigenous and African ancestors, with a particularly brutal violence against our women, and a continued legacy of psychological trauma perpetrated against us by the White colonizing man (and woman) and by the U.S, we would not have survived if it were not because we have learned to fight with our teeth and nails to improve our living conditions and create a space of love and sanctuary for ourselves and our children. Although many of us have only the means by which to fight within our own homes and families, giving all our strength and energy to put food on the table and create conditions that better our children's lives, there are also many who have been able to extend their fights to effect broader positive changes for our communities and to challenge structural conditions of exploitation.

What we have to recognize is that there is a reason behind the myth of the Latinx woman's complacency that has little to do with our actual experience of struggle and everything to do with quieting our historical legacy and learned impetus to stand up and fight for our rights. While the Boricua/Chicanx/Latinx activist is often invisible in the United States, it is our very ancestors and our own brothers and sisters of this generation across Latin America who mobilize in large numbers and regularly bring whole governments to their knees in order to create a better society. Consider that within the last 50 years there have been large-scale revolutionary movements, many of them as armed struggles, in almost every country in Latin America. And it is often the women who are the heart and soul of these movements because we know how to develop the relationships of trust and solidarity necessary to organize and unite.[15]

We have a similar history of activism within the United States, albeit less fantastic given the systematic erasure of our histories, cultures, and languages and the consistent threat of persecution, deportation, or incarceration that has increasingly become the staple of American society with its highly lucrative prison industrial complex and increased military tactics against civilian protests. The image of political "freedom" that the United States creates to the outside world can easily be contested when we recognize that in the society with the greatest inequality in the world, where some are starving and others make over a million dollars a day and black and brown bodies are systematically caged, there has never been any significant threat to the capitalist system.

Nonetheless, we have seen heroism in our communities at both national and local levels. Dolores Huerta, whose work with the Farm Workers' Union brought significant attention to their fight for better wages and healthier working conditions, is a model that many of us look to for inspiration.[16] Anaida Colón-Muñíz and Magaly Lavadenz have documented how education has been a field within which Boricua, Chicanx, and Latinx activists and scholar-activists have made important strides.[17] Lost to history until recently, the California landmark case of segregated schools brought to the courts and which paved the way for Brown vs Board of Education was the Méndez vs Westminster case, a class action suit brought on by five Mexican and Puerto Rican families against four school districts in Orange County on behalf of 5000 children.[18] In this case Ms. Méndez ran the rented family farm, which supplied money and time so that Mr. Méndez could work on the lawsuit. As I discussed in Chapter 5, too often men are able to dedicate time and energy to activist work because there are women who are home taking care of the family and other responsibilities that support radical change. These women's contributions to the cause are equally significant but are rarely recognized.

In our communities we have seen parents, children, and teachers fight for better schooling, bilingual education, and Chicanx, Latinx, and Puerto Rican Studies programs in colleges and universities.[19] In the Los Angeles area, women of our communities are involved in all sorts of organizing efforts, including immigrant rights, supporting Dreamers and DACA recipients, Ethnic Studies for high schools, fair housing, affordable health care, workers' rights, LGBTQIA rights, and a host of other concerns affecting our communities. What is harder to find are organizations on the radical left that actually recognize (not just in theory, but also in practice) that all of these problems of race, class, and gender are manifestations of interlocking systems of oppression and exploitation that we must address conjointly.

Latinx Women Activists

I had the opportunity to talk to four Latinx women activists from Southern California, each working with immigrant Latinx communities in a variety of contexts. Two of the women, Marisol and Cheyenne, are in their twenties and already speak about their experiences with a wisdom rooted in thoughtful reflection and community work. The other two have dedicated their lives to working with communities and challenging structures of oppression.

Marisol Ramirez is an organizer for a non-profit organization that aims to foster humanizing relations among community members and to provide support services that help the community thrive. She began working with and mobilizing the community for change while in high school and has continued working in a variety of programs on issues negatively affecting her community, including fair housing and immigration status.

Cheyenne Reynoso is an Orange County Native organizer with the Ocean Protector's Coalition for Native Nations and Indigenous Peoples and Resilience Orange County Project Associate and coordinator of Girls and Women of Color (GWoC), which aims to support the development of youth leaders that are empowered to create "social-systemic transformation while promoting healing, trauma-informed and culturally relevant practices..."[20] Cheyenne is of mixed Indigenous, Mexican, and White heritage but she identifies primarily as a Native woman.

Martha Sanchez is an organizer for Alliance of Californians for Community Empowerment (ACCE), "a multi-racial, democratic, non-profit community organization building power in low to moderate income neighborhoods to fight and stand for economic, racial and social justice."[21] Martha came to the U.S. as an unauthorized worker with her husband, first-born son, and pregnant with her second. Her experiences are clearly defined primarily as a working-class immigrant Latinx woman and mother but also as a person who sought to better her own education, learn English and attain a college degree.

Anaida Colón-Muñíz is professor of education at Chapman University and coordinator of el Centro Comunitario de Chapman University in Santa Ana, which offers a variety of services to the community that is home to the largest Latinx immigrant population in the country. Among the programs offered are early childhood literacy, parenting, and mentoring for high schoolers. Anaida is a proud Puerto Rican woman dedicated to the development of bilingual education and other programs for Boricua, Chicanx, and Latinx communities. Through her scholarship and in her role as professor she teaches K-12 teachers and doctoral students to think and act critically upon the world.

Each of the four women spoke with pain and indignation about their experiences and understandings of oppression and exploitation. They recognized how their experiences were rooted in broader social structures as well as encased in personal histories that went back to their parents' and ancestors' experiences. Their stories reveal the dynamic and complex interplay of class relations, racism, sexism, cultural differences and cultural pride, and immigration status. Above all, the stories portray critical and reflective women with tremendous resiliency, courage, strength and hope. If we take these women to represent the tremendous potential for criticality and commitment to changing the world that is to be found among Native women and Women of Color in the world, then we can believe that the future holds a wealth of promise.

Marisol: Activista de su communidad

We grew up in poverty. At one point the whole family lived together, eleven of us in a two-bedroom apartment. The neighborhood was poor and not that uplifting. One time my brother came to pick me up from junior high. We didn't have a vehicle so my uncle had lent my brother his car. The car looked so bad and made a lot of noise. I was so embarrassed. I was shrinking into the seat. I was ashamed to be seen by my friends in a car like that. My brother called me out—"Are you embarrassed that we're in this car?" I asked myself, why should I feel bad if this is the way it is for us? But I still felt embarrassed; I couldn't help it, that's how I felt.

My mom was always working. She used to take the bus to another city to work just because the pay was a little higher there. Back in Mexico, my mother was doing ok financially. She had a good job. You can see from pictures that she had nice clothes. My dad was the one who wanted to come to the U.S. for work and my mom wanted to keep the family together. In the U.S. is where my mom came to wear tennis shoes for the first time and here it is all she ever wears. It's symbolic of the amount of labor she came to do.

My dad was not that present. He had diabetes, which I think affected his mood and temperament. After my mom arrived was when she realized my dad was financially unstable. He had lost his job and was renting in someone's garage. He was often in a depressed state. This was not who he had been in Mexico. It's part of the immigration experience. My brother and sister were a little older so they practically raised the rest of us since my mom was always working.

I have learned a lot through my family's stories. My Tía Martha, for example, was very strong—a fighter. When she came to the U.S. she was an important presence for me. I was eleven when my aunt passed away so I took her death really hard, but also because that was my first understanding of what borders do to affect families, what immigration status really means. My dad was able to fix his papers in the 80s and get his residency in the first reform. My mother and my brother and sister were able to fix their status when they came to this country. But mi Tía Martha came later and was only able to bring one of her children and the other three were left behind. Back then it was before internet, mi Tia Martha would always send letters and sometimes we would get a prepaid phone card but it was ridiculously expensive.

When we knew that she was going to pass, we got a call in the middle of the night and I remember me and my little sister ran down the street so we could get to my aunt's house. She looked like she was in pain and her eyes were shut and she would vaguely tell you what she wanted. I've never seen someone take such a long time to die. What she wanted was to talk to her kids in Guadalajara and say goodbye because she dreamed of being able to see her kids. She took turns speaking to each child on the phone and when she finally said goodbye to her son, she took a deep breath and then exhaled and that was the end. That was so hard for me to see how she could hang on just to hear her family's voice. This is what coming to a different country for a better life means. This is what it does to families. It tears families apart.

My mom is a different kind of strong. One time my dad owed twenty dollars to this man and one day the man came to collect his money. My dad said he didn't want to answer the door but the man heard him from outside and insisted. A really frightening argument ensued. My mom was very brave. She insisted on confronting the man and give him the 20 dollars so he would leave us alone. She went up to the man's door and said, "Tenga, aquí tiene sus 20 dólares y no vuelva a molestar a mi familia." I can't believe she had the courage to do that.

My mother had a rough childhood. Her father was wealthy and when he and my grandmother split up he took her from my mother. She was raised by her dad's mother. She was not allowed to see her mother. She says she knew her mother and sisters loved her because they would sneak notes and risk going to see her. When her father died she ran away and went back to her mother. She says that's when she was able to be free.

When my brother was old enough to work, we finally moved into a little nicer neighborhood. It was only two blocks away but still better. There I realized that, when you are only exposed to so much, there's only so far you can see. In the new neighborhood I realized I could do more. I started doing things differently and that included being involved in the community. Because I was really friendly, people in the school office noticed and asked me to help with translating for parents with the staff and the principal.

Then, they asked me to be part of this group at school called Bridges, through Orange County Human Relations, that got different groups of students in school to talk about race, inequality, problems. There they invited me to a community meeting at St. Boniface church. Three of us said, "Yeah let's go!" The meeting was facilitated by the other non-profits. It was discussing housing and the lack of affordability. The housing developments that were being created in the city were not going to be accessible to working-class families. The rents were going to be too high. All the businesses that would be located underneath the apartment homes were going to be minimum wage jobs so the people that would work there wouldn't be able to live there. These issues resonated with me because of the neighborhood we grew up in. I thought, "This is the reason we can't progress as people."

Past that, the community forum engaged me in a lot of other circles and other campaigns that I ended up really pushing for. For example, the district elections in Anaheim, we were able to pass two measures that would allow for more representations for families in Anaheim. Before mayors or council members could live anywhere so, historically, they came from the richest parts of the city. Now by districts, they have to live in the area they represent. It allows for accountability.

I do a lot of organizing and house visits with the residents in the community. It's a tough road because I'm very young and then I'm a woman. It has its advantages and disadvantages. Being young people think, "What can you bring to the table? You lack wisdom." But being a woman you're seen as vulnerable and it's easier for other women in the community to confide in you. I think with every person that I've visited in the community there is this energy that you depict from the stories you hear. I ask myself, "What would be helpful or empowering that would encourage the other person to take something and apply it to their own life?"

It's empowering. The things I experienced as a child now as an adult I can help with. There are typical stories of landlords not taking care of the apartments to the extent that children are affected, sometimes with rashes all over their bodies because the tub needs to be replaced. Also, people who need help with resident status issues, helping with DACA forms. It's energetic to see that there's more that I will be able to do when I finish college. Of course, my involvement in my community may be why I haven't finished college yet but how can I say, "I'm going to stop now when there are people that are counting on me?

Cheyenne: A Native Womxn's Story

My mom is White and Native—her father's side is Oklahoma Choctaw, Mississippi Choctaw and Cherokee and Creek. On my Dad's side he's Mexican. I grew up involved with our Native community in Orange County and in L.A. I identify as Native first because of my mom. For years I've been culturally focused. That is what has driven me—learning about my identity as a Native womxn.[22] There is a lost history due to colonization and relocation—of not knowing who I am or where I come from. I struggled with identity a lot, being a Person of Color and an

Indigenous womxn, because I didn't have access to that history. Having a son made me want to know more because I want him to know where he comes from and who his ancestors are—to take pride in his culture and heritage. It has been a generational struggle of connecting our histories and heritage because of the influence of the U.S. government and colonization. Organizations like Ancestry.com are usually for "mainstream White people"—folks who are descendants of the first immigrants. My ancestors were made up of confederate soldiers, colonizers and Native womxn. What Native person or Person of Color isn't mixed? I don't say that to take it lightly or write it off but more so to show the power of resiliency within us. Not being able to access this history adds to the story. People have still survived and always will.

My involvement in activist work definitely emerged out of hurtful experiences. We have to fight against the idea that we're not human or don't exist. I remember being teased in school for my name. I love history but school history I hated because it was European history. When we would take field trips and my mom was a chaperone, she would raise hell because they would say things like "sit Indian style" or mimic the Indians, "la, la, la." It was done for students to have fun but really it was mocking everything we were supposed to be, it was mocking the idea of my ancestors' survival and our existence.

I think my cultural focus came from growing up and not having a community of Native people within the school system and the silent violence of people not ever acknowledging you—that active, repetitious, you don't exist, you don't exist, and if you do exist, you're going to be punished for it because we have to validate our norms.

At first, I was ashamed of my mom for speaking out. Now I'm glad that she duked it out with so many people. That helped me see that I need to do something, to say something. I have a different way of going about it but her strength and constant fight to stand for what is right laid a foundation for me. It made me think, "Are you going to be comfortable or are you going to stand up?"

Even today, I took my son to the dentist and he was being good; he let them do x-rays so she says I have a surprise for you, Do you like cowboys and Indians? To this day they're still handing out those horrible toys. Of course, I want to ask, "Why do you have this and why are you giving it to children?" But with my son, he doesn't like conflict. He just has a different manner about him and I want to navigate the space showing him that it is ok to question things and address issues in the way he feels comfortable. Do I say, "No, we don't play with that stuff?" She handed him the pack. So, I said, "Ok little one, there's only one rule if you're going to play with this—the Indians always win!" I opened it and, of course, they were the stereotypical red Indians. And I said, "Look they're doing medicine dances."

We have devastating histories, but also beautiful histories. There's a point to keeping Indigenous womxn and Womxn of Color down but it also reveals the weakness of the system. Missing and murdered Indigenous womxn is a huge epidemic. It is traumatizing to know that the system that is in place thrives off of our pain and death. But a lot of communities have their stories and knowledge to fall back on. We may be fucked in this society but our communities have systems in place to help combat these things and heal—we exist and will continue to beyond this system.

Of course, Womxn of Color bear the brunt of the shit that no one wants to see—the products of the capitalist system. And there's an extra tinge with Black womxn and local Native womxn. I'm a working-class single mother, a first generation college student. I have all that. But living on the land that was taken from you; holding the history and violence of this land that Acjachemen and Tongva ancestors lived and existed on and the land that they are still digging their bodies up on is another level of normalized constant violence. Local Native Nations have never been given justice. There will never be justice on stolen lands. I don't think it's a surprise where we are in this society. That is why it is so important to continually acknowledge and incorporate local Native voices within the work that we do and the spaces we create.

My mom is a very passionate person. We are sensitive and react to things. I learned to NOT react because it was a sense of survival. I think seeing abuses by men toward my mom or other womxn and then experiencing that as I got older; realizing that at certain points in my life a man could have gotten away with whatever they wanted to get away with, is a very scary concept. Wow, this person can do that and he knows it. Or a man feeling empowered to say something very violent to me and then being validated by the state. For me that has been a great fear, especially now having a son, and thinking what they can take away from me, but also what they can do to me. Would I be able to protect myself, let alone a child? That's not paranoia—that's just the reality of being a womxn.

These questions have made me go in the direction of community justice or social justice work on different levels. I did a lot of youth organizing with Native youth and POC youth in college and I also worked on the East coast with Native college students after graduating. I went to UCI (University of California, Irvine) and I became interested with Sacred Sites Protection work and the local history of injustice, which awoke me to the reality that local Natives are very different from my experience as an urban Native who was historically disconnected from my ancestral homelands. It made me realize that we have a responsibility to local Native Nations because we're also settlers in some way. It may not be the colonizing settlers but we definitely are a part of that system and we have a responsibility to uplift those voices and make sure that we are actively combating settler colonization in the work that we do in our lives.

I work for Resilience Orange County, The Ocean Protectors Coalition of Native Nations & Indigenous Peoples, and with Sacred Places Institute for Indigenous Peoples. With Resilience Orange County we work with a highly Latino undocumented population. I work with young Womxn of Color talking circles and I also manage the budget work and details— the tedious things— but which are necessary. My time coordinating powwows in college assists my work with budgets and events. I feel as though I incorporate a lot of the hard lessons I learned as a student into the work I do now with local Native Nations and local Communities of Color. I also work alongside badass local Native women to advocate for the environment and protection of sacred sites, land, water and representation/acknowledgement and the need to incorporate local Native women and Nations within work that is being done on their homeland. They know better than anyone what is best for their homelands and how to protect it! Through my work I have realized that Intersectional work is necessary and essential within community work.

So, I think these personal experiences with trauma that we can't address— because where do we address them from?—is also a personal investment because I'm a Womxn of Color. My own history as I grow is becoming more accepting of myself and has helped me practice being humane. Being a woman connects us as well.

The work we do with GWoC (Girls and Women of Color) and with Sacred Places Institute for Indigenous Peoples is very collaborative. There's beauty in collaboration. I don't think that anything I've done has been just me, but rather through working with community. I am invested within these communities because they are a part of me. I try to address the work I do as more than just solidarity work. I may not be Indigenous from Acjachemen Homelands and I may not be an undocumented community member; but these are people, especially women, who are a part of the community that I and my son live and survive within. It is important that we realize that. It is essential that we engage with intersectional work for ourselves and for our future generations.

Martha: Indocumentada e invencible[23]

Yo soy una madre de tres hijos, que ya están todos en la universidad. Vinimos a este país a buscar un futuro. Mi esposo había perdido su trabajo, yo estaba embarazada, y no teníamos medios para sobrevivir. Fue difícil cruzar la frontera, como todas familias que toman riesgos tremendos. La meta principal era sobrevivir, trabajar un poco, ganar dinero, y regresar.

Yo tenía ganas de superarme. Yo siempre tuve ese deseo de servir. Yo quería ser como la madre Teresa. Yo quería ser monja y servir como ella o ser doctora pero no pude seguir estudiando porque mi mamá estaba aquí en los Estados Unidos para sostenernos. Éramos siete. Yo me quede encargada de la casa. Tenía como 12 años.

Cuando mi hijo entro en Headstart parte de los requisitos era que los padres tienen que ser voluntarios. Entonces yo dije, "¡Bien! Me encanta la idea. "Y me empecé a involucrar y a cultivar ese sentimiento de ayudar. Luego cuando empezaron la escuela primaria nos mudamos aquí al Sur Centro de Los Angeles. Nos dimos cuenta de que estábamos condenados a vivir en esta área del Sur Centro debido a una ley que ya no está explícita pero todavía se practica que se llama "redlining." No nos daban préstamos para comprar por otras áreas. Este es un área con industria de químicos, calles destrozadas, sin parques o árboles para limpiar el aire. Los niños desarrollaban problemas de respiración. Un día me di cuenta que una compañía que usaba químicos carcinógenos estaba operando frente a la escuela de mis hijos.

Cuando yo empiezo a investigar recibo una invitación para ir a una junta en la escuela para hablar de esa compañía. En la junta el director de la escuela me manda a callar. Me dice que la junta no era para mí sola. Pero si yo era la única con preguntas es porque los demás no sabían que preguntar. Dije, "¡Wow!" Después de ocho años de lucha agresiva, la compañía cerró. El lugar frente a la escuela se transformó. Pero ahora viene la posibilidad de gentrificación—el desplazamiento de la clase pobre por la burguesía.

En este proceso empiezo yo a tener confianza en mi voz. Mi naturaleza de ayudar para cambiar lo que está mal. Yo siempre he pensado que la educación es el boleto para lograr mis sueños. Mientras trabajaba come activista aprendí inglés, hice mi GED, luego terminé el colegio, fui a la universidad y agarré mi bachelor's. Poco después, casi 20 años de espera, logre convertirme en residente legal.

Mi esposo trabajaba de noche y dormía durante el día entonces él no sabía en realidad lo que yo hacía, ni siquiera que había estudiado. En la casa de mi esposo pensaban que una mujer cerca de los libros es peligrosa. Le decían, "No dejes que lea tanto porque después no la puedes controlar. La mujer con estudio se te va de las manos." Es difícil porque también el estudio pone barraras con la familia. Es como caminar sola.

La organización en la que me involucre al principio ACORN tenía muchos problemas entonces un grupo de nosotros formamos otra organización ACCE, que ha crecido bastante. Hace dos años surgió la oportunidad de trabajar con las escuelas y a mí me apasiona tanto la educación que yo dije este trabajo es para mí. Mi trabajo es dirigir una campaña que está enfocada en la creación de escuelas comunitarias que ofrecen programas después de escuelas, arte y deporte, enfermeras, consejeros, centro de padres y de bienestar social. También estamos buscando que las escuelas tengan más voz en la decisión del presupuesto escolar. Ya logramos una resolución en el distrito escolar aceptando las escuelas comunitarias como un modelo nuevo de escuelas públicas. Me apasiona hablar con los padres de que debemos defender nuestro sistema escolar que no es regalo, lo pagamos. Hay personas infiltradas cuando hacemos acciones y tratan de infiltrar nuestro pensamiento. Estamos compitiendo en un mundo de hombres blancos que no les importa ni siquiera sus mujeres Blancas. ¿Por qué se van a preocupar por una Latina?

Lo que me impulsa a ser activista es saber que se siente ir a la cama sin comer; estar tres o cuatro días sin comer; vivir una extrema pobreza, sin ropa limpia porque ni siquiera hay jabón para lavar; ir a la escuela sin abrigo y decir, "Oh no, no tengo frío"; Y cuando te preguntan "¿Por qué no comes?"—obviamente es que no tienes que comer. Yo me la pasaba mordiendo los borradores porque tenía hambre. Yo comía tierra y tenía que pelearme con mis hermanos mayores—pero pelear fuerte—para que no se comieran todo y alcanzara para los más pequeños. Eso se tiene que vivir para poder entenderlo.

¡Si no me vencí antes, ¿por qué ahora? El miedo no se va. Aprende uno a vivir con él. Está bien tener inseguridad, dudar pero no dejes que el miedo te paralice. *Si uno vive todas esas experiencias, cuando es adulto y adquieres un pode, esas experiencias se convierten en en armas, ¡uhf! Yo no veo mi pasado como triste o doloroso. Lo veo como oportunidades para seguir ayudando. Yo sé cuándo me cuentan, "Nos van a desalojar."; lo que se siente ser rechazado, repudiado, oprimido.* ¡Híjole, yo estoy con ellos!

Somos gente común que de verdad ama el cambio, ama la comunidad. Si en verdad queremos alcanzar un cambio tenemos que ir a la comunidad, al Corazón que es la comunidad—los pobres—y hablar su idioma. Creemos que para llamarnos comunidad hay que unirse mano a mano, hombro con hombro, reconocer los valores, las fortalezas y las fragilidades de cada miembro, fortalecer al frágil es lo que nos hace especiales. No estamos escalando uno sobre otro sino caminando con los brazos unidos y creemos que cada comunidad tiene una fuerza única y poderosa por eso vamos de puerta en puerta. La voz más chiquita, la más frágil puede hacer el cambio más grande en el planeta y estamos buscando esa voz todo el tiempo.

Anaida: Toda una vida en acción

Growing up in a working-class family from Puerto Rico, my mother transitioned into her new life in New York City as a seamstress in a factory. In Puerto Rico it was different. She worked embroidering negligees that she would pick up at from a taller location. There, you would pick up the garment and take the work home. She would spend weeks embroidering one garment and get almost no money. Once in

New York, my mother continued to work in the garment industry, but now she had to go into a sweatshop. I remember going into the factory and noticing the loud noise and heat. It was strange because my mom was always dressed up, so she would dress up for work with her spiked heels and change clothes because she would get sweaty. When I finally started teaching, I saw that we had to clock in and out and I thought, "Oh my God, this is just like a factory!"

We ended up coming to New York in the 50s because my father had an ulcer and it was recommended to him that there was better treatment in New York. Once there, he called my mom and said, "I'm going to send you the tickets to come. The rent here is really cheap and there are lots of jobs".

I went to several mostly Black and Puerto Rican schools for elementary and junior high, but there was one year, 6th grade that I ended up going to a White school. I was very intimidated because at the Black and Puerto Rican schools, girls were the more active and raised their hands, but at the White school it was mostly the boys who answered questions and were more aggressive. I noticed a big difference between the schools: In the Black and Puerto Rican school I was at the top of my class, but at the White school I was struggling to keep up, and when I went back to the Black and Puerto Rican schools, I was riding along because the expectations were so much lower. When I got to high school they were integrating schools so they shifted me from my local Black and Puerto Rican school to a White school where I was bused in and we were like .01% of the population. I guess everywhere we went after that too. But I felt like I had gotten involved in two different worlds. I even wrote an essay for which I received an award, "A Citizen of Two Worlds"—about living two parallel lives.

But I got very involved with school. My father was strict so they only way I could have fun was doing things through school, especially ASPIRA,[24] which was great because I met Puerto Rican kids from all different high schools that were Aspirantes and we started a Puerto Rican chorus, did a little theater, and they taught us a lot about our background and cultural pride. But I was still really colonized. I felt the United States was untouchable, that it was perfect. I lived in this little bubble. This was during the Vietnam War and everyone was protesting. But even though I was active and culturally aware, politically I was conservative. I had learned about Puerto Rico but I didn't think of it in a critical way. I thought of it more as that's my culture, I'm so proud. But I was so loyal to the U.S. I was class president and I remember stopping students in the hallway when they were walking during the national anthem 'cause I thought it was so disrespectful.

I was very aware about racism. I knew racism existed that the darker you were the harder you had it in life. And I had this fervent Puerto Rican nationalism, but I *wasn't all out Independendista then. On U.S. militarism, I still felt that even though the Vietnam War was going on that there was a reason for it; I didn't have political consciousness.*

As I got older I could see the change in me, there were just too many contradictions. I started to feel very angry. My consciousness was awakening. I remember drawing, and I'm not an artist but I expressed myself that day, a White man sitting at a dinner table with a plate in front of him with the names of countries from Latin America—the White man devouring Latin America for his own nutrition and benefit.

In SUNY Binghamton, where I did my undergraduate work, I joined a small group called Azabache and we were very involved with asserting our identity and being respected, so we did cultural activities but we also did political activities. One of them was during Wounded Knee when the United States isolated The Oglala Lakota because they wanted the black gold from the hills. It was another example of the avarice. So, we invited the chiefs to come and speak and we did a little theater in protest. Then we organized a food bank to support and would sneak it in.

We also protested when the U.S. went into Cambodia. I had a professor who would read the names of all the soldiers who had gotten killed that day as a memorial. But it used to leave me cold inside when every other name was a Latino last name, because I knew that a lot of the people being sent were Latinos. One day my Cuban friend and I went to a protest. It was a big deal. There were protests everywhere in the universities and in the streets. Everyone was getting arrested. The first wave of protestors had been mostly male students. Then it was the professors. So finally, the third was when the women- all the women's organizations went. You would likely be arrested if you stepped out of the boundaries that the permit for protesting set. I told myself—we're either in this protest or we're not. Luckily, they stopped processing fingerprints because they had arrested so many people. Otherwise I would not have been able to be a teacher.

At that time there were so many protests for everything—women's rights, Latino rights, Black rights. SUNY Binghamton in New York where I did my undergraduate program was a predominantly White school. We were the recipients of the fact that they were opening up admissions for more Latinos in universities throughout the state and a lot of heads got busted to make that happen. I was a beneficiary. We were like 30 Black and Latino students in a school of 4000. So we were very small.

It was a time of a lot of people exploring drugs and the sexual revolution. This was 1969–1973. There were a lot of protests for everything—women's rights, Latino rights, Black rights. So we fought for the Latin American and Caribbean Area Studies Program, which was our ethnic studies program at the time. The Black students had been able to get the African-American Studies Program and we had not been able to get ours. So I was one of two students who was on an interdisciplinary committee working on this, but it took a whole year before anything happened and we wanted it before we graduated. We got tired of waiting so one day our group, Azabache, and the Black Student Union got together and did a stand-in around the committee that was meeting, and that day we got the program! I became the second person to take the major.

I grew up in a family where my father was part of the union movement. He was a representative when the AFL and CIO joined and he had come to the U.S. to participate as a delegate. He always believed in workers' rights. He was also an active nationalist in Puerto Rico with Pedro Albizu Campos. So we had that strong nationalism in our own home. We were always taught to have pride in our Spanish language, in our culture, to respect others, and to speak up when we saw injustice. He was part of the carpenters union. His company went on strike when he was a foreman. One evening it was so cold, so there were only two people out there picketing, but he didn't stop, he didn't stop. Another time we were at a counter waiting to order food and there was a Black man sitting also, and we saw that the server kept going to another person and then another and then he came to us. My father said, "No you have to go to him first" (referring to the Black man). My mother was also a very dedicated worker but she didn't take B.S. I remember a story of one time when the boss spoke badly to her, she went quietly to the back, picked up her things and left. She never went back. So, even though I would get really nervous and I would tremble inside, I always felt like I had to do what was right.

I never wanted to go into education. I believed the powers that be were directing Latino students into social work or teaching. But after I graduated from Binghamton I met someone from the NY State Bilingual Education Department, and this was 1973 or 1974 and we became friendly because she was Puerto Rican, and I started to learn more about education and bilingual education, and that's when I thought, 'Oh, maybe education is not a bad place to be because there's a lot happening here and I can see making a difference.'

That's when in 1973 I decided to go to Bank Street College and Teacher Corps and get my master's degree in education. We worked as interns in a high poverty area, with high rise projects and tenements, and the school was falling apart. It was an intense experience. A group of us got turned on to Freire so we created our own circle and read and discussed Pedagogy of the Oppressed, and we created a critical curriculum. And for my master's project two of us created a summer school program and we did like an action research. When I finished my internship, the school had a position for a bilingual teacher and they wanted me to come back.

Teaching is activism in the schools, changing lives. Activism can't be just action, you also have to reflect and see how things are connected. There has to be greater understanding that you're doing this for a particular purpose. It has to be for the betterment of the people, related to shifting power or creating social change. For me it's a way of life.

Learning From Chicanx/Boricua/Latinx Women's Stories

Although the four women and their stories are considerably different, there are important ideas that they teach us. Of significance is the need to highlight the different experiences of oppression that they have endured as well as the ways they make sense of these experiences and the ways that they turned those experiences into "*armas*" (tools) to develop courage and resilience and to inform the ways that they connect with and learn from the communities with whom they work. While sharing painful experiences, there was tremendous energy that exuded from the women as they told their stories, which is evident as we read them. They are hopeful because they have seen that changes—even if small ones—can and do happen.

The women also evidence diverse levels of, but consistent engagement with, notions of recognition, identity, material conditions, local and structural dimension of race, class, and gender dynamics and capitalist relations. This suggests that attempts to create linear stages of development with respect to recognition, courage, agency, and action will miss the ways in which these complex processes work together and support each other.

An important learning is that all of the women *learned* to be courageous and to stand up. Three of the women speak about learning by seeing their parents stand up, whether for others or for themselves. Even though they may have felt shame in their youth, the agency they observed in their parents inspired them as adults. For Martha, her model was not a person present in her life but a figure of selflessness and service—Mother Teresa—whom she wished to emulate. This is important because it tells us that we need to make sure that our children and our students have opportunities to see people acting courageously and internalize the commitment to act as Anaida who said, "I always felt like I had to do the right thing."

The women speak of "trembling" and that the fear "*nunca se va*" (never leaves you) but that we must not allow it to paralyze us. Too often people

believe that those who have changed the world for the better are extraordinary superheroes that live by standards impossible for us to meet. This is, of
course, the fallacy that we are led to believe because so much of our learning related to social movements surrounds key figures and rarely do we hear
about the hundreds and thousands who have organized and worked tirelessly
often for years and in different ways to build a movement. The Civil Rights
movement did not just happen. It grew to national awareness and stimulated
numerous movements to the spotlight but there were numerous groups that
had been working toward these efforts long before the 60s came and these
same groups have continued to work, perhaps re-organized, morphed into new
movements, or been picked up differently by the next generation. It is no
accident that a spotlight is placed on a few key figures whereas the majority
of people that go unnoticed are the ones who do the daily work of knocking
on doors, talking to people, raising consciousness, mobilizing, and making
the small changes that eventually raises our hopes, vision, and power to make
larger changes. This invisibility often stops us from believing that we too can
make a difference. Of course, Dolores Huerta is an amazing person, full of
courage and strength, but she was once in many ways similar to most Chicanx
youth today.

Another important theme that emerges from these stories is the significance of grassroots organizing, working with the people but not just for the
sake of growing in numbers. Of course, mobilizing large numbers is important,
but what is also important is that the people are the ones who have lived the
realities that we are seeking to change and thus they know first-hand what
needs changing and how best to go about it. Their ideas, strategies, perspectives are rooted in the reality that sometimes those of us who have moved into
spaces of power (i.e. the university) can easily lose sight of or fall out of touch
with the people. An important point is that the women describe working
with communities in a way that resembles the concept of horizontalidad that
I discussed in the previous chapter—a decentralized organizational style with
collective decision-making instead of leadership—that has developed out of
the Zapatista Movement and is growing across numerous contemporary organizations and movements. This approach suggests a different ontological and
epistemological clarity—the idea that the knowledges they bring and their
ways of coming to know the world differs from traditional western approaches
which have ruled organizational structures for centuries and, given the conditions of today's world, have not proven effective.

Notes

1. Latinx is an umbrella term referencing any person of Latin American descent. Chicanx has generally been used by the Mexican American community to highlight their colonized history and connotes an activist orientation and political resistance. It was popularized during the Chicanx Movement of the 60s. However, newer generations of Mexican immigrants as well as immigrants from other Latin American countries are choosing to identify as Chicanx in acknowledgement of the colonial relations that exist between the U.S. and Latin America. Boricuas are persons from Puerto Rico and of Puerto Rican descent whose experiences of colonization are distinct given that Puerto Rico remains a conveniently "forgotten" U.S. colony.
2. Gloria Anzaldúa, *Borderlands La Frontera*, 15.
3. Lilia D. Monzó, "Marx in the Age of Trump: Reaching Out to Communities of Color."
4. See discussion in Peter Hudis, *The Alternative to Capitalism*.
5. Raya Dunayevskaya, *American Civilization on Trial: Black Masses as Vanguard*.
6. Lilia D. Monzó and Peter McLaren, "Marked for Labor: Latina Bodies and Transnational Capital—A Marxist Feminist Critical Pedagogy."
7. Michael A. Lebowitz, "What Makes the Working Class a Revolutionary Subject?"
8. Deborah P. Kelsh, "The Pedagogy of Excess."
9. Lebowitz, "What Makes the Working Class?"
10. Ibid, para. 4.
11. Paulo Freire, *Pedagogy of the Oppressed*.
12. Charles Post, "The "Labor Aristocracy" and Working-Class Struggles."
13. Karl Marx, cited in Lebowitz, "What Makes the Working Class?"
14. Ibid.
15. See Chapter 5 for women's roles in a variety of revolutionary movements.
16. Magaly Lavadenz and Anaida Colón-Muñíz, "La Lucha Sigue: An Interview with Dolores Huerta."
17. Anaida Colón-Muñíz and Magaly Lavadenz, eds., *Latino Civil Rights in Education: La Lucha Sigue*.
18. Sandra Robbie, "The Meaning of Méndez."
19. Colón-Muñíz and Lavadenz, *Latino Civil Rights in Education*.
20. Girls and Women of Color (GWoC), https://resilienceoc.org/gwoc/
21. Alliance of Californians for Community Empowerment (ACCE) Action, http://www.acceaction.org/#
22. Cheyenne Reynoso, the author of this story, uses a non-traditional spelling of womxn as an empowering way of negating the historical treatment of womxn as appendages to men.
23. Although Martha is completely fluent in English, we spoke during the interview/conversation in Spanish. I've kept it in the text in Spanish to honor our primary language and to be true to her words. The English translation appears as an appendix.
24. ASPIRA of NY is a non-profit dedicated to serving Puerto Rican/Latino youth in NYC.

Bibliography

Anzaldúa, Gloria. *Borderlands/ La Frontera—The New Mestiza*. San Francisco, CA: Aunt Lute Books, 1987.

Colón-Muñíz, Anaida and Magaly Lavadenz, eds. *Latino Civil Rights in Education: La Lucha Sigue*. New York, Routledge, 2016.

Dunayevskaya, Raya. *American Civilization on Trial: Black Masses as Vanguard*. Chicago, IL: News and Letters Committee, 2003.

Freire, Paulo. *Pedagogy of the Oppressed, 30th anniversary edition*. New York: Bloomsbury, 2000.

Hudis, Peter. *Marx's Concept of the Alternative to Capitalism*. New York: Haymarket Books, 2013.

Kelsh, Deborah P. "The Pedagogy of Excess." *Cultural Logic: Marxist Theory & Practice* (2013): 137–156. https://ojs.library.ubc.ca/index.php/clogic/article/view/190896/188481

Lavadenz, Magaly and Anaida Colón-Muñíz. "La Lucha Sigue: An Interview with Dolores Huerta." In *Latino Civil Rights in Education: La Lucha Sigue*, edited by Anaida Colón-Muñíz and Magaly Lavadenz, 109–120. New York, Routledge, 2016.

Lebowitz, Michael A. "What Makes the Working Class a Revolutionary Subject?" *The Monthly Review 64*, no.7 (2012). https://monthlyreview.org/2012/12/01/what-makes-the-working-class-a-revolutionary-subject/

Monzó, Lilia D. "Marx in the age of Trump: Reaching out to Communities of Color." *International Marxist Humanist Organization*, Feb. 1, 2017. https://www.imhojournal.org/articles/marx-age-trump-reaching-communities-color-lilia-d-monzo/

Monzó, Lilia D. and Peter McLaren. "Marked for Labor: Latina Bodies and Transnational Capital—A Marxist Feminist Critical Pedagogy." In *Race and Colorism in Education*. Edited by C. R. Monroe, 63–86. New York: Routledge, 2017.

Post, Charles. "The 'Labor Aristocracy' and Working-Class Struggles: Consciousness in Flux, Part 2." *Solidarity*, September-October, 2006. https://solidarity-us.org/atc/124/p129/

Robbie, Sandra. "The Meaning of Méndez." In *Latino Civil Rights in Education: La Lucha Sigue*, edited by Anaida Colón-Muñíz and Magaly Lavadenz, 58–64. New York, Routledge, 2016.

· 7 ·

GENDERED AND RACIALIZED CAPITAL

Tensions and Alliances

Am I free to roam? ... do I remain the unsettled native, left to unsettle the settled spaces of Empire?

—Irene Watson[1]

This book is about the revolutionary history and potential of racialized women. Specifically, it outlines some of the conditions of oppression that these diverse communities of women have long experienced, which give impetus, courage, and hope. These are histories of struggle that can be engaged toward creating solidarity and a collective front against the capitalist, racist, misogynist and heteronormative structures that create oppressive conditions beyond the imagination.

The capitalist system and the settler-colonial project it spawned in North America remains intact through patriarchal and racialized structures of dispossession, territorial control, the prison and military industrial complexes, the hyper exploitation of predominantly "alien" labor, perpetual war, and global market and international trading machinations that sustain its accumulation. The diverse ways in which different racialized communities have come under the perpetual gun of capitalist relations and a patriarchal, White supremacist class creates divisions among and between us, creating conditions

wherein oppressed communities are at times complicit with capitalism, imperialism, and colonialism in the oppression of other racialized communities.
Certainly, the patriarchal structure in which all communities participate supports the processes of racialization, colonization, and capitalism. Although
some authors argue that the concept of racism must be pluralized to distin-
guish the diverse ways they are structured, I believe that the more important
theorization is that which links these patriarchal "racisms" to explain how
together they maintain a global system of capital accumulation for a propor-
tionately very small, predominantly White, capitalist class.

Although crude (class reductionist) Marxists would like to presume that,
as the working class, we are all in the same perilous conditions and benefit
similarly from the breakdown of capitalism, the diversity of interests, oppositional tensions, and what is just for these differently oppressed communities
require both theoretical and practical articulations and they must be engaged
with the communities, and for my focus, with the women, who live out these
oppressive realities. The relevance of a revolutionary critical pedagogy and
Marxist-humanism to diverse communities is dependent on the extent to
which we are willing to engage questions of racialized and gendered specificity in relation to the broader structure of capitalism and to begin to develop
viable possibilities for the liberation of all peoples and life forms. This is a
long-term project; one that must be developed dialectically with the ongoing
struggles for more immediate (even if only limited) relief from suffering and
instantiation of agency and dignity.

In this chapter I draw on Evelyn Nakano Glenn's unitary theory of racialized and colonial oppressions in the context of North American settler colonialism, with specific focus on the U.S. Her work is a brilliant and thoughtful
articulation of how diversely racialized communities have been incorporated
into the settler-colonial project—a project deeply rooted in capitalism and
"so-called primitive accumulation." The diverse "racisms" and their relationship to capital and the colonial project create tensions between and among
diverse communities, including among women, for whom conditions of
exploitation are both exacerbated and manifest in gender-specific ways. Here,
I address specific tensions that divide diverse racialized women but that also
create potential alliances. My goal is to provide a space where these various
articulations come together for a more holistic understanding. My hope is
that a Marxist-humanist lens may provide some insights that will extend the
conversation to a dialectical approach that articulates both immediate and
long-term praxis to remake the world.

Capitalism, Colonialism, and Racialization: Toward a Unitary Theory

Marx's theory of primitive accumulation recognizes imperialism and colonization to be a *continual* process by which the capitalist extracts ever-increasing amounts of surplus value from the worker. Indigenous scholars argue that colonization has more to do with land appropriation than the exploitation of workers; however, this reality is not incompatible with the need for workers to create value.[2] In Chapter 2, I provided a more extensive discussion of Marx's theory of "so-called primitive accumulation." Here, I want to point out that for the capitalist, land is a source of wealth—the means of production—through which workers create value, thus enriching those who make the land "their property." However, contrary to many misrepresentations of Marx's work that he saw land as mere resources to be manipulated by humans, Marx specifically challenges the ways in which the fertility of the land is exploited as it is turned into a mere tool of production and instead argues that a significant "rift" occurs when the "metabolic" relation between humans and nature is severed.[3] Here, I turn to more contemporary theorists in order to understand the historical conditions that have led to the continued appropriation of Indigenous lands and to a process of patriarchal racialization that has facilitated settler colonialism and increased accumulation through imperialism and structural colonial relations between the Global North and South.

Evelyn Nakano Glenn has developed an important framework for explaining the settler-colonial experience and the diverse ways in which racialized groups, and women among them, have been incorporated into the colonial-settler state's agenda for capital accumulation.[4] Indigenous scholars have long established that settler colonialism differs from colonialism in that the latter sought to exploit the land and peoples but to take their stolen riches back with them. In contrast, settler colonialism is characterized by the colonizers' intent to settle in the colonized land and to maintain a strict separation of and continual attempt to eliminate Indigenous nations in order to remove Indigenous claims to lands and create an "uncontested" settler-state.

In his chapter on primitive accumulation, Marx describes how colonialism supports greater and greater accumulation through the appropriation of land and other resources and the hyper exploitation of colonial labor.[5] For settler colonialism this remains the case. However, by choosing to settle in colonial lands, they seek to normalize their own cultural ways. This "cultural invasion" cannot take hold when a large population of Native peoples remains.[6] Numerous Indigenous scholars point out that the settling project is predicated on the elimination of Native peoples who were depicted by the first White colonizers as subhuman, foreclosing the possibility of co-existence.[7] Since Indigenous peoples were unwilling to give up the lands with which they and their ancestors have lived and built kin relations for thousands of years, their total extermination became the end goal. While the first process of extermination involved genocide, later approaches have involved epistemicide, cultural assimilation, and or the Whitening of the race (miscegenation), with the end goal of eliminating Indigeneity.

Women have been especially targeted in the context of conquest, war, and genocide; their rape, theft, and enslavement has become a weapon of war, a sexualized violence against not only women but women of a particular race, culture, ethnicity and a process (rather than an act) which aims to terrorize women and demoralize and emasculates men.[8] Patriarchy was introduced into otherwise more egalitarian Indigenous societies through the Imperial imaginary, wherein the White man was made into the epitome of human development through conquest and genocide.[9] The process of colonizing the Americas have been well documented, with horrific stories of the way women were raped and enslaved. Later attempts at elimination of Indigenous peoples and culture directly targeted women via sterilization, forced adoption, foster programs, and boarding schools.[10] The settler-colonial logic of elimination targets women especially, since they are often the primary caretakers of children and carriers of cultural traditions and knowledge systems to the next generation. Today, there remains a consistent problem of the disappearance of and murder of Indigenous women. This phenomenon has to be examined through the lens of a long history of patriarchal colonial genocide and violence.

But if settler colonialism is bent on eliminating Indigenous peoples, then it requires not only land (sources of wealth) but also labor. Only labor can create value for the purposes of accumulation of capital. Although Native peoples as well as indentured Whites were enslaved labor, a structure predicated on the elimination of the Natives must find a way in which to create a new workforce and justify their exploitation.[11] The transatlantic slave trade and the process of racialization served this capitalist purpose.

Scholars of the growing "Afro pessimism" tradition, including Frank B. Wilderson III, Orlando Patterson and Jared Sexton, argue an anti-Blackness exceptionalism that challenges the logic of racism as a structure applicable to all non-Whites and the logic of capital premised on the exploitation of labor, since Black slaves cannot be reduced to labor in the way that other workers can.[12] Partially conceding to this argument, Iyko Day points out that the logic of elimination that is applied to Indigenous peoples and the "terror formation" applied to Black peoples does not suggest production and capital accumulation to be the foundational process at work in the settler-colonial state.[13] I agree that the logic of capital alone cannot explain the atrocities committed against Indigenous and Black slaves. I also agree that diverse racial groups have been incorporated differently—have a different function—in the logic of capital; however, I would argue that these diverse racisms are linked to White supremacy and to a broader capitalist system. In Chapter 2, I argued that race and class are dialectically related and that Marx's dialectic and his critique of capital, which includes the role of colonialism, offers important insights to making sense of how these logics work together. While it is certainly true that Black slaves were property, they were also "workers" in the Marxist sense of the word, which is that they created value. Although slaves experienced the ultimate form of dehumanization—they *did* create value (monetary value).[14] This is why the slave trade (and not cotton) was the greatest industry of production during the slave era.[15] Unlike Indigenous peoples who were earmarked for extinction, Black slaves were earmarked for growth, with the rape of Black women to produce more and more slaves a central feature of American slavery.[16] As opposed to Indigenous peoples who must show significant amounts of "red blood" to receive their rightful due of land and resources, Blacks have been made thus by a minimalist amount of "Black blood." This has ensured the continuation of Blackness as a precondition to a continually growing pool of highly exploitable labor.[17] While the Afro-pessimist argument that precludes any commensurability between the oppression of Black peoples and that of other non-Black People of Color may be valid in so far as it has been produced through specific historical relations, it is my belief that we can establish the horrific and long-standing violence of anti-Blackness without embracing an "oppression Olympics" that has only served to create divisions between diverse groups rather than to embrace a unifying politics that aims for the liberation of all peoples. While racisms differ in their purpose and manifestations and even the brutality with which they are deployed, they are linked in ways that support a broader global social, economic, and political system.

Marx attempted to explain the actual process by which capitalism functioned and maintained itself. The binary of worker and capitalist was a way to strip the process to its essential components. This does not preclude there being other categories of peoples nor does it suggest that all groups would fit nicely into these categories. Certainly, Marx realized that there would be other people that did not fit neatly into the worker/capitalist binary. Nor does it preclude that there be other forms of oppression that would interact with the capital logic as racism, patriarchy, and other structures of oppression have done. However, that these other oppressions exist and interact does not change the fact that capitalism persists because labor produces and creates value. Indeed, the unifying theory that Glenn develops explains how diverse groups replace and impact each other, such that both capitalism and racism remain intact, along with other structures of oppression. While a crude class-reductionist Marxism may presume that racism would end at the collapse of capitalism, Marxist-humanists recognize that racism, although developed to justify slavery, took on a life of its own that has persisted beyond slavery, creating conditions of inequality, lack of opportunity, and relations of domination that are today not solely a function of or tied to class.[18]

Scholars Manu Karuka, Iyko Day, and others have begun to trouble the binary settler/Indigenous to make room for racialization and racism and specifically the long history of Black slavery and anti-Blackness in the U.S. context.[19] This work has provided important insights into the parallels and conflicts that arise from the different oppressions of Indigenous groups and Black Americans within settler-colonial capitalism, as well on the ways in which solidarity can be built and both groups can flourish in co-existence. Some scholars, including Evelyn Nakano Glenn and Iyko Day, are doing groundbreaking work in developing a unifying theory that explains how various racial and ethnic groups have been incorporated into what bell hooks terms White supremacist capitalist patriarchy.[20]

Evelyn Nakano Glenn characterizes other groups under settler-colonial rule in the United States as the "exogenous other," including Chicanx, Mexican im(migrants) and Chinese peoples.[21] For example, Glenn argues that the predominantly Mestizx people of the U.S. Southwest, previously colonized under Spanish rule and later colonized a second time via U.S. western expansion and the Mexican-American war, cannot be considered either Native nor settler. Vélez-Ibáñez explains that at the time of the U.S. invasion into what is now the Southwest U.S., the area was significantly inhabited by Mestizx peoples with Spanish and Indian ancestry. Anglo settlers dispossessed Mexican farmers and agriculturalists of their land through various legal and extra legal means, including taxation, delaying land grant claims, and outright theft, which pushed Mexican workers into seasonal migratory wage work as sheepherders, vaqueros, and later in mining, railroad construction, and agricultural field labor.[22] Up until the 1930s the border with Mexico was not legally policed and migrants traveled across the border to and from the U.S. freely. Large agribusinesses replaced small farms, which required a large mobile labor force that would move with the seasons. These businesses welcomed a highly exploitable, Mexican migratory labor force.[23]

The treaty of Guadalupe Hidalgo promised the Indigenous and Mestizx peoples of the Southwest U.S. citizenship.[24] However, the colonizers could not fathom giving citizenship to Natives; therefore, the Mexican people of the Southwest were racialized White. Eventually, Mexicans, often darker skinned, came to be renamed as ethnic minorities in order to separate them from "pure" Whites. The predominance in agricultural "stoop labor" came to define them with epithets as "dirty Mexicans."[25] Glenn identifies four ways which Mexicans have been subjected to settler-colonial control: (a) containment, (b) erasure or cultural assimilation, (c) terrorism, and (d) removal, such as deportations.[26]

Although traditional forms of colonization differ from settler colonialism, they were no less violent or genocidal. However, under classical colonialism, the goal was to conquer in order to erect and maintain relations of domination but not necessarily to eradicate the Indigenous peoples. In "Spanish America," for example, although clearly evidencing the belief in White race superiority and a violent disdain for the Indigenous nations and the African slaves that were transported as property, as well as their cultures and beliefs, there was significantly greater mixing of peoples. Initially, miscegenation occurred through the common patriarchal use of raping Indigenous women as a violent tool of conquest and later through the notion of creating a "cosmic race" that would be increasingly improved by Whitening it.[27] Consequently, a new majority of Mestizx peoples was born with a similarly racialized hierarchy, wherein Indigenous and Black peoples have tended to be among the poorest and those who were more direct descendants of the Spanish colonizer inherited their stolen riches and positions of domination. Colorism has ensured that patterns of racialized patriarchy, even among a mixed-race people, have persisted in neocolonial contexts, defining economic opportunities and gendered life chances in Latin America and other nations colonized by the White man.

In the Global South, neo-colonialism defines social, economic, and political relations to Empire. The economic dependency of the Global South on the North is secured through western corporate investments, trade agreements, transnational capital, political intervention, invasion and war, or the mere threat of these.[28] The result is the Global North's consistent encroachment on the Global South's lands and resources and an unparalleled exploitation not allowed in the presumed "civilized" Global North, where protections for workers exist to justify a false narrative of democracy and benevolence. Of course, it cannot be overstated that these "protections" come at a cost to the most vulnerable in the so-called "developing world," who are pushed off their lands and into crowded cities where work is scarce, violence high, and lives grow increasingly precarious. That people will seek safety and dignity by migrating to the places where they perceive these may be found—the "developed" world—is to be expected. These im(migrants) become the scapegoats of economic crisis or social upheaval, with laws and policies aimed at curtailing migration, denying refuge, and deporting people who have spent years giving their hard and poorly paid labor, taxes, and cultural enrichment to a country that for some is their only "home."[29]

There are sufficient parallels in the ways diverse racialized communities experience class, racism, and other oppressions, to name our common enemies: capitalism, colonialism, imperialism, patriarchy, and racism. Yet there are also differences, which pit us against each other, particularly as we fight for limited resources. Below I discuss some of the issues that create important tensions between and among Women of Color and Indigenous women. I believe understanding how these oppressions are linked to support the overarching structure of a White supremacist, patriarchal capitalism will help us recognize our common interests and to understand that the tensions we experience are often created by applying the logic of capital. Unfortunately, full reparations for the atrocities committed against specific groups cannot be met without denying another group's needs. Thus, we have to do the best we can to try and co-exist and ameliorate conditions for all of us within this structure while simultaneously building alliances to bring down the capitalist structure that feeds off of our pain and humiliations. We have to create a socialist imaginary wherein everyone's actual needs are met, including the need for place, food, shelter, education, healthcare, dignity, creative labor, and love.

A Contested Terrain

Land and space is an important source of contention in settler-colonial states. All people seek to have space where they can be safe and feel at home; where their ontological and epistemological ways are not marginalized, perceived perverse or unnatural, or subjugated. This is especially true for women who are made into pawns of war and conquest. The settler-colonial logic of elimination of Indigenous peoples impact women in very different ways since the patriarchal order established through state laws and policies have significantly infringed upon their pre-colonial roles and rights. The patriarchal order established by the colonial settlers, after centuries of continuous infringement and replacement of the matriarchal lineage, have significantly shifted power in Indian reservations and in the household to men. Thus, Indigenous women within a settler society are often subject to the patriarchal laws of the state but also to those transferred by the state onto Native men. The result has been that tribal governance in most nations is heavily male dominated and women sometimes do not hold the right to vote or hold office.[30]

Sovereignty over particular lands can mean freedom to be a self-determining nation, constructing their own government and systems and thus the opportunity for Indigenous women to re-establish their traditional ways and/ or create new ways without the constant threat of the state that functions through the logic of elimination. Manu Karuka comments that in North America, the justification for the settler state is built on a mythologized *terra nullius*, the idea that the land was free of peoples and/or "civilization," and thus waiting to be taken.[31] The appropriation of lands by the colonizer and forced removal of Indigenous peoples from the land with which they have survived for thousands of years was key to the genocides of entire peoples, languages, knowledges, and cultures and to the establishment of patriarchal structures that gave Indigenous men some semblance of power but created the gender antagonism, that although perhaps already present, took on new sociohistorical significance and properties under capitalism in the colonial state. Land is recognized as key to Indigenous survival, but especially to women. The goal of sovereignty has, thus, defined Indigenous movements since the arrival of the first colonizers. In today's environmental crisis, Indigenous struggles for land are also about preserving water supplies.

Joanne Barker documents that women have always been key players in these struggles, especially under the Canadian Indian Act, which redefined Indigenous women who married non-Indian (or non-recognized Indians) as non-members of their nations, with no right to reservation lands or resources.[32] Barker makes very evident that women in Canada have been at the center of struggles for self-determination, land rights, and against The Indian Act. They have been big supporters of maintaining Native governance structures. However, patriarchal structures that are meant to control women in the service of capital and colonial rule create conditions that split women's loyalties. Barker points out that Indigenous women have often been made to choose between their rights as women and the preservation of Native cultures and governance. Drawing on their male privilege, Native men have some-times argued that their communities have never been sexist since they were historically matriarchal. Women are made to feel disloyal if they challenge the sexism that exists within Indian reservations and their laws and structures. These gender struggles among Indigenous communities often limit the poten-tial to obstruct capitalist-colonial structures.

The Black Liberation movement has also, at different times, attempted to claim the right to land. In particular, According to Karuka, Black liber-ationists have argued for a place where people could stay and live.[33] During Reconstruction their goal was crucial to the moment—to find safety, dig-nity, and self-determination and they were ready to leave to go where they needed to go to make that dream of place reality. In the early 20th century, a "back to Afrika" movement grew wherein many Blacks from the South and working-class Blacks emigrated to Africa. The Black Power Movement of the 60s, following Malcolm X, called for more than civil rights. They also sought self-determination and influenced the idea of making the Black Belt the "'his-torical homeland ... where the African-American people were moulded into a nation of people through the process of capitalist development inside the United States of America.'"[34]

The struggle for land and self-determination has at times created important tensions between Black and Indigenous peoples. Karuka points out that this land, in which Black slaves produced the lucrative cotton industry that facil-itated advanced capitalism, had been previously made rich and fertile through its relations to Indigenous peoples.[35] Indigenous scholars critique the lack of acknowledgement of previous Indigenous existence and genocide that accom-panies some Black claims to lands. Karuka specifically critiques Megan Kate Nel-son for depicting Black maroon settlement in the southeastern borderlands from 1750–1845 as an act of appropriating *terra nullius* or empty lands, even though these were Muscogee ancestral lands ceded in treaties in 1814 and 1826 before complete Indigenous removal from the land in the 1832 Treaty of Cusseta.[36]

Some Indigenous scholars, including Candace Fijikane and Patrick Wolfe, who adhere to the traditional binary of Indigenous/Settler relations argue strongly that settler colonialism is a structure defined by this binary, such that all non-Indigenous peoples are settlers, regardless of whether the settling was intentional or forced, as in the case of Blacks slaves.[37] While these scholars recognize the processes of racialization and sympathize with the oppressions that force migration, they nonetheless argue that everyone other than Indigenous peoples is complicit with settler colonialism. Candace Fujikane prescribes that settler allies must support and work to challenge the settler-colonial state and restore the lands to its "rightful" Indigenous owners.[38] Fujikane points out that, according to Haunani-Kay Trask, an important leader of the Hawaiian Sovereignty Movement, "the United Nations Declaration on the Rights of Indigenous Peoples distinguishes [I]ndigenous peoples from all others on a particular land base by their [I]ndigenous human right to self-determination and self-government; minority populations do not possess this right."[39] However, Black communities, descendants of slaves who live under perpetual persecution as well as other groups forced into migration, cannot be treated as the colonizers. Furthermore, they also *need* spaces to survive and to live with safety and dignity. For Indigenous people to adopt a propertied relation to land is to accept the capitalist logic of the colonizer—that land is property.

The Black Panther Party eventually shifted from a nationalist movement to developing socialist ideals. They began to move toward building an international movement and solidarity with the "third world." Huey Newton, specifically, of the Black Panther Party, envisioned a radical concept of self-determination—one that encompassed a "worldliness" that would eliminate boundaries and benefit all people (not peoples).[40] While the struggle for immediate concessions to land and space continue we must engage the broader challenge to eradicate the system that consistently subjugates racialized communities and women.

A related source of conflict has been the ways in which civil rights law has typically been used toward the right of racialized and ethnic minority communities, perhaps with the presumption that Indigenous peoples are also supported through these laws. Of course, this may be true in many cases, but not in all. Fujikane explains how civil rights law has often been used against Indigenous peoples' claims to land and other resources. An instructive case is that of Hawaii, which is a two-time settler-colonial state. The first settlement took place as James Cook facilitated with European arms to unite the Islands into one Kingdom under the rule of Kamehameha. Fujikane explains that Hawaii's first colonization brought different Asian groups as slaves who faced horrific conditions. The U.S. settlement that came later, followed by the civil rights movement of the 60s and Ethnic Studies, in particular, gave Asian minorities in Hawaii greater opportunities but invoked the rise of multiculturalism as a social justice endeavor that gave settlers a claim to Hawaii that ignores the original Hawaiian inhabitants. Fujikane explains:

> In settler societies, the issue of civil rights is primarily an issue about how to protect settlers against each other and against the state. Injustices done against Native people, such as genocide, land dispossession, language banning, family disintegration, and cultural exploitation, are not part of this intrasettler discussion and are therefore not within the parameters of civil rights.[41]

For example, Harold Rice, a rancher of European descent, won the case of Rice vs Cayetano by invoking the 14th and 15th amendments. Rice sued the State of Hawaii for the right to vote in elections for the board of trustees of the Office of Hawaiian Affairs, which previously restricted voting to only Hawaiians or Native Hawaiians. The result was that non-Natives were granted voting rights on elections for an agency that handled the disbursement of funds and benefits to Native Peoples.[42]

The civil rights movement was instrumental in striking down Jim Crow and in passing laws and policies that increased minority participation in contexts of power, including affirmative action and bilingual education. However, it has become clear that many of these gains have been reversed or reconstituted to maintain racialized and gendered relations of domination. Fujikane argues that while civil rights presuppose a capitalist system that can be made fair or more just through laws that equalize conditions, Indigenous self-determination requires a complete change to the structure of settler colonialism. I would argue that this change must be global in scope, such that we develop different social relations across international spaces, thereby negating the capitalist need for imperialism and colonialism.

However, this transformation cannot presume to take us back in time and return us to a pre-capitalist and pre-colonial world. Even without borders or ownership of land, we will all still need space to live and grow. A "politics of refusal" acknowledges the history of land appropriation but reconsiders the question of land "rights" and argues instead for creating alternative visions that are in concert with Indigenous values and knowledges, which challenge the very system of capitalism which has created horrific realities of violence and pain for Indigenous people but also for Black communities, migrants, and other peoples who seek refuge in other countries from poverty, hunger, violence and destruction.[43] My own belief is that we need to challenge both the capitalist system and any immediate solutions that stem from the same capitalist and colonial logic; these will merely produce new forms of oppression rather than transforming structures toward liberation.

Race, Whiteness, and the Model Minority Myth

In the U.S., class inequality is structured along racial and gender lines, with Black, Indigenous, and Latinx women (especially undocumented) facing the greatest poverty and humiliations.[44] The low-income urban communities that are densely populated Black or Brown lack the social and economic resources to support class mobility. Schools are underfunded, sometimes falling apart. Teachers are underpaid, overworked, and usually within their first few years of teaching, which means they have yet to master good teaching; yet they end up teaching in the communities where experienced teachers are most needed. This is often true in reservation schools too, which lack funding and resources. Persistent inequality permeates in these communities, affecting their education, employment, health, and social networks. Although Asian women and their communities, as a racialized group, fare much better and sometimes exceed the success of Whites, specific groups of Asians, including Hmong and Pacific Islanders, face similar economic and social constraints as Black, Indigenous, and Latinx communities.[45]

This persistent inequality across all markers of life chances is inconsistent with a society that prides itself as "having the greatest opportunities" and being "meritocratic"—ideals that are often touted as the cream of the capitalist system, even though significant evidence exists to the contrary. Marx posited two major antagonist classes: the capitalist who owns the means of production and the proletariat or workers who must sell their labor power to the capitalist class for survival. However, among the proletariat there are significant inequalities in terms of wealth, educational opportunities, access to resources, and overall life chances. White supremacy, racialization, genderization, and Indigeneity are all processes that limit opportunities. The capitalist system has proven to be quite efficient at creating barriers and points of contention among the working classes, by restricting access to resources and thereby pitting racialized communities against each other in competition for limited resources.[46]

The stereotypes associated with racialization, gender, and Indigeneity serve to justify these inequalities, by providing a means by which to rationalize why inequality persists even after years of continually working to narrow an achievement and wealth gap that nonetheless continues to widen. The model minority stereotype is one that society seems to have grabbed a hold of and, as if their life depended on it, cannot let go of, lest it unravel the neat associations that have been created to make the middle classes feel good about accepting a system that feeds off of the exploitation of others, the vast majority of whom are Women of Color and Indigeneity. Thus, the myth of the Asian "model minority" persists even though it has been challenged over and over and has been shown to exist as a tool that controls and limits Asian potential while simultaneously condemning other racialized groups to conditions of impoverishment by marking them "unteachable" sources of low-level brute labor.

The model minority stereotype marks Asians as over-achievers, "naturally" inclined toward sciences, mathematics, and technology, hardworking, compliant, and self-sufficient. Women are especially marked as docile, quiet, and obedient. These qualities are then used to explain their surpassing the dominant White group in the U.S., regarding educational achievement, college acceptances, income and wealth. In effect it disciplines Asians by channeling them to a particular economic sector, determining the identities they have access to, masking the struggles that some Asians face, and foreclosing support systems. These stereotypes also support the perception that Asians lack leadership qualities, which lead to the glass ceiling effect in relation to top-level leadership positions, despite their higher achievement levels. Asians interested in pursuing careers in fields other than the sciences or math have to convince others that this is really what they want to do and have to work twice as hard as others to demonstrate that they can be successful outside the sciences.[47]

The model minority stereotype is used to justify claims that racism, language barriers, and other external factors cannot be a factor in determining success since Asians face many of these same issues but are still able to create success for themselves and their children. This argument condemns communities that have faced a long history of disservice from the educational system, namely Black, Latinx, Chicanx, and Indigenous, as "failing" due to their own individual or cultural deficits. It also serves to discipline these communities to be more like the stereotype Asians who are perceived to follow the rules without question or protest.

Critical Asian scholars have long established this "model minority stereotype" to be a myth that serves as a "hegemonic tool." The Asian success story is not a monolithic story of all Asians as it is presented. People who make up this umbrella identity Asian are significantly diverse peoples of different countries, with different languages, cultures, and histories. Putting them all together as one category creates the illusion of a very successful racialized group that on measures of success, such as education and income levels, surpass the dominant group. However, when statistics are disaggregated by country of origin we come to see a very different picture of Asian performance. Disaggregating by country reveals that success in terms of both education and wealth relates generally to the class standing they held in their countries of origin, their prior access to schooling and English fluency, whether they were refugees, and their history of colonization.[48]

For example, when we consider the general characteristics of immigrants from India, we note that upon arrival they speak English, hold some professional degree, have some financial capital, and join an already financially and educationally prosperous ethnic enclave in the U.S. These factors facilitate legal entry into the U.S. and provide a much more seamless incorporation into U.S society for themselves and their children who then continue to excel in their schools with the support of an already wealthy and/or academically oriented community. In contrast to this general picture of Indian achievement are the experiences of the Hmong community.[49]

The Hmong people of Laos, often referred to as Miao or Meo in Asia, began entering the U.S. as refugees during the Second Indochina War (Vietnam War) and the Secret War in Laos. The U.S. military recruited the Hmong as guerillas to fight alongside American soldiers against the North Vietnamese Army (NVA) and Pathet Lao forces. When the U.S. finally pulled out of Vietnam, the Hmong people were forced to flee. Many resettled in the U.S. as refugees.[50] In general, the Hmong people have not fared as well as some other Asian groups, socially, economically, or educationally.[51] The Hmong faced significant economic and social disadvantages upon arrival, including poverty, a different language, lack of familiarity with U.S. culture and schooling, refugee status and secondary migration to develop enclaves where they could feel at home.[52]

Explanations for their lower achievement patterns have been similar characterizations to those levied against Black families and Mexican and other Latinx families, including individual and cultural deficits, and discontinuities between the home and school (or broader society) culture. The Hmong people have been depicted as "homogenous, fixed, savage and primitive in comparison to modern Western culture."[53] These "explanations" amount to the same deficit discourse that is meant to psychologize social and economic problems by blaming students, their families, and their cultures.

Hmong Americans, like other Asian groups, are rejected for their presumed "foreignness," according to Mia Tuan, even when they have been born in the U.S. However, their status is elevated when they perform their expected model minority stereotype. They are "whitened" or treated as "honorary Whites" when they behave in accordance with model minority expectations, not only in regards to achievement but in regards to compliance and acceptance of the dominant cultural norms. In contrast, when Hmong students resist, engage in student activism, or challenge the status quo in any way, they are "Blackened."[54]

This process of Whitening or Blackening Asians creates schisms between Asians and People of Color. The concept of "acting White" was first introduced to explain the rejection that academically successful Black students received from their Black peers.[55] According to Signithia Fordham and John Ogbu, who first coined the concept, Black students perceived other academically successful Black students to be "acting White," or adopting the characteristics typically associated with White culture and therefore "selling out" and/or behaving with a sense of superiority toward their less successful Black peers. The result was that many Black students "chose" to remain "underachieving" or hid their achievements in order to avoid rejection and ridicule. An important critique of this work was that the desire for success and hard work are not exclusively White cultural norms. However, while hard work or success are not sole attributes of the dominant group, the ways in which success is defined and the practices rewarded in schools with good grades and identification with intelligence are often culturally derived practices.

Becoming an "honorary White" further entrenches the schism that is created between Asians and Black and Brown communities through the model minority myth. The lack of trust and resentment felt toward the dominant group for the continual experience of White supremacy and the very real privileges that they receive and for the fact they control the resources that are unequally allotted in society is then transferred to some extent to the Asian community. Likewise, some Asians who may perceive themselves as enacting the model minority stereotype may assimilate to the White dominant group, developing the same value system and beliefs, including the deficit frame through which Whites view Black, Brown, and Indigenous communities.

Related to the notion of Asians as honorary Whites, Iyko Day discusses Asian female racialization in the context of Canadian-settler society as an example of her concept "alien capital," a concept that highlights her argument that Asians are always viewed as alien forms of capital—defined as racial outsider and a valuable source of capital.[56] In the settler-colonial context, the Asian is always "alien" or outside of the racial antagonism Black/White and the colonial antagonism settler/Indigenous. Day describes the context within which an image of a female Asian scientist in the newly designed one-hundred-dollar polymer banknote was replaced by a female with Caucasian features "peering through a microscope." Day points out that although the original had a female Asian scientist, which can be cause for concern given its stereotypical representation, the cause for concern that led to its replacement was that focus groups in Montreal and Charlottetown who previewed it indicated:

> ... her Asian appearance 'didn't represent Canada' and was 'exclusionary'... since the banknote did not represent other ethnicities. ... A banks spokesman indicated that the image of a 'Caucasian-looking woman' was substituted to 'restore neutral ethnicity.'[57]

Evidently from the comments that "justified" the replacement, Canada's multicultural society can only be represented through a Caucasian woman. Indeed the belief that Caucasian suggests some form of "neutral" ethnicity suggests Whiteness as the prevailing norm and others as marginal foreigners. The message is a clear reminder that even though the country may be growing multicultural, Canada is a settler-colonial society established as such by European-colonial greed and White supremacy.

Day continues her analysis of Asian racialization and its relation to capital as signified by the initial impetus by the bank to place a female image on its banknote. Here the Asian female represents great value in the sense of being thought worthy of being placed on the banknote but the reason for her worth is that she has great value as the most competent producer of value. This image represents the model minority Asian who surpasses even White success by their own dominant terms. In this sense the Asian model minority has the greatest value as a worker. Her labor power has greater worth than the labor power of others in society since she is believed capable of producing the greatest value. From the perspective that the system can work, the Asian model minority on the bank note represents the success of capitalism and mystifies and obscures the relationship of race to class by denying its negative impact of the life opportunities of People of Color and Indigenous communities.[58]

For some Asians this positioning is a source of pride. Ironically, however, the fact that she can produce greater value marks her as a greater source of capital. From a Marxist perspective all workers are capital—a source of wealth that the capitalist owns so that they can produce even greater value. Gender here plays an important part, since it is a depiction that suggests a common, although false, female stereotype of docility and one that is generally applied to Asian women specifically. Her presumed docility is an asset to the capitalist who seeks efficiency and obedience. The depiction is taken to suggest that the Asian female is the epitome of a good worker, making her labor power that much more valuable. She is a thing, a pawn of capital, that not only produces greater value and keeps the capitalist system churning but also a pawn in supporting the ideologies that sustain the system by making it seem fair, hiding the effects of racism, and psychologizing inequality.

Of course, like the model minority myth itself, this idea of the female Asian as the "good worker" is also a myth. Asian women, like all others, have been instrumental to social change efforts in their communities and within their families. If we believe as some do that some stereotypes have perhaps a kernel of truth, given the right conditions, then we should learn more about the Asian woman warrior, a classic of Chinese mythology. There is ample evidence of many Asian women who are resisting the stereotypes that are prescribed to them or transforming them to meet their own needs. While these capitalists racializations attempt to define our roles in this settler-colonial society and in the broader capitalist world, such that the system remains functioning to its accumulation ends, Asian women are fighting to define themselves in ways that make sense to them. Many Asian, Black, Latinx, Indigenous, Muslim, and women of all categories are recognizing that our experiences are not isolated but linked to that of other women and other communities and to broader capitalist social relations. It is my hope that making these links is one step toward creating the fissures that Holloway argues will one day "crack" capitalism and make a new world possible.[59]

Criminalizing Migration

Although the "immigration" debate is not about which group can claim land as property it *is* related to the question discussed above: Who has the right to a space where they and their families can exist and survive with dignity? The Mestizx peoples of the Southwest and of Mexico, more broadly, have a long history of searching for space. Carlos Vélez-Ibáñez demonstrates how this search for space has been a central theme in the Mexican literature and arts of the region.[60] Today's immigration debate also centers on Mexican and Central American im(migrant) communities that have a long history of colonial and imperial relations with the U.S. Although many people of other racialized groups and from many countries get caught in the crossfire and are similarly criminalized, the issue is often portrayed as the need to control the Mexican border from Mexican and Central American peoples who are coming to the U.S. "to take our jobs and resources."[61] While this debate forms part of a larger extremist White nationalist and White supremacist movement to rid the U.S. of non-White groups and/or re-establish domination for the White race in all sectors of society (something we have not really moved that far from yet),[62] my intention here is to focus on the Mexican and Central American (and Latinx and Chicanx) communities, which while having similar experiences to other immigrants, nonetheless face unique issues based on specific sociohistorical conditions. My goal is to present how these im(migrant) communities are feminized, villainized, and criminalized in ways that create schisms between them and other more established immigrant, Black, Indigenous, and Latinx/Chicanx communities. At the same time that this national debate and criminalization creates ruptures, it also presents opportunities to see the common racism and suffering that these communities face and to develop solidarity and create coalitions to work together and bring other allies along.

It is important to note that the term "immigrant," defined as choice settlement in another country, is purposely misleading when applied to peoples for whom migration was not a choice but the only solution. This term, applied to those groups who seek entry for reasons that do not satisfy U.S. refugee status (determined through specific political and anti-communist ideology), is meant to disguise the "host" country's involvement in the process of dispossession of land and resources of the Global South and its peoples. The migrant communities of Mexico and Central America are to varying degrees Indigenous. There is evidence that Native peoples have migrated throughout the Americas and across what is now the U.S. Mexican border for thousands of years. Studies indicate that common historical migration routes ran North-South without restriction.[63]

After the massacres that led to the Spanish colonization of the area that spans the Mexican-U.S. border, Northern Mexico was colonized a second time; this time it was the U.S. that brutally sought the land for their "westward expansion" through the Mexican-American war of 1846–1848. However, it was not until 1924 that the border became formally patrolled to prevent people from entering the U.S. Initially established to control Chinese immigration, under the Chinese exclusion act, Mexican migration was less restricted because it was seen as an aspect of the territory's sociohistorical legacy as well as because the Mexican people presented a "cheap labor" source. Furthermore, deportations before the 1920s was negligible. Mae M. Ngai argues that the "melting pot" ideology made it unconscionable to deport anyone who had already established themselves in the U.S. and presumably begun to "assimilate."[64]

However, border controls became increasingly restrictive as a result of successive immigration laws that criminalized unauthorized entry. In addition, attempts to streamline the process of deportations that were increasing, border controls became associated with having or not having "appropriate papers" rather the previous qualitative dimension of "undesirables."[65] This led to a much greater emphasis on territoriality and the notion of U.S. sovereignty in immigration debates. The legality of "papers" began to define one's ability to stay in the country more so than family relations, history in the region, or even labor needs. Immigration became also associated to prohibition with the bootlegging of Mexicans as a parallel; the latter being worse than the former. Thus, undocumented immigrants became the "least desirable aliens."[66]

The first border patrol agents were poorly trained and functioned as an agency of "pursuit and apprehension." They were given free rein to engage in the interior far north of the border. The U.S. Mexican border treated Mexicans as "dirty animals," and hosed them down before inspecting their papers for entry. Racial hostility not only defined the border patrol but also became further perpetuated through immigration law and border patrol policies.[67]

Although immigration has been a common global trend since colonial times, never has it reached the global proportions of today, with people needing to leave their countries of origins due to poverty, violence, war, displacement, political persecution, and environmental disasters. The "immigration" debate is actually a global phenomenon of gargantuan proportions, evidence of a capitalist system in crisis and the desperate attempts to correct it through imperial domination. However, the debate within the debate, which I focus on here, is about northbound migration.

The economic and social upheavals of Mexico and Central America are directly related to U.S. international policy. While there has always been migration from and to Mexico, the significant growth of the last few decades corresponds to the neoliberal order and NAFTA (North American Free Trade Agreement), which has displaced many, predominantly Indigenous farmers from their lands, created maquiladora industries, or foreign owned factories (mostly U.S. and Canada) in which hyper exploited workers, mostly women, slave long hours for wages that barely allow them to survive, and pushed out small local business with the introduction of foreign capital. The U.S-sponsored War on Drugs has only increased violence south of the border and the guns that supply the cartels are brought into Mexico from the U.S. Countries in Central America have suffered through the economic and political bullying of the U.S., including providing support and assistance to dictators and strongmen perceived to create conditions favorable to U.S. corporate and increasingly transnational corporate interests—all, of course, in the service of capital.[68]

Given the history of migration and guest worker programs, proximity and accessibility by land, and the existing enclaves that have been established, the U.S. is an obvious place for people to seek refuge from poverty, joblessness, and violence. Those who are able to secure legal entry do so and those who cannot enter without legal documentation, follow a thousand years-old ancestral tradition of migration in search of food. Once in the U.S. the majority of Mexican and Central American migrants find work in agriculture, construction, factories, or the service industry. They provide cheap labor and bolster the U.S. economy.[69]

White supremacy and White nationalistic fervor are staples of the U.S. settler-colonial state and gains momentum during times of economic or political upheaval, when people begin to look for scapegoats to justify why the so-called American Dream has not materialized for them. What we see today is that decades of a stagnant capitalist economy, the Great Recession of 2008, and a sense of hopelessness among the working class has led to a mentality of "it's either me or them," especially when we have a racist president spewing lies and vilifying im(migrants).

Today, many working-class Whites are looking around at a society that is increasingly multicultural where the Civil Rights movements of the 60s brought about significant social changes that allowed some People of Color to move into positions of power and they are wondering if without this multicultural society those positions would have been available to them or their children. They argue that they are the new victims of discrimination, with immigrants taking their jobs and resources. Although they reject any notion of having White privilege, they revile the loss or potential loss of these privileges that they perceive as natural rights. For some people the chanting, "You will not replace us!" that is heard at White nationalist rallies has not just racial but also economic resonance.[70]

While this is predominantly a White on Brown attack, there are many People of Color that, although they may not repudiate Latinx immigrants, do believe the dominant narrative that immigrants take their jobs and resources, that some form of border control is necessary, and who buy into the negative stereotypes about Mexican immigrants and perhaps even support deportations of undocumented immigrants because they "broke the law."

It is important to note that forced migration is a feminist issue. There are two important reasons for this. The first is that forced migration occurs as a result of and through a process that is defined by a patriarchal colonial capitalist order. The Other (individual, racialized group or Nation, or foreign state) is always feminized in comparison to the Imperial being who makes himself all powerful through the control of the Other's land, resources, and people. That in turn, the most vulnerable people in their own countries, in the migration process, and in the "host" country are women and children is a function of the patriarchal order that was established through the same colonial-capitalist order that, as discussed above, upset the gender balance and diluted the power that women held in pre-colonial Indigenous nations. The second reason forced migration is a feminist issue is a more obvious one; three-quarters of all im(migrants) to the U.S. each year are women and the treatment they receive and process of incorporation creates specific gender-related concerns. For example, according to NOW (National Organization for Women), although seventy percent of immigrant women attain legal status through a family-based visa, the number of women waiting to be reunited with their families is about four million and some have been waiting for decades. Lesbian, gay, bisexual and transgender im(migrants) are not allowed to sponsor their partners or children for legal status despite raising children or owning homes together. In addition, approximately 60% of undocumented women work predominantly in the informal labor market, such as child care, which may exclude them from requirements necessary for permanent residency. The remaining 40 percent work without pay in the home. Im(migrant) women, especially those that are undocumented and that have children to care for, are highly vulnerable to significant workplace abuses and partner abuses, including wage theft, sexual and physical assault.[71]

So is there any truth to the claims that immigrants take our jobs and our resources? Research shows that Mexican and other immigrants generally take jobs that Americans do not wish to do because the often back-breaking work is perceived not worth the low wages, poor working conditions, pesticides, or other conditions that threaten lives and wellness and also because most Americans perceive these jobs beneath them. Although the deportation of Mexican undocumented workers has risen to levels that signal a White nationalist agenda of hate and "elimination," approximately 160,000 guest workers were hired in 2016.[72] The state authorizes guest worker programs that are quasi-slave labor in particular sectors where production cannot be met by the U.S. existing labor force.[73] The Bracero Program, instituted during labor shortages, that brought Mexican labor to work in U.S. agriculture and the importation of Chinese labor for the construction of the railroad are well recognized examples of horrific abuses and exploitation of guest workers in the U.S.[74] Farmworker Justice documents that standards for a "prevailing wage" workman's compensation, adequate working conditions, and the right to a harassment-free environment are often not met and that wage theft and extreme abuses are common because their visas are tied to a single employer who controls where they live and most aspects of their lives. As in the case of undocumented women, women guest workers are even more vulnerable to sexual harassment and sexual assault. Numerous cases have been reported of guest workers who are lured by false promises of citizenship and later stuck in near slave conditions. Although guest workers are often hired year after year and take part in and contribute to a community they have no path for legalization.

Although proponents of stricter border controls argue that halting the unauthorized workforce would ensure that these industries begin to pay better wages and offer better working conditions, without "cheap labor" the labor-intensive agricultural sector of the economy would collapse and produce, meat, and milk would have to be imported. This would mean additional job losses for those who now work in making and selling fertilizer, food processing, trucking, and other related jobs that support the industry. Other industries would also go bankrupt without immigrant labor because Americans would demand wages that would quickly drain small businesses.

Research also shows that unauthorized worker pay taxes regularly as if they were authorized to work in the hopes that one day they may be able to file for legal status. Because of the fear of deportation, they rarely seek social services when they need them. The only social service regularly obtained by undocumented workers is schooling for their children. Since many of these children will only know this country as their own and will remain here their schooling is really an investment not only on them but also on their potential contribution to this country. This is very evident through the research on DACA (The Deferred Action for Childhood Arrivals), which was implemented by President Obama in 2012, which allows young people who immigrated as children before the age of 16 to work, go to school, and get a driver's license for two years, without worry of deportation. Studies have shown that DACA recipients have made an important contribution to the economy by opening businesses that employ both immigrant and US citizens.

Of course, the infamous Mexican border wall, that Trump campaigned on, will not only cost us billions of dollars but it will not prevent people from crossing the border. People from Mexico and Central America migrate north because they have no other recourse. The inexcusable lies spread about the Mexican people being "criminals and rapists" cannot be further from the truth. Studies show that Mexican peoples (documented and undocumented) are hard-working and courageous people who sacrifice their lives crossing the border, live for years in fear of deportation, and are highly exploited and abused by employers and others all to be able to feed their families and to offer their children an opportunity to have an education and live a life with dignity.

At the individual level, it is easy to see why the so-called immigration debate may be a source of tension between unauthorized workers and more established im(migrants), Latinx, Indigenous, and Black communities. Without knowing the facts, even when people have personally experienced the urgency of poverty and need, they may be inclined to reject another's reality and instead focus on their own fears of job loss, possible homelessness, and other social ills—all very possible in the context of a capitalist structure where individuals must fend for themselves.

There is a general belief that Latinx im(migrants) and Blacks are often at odds politically and economically. One aspect of these tensions is related to degrees of segregation. Black Americans had to fight hard against Jim Crow and yet they remain generally more racially segregated than immigrants overall, and Latinx specifically. Integrated communities tend to include more Latinx families than Black families. Integrated neighborhoods tend to be middle class and in this context Latinx tend to be more accepted than Blacks. This difference, however, is less evident in working-class communities. Instead, what happens in working-class segregated neighborhoods is that swelling immigrant enclaves sometimes push out Black neighborhoods. Another point of contention between Black and Latinx communities has to do with racial identification. While the majority of Latinx peoples in the U.S. are Mexican, which means they are generally Mestizx, descendants of Indigenous peoples and/or Black slaves, the majority of Latinx communities identify themselves as White on census data. Unfortunately, the racist perception of White as "improving the race" remains a strong ideology in Latin America.[75]

The most significant point of contention is the perception that im(migrants) displace Black workers. Large-scale data on this suggest that immigrants are good for the economy and in regards the Black community overall, there is little evidence of labor market competition. Immigrants seem to bring different skills, abilities, and interests. While small qualitative studies suggest the reverse, this is specific to low-skill labor and may have more to do with perception than actual displacement. While these tensions exist, Black communities have overall been very supportive of immigration, suggesting that a sense of solidarity with communities of color persists. Aspects of this may be that they seem to recognize some of the parallels between the experiences of Latinx im(migrants) and their own experiences of oppression. For example, that large sectors of the immigrant and the Latinx community, specifically, do not vote resonates with their own struggles over voting rights and the civil rights movement. Furthermore, with all the narratives about conflicts between Black and Latinx communities, strong bonds were forged during the Civil Rights Movement, from which many other groups drew strength and strategy to make their own demands heard.[76] Ironically the people that are most likely to be displaced by new im(migrants) are those who came not long before them. They tend to have the same skill set and to settle in the same industries. Yet im(migrants) vote very strongly in favor of im(migrant) rights. Of course, there are many who complain about or fear job loss but these numbers don't stack up to making any real mark.

Of significant importance is the fact that undocumented im(migrants) are being targeted for detention and deportation in ways that resemble the targeting of Black men and women for incarceration.[77] For Black communities whose men face significant overrepresentation in prisons and who live in fear of being killed by White police or being "the new slave" of the system, the excessive force and dehumanizing strategies employed by ICE against migrants whose only infraction is their unauthorized status, hits very close to home.[78]

Since the claims that immigrants are a financial burden are false, then what is pushing the anti-immigrant agenda? Aside from providing the important scapegoat that clears the U.S. government and the capitalist system from any culpability, im(migration) control is a highly lucrative industry—part of the global multi-billion dollar prison industrial complex that cages and controls primarily Black and Brown bodies. Consider that prisons are increasingly being privatized and that they often have a hand in electoral politics, monetarily supporting presidents and lobbying for their interests in order to secure the prison slave labor from which they make fortunes. One of the most influential and profit-making prison companies, GEO group, named "homeland security" and "immigration" among the main issues its lobbyists discussed with lawmakers.[79]

These excessive anti-im(migrant) policies and White nationalist narratives for the sake of corporate greed have taken on a strikingly cruel edge under the Trump administration. Many, of course, in the U.S. and around the world were appalled at the cruelty of separating families and literally taking babies from their mothers and caging asylum seekers as punishment for coming to this country in search of safety and a life with dignity for themselves and their children. The treatment and intimidation that many of these asylum seekers have reported, being put in chains and being told they would never see their children again, is unbelievable. These are crimes against humanity made more heinous by the fact that people come to the US seeking refuge from poverty, violence, and wars that the U.S. is highly implicated in creating and because we deploy false narratives of U.S. freedom and opportunity around the world that pulls people to our borders.

Attacks on im(migrants), however, may bring together documented and undocumented immigrant communities, political and environmental refugees and asylum seekers, and guest workers from around the world, including Mexico and Central America, Latin America, Asia, Africa and the Middle East. They find common interests around human rights, labor rights, language rights, access to education, family reunification, against deportations, against racism, and against the hyper exploitation of women in their communities. They also bring ties to international concerns in their respective countries of origin. Here we see the potential of coming together around multiple identities and intersections. Certainly, the thousands of Central Americans seeking asylum at the U.S.-Mexico border, mostly families with children, who are being kept in what amounts to concentration camps has the potential of drawing strong support from Japanese-Americans who remember a similar history of vilification and incarceration in internment camps during WWII.

The heart-breaking scenes of young children torn from their families and the criminal treatment they are receiving upon arriving at our borders and being denied entry for months thereafter has brought out people across multiple sectors to join massive demonstrations and publicly denounce this devastating injustice. Numerous women's groups, including the National Domestic Workers Alliance, the National Asian Pacific American Women Forum, Black Lives Matter, and the National Organization for Women have joined forces to keep families together and fight deportations. In a similar vein, the "Abuelitas Responden" was a movement of grandmothers travelling by caravan to the Mexican border that brought grandmothers across race and other identities in support of migrant families.[80]

Indigenous nations and organizations have also come forward in support of immigrants, even though there may be some who consider them "settlers." There seems to be a difference between theoretical arguments and what actually people stand up for. Indigenous peoples recognize the rights of every people to seek a place to live and work and when it comes to actual policies that can affect people immediately, there is a strong sense of solidarity among Indigenous peoples and immigrants. This is especially so in regards migrants from the Americas who the Indigenous people recognize to have Native ancestry.

Building Solidarity and Remaking the World

In this chapter, I have shown that there are significant tensions between racialized communities and even within them. Yet there is a long history of collectivizing between diverse racialized communities at key moments in history. As Cedric Robinson has shown, the first point of refuge for Black slaves running away was the Indian Reservation where Indigenous people and Black peoples forged important resistance movements.[81]

This solidarity is being evidenced today, as injustices mount against all those who are marginalized and exploited within the settler-colonial state. The injustice and violence experienced by the Sioux Nation regarding the Dakota Access Pipeline drew people in support of Indigenous rights from many parts of the United States and from many racial and cultural backgrounds. Keedra Gibba, a Black woman who visited Standing Rock in support of the Sioux Nation against the Dakota Access Pipeline, reflects:

> The same white supremacist ideology that fuels some Indigenous people's anti-Blackness is the same ideology that was at the root of my ancestors' actions as "Buffalo Soldiers."[82]

I would add to Gibba's analysis that "White supremacist ideology" is closely tied up with capitalism and colonialism. Gibba continues:

> As a "stolen person on stolen land," I am rooting for Indigenous peoples' sovereignty. The struggle at Standing Rock has reminded me that we as a people are dependent upon the land rather than owners of it, a philosophy embraced by my African ancestors nearly 200,000 years ago. This knowledge still runs in my blood. ... We too understand that water is life.[83]

I believe these are the connections that we need to be making in order to build coalitions that challenge the capitalist system that is central to human suffering and that pits us against each other. Obviously bringing down capitalism will not necessarily solve the various contentions discussed in this chapter, particularly around land and making space for everyone but self-determination, freedom from property and domination, and the recognition of mutual responsibility to human beings and to the Earth will not happen as long as capitalism is allowed to structure our lives.

Some scholars have begun thinking about what it would mean to reconcile some of these tensions. Manu Karuka argues in favor of Black and Indigenous self-determination as opposed to liberation and sovereignty, which Karuka claims are divisive goals that do not account for the human rights and needs and the histories of oppression that each group has suffered. Karuka argues that such goals have kept us from advancing a humanistic co-existence built on solidarity as peoples that have both been and continue to be treated with a genocidal violence by the very fact that it attempt to structure forms of reparation and space through the same logic of capital and colonialism—a logic of individualism, property, and competition.

According to Leanne Simpson, "treaty processes" existed long before colonization between Indigenous nations based on the "common Indigenous ethics of justice, peace, respect, reciprocity, and accountability" and "grounded in the worldviews, language, knowledge systems, and political cultures of the nations involved."[84] In her analysis of the Haudenosaunee and Nishnaabeg Nations, Simpson points out that Gdoo-naaganinaa, the Dish with One Spoon treaty, binds them to sharing their resources and trading while honoring each other's political and cultural forms. Simpson's analysis of early treaties points to Indigenous beliefs that the treaties were an invitation for the Eurocanadians to learn the Indigenous way of life and how Indigenous people related to the land while also sharing their own technologies, which is certainly not what the White man sought. Simpson argues that for the Nishnaabeg Nation, self-determination means living "the good life," which is based on developing relationships "that when practiced continually and in perpetuity, maintains peaceful coexistence, respect, and mutual benefit."[85]

Notes

1. Irene Watson, "Settled and Unsettled Spaces: Are We Free to Roam?"
2. For a critique of Marx's theory of primitive accumulation, see Glen Sean Coulthard, *Red Skin, White Masks*.
3. See John Bellamy Foster, "Marx's Theory of Metabolic Rift."
4. Evelyn Nakano Glenn, "Settler Colonialism as Structure."

5. Karl Marx, *Capital*, Vol. I, chapter 26.
6. Paulo Freire, *Pedagogy of the Oppressed*, chapter 4.
7. See the works of Indigenous scholars Joanne Barker, Glen Coulthard, Mishuana Goeman, Sandy Grande, Evelyn Nakano Glenn, Audra Simpson, and others.
8. Andrea Smith, "Not an Indian Tradition."
9. Ramon Grosfoguel, "The Structure of Knowledge in Westernized Universities."
10. Karen Stote, "The Coercive Sterilization of Aboriginal Women in Canada"; Victoria Haskins and Margaret D. Jacobs, "Stolen Generations and Vanishing Indians."
11. Glenn, "Settler Colonialism as Structure."
12. See Orlando Patterson, *Slavery and Social Death*; see Frank Wilderson III, *Red, White, & Black*; see also Jared Sexton, "People-of-Color Blindness."
13. Ibid., 115.
14. Ken Lawrence, *Karl Marx on American Slavery*.
15. Roger L. Ransom, *Conflict and Compromise*.
16. Edward E. Baptist, *The Half Has Never Been Told*.
17. Glenn, "Settler Colonialism as Structure."
18. Peter Hudis, "Rethinking the Dialectic of Race and Class."
19. See Manu Karuka, "Black and Native Visions of Self Determination." See also Iyko Day, "Being or Nothingness."
20. Glenn, "Settler Colonialism as Structure"; Iyko Day, *Alien Capital*.
21. Glenn, "Settler Colonialism as Structure."
22. Carlos G. Vélez-Ibáñez, *Border Visions*.
23. Mae M. Ngai, *Impossible Subjects*.
24. Ibid.
25. Ibid., 131.
26. Glenn, "Settler Colonialism as Structure."
27. Gregory Velazco y Trianosky, "Mestizaje and Hispanic Identity."
28. William I. Robinson, *Latin America and Global Capitalism*.
29. Patrisia Macías-Rojas, *From Deportation to Prison*.
30. Diane-Michele Prindeville, "Feminist Nations?"
31. Manu Karuka, "Black and Native Visions of Self Determination."
32. Joanne Barker, "Indigenous Feminisms."
33. Karuka, "Black and Native Visions of Self Determination."
34. Ibid., 87.
35. Ibid.
36. Ibid.
37. Candace Fujikane, Introduction to *Asian Settler Colonialism*; Patrick Wolfe, "Recuperating Binarism."
38. Fujikane, Introduction to *Asian Settler Colonialism*.
39. Ibid., 4–5.
40. Karuka, "Black and Native Visions of Self Determination."
41. Haunani-Kay Trask, *From a Native Daughter*, 25.
42. See Rice vs Cayetano, Legal Information Institute, Cornell University Law School, https://www.law.cornell.edu/supct/html/98-818.ZO.html.
43. Glenn, "Settler Colonialism as Structure."

44. According to Bureau of Labor Statistics (BLS) data, income averages reveal that women earn, on average, less than their male counterparts across all racial groups and that Black, Indigenous, Latinx, and Pacific Islander (racialized as Asian) women and men earn less than White and Asian women. See Worldatlas, "Income Inequality by Race and Gender in the U.S." See also, AAUW, *The Simple Truth About the Gender Pay Gap*. Another measure is put out by Urban Institute, which shows overall wealth of Blacks and Latinx communities significantly below that of Whites. See Urban Institute, "Nine Charts About Wealth Inequality in America."

45. Christian Edlagan and Kavya Vaghul, "How data disaggregation matters for Asian Americans and Pacific Islanders"; see also Worldatlas, "Income Inequality By Race and Gender In the U.S."

46. Lilia D. Monzó, "Marx in the Age of Trump."

47. Frederick T. L. Leong and James A. Grand, "Career and work implications of the Model Minority Myth."

48. Stacey J. Lee and Kevin Kumashiro, *A Report on the Status of Asian Americans and Pacific Islanders in Education*.

49. Ibid.

50. Stacey J. Lee, Choua Xiong, Linda Marie Pheng and Mai Neng Vang, "The Model Minority Maze: Hmong Americans Working Within and Around Racial Discourses."

51. Stacey J. Lee and Kevin Kumashiro, *A Report on the Status of Asian Americans and Pacific Islanders in Education*.

52. Ibid.

53. Stacey J. Lee et al., "The Model Minority Maze: Hmong Americans," 3.

54. Mia Tuan, *Forever Foreigners or Honorary Whites?*

55. Signithia Fordham and John Ogbu, Black students' school success: Coping with the "burden of 'acting white.'"

56. Iyko Day, *Alien Capital*.

57. Ibid., 3.

58. Ibid.

59. John Holloway, *Crack Capitalism*.

60. Vélez-Ibáñez, *Border Visions*.

61. It is necessary to note here that the Muslim community has also been falsely and severely criminalized and targeted in the U.S. I will, however, focus here on the criminalization of the Mexican and Central American im(migrants) that have a unique colonial history with the U.S.

62. Ronald W. Walters, *White Nationalism, Black Interests*.

63. Vélez-Ibáñez, *Border Visions*.

64. Ngai, *Impossible Subjects*, 56–75.

65. Ibid.

66. Ibid.

67. Ibid.

68. Ibid.

69. Ibid.

70. Walters, *White Nationalism, Black Interests*.

71. NOW, "Immigration as a Feminist Issue." Retrieved Nov. 19, 2018, https://now.org/resource/immigration-as-a-feminist-issue/; Mary Bauer and Mónica Ramirez, *Injustice on Our Plates*.
72. Ibid.
73. Etan Newman, *No Way to Treat a Guest*.
74. Ibid.
75. Mary C.Waters, Philip Kasinitz, and Asad L. Asad, "Immigrants and African Americans."
76. Ibid.
77. Patrisia Macías-Rojas, *From Deportation to Prison*.
78. Michelle Alexander, *The New Jim Crow*.
79. GEO Group spent $350,000 on lobbying during the first quarter of 2017. Federal filings show that a subsidiary of GEO Group also donated $250,000 to President Trump's inaugural festivities and another $225,000 to a super PAC that supported his election. In federal filings, GEO Group named "homeland security" and "immigration" among the main issues its lobbyists discussed with lawmakers. The increase in lobbying come as Trump attempted to push Congress to allocate $1.4 billion for the initial construction of the border wall and add $4.5 billion to the already-massive budget for immigration enforcement, including $1.5 billion to expand the nation's immense network of immigration jails. See Mike Ludwig, "Trump's Immigration Budget Is Based on Xenophobia, Not Facts"; Mike Ludwig, "Private Prison and Border Security Contractors Lobby Congress Over Trump's Border Wall."
80. Lornet Turnbull, "Caravan of Grandmothers Heads to Mexico Border."
81. Cedric J. Robinson, *Black Movements in America*.
82. Keedra Gibba, "Stolen People On Stolen Land: Standing Rock and Black Liberation," para. 7.
83. Ibid., para 12–13.
84. Leanne Simpson, "Looking After Gdoo-naaganinaa," 29.
85. Ibid., 35.

Bibliography

AAUW (American Association of University Women). *The Simple Truth About the Gender Pay Gap*. Fall 2018 Edition https://www.aauw.org/aauw_check/pdf_download/show_pdf.php?file=The_Simple_Truth

Alexander, Michelle. *The New Jim Crow: Mass Incarceration in the Age of Colorblindness*. New York: The New Press, 2010.

Baptist, Edward E. *The Half Has Never Been Told: Slavery and the Making of American Capitalism*. New York: Basic Book, 2014.

Barker, Joanne. "Indigenous Feminisms." In *the Oxford Handbook of Indigenous People's Politics*, edited by José Antonio Lucero, Dale Turner, and Donna Lee VanCott. Oxford University Press, Online publication, 2015. https://www.academia.edu/14991489/ Indigenous_Feminisms_2015_

Bauer, Mary and Mónica Ramírez. *Injustice on Our Plates*. Montgomery, AL: Southern Poverty Law Center, 2010. https://www.splcenter.org/20101107/injustice-our-plates

Day, Iyko. "Being or Nothingness: Indigeneity, Antiblackness, and Settler Colonial Critique." *Ethnic Studies 1*, no. 2 (2015): 102–121.

———. *Alien Capital: Asian Racialization and the Logic of Settler Colonial Capitalism*. Durham: Duke University Press, 2016.

Coulthard, Glen Sean. *Red Skin, White Masks: Rejecting the Colonial Politics of Recognition*. Menneapolis, MN: University of Minnesota, 2014.

Edlagan, Christian and Kavya Vaghul. "How Data Disaggregation Matters for Asian Americans and Pacific Islanders." Washington Center for Equitable Growth. December 14, 2016. https://equitablegrowth.org/how-data-disaggregation-matters-for-asian-americans-and-pacific-islanders/

Fordham, Sygnithia and John U. Ogbu. "Black Students' School Success: Coping with the 'Burden of Acting White,'" *The Urban Review 18*, no. 3 (1986): 176–206.

Foster, John Bellamy. "Marx's Theory of Metabolic Rift: Classical Foundations for Environmental Sociology." *The American Journal of Sociology 105*, no. 2 (1999): 366–405.

Freire, Paulo. *Pedagogy of the Oppressed, 30th anniversary edition*. New York: Bloomsbury, 2000.

Fujikane, Candace. "Introduction." In Asian Settler Colonialism: From Local Governance to the Habits of Everyday Life in Hawai'i, edited by Candace Fujikane and Jonathan Y. Okamura, 1–42. Honolulu, HI: University of Hawaii Press, 2008.

Gibba, Keedra. "Stolen People On Stolen Land: Standing Rock and Black Liberation." *Portside*. December 14, 2016. https://portside.org/2016-12-14/stolen-people-stolen-land-standing-rock-and-black-liberation

Glenn, Evelyn Nakano. "Settler Colonialism as Structure: A Framework for Comparative Studies of U.S. Race and Gender Formation." *Sociology of Race and Ethnicity 1*, no. 1 (2015): 54 –74.

Grosfoguel, Ramon. "The Structure of Knowledge in Westernized Universities: Epistemic Racism/Sexism and the Four Genocides/Epistemicides of the Long 16th Century." *Human Architecture: Journal of the Sociology of Self-Knowledge 11*, no. 1 (2013): 73–90.

Haskins, Victoria and Margaret D. Jacobs. "Stolen Generations and Vanishing Indians: The Removal of Indigenous Children as a Weapon of War in the United States and Australia,1870–1 940." In *Children and War: A Historical Anthology*, edited by James Marten, 227–241. New York University Press, 2002.

Holloway, John. *Crack Capitalism*. New York: Pluto Press, 2010.

Hudis, Peter. "Rethinking the Dialectic of Race and Class." Paper Presented at the Public Meeting of the International Marxist Humanist Organization, March 11, 2018.

Karuka, Manu. "Black and Native Visions of Self-Determination." *Critical Ethnic Studies 3*, No. 2 (2017): 77–98.

Lawrence, Ken. *Karl Marx on American Slavery*. Sojourner Truth Organization, 1976. http://www.sojournertruth.net/marxslavery.pdf

Lee, Stacey J., Choua Xiong, Linda Marie Pheng and Mai Neng Vang. "The Model Minority Maze: Hmong Americans Working Within and Around Racial Discourses." *Journal of Southeast Asian American Education and Advancement 12*, no. 2 (2017): 1–20.

Lee, Stacey J., and Kevin Kumashiro. *A Report on the Status of Asian Americans and Pacific Islanders in Education: Beyond the Model Minority Stereotype*. Washington, DC: National Education Association Human and Civil Rights, 2005.

Leong, Frederick T. L., and James A. Grand. "Career and Work Implications of the Model Minority Myth and Other Stereotypes for Asian Americans." In *Model Minority Myths Revisited: An Interdisciplinary Approach to Demystifying Asian American Education Experiences*, edited by G. Li & L. Wang, 91–115. Charlotte, NC: Information Age Publishing, 2008.

Ludwig, Mike. "Trump's Immigration Budget Is Based on Xenophobia, Not Facts." *Truthout*, March 17, 2017. https://truthout.org/articles/trump-s-immigration-budget-is-based-on-xenophobia-not-facts/

———."Private Prison and Border Security Contractors Lobby Congress Over Trump's Border Wall." *Truthout*, April 25, 2017. https://truthout.org/articles/private-prison-and-border-security-contractors-lobby-congress-over-trump-s-border-wall/.

Macías-Rojas, Patrisia. *From Deportation to Prison: The Politics of Immigration Enforcement in Post-Civil Rights America.* New York University Press, 2016.

Marx, Karl. *Capital*, Vol. I. Translated by Ben Fowkes. New York: Vintage Books, 1977.

Monzó, Lilia D. "Marx in the Age of Trump: Reaching Out to Communities of Color." *International Marxist Humanist Organization*, Feb. 1, 2017. https://www.internationalmarxisthumanist.org/wp-content/uploads/Monzo-women-rev.pdf

Newman, Etan. *No Way to Treat a Guest. Farmworker Justice.* Retrieved April 11, 2019. https://www.farmworkerjustice.org/sites/default/files/documents/7.2.a.6%20fwj.pdf

Ngai, Mae M. 2004. *Impossible Subjects: Illegal Aliens and the Making of Modern America.* Princeton, NJ: Princeton University Press.

NOW (National Organization for Women). "Immigration as a Feminist Issue." Retrieved November 19, 2018. https://now.org/resource/immigration-as-a-feminist-issue/.

Patterson, Orlando. *Slavery and Social Death: A Comparative Study.* Cambridge, MA: Harvard University Press, 1985.

Prindeville, Diane-Michele. "Feminist Nations? A Study of Native American Women in Southwestern Tribal Politics." *Political Research Quarterly 57*, no. 1 (2004): 101–112.

Ransom, Roger L. *Conflict and Compromise.* Cambridge, England: Cambridge University Press, 1989.

Robinson, Cedric J. *Black Movements in America.* New York: Routledge, 1997.

Sexton, Jared. "People-of-Color-Blindness: Notes on the Afterlife of Slavery." *Social Text 28*, no. 2 (2010): 31–56.

Simpson, Leanne. "Looking After Gdoo-naaganinaa: Precolonial Nishnaabeg Diplomatic and Treaty Relationships." *Wicazo Sa Review 23*, no. 2 (2008): 29–43.

Smith, Andrea. "Not an Indian Tradition: The Sexual Colonization of Native Peoples." *Hypatia* 18, no. 2 (2003): 70–85.

Stote, Karen. "The Coercive Sterilization of Aboriginal Women in Canada." *American Indian Culture and Research Journal* 36, no. 3 (2012): 117–150.

Trask, Haunani-Kay. *From a Native Daughter: Colonialism and Sovereignty in Hawai'i.* Honolulu: University of Hawai'i Press, 1999.

Tuan, Mia. *Forever Foreigners or Honorary Whites?: The Asian Ethnic Experience Today.* New Brunswick, NJ: Rutgers University Press, 1998.

Turnbull, Lornet. "Caravan of Grandmothers Heads to Mexico Border." *Truthout*, July 13, 2018. https://truthout.org/articles/caravan-of-grandmothers-heads-to-mexico-border/

Urban Institute. "Nine Charts About Wealth Inequality in America (Updated)." October 5, 2017. http://apps.urban.org/features/wealth-inequality-charts/

Velazco y Trianosky, Gregory. "Mestizaje and Hispanic Identity." In *A Companion to Latin American Philosophy*, edited by Susana Nuccetelli, Ofelia Schutte, and Otávio Bueno, 283–296. Malden, MA: Blackwell Publishing, 2013.

Vélez-Ibáñez, Carlos G. *Border Visions: Mexican Cultures of the Southwest United States*. Tucson: University of Arizona Press, 1996.

Walters, Ronald W. *White Nationalism, Black Interests: Conservative Public Policy and the Black Community*. Detroit, MI: Wayne State University Press, 2003.

Waters, Mary C., Philip Kasinitz, and Asad L. Asad. "Immigrants and African Americans." *Annual Review of Sociology* 40 (2014): 369–390.

Watson, Irene. "Settled and Unsettled Spaces: Are We Free to Roam?" *Australian Critical Race and Whiteness Studies Association Journal* 1 (2005): 40–52.

Wilderson III, Frank B. *Red, White, & Black: Cinema and the Structure of U.S. Antagonisms*. Duke University Press.

Wolfe, Patrick. "Recuperating Binarism: A Heretical Introduction." *Settler Colonial Studies* 3, nos. 3–4 (2013): 257–279.

Worldatlas. "Income Inequality by Race and Gender in the U.S." Retrieved Nov. 17, 2018. https://www.worldatlas.com/articles/income-inequality-by-race-and-gender-in-the-u-s.html

· 8 ·

PEDAGOGY OF DREAMING

That's the power of imagination, peeking beyond the fence of your personal reality and seeing the possibilities thereafter.

—Helena María Viramontes[1]

Ultimately, cynicism is the great mask of the disappointed and betrayed heart.

—bell hooks[2]

This book has been my attempt to argue that transforming the world is our only salvation as a species being, both physical and morally, and that Women of Color—Indigenous women, Black women, Latinx women, Asian women, Middle Eastern women, Muslim women, Ethnic minoritized women, and all non-western women—present significant "revolutionary reason and force" to this gargantuan task. Not only do we bring the impetus that can come only from a place of enormous oppression and pain, but also, we bring an ontological, epistemological, and axiological diversity that may shed light on how to organize the world toward peace, equality, real democracy, freedom and love.

Without a doubt, this will require multiple and interlocking struggles; Women of Color are generally oppressed and exploited on three different axes—class, race, and gender—but many also face oppression due to sexuality, gender fluidity, religion, and/or other marginalized identities. Transforming the world requires us to develop an alternative to capitalism but it also requires that we eradicate all forms of oppression and exploitation. We cannot wait to establish more democratic economic formations to begin addressing the antagonisms that make us bleed figuratively and sometimes literally.[3] It requires a commitment to end racism and sexism and other oppressions for us to begin to trust each other sufficiently to work together to collectively confront capital; this is especially true in the industrialized world where state control and military power are enormous.[4] Even if we were able to pull it off, without a serious and evidenced commitment to equality and freedom—which requires a challenge to all oppressions—a socialist alternative would not be sustainable under a system that maintains relations of domination.

Karl Marx has given us a socialist imaginary. Through his work and ideas we can dream of developing a new humanism that develops our species being through new values and social relations that are built on equality and cooperation rather than competition and individualism.[5] It is his vision of the future that has left us some ideas of how to develop an economic system that is *actually* democratically controlled by the people, wherein every person is inherently equally valued and perceived as interdependent with all other live forms. But we cannot focus solely on transformation at broad levels of action; praxis is a dialectical process not only in the unification of objective and subjective transformation but also at the level of structural and interpersonal social relations. The revolutionary must live their lives to the greatest extent possible with coherence to their revolutionary ideals.

For this Paulo Freire has much to teach us. His philosophical analysis of the relations between oppressed and oppressors and his concrete engagement with praxis, hope, solidarity, and dreaming—dialectically defined concepts that move us to struggle not only in large movements and protests or in community actions projects, but within every sphere within our daily living—are at the heart of transformation. Few works have been as enlightening and inspiring to me as Freire's *Pedagogy of the Oppressed*.[6] I recall that reading it for the first time was a transformative experience and each subsequent reading of this and Freire's other works remind me that history is possibility and that it is up to us to dream up a world that honors our human potential to love and respect each other and to live with joy and awe. From there, of course, we must take action and transform the world to make our dreams come true.

Often touted as the greatest education philosopher of the 20th century, Freire's work espouses a profoundly humanist philosophy about how to live in this world as Subjects—human beings who act in the world—learning, loving, hoping, and dreaming. His work was about more than education in the formal sense but about how to walk with others, learning together and paving the path for this long and never-ending journey toward freedom.

Freire argued that we must name the truths of injustice, examining the social structures that oppress but also the individuals who, knowingly and sometimes unknowingly, enforce these structures that benefit some at the expense of the many; and this includes ourselves for we too, even amidst our activist work for social change sometimes find ourselves hopeless and alone, engulfed with our own pains and fears, which although very real, are debilitating to a political project that demands the affirmation of life and love.[7] The dehumanizing social relations that he articulates between oppressed and oppressors, which normalize and further entrench systems of domination by their very subtle insinuation into every sphere of our daily lives, awakens our indignation and our human desire to struggle for what is just. Freire argued that it is the human vocation of the oppressed to liberate themselves and their oppressors:

> This, then, is the great humanistic and historical fact of the oppressed: to liberate themselves and their oppressors as well. The oppressors who oppress, exploit, and rape by virtue of their power, cannot find in this power the strength to liberate either the oppressed or themselves. Only power that springs from the weakness of the oppressed will be sufficiently strong to free both.[8]

His hopefulness reflects an authentic faith in the oppressed to lead the way. It is through this love and trust that acknowledges our humanity that we become conscious beings for ourselves rather than for the oppressors. Education is, of course, an important context within which to engage a humanizing pedagogy. Yet pedagogy does not refer to teaching methods or techniques; rather it is a moral and political practice that develops our human capacities and vocation to engage the world as critical citizens.[9]

Paulo Freire was born and raised in Recife, Brazil to a middle-class family. An economic downturn pushed his family into poverty wherein he experienced significant deprivation and even hunger. This experience undoubtedly influenced his understandings of structural constraints and yet he denounced cynicism and fatalism. He grew to understand that amidst sociohistorical and economic constraints we have agency to change the course of history. Like the women who shared their stories in the previous chapter, Freire also had a model of agency early in his life; with no financial means to send the young

Paulo to high school, his mother set out to find him a school that would grant him a scholarship and succeeded in doing so.[10]

Paulo Freire grew up to become a great educator and to develop a highly successful approach to literacy education that contextualized the development of literacy within historical economic, social, and political structures. Rather than the mere communicative tool that is presumed and presented as a neutral skill, Paulo recognized literacy as both reflective and constitutive of particular histories and socioeconomic and political positionings.[11] Seen in this light literacy is a way of knowing the world that brings forth an ontological clarity or conscientizacao, which has the power to mobilize the oppressed to transform the world.[12] Once recognized as a process for liberation, it is easy to understand why literacy has been purposely kept from the most oppressed communities or distorted into a set of discreet skills divorced from its key role in our understanding and development of the social relations with which we make history. In the sense that to be human is to be a Subject,—an actor in the world and not an object to be acted upon—understanding the world and our roles within it is a humanizing pedagogy. Freire dedicated his life to developing this literacy among poor, oppressed and exploited communities. In the process he developed a philosophy of liberation that engages an ethical praxis toward the humanization of the oppressed, which involves the dialectical transformation of our objective world and of our subjective selves.[13]

Freire drew heavily from Marx, particularly on his dialectical approach, his understanding of our human vocation to struggle for freedom, and in the development of praxis in the context of revolutionary struggle. Yet Freire challenged the western neglect of the body and spirit as ways of knowing, invoking the heart, emotions, and faith as key to making sense of and engaging in the world. While Marx dissected the capitalist system and articulated it as a series of social relations that were exploited for the purposes of capital accumulation, which in the process alienated and deformed humanity, Freire focused on the *interpersonal social relations* that as a result of capitalist production are steeped in relations of domination and are generally reproduced. Freire gave us a way to begin to dialectically transform these social relations by engaging an ethical praxis and developing ontological clarity, epistemological sophistication, and the impetus to walk the path to freedom.

Freire's humanizing pedagogy has been adapted in many parts of the world. In North America numerous scholars, including such giants as Henry Giroux, Peter McLaren, Donaldo Macedo, and Antonia Darder have extended his work under the umbrella of critical pedagogy.[14] Solidified as a specific area of studies in education, critical pedagogy is sometimes taught in progressive colleges of education with the goal of engaging teachers as Subjects in the world who can recognize the role of education in capitalist production processes and engage a humanizing pedagogy with their own students.[15] Many of these teacher educators have gone on to develop a critical pedagogy in their own primary and secondary school classrooms. As an educator I believe and have seen that classrooms can develop into transformative spaces when teachers engage with their students as human beings with a curiosity to know each other and the world.[16] But I also believe that to learn and be curious is a human vocation that is engaged with every breath we take no matter in what context we find ourselves.

In a way Marx guides our understanding of the deformation of humanity in capitalist relations and other antagonisms and Freire elucidates how we can begin the process of changing these social relations, creating contexts that humanize in the process of revolutionary praxis. As often happens when someone and or their work threatens those in power, Freire's humanizing philosophy has been domesticated. For example, his articulation of dialogue as epistemology—a way of knowing that can access the ontological reality of the oppressed—has been degenerated to a mere approach at better communication or making students feel valued. Others have argued that critical pedagogy is "just good teaching," abstracting it from its political project. Donaldo Macedo, who has introduced much of Freire's work to the English-speaking world, has often challenged this violent distortion of Freire's concepts, arguing that Freire always envisioned his *Pedagogy of the Oppressed* to have the goal of transforming society into a classless world.[17] Antonia Darder concurs with this analysis stating:

> ... Freire's work was "unabashedly grounded in Marxist-socialist thought. Without question, when Freire spoke of the "ruling class" or the "oppressors," he was referring to historical class distinctions and class conflict within the structure of capitalist society—capitalism was the root of domination. ... However for Freire, the struggle against economic domination could not be waged effectively without a humanizing praxis that could both engage the complex phenomena of class struggle and effectively foster the conditions for critical social agency among the masses.[18]

Indeed, if we examine his work with disenfranchised communities we learn that Freire was always concerned with their conditions of illiteracy as both a consequence and basis of poverty and how this poverty serviced the oppressors. Of course, Freire recognized other forms of oppression and resisted crude misrepresentation of Marx's works that were class reductionist and non-dialectical. He recognized oppression as manifested through a set of interlocking systems that include class, race, gender and other forms of oppressions and historically specific in their manifestations to the capitalist mode of production.[19] In an attempt to bring back the Marxist roots of Freire's work, Peter McLaren, following the work of Paula Allman, has developed a revolutionary critical pedagogy, which has a more focused lens toward challenging capitalist relations in favor of a socialist alternative.[20] Revolutionary critical pedagogy emphasizes how racism, sexism, and other antagonisms are produced within and hold up capitalist relations.[21]

Scholars and teachers who misrepresent Freire's philosophy of liberation and use it as a "feel good" education fail to grasp that authentic love of the oppressed—whether it be the poor, women, People of Color, LGBTQIA— means recognizing them as human beings deserving of the right to see reality for what it is, the possibilities for change that exist, and their own capacity to act in this world toward human goals.[22] Anything less is an education that preserves the structures of oppression and makes teachers complicit in this process.

One of my greatest disappointments in life is never having met Paulo Freire. Although embodying human frailties as we all do, by all accounts of the many who loved him, he lived out what he professed to the world—an openness of spirit, joyful in life, filled with hope and faith in humanity, and uncompromising in his quest for justice. However, I have been very fortunate to come to know a number of people who, by their own confession, were touched forever by the hand and love of Paulo Freire. They often share their stories of Freire and of their time with him with nostalgia and deep admiration.[23] His name is never far from their lips. Many recognize love to be an enduring facet of Freire's philosophy. Peter McLaren describes the dialectical way in which Freire embodied love:

> For Freire, love is preeminently and irrevocably dialogical. It is not an attachment or emotion isolated from the everyday world; rather it viscerally emerges from an act of daring, of courage, of critical reflection. Love is the fire that ignites not only the revolutionary but also the creative action of the artist, wielding a palette of sinew and spirit on a canvas of thought and action, its explosion of meaning forever synchronized with the gasp of human freedom.[24]

Antonia Darder points out his enduring passion for life and to be alive:

> For Paulo Freire, life was unquestionably his most enduring passion ... to be passionate and to love in the midst of all our fears, anxieties, and imperfections truly constituted powerful expressions of our humanity. ...[25]

Henry Giroux points out his enduring faith in humanity and commitment to struggle:

> His very presence embodied what it meant to combine political struggle and moral courage, to make hope meaningful and despair unpersuasive. Paulo was vigilant in bearing witness to the individual and collective suffering of others, but shunned the role of the isolated intellectual as an existential hero who struggles alone. For Freire, intellectuals must match their call for making the pedagogical more political with an ongoing effort to build those coalitions, affiliations and social movements capable of mobilizing real power and promoting substantive social change.

Donaldo Macedo reminds us that when we need inspiration we can look to Freire:

> His words of wisdom, his penetrating and insightful ideas, his courage to denounce in order to announce, his courage to love and "to speak about love without fear of being ascientific, if not antiscientific," his humility and his humanity make him immortal—a forever present force that keeps alive our understanding of history as possibility.[26]

To hold such love and hope in a world fraught with pain can only happen when we dare to dream of a future wherein every human being lives with love and dignity—a classless society founded on equality and freedom—and to believe fully in our capacity as human beings to make this dream come true. We move to act toward our humanization, and take the necessary risk this undoubtedly requires, when through our dreams of the future we can see that we have the potential to be so much more than we are—to be a people who inspire love and hope and courage. It is this dreaming that allows us to trust in the people who have for too long been judged deficient and to open ourselves to see and understand the broader structural relations that have led to such positioning. Although praxis is often discussed in terms of broad-based struggle, dialectically speaking, praxis is also about the change that happens within us as we struggle and change our objective social conditions. A vision of the future is a necessary aspect of our humanity since our impetus to act has to have some sense of what we are acting for and where we are walking to. Without dreams we flounder.

In 2014, I had the honor to meet and spend a week with Nita Freire who visited our campus for the renaming of the Paulo Freire archives at the Leatherby Library. According to Donaldo Macedo, Nita Freire is the most authentic and competent of Freirean scholars not only because of her intimate relationship with Paulo Freire as his wife, but also because they engaged a deeply dialogical relationship that deepened and extended Freirean concepts.[27] This is quite evident in *Chronicles of Love* wherein we see Nita and Paulo Freire living out the pedagogy they espouse(d) in their daily lives.

Meeting her, I was immediately enthralled by her beauty and grace. I observed that she walked through our campus that week with a penetrating gaze and a curiosity that seemed to touch our souls beneath the surface of our daily chatter and niceties. She carried a quiet confidence that can only stem from a profound clarity and wisdom, perhaps made more evident because the slight language barrier led us to communicate beyond words—through expressions of joy, concern, and love. A dream of mine is to one day walk with the grace she displayed and it is with that dream that this project developed.

In this chapter I develop a pedagogy of dreaming as an essential aspect of our political project to create a new society. We are often led to believe that dreaming is a distraction or even an obstacle. Here I argue that in fact dreaming is an aspect of moving forward in the world and the denial of its existence and its capacity to help us understand and make history serves capitalist interests. For Indigenous women and Women of Color, dreaming may allow us to perceive our right to exist in the world as human beings beyond our historical experience. I end this chapter with a section inspired by Nita Freire, and aimed at Women of Color on "walking with grace"—engaging a pedagogy of dreaming that nourishes our spiritual vocation to walk courageously into the future with a profound political commitment to human freedom.

Why Dreaming?

History as development and possibility demands that we dream. I am not referring to subconscious images during sleep but rather to a vision of the future that reflects our desires.[28] By development, I do not mean the distorted capitalist version that ties human growth to capital accumulation but rather growth in our capacity to be human and in our social development as a people to ward off disease and human suffering. Over and over again in Freire's work we find the idea that humanity can be continuously improved, that we are always unfinished and on a journey to becoming more fully human. Marx, before Freire, espoused a similar ontological understanding. Although he developed a communist imaginary he never expressed this to be the end of history, rather it was the next phase in our continuous human quest for freedom.[29]

History as possibility recognizes our human agency to choose and take the steps that set us on a particular path to the future. In the Hegelian sense of the positive always being held within the negative, Marx argued that socialism would emerge from the womb of capitalism. Yet this does not suggest that there is nothing new to be created; instead, it means that aspects of the future are contained within the present such that the negation of the present conditions of inequality, injustice, racism, sexism, and ultimately capitalism will highlight its opposites. If we look we can see this everywhere. I fully believe that most human beings in the world have a tendency toward goodness and justice but these tendencies are easily clouded by the existence of the negative that dominates our world—fear, greed, narcissism—all created by a system that feeds off of these conditions.

This first negation, however, is never sufficient. Merely acknowledging and asserting our human right to freedom will not bring down the oppressive structures of our world. We need a double negation—the negation of the negation is a decisive STRIKE that brings down the capitalist system and allows us to create a new society. It is my hope that this new society will be in the image of Marx and Freire's vision—a classless, anti-racist, anti-sexist system that denounces all forms of oppression and develops freedom, equality, and value for all life forms, including the Earth that sustains us; however, this is not predetermined. Structures develop conditions of possibility that we as human beings generally make choices within but that we can also chose to destroy.

While there are elements of this new society in the current system—free lunch programs, for example—these would not be adopted in the same manner. Certainly, in a society that recognizes the inherent value of every person, we would want to establish a system of food distribution that was accessible to everyone, not just students and not just for school lunch. The progression of history as continuous movement requires that we create and this requires that we dream. While some acknowledge that history informs our present, few recognize that in fact the future also informs our present. It is through dreaming that we know what steps to take to move forward.

Yes, it is common to fear ridicule when we talk about dreaming. In our society dreamers are often believed to be "failures," or people who "don't get things done." Students are often told to "stop day dreaming and get to work." The popular and sarcastic phrase "dream on" suggests that a particular idea or desire is impossible or will never happen. Instead, those who fear the ridicule of a society that defines rationality narrowly will call this "envisioning" or "imagining."

Yet dreaming is not always as we've been made to believe: pure fantasy. Our dreams are often reconfigurations of what already exists in the world and thus plausible alternatives to the way things are. However, even when our dreams are fantastic—flying, for example—they can reflect a deeper desire that can be fulfilled in realistic ways. Vygotsky showed that children's play, especially their use of the imagination and fantasy play, were important ways in which children began to make sense of as well as critique the world around them.[30]

Importantly dreaming suggests a belief in the possibility to achieve that which does not yet exist. This is an important stimulant for creating hope and impetus for changing the world. In that it presents desired outcomes, dreaming can gives us courage to move forward. It can create opportunities for rehearsal and planning. It can provide a visual representation, making the realization of our dreams that much more plausible. Without dreaming, we move in darkness and perhaps in circles without a clear direction because the fear of the unknown can be overwhelming—like entering into a pitch-dark room without any sense of what lies in wait. Without dreaming we can become paralyzed and hold onto the familiarity of what is—too afraid to trust in the unknown to take the necessary next step.

For some people dreaming can produce fear, especially for those who do not see history as possibility. It requires courage because in our dreams we see our desires actualized and later cannot pretend to be happy with a reality that is less than satisfactory. When we dream of a loving encounter we can no longer pretend that a less beautiful encounter is acceptable. Dreaming then gives us fresh insights into the problems that exist in the world as it is. Dreaming allows us to articulate not only the limitations of what we now experience but also what new social relations we can create.

In *Marx's Alternative to Capitalism*, Peter Hudis examines Marx's many works in search of any clues to his vision of the new society that he believed would develop out of the ruins of capitalism. While he did not use the term dreaming it was precisely by envisioning what could be possible in the future that Marx developed his conception of a new humanism. According to Hudis:

> Marx definitely understood his role as delineating the "law of motion" of capitalism toward its collapse, but the very fact that he analyzed it with this aim in mind, suggests that he approached his subject matter with a conception of the necessity for its transcendence.[31]

Imagining the transcendence of capitalism is undoubtedly a projection of the future. However, for Marx, dreaming was not a utopian fantasy. Rather, Marx insisted that the new society would emerge out of the womb of capitalism.

Thus, elements of the new society were embedded in today's reality. Hudis comments:

> Normative considerations are as inescapable as language itself, precisely because what *ought* to be is inscribed within what *is*. It is not impossible to avoid reflection about the future nor is it desirable to avoid it—at least so long as such reflection has some grounding in *reality*.[32]

For example, Hudis argues that Marx's greatest concern was the alienation of human beings under capitalism. According to Hudis, Marx perceived that any new society must transcend capital and cease to create conditions wherein human beings were controlled by that which we ourselves produce.[33] To dream a new society wherein human beings do not experience alienation is not a dream that emerges out of thin air. Marx explained that we experience alienation in the process of commodity production—the commodity always has use value but it ceases to be recognized as embodying the creativity and energy of the human producer and instead gains an exchange value that is used against the human producers to confine them as slaves in the capital relation.[34] However, Marx recognized that not all production was commodity production. Within capitalism, examples of the production of use value without exchange value continue to exist, although mostly in personal relations. One example of the economy of use value can be found in food sharing cooperative gardens, wherein community members collectively manage the garden and grow fruits and vegetables for consumption. Often these cooperatives establish community kitchens and other share and trading practices. Unfortunately, such cooperatives are rare. Often the cooperatives turn to selling the products they produce and sharing the profits collectively. Although this can still have elements of use value production, it takes on aspects of value production as it enters the market. Of course, all examples within capitalism, though, run the risk of developing relations of domination and other aspects of capitalist relations. Nonetheless, we can see that Marx did not pull his ideas out a hat but drew from existing elements. How the economy could be organized to produce only use value is something Marx purposely did not discuss, lest his ideas be taken as prophetic rather than possibility.[35]

We find a similar pattern of possibility embedded in Freire's many works. As Giroux has often said, Freire provided us with a "language of critique and possibility."[36] Possibility, of course, is a project of the future. Indeed, it could not be otherwise for critique carries always some idea of how something can be better, even if how to make it better has not yet been worked out. Freire was explicit on the power of dreaming:

> There is no change without dreams just as there are no dreams without hope … the understanding of history as possibility rather than determinism … would be unintelligible without dreams. … Risk only makes sense when I run it for a valuable reason, an ideal, a dream beyond risk itself.[37]

Freire professed the possibility that exists in a humanizing education that transcends the dichotomous teacher-student relation in which teaching and learning are perceived separate processes. This humanizing education perceives learning a process involving mutual curiosity, dialogue, and praxis. The concepts Freire developed are not fantastic aberrations of reality but rather contain elements that can be evidenced in traditional classrooms but that occur perhaps spontaneously when perceived notions of what it means to be a teacher or student are relaxed and our human capacity to love and to see the value in the other emerges momentarily before we are immediately reminded of our prescribed teacher role.

Unlike Marx, Freire did not shy away from talking about dreaming, love, or hope. He embraced these concepts that are too often believed to be absent of scientific rigor because they are difficult to measure in traditional quantitative forms. However, Freire was keenly aware of different ways of knowing and thus embraced the use of constructs that allowed him to express a humanizing pedagogy in ways that, although difficult to measure, are indeed aspects of how human beings actually engage in the world. Although few of us may discuss our dreams or use the concept in our scholarly work, almost everyone likely recognizes and engages this activity in one way or another in their lives.

Freire followed Marx's lead in terms of recognizing human beings as the makers of history in whom agency—the ability and willingness to act to change the world—was our human vocation. But Freire recognized that the development of agency requires a humanizing pedagogy—one that transforms the dehumanization that we have experienced for centuries under capitalism and other structures of oppression. Freire argued that a humanizing education requires us to engage in the act of hoping and loving—human emotions deformed by commodity production but capable of being reinvented through an ethical revolutionary praxis.[38]

Paulo Freire was not only a dreamer of new worlds but also a dreamer in *this* world. His dreaming evidences the possibilities for transforming the world in developing a pedagogy of dreaming. In everyday stories of living and through Nita Freire's brilliant analysis—striking in its subtleness—we learn that dreaming helped to develop Freire's enduring patience, hope, and courage.[39] Donaldo Macedo points out that although Freire felt deep rage at injustice, it was his idealism—his "unyielding belief in utopia as possibility"—that shielded him from any sense of fatalism or cynicism.[40]

Dreaming as Epistemology: Challenging Temporal "Rationality" and the Politics of Now

History is generally conceived of as the past, that which already has taken place, a set of static events that occurred at a particular point in time. Indeed this is generally how we teach history. But history can be conceived more accurately as a process; most events can be traced back for years and have not only lasting effects on the present but guide our development toward the future. Thus the past and the present are always embedded in the future. In addition, and contrary to what we have been led to believe, the future is also an aspect of the present and the past since it is our quest for particular developments that propel us forward in specific directions. This conception of history gives great agency to human beings and allows us to better see the significant changes that we have accomplished as well as the process of long struggle, with many smaller struggles embedded, that we have forged. From this perspective a "failed revolution" can be seen as merely stalled or derailed. It can also be viewed as one of many revolutions moving in the same direction, providing different insights for future generations that continue the long struggle.

We can see how this conception of history can be problematic to the status quo, which would like us to believe that the past remains in the past and that we cannot do much about the future. Instead the future is individualized, making us believe that one's future is isolated from the future of others and of the world we live in. This individualistic orientation supports capitalism by precluding any collective activity. It is a western perspective on history wherein the past, present, and future are distinct. This approach serves the capitalist class's hegemonic control since it encourages immediate gratification, apathy and inertia for broad-based change, and systematically erases the history of struggle that has always been in existence and that transcends our own time and space.

Today we seem to have developed an obsession with the present—to make sure we don't miss out on what is happening *now*. We are told that a look at history just stirs up bad blood and a look at the future is a waste of time. The present is what matters and if we spend too much time remembering or dreaming then we will miss out on today. The current popularity in understanding that "the present is a gift" is another ploy by which to dismiss the complexity of time and abstract it from the past and future. This non-dialectical approach to time is being popularized among the middle classes as self-care—a now lucrative industry of the middle classes whose growing economic precarity, increasing productivity demands, and an ethos that associates our worth as human beings with how much money or goods we have accumulated, is resulting in high levels of stress and unhappiness.[41] A focus on the present allows the middle classes to turn inwards for relief and satisfaction while also spending their money on self-help classes, yoga, and other co-optations and exoticized Eastern wellness approaches. The popularity of Asian wellness approaches allow the predominantly White middle classes to believe that multiculturalism is on the rise and racism is being eradicated (even though the working class is still predominantly made up of People of Color). The White middle classes who exploit the Asian wellness industry believe themselves culturally progressive while simultaneously placing Asian communities at their service.

This focus on the present suggests we are wasting our lives if we contemplate the past or dream of the future. The consequence is the erasure of past atrocities against Indigenous peoples and People of Color and the possibility of recreating these in the future. The break from the past attempts to suggest that things have significantly improved. Yet we see clearly today that the struggle for civil rights of communities of color, Indigenous communities and for women have taken a turn back toward a past that was outwardly racist and misogynist.[42] Yet the past is always present—in the memories of those who have suffered and whose ancestors were enslaved and/or massacred and on whose blood and pain lays the very foundation of industrialization and capitalism.

Of course, a focus on the future puts us on a path toward transformation. The White supremacist capitalist class (the men especially) are happy with the way things are. They want things to stay the same. A focus on the present abstracted from the past and the future renders us passive and unchanging. Surprisingly this focus on the present is being touted as an aspect of the Buddha teachings. Although Buddha did teach about self-discipline and appreciation for our lives in the present, he did not disavow our responsibility to the people around us. Some would say he was a social activist in his own way, challenging the caste system and professing equality for women. His support of stillness of the mind through meditation was not meant to be a form of incubation from or rejection of the outside world. On the contrary, Buddha professed self-discipline and the rejection of greed and earthly desires as a way of reaching clarity about human suffering in the world in order to develop compassion for others and create conditions that alleviated suffering. While his approach did not involve the more common social activism of today, such as protesting and striking, his teachings do not support the new age focus on commodified feel-good therapies that distract us from the world's pain. This distortion has lent acceptability and legitimacy to an industry that has been coopted from ancient eastern traditions and commodified primarily for western consumers. This abstraction from the more dialectical understanding of time obscures our active role in making history.

Another way in which western conceptions of history aid in maintaining the status quo and discourage dreaming is through the measurement of time in equal increments. This notion of history generates a belief that change is so incremental that life is experienced as static, with each day leading us to the next in a monotonous routine that seems predetermined and outside of our control. This approach to history precludes the need to re-examine the past in light of the future. Dreaming that we can create a completely new society when most of our days are so routinized that they look exactly the same across months and sometimes years, seems implausible. Of course, capitalist society organizes our lives through lock-step routines that increase efficiency and productivity in order to maximize capital accumulation. This western notion of time serves hegemonic control as it encourages immediate gratification, apathy and inertia for broad-based change, and invalidates attempts at broad goals for the betterment of humanity beyond our own time and space. The belief that everything happens in lock-step supports complacency and inaction—the belief that we will end up where we need to be—that history determines our fate rather than that we determine history.

Walter Benjamin reconceptualizes history as messianic moments— moments that are so extraordinary that they rupture the course of history. He uses the "angel of history" as a metaphor to the new vantage point that allows us to understand the past and to envision the future. Messianic moments are, thus, revolutions—a praxis that galvanizes us to chart a new course in history. To conceive of history in this way is to see ourselves as the makers of history and to gain hope and agency that we can change the world because we always have. Messianic moments are not in step with development and therefore require willful action on our part as human beings. Walter Benjamin's angel of history is the prophet who can decipher the rubble left behind and lead us to the next messianic moment.

For Indigenous women and Women of Color dreaming is especially important epistemologically since we cannot know a past or a present without oppression—in every context of our lives we are oppressed and exploited. Only through dreaming can we recognize the possibility of our freedom and envision a future where we are treated as fully human.

Dialogue Beyond Words: Finding the Silence That Let the Other Speak

Dialogue as Freire meant it to be, an epistemological encounter, can be very difficult to achieve. It requires a reconceptualization of how we move through the world. The relations of domination that exist across our world and that are facilitated by the insistence of binaries—teacher/student, parent/child, man/woman, White/Person of Color, straight/gay—preclude the kind of epistemological encounter that Freire sought to create through dialogue. In a Freirean sense, dialogue is a way of knowing that engenders curiosity in the Other and respect for their culture and knowledge. To dialogue is an epistemological encounter that both reflects and develops each person's humanity. When we dialogue we listen fully to the other person and in doing so affirm that we have something to learn from them and that they have something worth teaching. For the oppressed this is a critical statement of validation of their humanity. Yet Frantz Fanon's insightful critique of Hegel's master/slave dialectic warns that the racialized woman cannot gain freedom from reciprocal recognition since under the White supremacist and patriarchal, settler-colonial logic, we are seen as subjugated, gendered colonized objects.[43] We must seek instead self-recognition and mutual recognition in our own spaces of belonging, such that through a "politics of refusal" we can engage with our oppressors on our own terms.

Nonetheless, dialogue can be had among our own communities and in this way develop a mutual recognition among ourselves. The fact that our histories of oppression have made us don a White mask and develop a certain degree of Whiteness to succeed in schools and society means that we have had to reject or submerge our subaltern. As noted throughout this book these are knowledges that we need to recover, such that they can provide new insights and ways of engaging in the world that may support human liberation and the development of new social relations.

An important consideration is that among the oppressed there are oppressors. Most Indigenous women and Women of Color face multiple axes of oppressions—generally class, race, and gender oppressions, but additional ones as well. Although dialogue is meant to break down these oppressions by providing the contexts within which the oppressed is heard and their ideas valued, it often occurs that power mediates form—in this case speaking and listening rituals and practices. When it comes down to taking part in dialogue across race and gender dialogue, is extremely difficult to achieve. We have developed very different interactional styles that reflect systems of domination, especially along gender lines.

For example, too often in western dogma learning across different perspectives is believed to take place through debate. Debates can be described as different camps that make their arguments for a particular case. There is a clear win/lose dynamic to debates. Positions are taken and supported or rejected. There is little room for nuance. Debates are generally speaking a White man's game wherein doubt is considered a weakness and nuance is considered murky ground that obfuscates meaning rather than elucidating it. Debates presume one correct answer and one appropriate and natural objective perspective. Debates are often a show of male intellectual prowess. Those who have a different interactional style are perceived as less intelligent. Although Freire was clearly not suggesting dialogue as debate I have seen many on the left revel over "a good debate."

Women and Women of Color, especially, often face the practice of "mansplaining" wherein men perceive the need to have things explained to us.[44] This is a common practice that on the surface seems an attempt at being "helpful" but in reality is frustrating and sexist since it reflects a clear supposition that women are not as knowledgeable or quick to understand. An aspect of this is related to differences in ontology—or how we understand reality. Many men, I've noticed, present information as fact whereas women often present information as their perspective or evolving (what we understand at a specific point in time, given our experience or existing research). These ontological differences among men and women are even reflected in academic fields, with fields that tend to be male dominated being more positivistic whereas fields with greater numbers of women emphasize the social construction of knowledge and the diversity of perspectives.

Once at a small dinner party where only women were in attendance (it just turned out that way as the only man invited did not attend), the topic of gender bias in student perceptions of their teachers came up. One White woman explained that when co-teaching a class with a White man she had noticed that he always spoke to the class with such assurance that it appeared as if he knew everything about the topic whereas in her own teaching she often presented information in a way that left the topic open for student perspectives to emerge and provided information in a way that made clear that this was what was known at the time rather than concrete facts. The women sitting around the table all nodded and began to discuss how their teaching styles also followed this pattern. In our discussion it was clear that all of us recognized that our way of teaching was not a function of lack of "expertise" or lack of confidence, but of a different way of knowing the world. Freire argues that an important aspect of dialogue is doubt and humility:

> How can I dialogue if I always project ignorance onto others and never perceive my own? … At the point of encounter, there are neither utter ignoramuses nor perfect sages; there are only people who are attempting, together, to learn more than they now know.[45]

These concepts, doubt and humility, are antithetical to western notions of the imperial being that represents "man" as White, wealthy, and heterosexual[46] Rather, these constructs are often associated with women and People of Color. Yet these concepts from a Freirian perspective suggest wisdom in understanding that no person can know everything, that multiple perspectives of the same reality exist, that ontological diversity exists because our positionality in the world grants us access to different experiences and different levels of intimacy with these experiences, and that knowledge is socially constructed and evolves over time. The oppressor believes they know everything and the oppressed know nothing. This happens also among the oppressed; the oppressor who, in their position as oppressed, feels compelled to exert dominance over another, replicates relations of domination among the oppressed. For true dialogue to occur the oppressor must be disarmed of their arrogance, relations of domination must be challenged, and a level of trust must be developed. This is very evident to me as I've observed interactions among students, faculty, and even families. The person with greatest power arrogantly expresses their thoughts without considering the impact they may have and the person with least power carefully chooses their words, often leaving the most important comments unstated. Indigenous women and Women of Color have a long history of distrust of men and White peoples and with good reason. Our unde-sired words have historically been sufficient excuse to abuse us with impunity.

Language has for too long been used as a tool of the oppressor—perceived as that which makes us a "more evolved" animal than all others and restricted from the oppressed or judged hierarchically throughout history. For example, the languages of Indigenous peoples (and thus the ability to communicate with one's own ontological and epistemological ways) have been stolen or restricted. Immigrant populations have often attempted to retain their lan-guages only to find it outlawed or undervalued. Yet our perspectives and ideas as racialized women at the intersections of oppression and exploitation are crucially necessary at this time in history when we are headed toward destruc-tion and when the western ways we have been heeding for centuries do not seem capable of challenging the status quo. How to bring these ideas forward in spaces still dominated by our oppressors—whether it be White persons or Men of Color—is an important challenge.

An important note is that to recognize diverse knowledges does not equate with subscribing to a postmodern perspective of multiple realities that are perceived as relative, such that oppression and exploitation become only actual phenomena for those who perceive it.[47] This approach fails to recognize an objective reality outside of our subjective perceptions. From a Marxist perspective, universality—totality—exists but this does not preclude the existence of cultural differences, experience, and identities that bring us to know aspects of the world differently. Thus, we can speak of Indigenous knowledges, as opposed to western, because they pertain to phenomena that are more directly related or impactful to non-western peoples, because they may be imperceptible to western peoples, or because they may not be deemed worthy of study. In this sense knowledges are not relative due to multiple real-ities but rather indicative of differences of experiences, cultural differences, differential access, and different sociopolitical and economic positionings. It is critical to recognize that in the case of competing realities regarding partic-ular phenomena a critical approach does not support a notion that multiple accounts are equally valid but rather that there are inherent interests and ideologies guiding each, often ones that support the status quo and others that reflect the interests or viewpoints of the oppressed. Peter McLaren explains:

> I believe that we can't understand isolated bits of experience adequately without the whole—the absolute. We need to ask what makes experience possible, why do cer-tain experiences count more than others, and what are the conditions of possibility for certain types of experiences. We read these dialectically against the absolute.

But here I must make a caveat. Quijano warns us that when thinking about totality, or sociohistorical totality, we need to avoid the Eurocentric paradigm of totality. We can do this by thinking of totality as a field of social relations structured by the heterogeneous and discontinuous integration of diverse spheres of social existence, every one of which is in turn structured by its own historically heterogeneous, temporally discontinuous and conflictive elements. Each element, however, has some relative autonomy and can be considered a particularity and singularity. But they move within the general tendency of the whole. We can't think of totality as a closed structure.[48]

This ontological and epistemological complexity adds to the already difficult task of dialogue across relations of domination discussed above. One possible solution is to create other epistemological encounters. Chicana feminist theories and Africana theories critique the western practice of dismissing ways of knowing that are based on body sensation, emotion, and intuition.[49] As discussed by decolonial theorists, western epistemology is rooted in the imperial being, which developed notions of superiority for conquering the world and established an "objective Truth" based on their own ways of knowing and being, rendering all Others subhuman.[50] This "Truth," which claimed mind over matter, was thought to occur in the head severed from the body politic. Indigenous knowledges and ways of knowing grounded in their ancestral lands and in the subjective experiences of colonization were defined as irrational. Yet there is no doubt that thinking is eased by our physical comfort, emotions, and feelings of love, pain, and anger.

In my own experience working with Latinx communities I have found that I can best convey my deep respect for them and their histories and experiences through the building of relationships that go far beyond engaging only for the purposes of a research project. Here it is not necessarily the dialogue that we engage in that conveys this respect but the willingness to build relationships, share personal stories, question my own thinking aloud in light of their perspectives, and allow myself to love and be loved. Indeed, Freire expressed how touching and caressing Nita's hands while engaging in an intellectual discussion with colleagues facilitated his thinking. Here he was pointing out that our ability to think and know is intricately connected with our bodies, emotions, and feelings.[51] Most importantly, it is in praxis—*acting and (not just) reflecting with* the Other and following *their* lead to transform social conditions that we exemplify beyond doubt a commitment to and faith in the Oppressed.

Some of these ideas are put into practice in "prefigurative" spaces wherein radical transformations are underway that begin to develop new social relations. Prefiguring is founded on the recognition that it is insufficient to work to dismantle capitalism and other structures of oppression in our world, but that it is necessary to simultaneously engage in creating the social relations that we envision existing in a classless, anti-racist, anti-sexist society that stands against oppressions based on sexuality, gender, religion, and all other ways of being. Prefiguring recognizes the dialectical tensions that necessarily exist between micro and macro level social change efforts as well as in the breaking down of the old and creating the new society. Both approaches are always simultaneously taking place, whether in organizational structures of social movements or in critical pedagogical classrooms and educational contexts. As these tensions and contradictions get played out we learn to develop more democratic spaces, dialogical encounters, and to develop among ourselves the new values and ways of engaging in the world that we envision and that can only be produced in the process of acting upon them.[52]

To bring us back to the significance of dreaming it is critical to recognize that we need a purpose for creating these epistemological encounters. Without a vision of possibilities beyond the existing social structure, conserving Indigenous and community based knowledges will be merely for our own community's enrichment and perhaps unlikely to have the significance to others that it does to us. It is only when we truly believe in the possibility of other creation that we develop the courage to take the necessary risks to show our vulnerability, our doubts, and thus create the dialogical spaces and other "loving encounters" for new ontological and epistemological insights to emerge.

Red Love: Beyond the Bourgeois Family

One of the most intriguing and exciting aspects of the socialist imaginary is the development of the socialist family and the reconceptualization of the loving relation between partners, parent/child, and others. Under capitalism the bourgeois family is recognized as one of the most oppressive and exploitative institutions for both women and children.[53] Marriage is an economic contract that historically defined wives and children as property, granting men legal right to make use or dispose of women and children at will. Today women in many countries have made important gains regarding their legal rights within the family and children have been granted legal protection from abuse and other rights, but marriage remains an economic construct tied to property rights, tax laws, spousal supports, and inheritance rights. Relations within the family are held to particular expectations and societal norms that have yet to transcend this history, with the abuse of women and children in the home reaching epidemic proportions across the world, including in the industrialized world where women have greater access to education.

This is not surprising within the totality of capitalism, wherein everything takes on the properties of the commodity—things to be bought, owned, and sold—with exclusive rights given to the proprietors. As with all other relations under capitalism, relations in the family are defined by domination and sub-ordination, with men in the position of dominance and women and children as subordinates. The family is, thus, a microcosm of the larger society's social relations of production whose function is to produce the next generation of workers and their labor power, including their acceptance to relations of dom-ination and the values necessary for capitalist production, such as a strong "work ethic," competition, individual ownership, capital accumulation, and consumer habits. Women are key to family production and therefore they and their bodies are controlled to ensure the maintenance of the system.[54]

The socialist dream of a new humanism would require a family structure founded on equality of worth between family members and relationships built on comradely respect, mutual caring, and responsibility toward each other. The goal would be that people would engage in creative labor beyond neces-sity such that immediate needs of food, shelter, health care, and education would be accessible to all regardless of family relations. Such a family context sows the seeds "for a love that seeks to know the Other, that cannot conceive of violating an Other, that recognizes their own development as a function of the Other, and that validates the Others' differences."[55] Within this socialist family, racism and other forms of domination and exploitation have no place. They cannot be bred under a structure that is founded on and perpetuates material equality and the inherent worth of every human being and other life forms.

Alexandra Kollontai was a vocal Marxist critic of the bourgeois family. She argued that love should not be a binding material contract and instead supported the development of "a new communist sexual morality of free, open and equal relations of love and comradeship.[56] By this Kollontai meant that love could not be forced and should not become a burden or used as leverage for social control. Further, as free and open relations would have it, feelings of possession, common in relationships under capitalism, would cease. While a person who decided to leave another may feel disappointed or pained, the sense of being wronged or betrayed would no longer apply, relieving partners from guilt and social pressures to remain in unwanted relations. In Kollontai's words:

Love is a profoundly social emotion. Love is not in the least a private matter concerning only the two loving persons: love possesses a uniting element which is valuable to the collective.[57]

As a "social emotion," love reflects socially constructed values and norms, which are dialectically related to material conditions and the mode of production. Within a socialist alternative people would be able to decide on their loving relations without worry over conventions or the impact that these decision would have on their economic well-being. Unfortunately, Kollontai's emancipatory contributions regarding the socialist family and loving relations were distorted into a form of promiscuous "free love" and her ideas were discredited.[58]

Erich Fromm also argued that love was distorted within capitalist relations. He theorized love as a force that unites us with another while not losing one's individuality. He argued that loving should not be a societal obligation or an economic determination:

... mature love is union under the condition of preserving one's integrity, one's individuality. Love is an active power in man; a power which breaks through the walls which separate man from his fellow men, which unites him with others; love makes him overcome the sense of isolation and separateness, yet it permits him to be himself to retain his integrity. In love the paradox occurs that two beings become one and yet remain two.[59]

Alain Badiou with Nicolas Troung develop this argument further and their ideas are especially fruitful for conceiving how love relates to the formation of a new humanist world that values our diversity of experiences, while ceasing to create false binaries upon which to build hierarchies:

In love ... you go to take on the other, to make her or him exist with you, as he or she is ... [It] is a quest for truth ... from the perspective of difference.[60]

What Badiou and Nicolas Troung describe sounds very much like the epistemological encounters that Freire theorized via dialogue. Here we have an example of what I earlier may be needed given the difficulties I've witnessed in creating authentic dialogue across diversity and even among the oppressed—an epistemological encounter based on the loving relation. This loving relation need not be between romantic lovers but can extend to friendships, colleagues, and even to the way in which we relate more generally to humanity. Of course, this now begs the question as to who would constitute members of a "socialist family."

Here again, we can see that the current society holds elements of the new; economic realities often demand extended family formation and painful experiences that the bourgeois family, with its abusive dogmas, engenders have led way to the reconstruction of families, including "choice families" with non-blood related members and "blended families" with divorced parents and their new partners.

In some cases the socialist alternative to the bourgeois family has been misdirected toward the disintegration of the family altogether. It is true that the family has proven resistant to dissolving the division of labor and gender relations of domination. However, I would argue that part of that resistance is that the societies that have attempted to dissolve the division of labor have not really had a clear focus on creating conditions that changed men's lives. For example, the goal of socializing domestic work and childcare in "working communisms" (or state capitalisms)[61] has brought many women out into the workforce and even into traditionally male dominated fields but they have not really done much to encourage a value for the "caring work" that is typically left to women, such that men would find satisfaction (and not ridicule) for this transition.

In the case of the Russian Revolution it has been documented that one of the major shifts in family law that was presumably to support women was to end the practice of adoptions. This policy created chaos with thousands of children uncared for and on the streets. It was a policy that eventually had to be rescinded.[62] While we want to challenge the division of labor that has traditionally relegated women to *only* caring work, we also must challenge the devaluation of traditional women's work. While caring work has served to confine women to the private sphere and unwaged work, it is not devoid of intellectual labor as has often been presumed. The family context certainly creates significant "drudgery"[63] for women but it is also an important and wonderful source of pride and satisfaction for many women. To suggest the dissolution of the family or the socialization of childcare such that women would be "freed" from having to care for their children trivializes the significant love, beauty, and intellectual elements of caring for and raising the children who will form the next generation. Such descriptions and attitudes about the work that women have been doing for centuries is as sexist as the division of labor itself.

It is important to note not only what a socialist family structure would look like for women but also what it would look like for Women of Color. Although a socialist society would be organized to provide for the basic necessities of all its citizens, it is critical to note that the family, although oppressive under capitalist logic, can be perceived as an important source of economic, social, emotional, and spiritual support among communities of color and Indigenous communities, especially as they deal with exploitative and racist conditions and attitudes from the White dominant group. Rather than a full dissolution of the family, which I believe will be quickly rejected by many women and especially Women of Color, it behooves us to recognize the positive that exists within the family and expel out the negative. A socialist family can become a context of epistemological encounters where equal and free human beings learn from each other, care for each other, and respect each other and wherein they enter into familial relationships willfully without pressures to remain beholden to each other by necessity or social convention. As Sandy Grande poignantly expresses in relation to caring for her mother, the "relations of mutuality" that are developed in families during the most trying of times move us beyond our capitalist obsession with the self, which defines caring work as subtractive, toward a recognition of the self in relation to others.[64] Relations of mutuality sustain us in the most difficult of times, materially, emotionally, and spiritually. It is this connection with others defined by love, respect, and social responsibility and enacted as a foundational element of everyday functioning that is at the heart of my socialist family imaginary.

Walking With Grace: Musings From This Latinx Woman of Color

I want to end this book by addressing the majority of Women of Color and Indigeneity. For many of us recognizing our potential to revolutionary praxis and our strengths and courage does not come easily. To varying degrees we have internalized deficit narratives, disdain for our ways of being and thinking, deep seeded fears of our physical and emotional safety, guilt for succeeding in a dominant White male world, and an uncritical gratitude for everything, including for being allowed to breathe. I want to argue that it's time we challenge the narratives, ideologies, and normalized gendered and racialized practices that are meant to keep us "in line." We are as human as anyone else and beyond that we are living beings with the natural right, as all living things deserve, to exist free of fear and violence and to receive respect and appreciation for our contributions to the world. In this section I explore some thoughts about what it may mean to be an a racialized woman who dreams of a future wherein we are seen and experience the world as fully human and living beings. What does it mean to walk in today's world with that dream firmly planted in our minds and hearts? What would we do the same? What would we do differently? How do we learn to dream big and yet live with the humility of knowing that we cannot make our dreams come true alone—that we must bring other Indigenous women and Women of Color and other male and White allies with us on this journey.

I was inspired to write this section through my interactions with Nita Freire during a short week when she visited our campus. Of course, I was a little awe struck, but I was also authentically drawn to her quiet confidence, the dignity with which she carried herself, the humility with which she interacted with all those who sought to meet and greet her, the gentle demeanor that also held strong philosophical convictions. I thought at the time and continue to think that this is who I want to be as I grow in age and, hopefully, in wisdom. And the term that I kept coming back to without even really knowing much about from whence it came was "grace."

Grace is a biblical concept often interpreted as a gift of the divine bestowed upon humanity. In Christian terms, "by the grace of God" refers to the beneficence by which God gave his life to spare ours.[65] In popular usage "to have grace" refers to engaging with humility, generosity, and kindness but, for some, infers a spiritual dimension that guides our values and the way we move about in the world. Although some scholars associate spirituality with concepts or ideas that have been taken up or developed by religious doctrine— such as this notion of grace, spirituality need not be associated with religion. Certainly, from whence concepts emerge is important but they can be taken as conceptual foundations that can be developed for other purposes and uses, which is what I and others have done with the concept of grace. Indeed, many people seem to subscribe to an anti-religious spirituality.[66]

An important clarification is that Marx's materialism is not incompatible with spirituality. It is true that Marx rejected religion and religiosity—the institutionalized appropriation of spirituality that has so often throughout history been in cahoots with the ruling class and has been used to justify social injustices as part of "God's bigger plan" and to develop a pedagogy of resignation.[67] However, Jose Miranda has made a convincing argument that Marx was guided by a strong moral conviction and that his ideas and impetus for a new communist humanism were rooted in early Christianity that aimed to transform humanity.[68] Miranda quotes multiple passages in which Marx's comments position his ideas in sync with early Christianity.[69] He also cites Eleanor Marx who in her book, *Erinnerugen an Marx*, discusses how Marx himself taught her "… the story of the "carpenter's son who was put to death by the rich." In the same passage she states, "I often heard him say: despite everything, we can forgive Christianity many things because of the fact that it has taught us to love ..."[70]

Peter McLaren also takes up this argument demonstrating through scriptures that Jesus Christ was a communist in the sense that he was adamantly against inequality, condemned the rich, and professed that the Kingdom of God was to be created on Earth:

> Jesus does not condemn wealth in the absolute sense, as when the wealth of the whole people is praised in Deuteronomy 28: 1–4. But when Jesus says, 'Happy are the poor' and 'Woe to you the rich,' he is attacking the fact that some people are poor and others are rich. ... Jesus's 'inexorable reprobation' to which he subjects wealth refers not to absolute wealth but to differentiating wealth, that is, to relative wealth, and Jesus does so 'implacably,' 'intransigently,' and 'inexceptionably.' (Miranda, 2004, pp. 21–22).[71]

McLaren continues:

> The Bible makes clear through Jesus's own sayings that the kingdom is not the state of being after death; rather, the kingdom is now, here, on Earth. Essentially Jesus is saying that, 'in the kingdom there cannot be social differences—that the kingdom, whether or not it pleases the conservatives, is a classless society.' (Miranda, 2004, p. 20)[72]

Paulo Freire too was highly influenced by liberation theology, which McLaren points out did not go far enough in its denouncement of inequality, making the poor only a "preferential option" rather than a "responsibility."[73] Yet for Freire, liberation theology was a springboard for his ideas, which, as we saw earlier, developed concern and commitment to the poor and oppressed into a living spiritual praxis.

I cannot state strongly enough that the communist and moral teachings of Jesus Christ that McLaren and Miranda support had nothing to do with the savagery and barbarism of the colonial being that claimed to draw inspiration from Christianity to engage in a project of mass genocide against Indigenous peoples to dispossess them of land and resources. There is no doubt that this perversion of Christ's teachings has made most of us on the left wary of engaging the spiritual dimension of our human nature. Indeed, it may appear to some a contradiction to engage a politics of spirituality to challenge capitalist social relations. However, Indigenous communities have never shied away from their spiritual connection to land and life and see it as deeply tied to their courage, strength, and survival as a people.

It is undeniable that many activists and scholars carry a strong spiritual humanism. Few have taken the risks that Freire took in not only talking about love, hope, courage, but also developing an entire educational philosophy around these constructs. Yet as we saw above with McLaren, many critical pedagogues and others on the radical left are beginning to realize that not only is it honest to publicly name these feelings that on a personal level are crucial to how we engage in the world, but also that a focus on spirituality may bring forth the subaltern knowledges that western imperialism has destroyed or submerged.

"Political grace" draws upon our spirituality to unearth and develop these lost subaltern epistemes toward a liberatory praxis. Wes Rehberg defines "political grace" as grace directed toward the oppressed:

> Grace, the gift of the divine, which is ever present and offered feely in its givingness, is political when it 'favors' people under abasing domination to reflect on their condition politically and to seek a political solution to their subjugation and oppression. Grace is a relationship with the divine, which, when accepted and acknowledged, transforms a human and human relations ... a gift of the spirit ... or can be considered an opening into a dimension which humans can't describe but know as something beyond their faculty to reproduce without help from beyond, a beyond that seems to be beyond the horizon of life but with which humans identify and of which they may feel a part.[74]

Antonia Darder further develops the notion of political grace "... as an integral spiritual force within the commons that can serve to better propel revolutionary movements for a more just world."[75] Darder emphasizes that political grace is rooted in community and collective ways of knowing. The goal in this concept is to move us one step further in the recovery of subaltern epistemes by engaging the spiritual connection and drive toward our search for freedom. With political grace driving our search for epistemological and ontological clarity, we come to recognize that this search is not only a necessary means to validate diverse peoples or even to move us in the direction of freedom, but that this is an historical process that is impelled not only by our commitment to develop our material human potential but that it is a Divine intervention that demands our full commitment.

Darder warns that our continued dismissal of spirituality as a guiding force for liberation merely because it is seen as "unscientific" from a scholarly perspective plays into capitalist interests. In her words, political grace is:

> A collective spiritual dimension that must manifest and unfold within our pedagogical and political praxis of community, if we are to genuinely extend our criticality beyond limiting and narrow allegiance to Western precepts of rationality.[76]

Darder points out that from a critical pedagogy perspective, grace is a spiritual connection that emerges with the said task of bringing forth a political project of liberation. Her point here is that it is in the process of our political project for liberation that political grace emerges. This is critical because she does not let us off the hook by suggesting that political grace comes forth to propel us to act. On the contrary, it is we, as human agents, who create the spiritual connection that develops into political grace.

The theoretical ideas that Darder establishes above are crucial to this work which has sought to encourage Indigenous women and Women of Color to not only be seen, but also to see ourselves and our knowledges and ways of engaging in the world as crucial to creating a better world.

To walk with grace, then, to me means that we move in the world with a deep and uncompromising commitment to creating a new humanism. Dreaming, of course, is crucial in this process, as I've already discussed above. But I would argue that our dreams must reflect an authentic view of ourselves as fully human and this dreaming must not only reflect our desires but also be connected to how we truly see ourselves in the world today. Thus, to dream of ourselves as fully human and deserving of freedom and equality we must begin to enact this dream today. Only in this way do we come to understand that our dreams *can* come true. As Darder points out above there is a grounded engagement to spirituality that I would argue holds true for dreaming as well. For racialized women, given our histories of hyper oppression and exploitation, this is a difficult task, but certainly not an impossible one, as my dreams consistently confirm. Peter McLaren expresses this idea quite beautifully:

> We need to stare boldly and unflinchingly into history's grim visage and assume our narrative space within the very contours of its flesh, a space where we can speak our own stories, listen loudly to the stories of others, and dream our own dreams without the dead letter of bourgeois ethics weighing like a nightmare on minds still capable of envisioning, still willing to hope, still intent upon constructing a space of difference, a space of possibility. That space does not wait for us, beckoning us to occupy it or thinking that we will one day stumble into it. There is no act of grace suddenly bestowing the path for us. We require an ultimacy of commitment, an unbending intent, a continually renewed effort to exert a defamiliarizing sway in the sea of the ordinary. It is a space that must be fought for and defended, a contestatory terrain where hope will always remain the enemy of despair. I call this building an arch of social dreaming.[77]

McLaren reminds us that grace does not just "suddenly" appear, that we must not assume a space of waiting. Grace shines upon us in the process of struggle. It bestows energy and drive to aid in our commitment and it can be an important source of solidarity and community but it requires us to act with agency, to rage against injustice, and to reach decisively for our dreams. To walk with grace is thus a continuous decolonizing project. Alyosha Goldstein elaborates:

> As Grande contends "Decolonization' (like democracy) is neither achievable nor definable, rendering it ephemeral as a goal, but perpetual as a process' (p. 166). Decolonization is thus a shifting configuration of strategies and actions, not an event, even as it is nonetheless eventful. Decolonization is a means without end. It is a creative response that necessarily exceeds legibility and reconciliation from the perspective of the conditions from which it arises … [It is] a collective overcoming and becoming in perpetuity by Indigenous peoples.[78]

As a Woman of Color, I have found that it is difficult to live in this world. In every context I am reminded that there may be negative consequences for being me, including ridicule, negative judgment, false generosity, or worse—all symptoms of capitalist relations. For me this is often felt as an academic where I seem to speak a completely different language or live out different values than my colleagues and students. Here I confront more often than not violent confrontations of class, race, and gender. By violent I do not necessarily mean physically violent (although this happens too to some of us), but more generally it is an epistemic violence that defines my ideas or ways of engaging as "inappropriate," "out of the norm," or "unnatural." Of course, this happens as well in the contexts of my own home where gender relations prevail, even under the most presumably "egalitarian" contexts.

I'm talking about the things that are so normalized that they become "common sense" and are perceived neutral and unrelated to the logic of capital—status and hierarchies, production for the sake of production, compartmentalization, work "ethic," recognitions and awards that mark some as better than others, assumptions that merit is "objective"—who designed the criteria? Although I focus here on the epistemic nature of this assault, epistemology is dialectically related to material conditions, such that the discourses and values we perceive as appropriate result in projects, programs, opportunities, and other material realities that hold up capitalist production processes.

Although I often name these westernized assumptions of neutrality and stake a value for my own subaltern ways, I recognize that there have been many occasions in which I just let it go. There is a practical consideration that since "common sense" derives from ruling class interests, every expected behavior and value will likely reflect a western episteme and capitalist interests (read male and White). Thus, the sheer number of times in which I would need to name this violence would render my critiques "unreasonable" and even produce the roll of dominant eyes. So there is a value system that we develop, often unstated and perhaps unexamined, in which there are certain grave examples of violence in which we recognize as critical scholars that to not name injustice is tantamount to taking part in it. And then there are the presumed "smaller" everyday occurrences wherein you can't really decipher what the social cost is, except that it gnaws at us when we say nothing. Here I want to invoke Sandy Grande's concept of "refusal and survivance," meaning that we must refuse to accept our continued colonization and instead develop strategies to take back what has been stolen from us. Refusal involves no longer accepting the negation of our ontological and epistemological clarity and the erasure of our histories of oppression and genocide but it also and importantly means the refusal to accept a liberal politics of recognition or reconciliation that acknowledges our existence as valued cultural identities and the "wealth" of our traditions while doing little to transform the structures that continue to disproportionately impact us materially.[79] For Indigenous peoples, refusal means accepting nothing less than sovereignty. We cannot forge survivance upon only an ideological acceptance of our right to exist as peoples but must demand the structural changes that must take place in order to support our survival—this means the elimination of structures that are actually killing us—capitalism, racism, sexism and other antagonisms—and that limit our ability to thrive economically, socially and psychologically.[80] This must be a collective effort that builds solidarity and in doing so not only more effectively challenges western ways, which ultimately is necessary to bring down capitalism (there is value in numbers) but also affirms our more collectivist ways of moving in the world. There is something very significant in acting as agents on our own behalf—indeed, this is one important aspect of what it means to be human. Our dreams begin to feel plausible as we begin to enact them strategically at every opportune moment.

It is also time to develop a thicker skin. We will often be judged anyway; thus, we might as well get comfortable with the labels that are often meant to keep us quiet or "in our place"—"arrogant," "sensitive," or "radical." It's time to own these as badges of struggle. To refuse is not only an outward exercise of agency but an inward one as well. We must refuse to accept our own internalized oppression as well and move toward our dreams unapologetically and with determination. Of course, we are still vulnerable as Indigenous women and Women of Color, so we need to be both savvy and courageous.

We cannot challenge everything at once but we can begin to chip away at the normative trends that follow the logic of capital. We must also be reflective of our own complicity taking up the logic of capital. We are not immune to it. We too practice relations of domination and must learn to treat others humanely and with equity. The mantle of criticality sometimes lends itself to judgments of others who are presumed "less critical" or "less engaged." While there is no doubt that some people engage a "false pedagogy" or a "cheap pedagogy," responding as a humanist means doing so with compassion—asking without judgments but with curiosity to understand. Creating epistemological encounters through dialogue, relationships, and love may help us find the way.

As we begin to move among the left, we come to find that people are conscious of our histories of oppression. They have learned the discussions of intersectionality and are prepared to do the "right thing" and make sure that we are not left behind, that our speaking times are not taken up, that our ideas are not dismissed. This "protectionism" can sometimes be a false generosity that fails to acknowledge us as human. Another way in which this *multicultural* hero presents himself is by "inclusion" but this is an inclusion that inscribes a different dehumanizing dimension—that of exerting power over us. This multicultural hero attempts to explain how important it is that our voices be heard and *demands* our presence without recognizing that as racialized women we have, generally speaking, many more demands than most men and White women. Class, race, and gender increases the demands made upon us (in terms of workload but also emotional toll) while also diminishing the social and economic resources at our disposal. And on top of these we have the "responsibility" to make ourselves heard across a spectrum of activities because society has not reached out to find or allowed access to many more of us who can share in the task and who also have the right to those opportunities. Some of these multicultural heroes mean well and only need to be told what to Women of Color is obvious but some just want to be heroes at our expense.

Part of our dehumanization lies in our internalized oppression—the lies we have internalized that we are not as smart, beautiful, or deserving as the White man and woman. This internalized oppression is often manifested in feelings of guilt, fear of lost opportunities, or fear of negative judgments. Walking with grace means walking without the fear and guilt that is running us ragged and make sure that the younger women who are coming behind us are not made to feel fear and guilt either.

I strongly believe that this means we need to find time and spaces for healing on our own and with each other. Healing is a critical component to finding our voices and recovering our community ways. Of course, meeting our economic survival needs is a first step in healing. The next step is to find ways to heal emotionally and psychologically. We cannot make the spiritual connection with others or love humanity if we cannot see that there *is* love in the world. And we need to be truly validated as ourselves to challenge the internalized oppression that has been developing over generations of oppression and exploitation. To stand up against the status quo alongside people who believe in the same things I believe in is thrilling and empowering; to do so in spaces where I am a lone voice is much more difficult but nonetheless necessary. It becomes easier after engaging regularly among people who validate and uplift me. Activism is in the streets but it is also in the heart.

The final step is to charge against capitalism and the various antagonisms that have claimed so many lives, especially those of Indigenous peoples and People of Color across the world. While the first two steps are necessary, it is not an accident that they are discussed theoretically as ends in and of themselves—reforms aimed at creating greater opportunities, closing the achievement gap, and drawing on our funds of knowledge are all important but insufficient to creating a more human world.

In this world of impending doom, where bombs are seemingly going off everywhere, except in the places that are often sending the bombs, and where millions of people live in dire poverty and endure unimaginable suffering and humiliations, there is still hope and beauty and goodness. Most of us can find multiple examples of this beauty everyday here on Earth. We can see much more of this beauty as we dream a world where love and justice prevail and every one of us treats the other as the creative human beings that we were meant to be and recognizes our inherent worth and interdependence. To make this dream reality we will need to forge a revolutionary struggle that brings down capitalism and the patriarchal and racist structures that support it. Indigenous women and Women of Color bring vital elements to this struggle—experiences, ways of knowing and engaging in the world, theories about what it will take to free the world of oppression, impetus, strength, courage, perseverance, and love. It is my dream that all of us, Indigenous women and Women of Color, may harness these gifts in this world so that we may *walk with grace* into the next.

Notes

1. Helena María Viramontes, "Nopalitos: The Making of Fiction," 292.
2. bell hooks, *All About Love: New Visions*, xviii.
3. Lilia D. Monzó and Peter McLaren, "Red Love."; Lilia D. Monzó and Peter McLaren, "Challenging the Violence and Invisibility Against Women of Color."
4. Peter McLaren, *Pedagogy of Insurrection: From Resurrection to Revolution*.
5. Marx, Karl, *The Economic and Philosophic Manuscripts of 1844*.
6. Paulo Freire, *Pedagogy of the Oppressed*.
7. Paulo Freire, *Pedagogy of Hope: Reliving Pedagogy of the Oppressed*.
8. Freire, *Pedagogy of the Oppressed*, 44.
9. Henry Giroux, "Rethinking Education as the Practice of Freedom."
10. Ana Maria Freire Araújo, *Chronicles of Love: My Life with Paulo Freire*.
11. Paulo Freire and Donaldo Macedo, *Literacy: Reading the Word and the World*.
12. Freire, *Pedagogy of the Oppressed*.
13. Paulo Freire, *Pedagogy of the City*.
14. Antonia Darder, et al., *The Critical Pedagogy Reader 3rd ed.*
15. Peter McLaren, *Life in Schools, 6th ed.*
16. Suzanne SooHoo, *Talking Leaves: Narratives of Otherness*.
17. Donaldo Macedo, introduction to *Pedagogy of the Oppressed, 30th anniversary ed.*
18. Antonia Darder, *Reinventing Paulo Freire: A Pedagogy of Love*, 39.
19. Macedo, introduction to *Pedagogy of the Oppressed*.
20. Peter McLaren, *Pedagogy of Insurrection*; Peter McLaren, *Life in Schools*; Peter McLaren, *Rage and Hope*; Paula Allman, *Revolutionary Social Transformation*.
21. Lilia D. Monzó, "Marx in the Age of Trump."; Lilia D. Monzó, "Women and Revolution."; Lilia D. Monzó and Peter McLaren, "The Future Is Marx."
22. Lilia D. Monzó and Robert S. Rueda, "Professional Roles, Caring, and Scaffolds."
23. Tom Wilson, Peter Park, Anaida Colón-Muñíz, *Memories of Paulo*.
24. McLaren, *Life in Schools*, 239.
25. Darder, *Reinventing Paulo Freire*, 34.
26. Macedo, introduction to *Pedagogy of the Oppressed*, 26.
27. Donaldo Macedo, introduction to *Chronicles of Love: My Life with Paulo Freire*.
28. Although I do not address this here, there are critical scholars attempting to understand how our subconscious imagination can support a justice agenda.
29. Dunayevskaya, *The Marxism and Freedom*.
30. L. S. Vygotsky, *Mind in Society: The Development of Higher Psychological Processes*.
31. Peter Hudis, *Marx's Concept of the Alternative to Capitalism*.
32. Hudis, *Marx's Alternative to Capitalism*.
33. Ibid.
34. Karl Marx, *Capital*, Vol. I.
35. Hudis, *Marx's Alternative to Capitalism*.
36. Henry Giroux, *On Critical Pedagogy*.
37. Freire, *Pedagogy of Hope*, 91.
38. Ibid.

39. Freire Araújo, *Chronicles of Love*.

40. Macedo, introduction to *Chronicles of Love*.

41. Erich Fromm, *To Have or To Be*.

42. Lilia D. Monzó, "White Supremacy, Hate, and Violence in Charlottesville."

43. Frantz Fanon, *Black Skin, White Masks*.

44. Rebecca Solnit, *Men Explain Things to Me*.

45. Freire, *Pedagogy of the Oppressed*, 90.

46. Ramon Grosfoguel, "The Structure of Knowledge in Westernized Universities."

47. Dave Hill, et al., *Marxism Against Postmodernism in Educational Theory*.

48. McLaren, *Pedagogy of Insurrection*, 235.

49. Dolores Delgado Bernal, "Learning and Living Pedagogies of the Home."; Cynthia B. Dillard, D. Abdur-Rashid, and C. A. Tyson, "My Soul is a Witness."

50. Grosfoguel, "The Structure of Knowledge."

51. Freire Araújo, *Chronicles of Love*.

52. Miguel Zavala and Noah Asher Golden, "Prefiguring Alternative Worlds."

53. Alexandra Kollontai, "Communism and the Family."

54. For more on women's roles in capitalist production, see Chapters 2 and 3.

55. Monzó and McLaren, "Red Love."

56. Teresa Ebert, "Alexandra Kollontai and Red Love," para. 16.

57. Alexandra Kollontai, "Make Way for Winged Eros," 278–79.

58. Ebert, "Alexandra Kollontai."

59. Erich Fromm, *The Art of Loving*, 19.

60. Alain Badiou with Nicolas Troung, *In Praise of Love*, 19–23.

61. Raya Dunayevskaya, *A Marxist-Humanist Theory of State Capitalism*.

62. Wendy Zeva Goldman, "Women, the Family, and the New Revolutionary Order."

63. Leon Trotsky, *Women and The Family*, 2nd ed.

64. Sandy Grande, *Red Pedagogy*, xvii.

65. Wes Rehberg, *Political Grace: The Gift of Resistance*.

66. Rebecca Gianarkis, *Spiritual but Not Religious*.

67. Michael Rivage-Seul, *The Emperor's God: Imperial Misunderstandings of Christianity*.

68. Jose Miranda, *Marx Against the Marxists: The Christian Humanism of Karl Marx*.

69. Miranda, *Marx Against the Marxists*.

70. Cited in Miranda, *Marx Against the Marxists*, 225.

71. McLaren, *Pedagogy of Insurrection*, 105.

72. Ibid, 106.

73. Ibid, 106.

74. Rehberg, *Political Grace*, para. 15.

75. Antonia Darder, "Political Grace and Revolutionary Critical Pedagogy," para. 3.

76. Darder, "Political Grace," para. 3.

77. Peter McLaren, "Critical Pedagogy: Constructing an Arch of Social Dreaming," 28.

78. Alyosha Goldstein, "Colonialism Undone: Pedagogies of Entanglement. Response 2," 46.

79. Glen Coulthard, "Subjects of Empire: Indigenous Peoples and the 'Politics of Recognition.'; Jodi Byrd, *The Transit of Empire*.

80. Sandy Grande, *Red Pedagogy*, xvii.

Bibliography

Allman, Paula. *Revolutionary Social Transformation: Democratic Hopes, Political Possibilities, and Critical Education*. Santa Barbara, CA: Praeger, 1999.

Badiou, Alain with Nicolas Troung. *In Praise of Love*. New York: The New Press, 2009.

Byrd, Jodi. *The Transit of Empire: Indigenous Critiques of Colonialism*. Minneapolis: University of Minnesota Press, 2011.

Coulthard, Glen. "Subjects of Empire: Indigenous Peoples and the 'Politics of Recognition' in Canada." *Contemporary Political Theory* 6 (2007): 437–460.

Darder, Antonia, "Political Grace and Revolutionary Critical Pedagogy," Rizoma Freireano, no. 21. (2016). http://rizoma-freireano.org/political-grace-21

———. *Reinventing Paulo Freire: A Pedagogy of Love*. Boulder, CO: Westview Press, 2002.

Darder, Antonia, Rodolfo D. Torres, and Marta P. Baltodano. *The Critical Pedagogy Reader, 3rd edition*. New York: Routledge, 2017.

Delgado Bernal, Dolores. "Learning and Living Pedagogies of the Home: The Mestiza Consciousness of Chicana Students." *International Journal of Qualitative Studies in Education* 14, no. 5 (2001): 623–639.

Dillard, Cynthia B., D. Abdur-Rashid, and C. A. Tyson. "My Soul is a Witness: Affirming Pedagogies of the Spirit." *International Journal of Qualitative Studies in Education* 13, no. 5 (2000): 447–462.

Dunayevskaya, Raya. *The Marxist-Humanist Theory of State Capitalism*. Chicago, IL: News & Letters Committee, 1992.

———. *Marxism and Freedom: From 1776 until Today*. Amherst, NY: Humanity Books, 2000.

Ebert, Teresa. "Alexandra Kollontai and Red Love." *Solidarity: A Socialist, Feminist, Anti-Racist Organization*, July-August, 1999. http://www.solidarity-us.org/node/1724.

Fanon, Frantz. *Black Skin, White Masks*. New York: Grove Press, 2008.

Freire, Paulo. *Pedagogy of the City*. New York: Continuum, 1992.

———. *Pedagogy of Hope: Reliving Pedagogy of the Oppressed*. New York: Bloomsbury, 1994.

———. *Pedagogy of the Oppressed, 30th anniversary edition*. New York: Bloomsbury, 2000.

Freire, Paulo and Donaldo Macedo. *Literacy: Reading the Word and the World*. Westport, CT: Bergin & Garvey, 1987.

Freire Araújo, Ana Maria. *Chronicles of Love: My Life with Paulo Freire*, New York: Counterpoints, 2001.

Fromm, Erich. *The Art of Loving*. New York: Harper & Row, 1956.

———. *To Have or To Be*. New York: Bloomsbury, 1976.

Gianarkis, Rebecca. *Spiritual but Not Religious: On the Collection of Spirituality and the Creation of Spiritual Narrative*. Hosfra University, Religious Studies Department, Unpublished Thesis, 2013.

Giroux, Henry. *On Critical Pedagogy*. New York: Bloomsbury Academic, 2011.

———. "Rethinking Education as the Practice of Freedom: Paulo Freire and the Promise of Critical Pedagogy." *Policy Futures in Education* 8, no. 6 (2010): 715–721.

Goldstein, Alyosha, "Colonialism Undone: Pedagogies of Entanglement. Response 2." In *Red Pedagogy: Native American Social and Political Thought, 10th anniversary edition*, Sandy Grande, 43–48. New York: Rowman & Littlefield, 2015.

Grande, Sandy. *Red Pedagogy: Native American Social and Political Thought*, 10th anniversary edition. New York: Rowman & Littlefield, 2015.

Grosfoguel, Ramon. "The Structure of Knowledge in Westernized Universities: Epistemic Racism/Sexism and the Four Genocides/Epistemicides of the Long 16th Century." *Human Architecture: Journal of the Sociology of Self-Knowledge 11*, no. 1 (2013): 73–90.

Hill, Dave, Peter McLaren, Mike Cole, and Glenn Rikowski, eds. *Marxism Against Postmodernism in Educational Theory*. Lanham, MD: Lexington Books, 2002.

hooks, bell. *All About Love: New Visions*. New York: William Morrow Paperbacks, 2018.

Hudis, Peter. *Marx's Concept of the Alternative to Capitalism*. Chicago, IL: Haymarket Books, 2013.

Kollontai, Alexandra. "Communism and the Family." In *Selected Writings of Alexandra Kollontai*, edited and translated by Alix Holt, 250–260. New York: Norton, 1977.

———. "Make Way for Winged Eros: A Letter to Working Youth." in *Selected Writings of Alexandra Kollontai*, edited and translated by Alix Holt, 276–292. New York: Norton, 1977.

Kruks, Sonia, Rayna Rapp, and Marilyn B. Young, eds. *Promissory Notes*. New York: Monthly Review Press, 1989.

Macedo, Donaldo. Introduction to *Chronicles of Love: My Life with Paulo Freire*, Ana Maria Freire Araújo, 1–9. New York: Counterpoints, 2001.

———. Introduction to *Pedagogy of the Oppressed, 30th anniversary edition*, Paulo Freire, 11–27. New York: Bloomsbury, 2000.

Marx, Karl. *Capital*, Vol. I. Madison Park: Pacific Publishing Studio, 2010.

———. *Economic and Philosophic Manuscripts of 1844*. Translated by Martin Milligan. Moscow: Foreign Language Publishing House, 1961.

McLaren, Peter. "Critical Pedagogy: Constructing an Arch of Social Dreaming and a Doorway to Hope." *The Journal of Education 173*, no. 1 (1991): 9–34.

———. *Life in Schools: An Introduction to Critical Pedagogy in the Foundations of Education*, 6th edition. New York, Routledge, 2016.

———. *Pedagogy of Insurrection: From Resurrection to Revolution*. New York: Peter Lang, 2015.

Miranda, Jose. *Marx Against the Marxists: The Christian Humanism of Karl Marx*. Maryknoll, New York: Orbis Books, 1980.

Monzó, Lilia D. "Marx in the age of Trump: Reaching out to Communities of Color." *International Marxist Humanist Organization*, Feb. 1, 2017. https://www.imhojournal.org/articles/marx-age-trump-reaching-communities-color-lilia-d-monzo/

———. "White Supremacy, Hate, and Violence in Charlottesville –A Marxist Humanist Response. *International Marxist Humanist Organization*, Aug. 17, 2017. https://www.imhojournal.org/articles/white-supremacy-hate-and-violence-in-charlottesville-a-marxist-humanist-response/

———. "Women and Revolution. Marx and the Dialectic." *International Humanist Organization*, Mar. 31, 2017. Reprinted. https://www.imhojournal.org/articles/women-revolution-marx-dialectic-lilia-d-monzo/

Monzó, Lilia D. and Peter McLaren. "Challenging the Violence and Invisibility Against Women of Color—A Marxist Imperative." *Iberoamérica Social: Revista-Red de Estudios Sociales*, April, 2016. https://iberoamericasocial.com/challenging-the-violence-and-invisibility-against-women-of-color-a-marxist-imperative/

———. "Red Love: Toward Racial, Economic and Social Justice." *Truthout*, Dec. 18, 2014. http://www.truth-out.org/opinion/item/28072-red-love-toward-racial-economic-and-social-justice.

———. "The Future is Marx: Bringing Back Class and Changing the World—A Moral Imperative." In *International Handbook of Progressive Education*, edited by Mustafa Yunus Eryaman and Bertram C. Bruce, 643–670. New York: Peter Lang, 2015.

Monzó, Lilia D. and Robert S. Rueda. "Professional Roles, Caring, and Scaffolds: Latino Teachers' and Paraeducators' Interactions with Latino Students. *American Journal of Education*, *109*, no. 4 (2001): 438–471.

Rehberg, Wes. *Political Grace: The Gift of Resistance*. Wild Clearing, 2004.

Rivage-Seul, Michael. *The Emperor's God: Imperial Misunderstandings of Christianity*. Sun City, Arizona: The Institute for Economic Democracy Press, 2008.

Solnit, Rebecca. *Men Explain Things to Me*. Chicago, IL: Haymarket Books, 2014.

SooHoo, Suzanne. *Talking Leaves: Narratives of Otherness*. New York: Hampton Press, 2006.

Trotsky, Leon. *Women and The Family, 2nd edition*. New York: Pathfinder, 1973.

Viramontes, Helena María. "Nopalitos: The Making of Fiction." In *Making Face, Making Soul/Haciendo Caras: Creative and Critical Perspectives by Feminists of Color*, edited by Gloria Anzaldúa, 291–294. San Francisco, CA: Aunt Lute Books, 1990.

Vygotsky, L. S. *Mind in Society: The Development of Higher Psychological Processes*, edited by Michael Cole, Vera John-Steiner, Sylvia Scribner, and Ellen Souberman. Cambridge, MA: Harvard University Press, 1978.

Wilson, Tom, Peter Park, and Anaida Colón-Muñíz. *Memories of Paulo*. The Netherlands: Sense Publishers, 2010.

Zavala, Miguel and Noah Asher Golden. "Prefiguring Alternative Worlds: Organic Critical Literacies and Socio-Cultural Revolutions." *Knowledge Cultures 4*, no. 6 (2016): 207–227.

Zeva Goldman, Wendy, "Women, the Family, and the New Revolutionary Order in the Soviet Union." In *Promissory Notes: Women in the Transition to Socialism*, edited by Sonia Kruks, Rayna Rapp, & Marilyn B. Young, 59–81. New York: Monthly Review Press, 1989.

APPENDIX

Martha: Undocumented and Invincible[1]

I am a mother of three, who are all already attending university. We came to this country looking for a future. My husband had lost his job, I was pregnant, and we did not have any means of survival. It was difficult to cross the border, like all families that take tremendous risks. The principle goal was to survive, work some, make money, and return.

I wanted to make more of myself. I always had this desire to serve. I wanted to be like Mother Teresa. I wanted to be a nun and be of service to others like she did or to be a doctor but I was not able to continue my education because my mother was here in the United States to provide for us. There were seven of us. I was in charge of the house. I was about 12 years old.

When my son entered Head Start part of the requirements was that parents had to volunteer. I said, "Good. I love the idea." and I began to get involved and to cultivate that sense of helping. Later when they began elementary school we moved to South-Central Los Angeles. We noticed that we were condemned to live in this South Central area due to a law, that, although no longer explicit, is still practiced called "redlining." The Banks would not give us loans to buy property in other areas. This is an area with chemical industries, streets that are destroyed, without trees or parks to clean the air. The children would develop respiratory problems. One day I noticed that a company that used carcinogens was operating across the street from my children's school.

When I begin investigating I received an invitation to a meeting at the school to speak about that company. At the meeting the school principal silenced me. He said that the meeting was not solely for me. But if I was the only one with questions it was because the others did not know what to ask. I said, "Wow!" After eight years of aggressive struggle, the company closed down. The area across from the school was transformed. Of course, now comes the possibility of gentrification—the displacement of the working class by the bourgeoisie.

In this process I began to gain confidence in my voice, my nature to help change what is wrong. I have always thought that education is the ticket to achieve my dreams. While I was working as an activist I learned English, completed my GED, later I finished junior college and went to the university and got my bachelor's. Shortly thereafter, alter 20 years of waiting, I was able to become a legal resident.

My husband worked nights and slept during the day. He did not really know what I was doing, not even that I had gone to school. In my husband's home growing up they believed that a woman close to books is dangerous. They would tell him, "Don't let her read so much because later you will not be able to control her. An educated woman will slip from your hands." It's difficult because an education creates barriers in the family. It's like walking alone.

The organization that I first got involved with, ACORN (Association of Community Organizers for Reform Now) had many problems so a group of us formed a new organization that has grown a lot, ACCE Action (Alliance of Californians for Community Empowerment Action). Two years ago, an opportunity arose to work with schools and I am so passionate about education that I said, "this job is for me!" My work is to direct a campaign focused on the creation of community schools that offer after school programs—arts and sports, nurses, counselors, a parent and social wellness center. We are also looking for schools to have greater say in education budgets. We've already won a resolution in the school district accepting community schools as a new model for public schools. I'm passionate about speaking to parents about defending our school system, which is not a gift; we pay for it. There are people who infiltrate our movements when we take action and they try to infiltrate our thinking. We are competing in a world of White men who don't care about even White women. Why are they going to worry about a Latina?

What motivates me to be an activist is to know how it feels to go to bed without eating; to be three or four days without eating; to live with extreme poverty, without clean clothes because you don't even have soap to wash; to go to school without a sweater and say, "Oh no, I'm not cold"; and when they ask you "Why aren't you eating?"—obviously it's that you don't have anything to eat. I would bite the erasers because I was hungry. I ate dirt and would have to fight with my older brother—fight *hard—so they wouldn't eat everything and there would be enough for the younger children. You have to live that to be able to understand it.*

If I didn't give up then, why now? The fear doesn't go away; we learn to live with it. It's fine to lack confidence, to doubt, but don't allow the fear to paralyze you. If we live all those experiences, when you're an adult and gain some power, those experiences become arms. Uhf! I don't see my past as sad or painful; I see it as opportunities to continue to help and struggle. I understand when they tell me, "They are going to evict us!"; how it feels to be rejected, repudiated, oppressed. Hijole, I am with them!

We are common people who really love to make change, love the community. If we really want to make a change we have to go to the community, to the heart that is the community—the poor—and speak their language. We believe that to call ourselves a community we have to unite hand to hand, shoulder to shoulder, recognize the values, the strengths, and the frailties of each member. To strengthen the most fragile is what makes us special. We are not climbing one on top of another, but rather walking with our arms united and we believe that every community has a unique and powerful force that is why we go door to door. The smallest voice, the most fragile, can make the greatest change in the planet and we are always on the lookout for that voice.

Note

1. This is the English translation of Martha Sanchez's narrative printed in Spanish in Chapter 6.

INDEX

Narrative, Dialogue, and the Political Production of Meaning

Michael A. Peters
Peter McLaren
Series Editors

To submit a manuscript or proposal for editorial consideration, please contact:

Dr. Peter McLaren
Chapman University
College of Educational Studies
Reeves Hall 205
Orange, CA 92866

Dr. Michael A. Peters
University of Waikato
P.O. Box 3105
Faculty of Education
Hamilton 3240
New Zealand

WE ARE THE STORIES WE TELL. The book series Education and Struggle focuses on conflict as a discursive process where people struggle for legitimacy and the narrative process becomes a political struggle for meaning. But this series will also include the voices of authors and activists who are involved in conflicts over material necessities in their communities, schools, places of worship, and public squares as part of an ongoing search for dignity, self-determination, and autonomy. This series focuses on conflict and struggle within the realm of educational politics based around a series of interrelated themes: indigenous struggles; Western-Islamic conflicts; globalization and the clash of worldviews; neoliberalism as the war within; colonization and neocolonization; the coloniality of power and decolonial pedagogy; war and conflict; and the struggle for liberation. It publishes narrative accounts of specific struggles as well as theorizing "conflict narratives" and the political production of meaning in educational studies. During this time of global conflict and the crisis of capitalism, Education and Struggle promises to be on the cutting edge of social, cultural, educational, and political transformation.

Central to the series is the idea that language is a process of social, cultural, and class conflict. The aim is to focus on key semiotic, literary, and political concepts as a basis for a philosophy of language and culture where the underlying materialist philosophy of language and culture serves as the basis for the larger project that we might call dialogism (after Bakhtin's usage). As the late V. N. Volosinov suggests "Without signs there is no ideology," "Everything ideological possesses semiotic value," and "individual consciousness is a socio-ideological fact." It is a small step to claim, therefore, "consciousness itself can arise and become a viable fact only in the material embodiment of signs." This series is a vehicle for materialist semiotics in the narrative and dialogue of education and struggle.

To order other books in this series, please contact our Customer Service Department:

(800) 770-LANG (within the U.S.)
(212) 647-7706 (outside the U.S.)
(212) 647-7707 FAX

Or browse online by series:

www.peterlang.com